Anastasia

The Lost Princess

—

JAMES BLAIR LOVELL

St. Martin's Press
New York

Library of Congress Cataloging-in-Publication Data
Lovell, James Blair.
Anastasia : the lost princess / James Blair Lovell.
p.   cm.
Originally published: Washington, D.C. : Regnery Gateway, c1991.
ISBN 0-312-11133-9 (pbk.)
1. Anastasiia Nikolaevna, Grand Duchess, daughter of Nicholas II,
Emperor of Russia, 1901-1918.   2. Anderson, Anna.   3. Princesses-
-Russia—Biography.   I. Title.
DK254.A7L64   1994
947.08'3'092—dc20   [B]   94-2040   CIP

First published in the United States by Regnery Gateway.

First Paperback Edition: February 1995
10 9 8 7 6 5 4 3

for my children,
Ken, Stephanie, Tasha, and Winston

and to
Vivian Allison
the wind beneath my wings

and
Daniel C. Duncan

Contents

Contents

Contents

What is history but a fable agreed upon?

—Napoleon I

Preface to
This Edition

James Blair Lovell died on December 4, 1993.

At the time of his death, James was doing research for a new book that would document the events surrounding recent claims by scientists that the skeletal remains found in Siberia are those of Czar Nicholas; his wife Alexandra; their daughters Olga, Tatiana, and Marie; three servants; and Dr. Eugene Botkin. Early in 1993, a preserved section of small intestine from Anna Anderson was discovered at a hospital in Charlottesville, Virginia. A portion of this tissue sample was submitted for DNA testing to determine if it matched the DNA of known living descendents of the Czar's family. The new book was also to document the results of that testing.

Since James's death, the results of the DNA testing of the tissue sample have made news around the world. While they are not the results that James and many other close followers of the mystery expected—they were negative—neither are they the last word.

The real story of Anastasia continues to unfold. Numerous critics have suggested there may have been tampering, inadvertent or otherwise, with the tissue sample. Furthermore, many DNA experts acknowledge a significant margin of error in both the testing process and the interpreting of test results.

At press time, plans for a second DNA test were under way. Devout believers on both sides of this extraordinary story will watch with still-bated breath as Anna Anderson's remains are once again subjected to the scrutiny of science. Among those who will pay close attention to the test and its results are the members of James Blair Lovell's research and support team, including myself, Claire Sawford of The Creative Umbrella in London, and several researchers. We intend to carry out James's plan for the new book—and to continue his quest for the truth that began more than two decades ago.

In 1972, James met Anna Anderson, who claimed to be Anastasia Romanov, the youngest daughter of the last Russian Czar, and he became convinced of the validity of Anderson's claims and accepted her request that he write the true story of her life, which differed markedly from versions previously presented in films, plays, and books. The book you are about to read is the result of nearly two decades of research into her life.

A few days before James died, a dear friend asked if he was disappointed that he would not be alive to hear the results of the DNA testing. James sat up in bed, looked his friend in the eyes and said, "*No.* I know in my heart that the Anna Anderson I knew in Charlottesville was Anastasia, and neither my belief or my work needs public validation."

I am convinced that James and Anastasia found each other because they shared many characteristics. I'm also convinced that James, Anastasia, and her husband, Jack Manahan, are all watching—waiting to see the ending of a great, real story.

Kathleen Franzen
November 1994
Washington, DC

Introduction

___

You are my heir. To you alone I leave these truths. This is all I have to give, and to you I give it. How you tell the world is for you to decide, but you will do so in my name.

Анастаси

BLUE EYES. Many have tried unsuccessfully to capture the essence of their color, a haunting shade, identical to that of her father's eyes. No one, however, has described their arresting focus. When she fixed her gaze on you, she drew you immediately and completely to her. The color was as deep as her suffering, but there was also a glint, a luminescence, like the innocent anticipation in the eyes of infants who have just learned to focus on the world. Indeed, even as she trained those incredible eyes on you, she was also taking in everything around her. If eyes are truly portals to the soul, then hers revealed an intense sadness and an equally profound sense of wonderment.

Her eyes were even more commanding because of the rest of her face. It was old and wrinkled, and she made no attempt to disguise the soft, aging skin with any makeup. Her hair was cut in a page-boy style and often dyed an improbable, shocking shade of auburn. Equally astonishing were the clothes she wore. She made no effort to be fashionable. Colors and patterns clashed outrageously. Seldom did she adorn herself with jewelry. She preferred loose-fitting pants to dresses and skirts. Nothing fit her well, because she dressed for comfort and warmth. Although ever-conscious of having aged prematurely, she had long ago given up any attempt to disguise that fact.

She was petite, no more than five-feet, two-inches tall. As she sat and fixed her gaze upon you, she seemed to will her body to shrink even further. She expressed her assertiveness through her eyes, not her movements. The dichotomy was striking. Her gaze and voice would sometimes convey great animation, while her bearing remained entirely constrained.

She could sit for hours on a footstool with her back rigid and shoulders squared. Her hands would lie unmoving in her lap, one crossed delicately over the other. Her legs met at the knees and then crossed demurely at the ankles. She epitomized the flawlessly composed lady. Occasionally, when nervous, she would daintily raise one of her hands to cover her mouth and jaw. The gesture was not practiced, but it served to bring your attention back to those eyes. In them, you could sometimes read the anxiety and uncertainty of the small child she never fully outgrew.

Often, she would remain silent in this posture, reaching from time to time into the enormous pocketbook that always lay at her side. Bits of foil containing leftover food for her cats, tiny pieces of paper, and crumpled tissues spilled over the sides, barely covering a tattered paperback copy of an Agatha Christie novel. When she lost interest in the subject being discussed, she might pull out the book and begin reading, eager to lose herself in another world.

She could at other times be an engaging conversationalist, once you became accustomed to the idiosyncratic English she spoke in varying accents. She had what can best be termed a Germanic or vaguely Eastern European accent with various other linguistic influences, and her pronunciation revealed a formal training in correct but archaic locution. She often divided the word *again* into two distinct syllables, *a-gain*, reflecting the British inflections that crept into her words.

Her interests ranged widely. She could talk about the most obscure works of art with authority and insight. She delighted in recitations of arcane matters relating to European royal history. Photography was her particular passion, and any mention of a camera or a photo would invariably lead to many questions and long discussions of the art. She loved to look at photographs and seldom objected to having her own taken. She was especially cooperative if the photographer was using equipment she had never seen before. She would ask questions about how it worked and would want to study it closely. Indeed, she evinced a fascination for all types of gadgetry, from pocket calculators to children's wind-up toys.

She also enjoyed speaking of inconsequential matters. She loved gossip, whether it concerned film stars or the people next door. Despite the fact that her visage, frame, and voice were those of an old woman, her emotions were those of an adolescent. She told anyone who would listen of her desire to see Disney World's Magic Kingdom. She remembered the excitement of watching the giant ferris wheels spin over Myrtle Beach, South Carolina. "That was wonderful," she would recall, her eyes reflecting the joy her guarded gestures effectively concealed.

She favored meeting people in small groups, preferably only one or two individuals at a time. Above all, she feared public places. Even if no one knew her name, people couldn't help staring at her. She hated being touched and avoided crowds of any size. She disliked eating in restaurants and would rather wait in the car, reading or simply studying the scene around her, while others brought food to her.

She craved anonymity but had stopped using false names, because they had only aroused more curiosity about her and drawn more attention to her. In her later years, she wanted to be addressed by the name she was given at birth seven decades before, in imperial Russia.

She had been born into a world of incomparable luxury, but it had vanished long ago. She now shunned the formalities and rituals that others insisted her heritage required. Any visitor who bowed to her or called her "Highness" or "Grand Duchess" received a quick, polite nod followed by a bemused smile, especially if the person was much younger than she and had never known a time when kings and emperors predominated. She would later turn to a bystander and whisper, "Why do they say this? The world is now very different. Now I am just Anastasia."

THIS was the private Anastasia, an unassuming but nevertheless captivating old woman. She was polite but distant, creating the impression that she preferred to be left alone. How such a timid lady could have created such an intense and long-running controversy was difficult to understand.

For more than fifty years after her rescue from a Berlin canal following an apparent suicide attempt, she had been the center of

worldwide publicity. By the time she married Dr. John Eacott Manahan in 1968, her story had been told and analyzed by reporters,
historians, scholars, and the merely curious. Those who knew any
of the facts of her life could not help being struck by its tragedy.
Regardless of whether they believed she was truly who she said she
was, she had undeniably been hounded by the press and the public
throughout her adult life. To anyone who did believe her, the weight
of the misery she carried was clear.

Perhaps her most difficult ordeal had been the nearly forty years
of court cases fought in Germany. Public attention had focused on
her unrelentingly, as those who opposed her claim to be the daughter
of the last Russian czar stopped at nothing to discredit her. They had
accused her variously of being a mad Romanian actress, a demented
Polish factory worker, a highly skilled adventuress, a Soviet agent,
or simply a crazed fraud. She had endured the most scurrilous
insults about herself and her parents and friends.

But she seemed oddly indifferent to it all, never trying to explain herself, knowing that she was who she was. Secure in her own
identity, she never bothered to publicly refute those who accused
her, let alone to plead her case to the press. She left that task to the
friends and supporters who always surrounded her. They tried,
without success, to convince her to personally join the battle against
her detractors. Her friends were the ones who arranged for the press
coverage and insisted that she agree to interviews. As a result, the
public saw a woman very much different from the exotic and beautiful Russian princess they expected. Newspapers and magazines
published stark photographs of a haggard woman, and instead of
finding stories of intrigue on a grand scale, readers learned that she
spoke rarely and only reluctantly to the press. When she did tell
anecdotes, writers often characterized them as fantastical nonsense.
That many of her utterances turned out to be accurate was often
overlooked or quickly forgotten.

The public preferred the imaginary Anastasia. People found the
legend created by several successful motion pictures and Broadway
plays more palatable than the truth. Audiences were left with the
impression that there might indeed have been a daughter who had
survived the massacre of the Russian imperial family. If such a
woman had endured, however, she had long since overcome the

tragedy of being robbed of her family and heritage. In the fiction-alized versions, she had prevailed in the face of adversity and been rewarded for her struggle. To most of the world, the legendary lost princess had long ago found recognition, happiness, and romance.

Her real life was a shocking contrast to the one depicted on stage and screen. Rather than accept that fate could treat a young girl so cruelly, the general public preferred to believe in the mythologized Anastasia and to dismiss as a fraud the woman who had lived such a terrible reality.

She suffered several nervous breakdowns. She lived on charity, while watching liars and callous manipulators profit from her image. She disdained the commercialization of her name but harbored an intense desire to have her true story told.

She was acutely aware of the wide disparity between public per-ception and truth. Substantial proof of her authenticity had existed for years. Forensic confirmation of her identity came eventually, but people were reluctant to part with the fictional Anastasia. The Holly-wood image had become too pervasive to be dispelled by mere fact.

She attempted to write her own story several times. Each effort failed miserably, either because she did not have the stamina to finish the work alone or because other events overtook the project. None-theless, setting the record straight remained one of her most impor-tant aspirations. By the time she moved to Charlottesville, Virginia, she was sixty-seven and feared the truth would die with her.

MY first acquaintance with the story of the lost princess came at an early age. When I was four, my parents lived near Augsburg, Ger-many, not far from the little village where Anna Anderson resided. They hired a governess named Madame Philippe to care for me. A member of the ancient Lithuanian aristocracy, she had fled her native country for the West as Soviet troops advanced during the Second World War. Shortly after beginning her trek, she had discov-ered the bodies of her two sons, massacred by Russian soldiers. Delirious with anguish and horror, she had tried to drown herself in a nearby lake but had been saved. She managed to overcome her grief and walked the entire distance to Augsburg, carrying a few family jewels hidden in the hollowed-out heels of her shoes.

Madame Philippe saw her own tragic circumstances reflected in the stories she heard about the woman who claimed to be Anastasia. As she cared for me, Madame Philippe repeated the accounts of the young Russian grand duchess who had escaped the Bolsheviks with jewels sewn into the linings of her clothes. Anastasia had also made the long journey out of her war-ravaged land to Germany and had apparently tried to drown herself, only to be saved.

Like a favorite fairy tale, the story of the lost princess remained with me, and I often wondered whether there was any truth behind it. As a young man, I read an excerpt of the Anastasia legend in a magazine, and my childhood curiosity immediately became an adult fascination. I began reading all I could find about Grand Duchess Anastasia and her parents, the Russian Czar Nicholas II and his German-born wife, Alexandra.

IN THE spring of 1970, when I was reviewing books for a southern newspaper, I received a copy of a new book, *The Hunt for the Czar* by Guy Richards, to evaluate. The book piqued my interest, and I began a correspondence with the author, which lasted until his death. Richards did not believe in the authenticity of the woman who lived in Charlottesville, Virginia, and called herself Anastasia. He maintained that she was a complete fake and that if she had any connection whatsoever to the Romanovs, she was probably the child of a former servant employed in one of the Czar's residences.

I also became acquainted with another author, Naomi Hintze. I had favorably reviewed her novel, *The Stone Carnation*, and we had become friends. When I learned that she lived in Charlottesville, I told her of my fascination with the legend of the lost Russian princess and asked whether the woman who called herself Anastasia still lived in Charlottesville. Mrs. Hintze said that she did but that they had never met. Her friend Mabel Luman, however, had known the woman's husband, Jack Manahan, for many years. Almost jokingly, I asked Mrs. Hintze to ask Mrs. Luman to inquire of Dr. Manahan whether I could interview his wife. Although Mrs. Hintze doubted that such a meeting could be arranged, she promised to ask Mrs. Luman.

Within a few days, Mrs. Hintze called to say that Dr. Manahan was seriously considering my request and that I was to call him myself and apply directly for the interview. She warned that he was thought to be highly eccentric and very protective of his wife.

Manahan was very pleasant when I asked whether he and his wife would submit to an interview. He seemed to ponder for awhile, then asked, "Your name is James *Blair Lovell*? Blair *and* Lovell?"

When I assured him that it was, he said that he had once written a genealogical pamphlet about the Blair family and that he had recently begun researching a similar study on the Lovells. If I would answer questions about my families, he would allow me to meet his wife. I readily accepted the offer.

To prepare for the interview, I needed to find out more about the Manahans. The first person I contacted was J. Lewis Walker, III, my former English-literature professor at the College of William and Mary in Williamsburg, Virginia. We had remained in touch since my time at the College, and he had recently moved to Charlottesville to teach at the University of Virginia. I had not spoken with him since the move, and I called to let him know I would soon be in his city. When I told him the purpose of my visit, stunned silence followed. I asked whether he knew the Manahans.

"Know them?" he laughed. "I live next door to them. Dr. Manahan is my landlord."

As it happened, adjoining the rear of the Manahan property was a small apartment building, with a number of units rented to members of the university faculty, among them Mr. Walker.

Having lived there only briefly, he did not know much about the Manahans except that they were both very eccentric. He did agree, however, to vouch for me when he paid his May rent to Jack Manahan.

Armed with a camera and tape recorder, I arrived in Charlottesville on May 8, 1972. A college friend named C. Dean Latsios met my plane, and we drove to Naomi Hintze's house. From there we went to lunch at Farmington, the exclusive country club reportedly designed in part by Thomas Jefferson. Mrs. Hintze remarked that the Manahans were also members. At the appointed time, we drove to the Manahan house at 35 University Circle.

The small front yard needed mowing, but nothing else appeared unusual on the outside. Dr. Manahan awaited the three of us at the front door. Stepping into the formal entrance hall, we were suddenly in another world. Books were everywhere. The entrance hall was lined with bookshelves, and more volumes were piled on the floor. Carefully navigating around them, we entered a semi-circular living room crammed with thousands of books, old paintings, ancient mementos, expensive china ornaments, and relics of the Romanov dynasty. Priceless artifacts lay beside broken children's toys. Letters from European royalty were displayed alongside yellowed Christmas cards. There was no order in this room and no place to sit.

I turned on the tape recorder and, as we remained standing, Dr. Manahan discoursed for hours on the detailed history of Anastasia, his own theories of the events of her life, the subject of false Romanov claimants, his wife's legal cases, and a myriad of topics relating to her claim to be the genuine Anastasia. When I asked how to address her, he laughed and said, "Call her by her real name—Anastasia."

She appeared only briefly, nervously speaking a few words into my recorder and posing for photographs, then left the room. Manahan remained gracious throughout and, as my friends and I prepared to leave, presented me with a copy of *Rasputin: The Mad Monk*, by René Fülöp-Miller, which he proudly inscribed as being from himself and Anastasia.

Dean Latsios and I departed for Washington, D.C., that evening. On the road, we discussed the meeting and agreed that it had been interesting but inconclusive. We had absolutely no sense of whether Anastasia was genuine or false. But we had no doubt that Manahan believed in her story. Sometime during the drive, Dean said, "Did you notice the way she kept staring at you?" I had not.

I wrote nothing for publication about the trip. The story was all too dubious, and I expressed my reservations to Naomi Hintze about Mrs. Manahan's identity.

The following month, *Life* magazine carried an article entitled "The Czar's Shutterbug," containing hitherto unpublished photographs of the Russian imperial family on holiday. Among them were several of the teenage Anastasia. As soon as I saw her, I knew she was the woman I had met in Charlottesville. Comparing the pictures in *Life* with the ones I had taken in Virginia confirmed my opinion. More than half a century had passed between the time the *Life* pictures had been taken and the time I had taken mine, but the similarity was more than striking. It was distinct enough to be uncanny.

OVER the next several years, I remained in frequent contact with the Manahans. I also made an effort to speak with anyone who had even the slightest knowledge of the Anastasia mystery. My skepticism gradually melted, and I began to think that her story, or parts of it, must be true. The tale of Anastasia was one of fiction versus reality, and I became intrigued by the challenge of separating them.

In autumn 1976, BBC reporters Anthony Summers and Tom Mangold published *The File on the Tsar*, accompanied by a television documentary of the same name. The book presented new evidence that overturned the accepted account of the last days of the Romanovs. It also contained a long chapter on Anastasia of Charlottesville, which provided the first synopsis of evidence supporting her claim ever published by independent researchers. *The File on the Tsar* was an international best-seller and quickly took its place among the seminal works of Romanov scholarship. Although the authors did not overtly endorse Mrs. Manahan's claim to be Anastasia, they clearly believed her. The case they presented for her authenticity was concise and persuasive.

The Summers and Mangold book renewed public interest in Anastasia Manahan. That same year, a well-known writer contacted me, saying he had learned of my friendship with the couple and was interested in collaborating with her on a book about her life. He asked me to travel to Charlottesville and offer her a million dollars for the authorized version of her story. She rejected his offer and asked me to write her story instead. Her only request was that a "true movie" be made, if the book became successful. All the previous films of her life, she said, were the work of "creators," a word she used to depict liars, traitors, scandalmongers, and fictionists. She used many such code words to describe people and things, and I had to learn to decipher them, as well as to cope with her disjointed sentences and her tendency to go off on tangents. She also habitually exaggerated. She wanted to tell me a "thousand things" about something that had happened "X times" in her life. She had been involved with "masses" of people throughout her life, but what remained most important to her were her memories and her "precious goods," her phrase for the innumerable objects she had collected over the years. They included official documents, photographs, and letters, as well as priceless paintings and artifacts. Just as "precious" were scraps of paper and the broken bric-a-brac she never threw away.

She often described how she felt about people who had played important roles in her life. She talked about the people known as "Anastasians"—a term she never used—who supported her during the German court cases concerning her legal identity. Among these were Prince Frederick of Saxe-Altenburg, who helped her survive the postwar devastation of Germany, and Baroness Monica Miltitz, who had lived near her in Germany after the Second World War.

She also talked about the friends who had always been important to her. Gleb Botkin, a childhood friend who remained her strongest supporter, was perhaps the most significant person in her life. Other good friends included Harriet Rathlef, who had helped Anastasia in the 1920s, when she lay suffering in a German hospital, and the Madsacks of Hanover, who provided her with care and funds in the years between the First and Second World Wars.

Finally, she told me about Alexis Milukoff, a strange Russian emigre who came to her in the 1960s and tried to preserve many of her "precious goods" after she left Germany for Charlottesville.

Anastasia left me feeling both honored and burdened. Our conversations had given me a general sense of her as a woman, but the task of accurately portraying her incredible life story was a daunting responsibility.

As I continued my research, the word spread among those who followed Anastasia's story that I was planning to write her biography. I compiled thousands of pages of documentary evidence and interviewed scores of her contemporaries. But no matter how much I learned, I always felt that I did not know enough.

Quite unexpectedly, I managed to procure most of the materials that Alexis Milukoff had secreted in Germany after Anastasia settled in Charlottesville. They had not been seen for more than two decades and included photographs, paintings, and other documents that would help tremendously with Anastasia's biography. Of great interest among the documents were letters from Gleb Botkin. He had lived in the United States but kept in close contact with both Anastasia and Milukoff. She had always considered Gleb her "best friend" and most ardent supporter. His correspondence helped me to understand the concerns Anastasia expressed and the problems she encountered during a period of her life that had otherwise remained relatively undocumented.

Also included in the Milukoff collection were tape recordings he had made with Anastasia during the late 1960s. From my own conversations with her and from reports I had read, I knew that Anastasia's discussions tended to be discursive and trivial, so I did not anticipate learning anything new from Milukoff's tapes. Besides, before purchasing Milukoff's collection, I had inquired about his reliability. Everyone who had known him told me the same thing: he photographed and recorded virtually every aspect of his own life, regardless of its importance. The tapes of his conversations with Anastasia would probably reveal more about him than about her.

Nevertheless, as I intended to preserve all the materials, I acquired the services of Herman Badler to act as conservator of the tapes. Mr. Badler, a retired broadcast-engineering executive, had previously been Vice-President of Operations and Engineering for CBS in Washington, D.C. Before he examined the tapes, he cautioned me that because of their age and the fact that they were made of ¹/₂ mil mylar, a very thin and fragile tape, they were likely to have suffered significant deterioration and loss of sound quality. When he examined them, however, he found that, despite being about twenty-five years old, they had been well cared for and properly stored, and were in excellent condition.

Each of the twenty-six reel-to-reel tapes contains four separate monaural sides, or tracks, which require playback on either vintage equipment or a state-of-the-art, studio-quality machine. Inside each of the tape boxes were loose sheets of paper on which Milukoff had made extensive handwritten notes. There he had listed when and where the recordings were made, and the full names of participants, other than Anastasia and himself. In addition, he had written summaries of the contents of each track, with numbers corresponding to the counter on his recorder. I stored the tapes as Mr. Badler recommended, in a cool, dry closet, each box standing on end.

One afternoon, while leafing through Milukoff's scrapbooks, I opened the closet, randomly chose Tape Five, and put it on the tape player. I began listening absent-mindedly but soon realized that I had stumbled onto something important. As I heard Anastasia agree that henceforth these tapes would form the basis of her authorized biography, to be written by Milukoff, I closed the scrapbook.

"And then I am born at Peterhof. Nineteen-hundred-one. Fifth of June at the Russian date. I know one thing, that I am sure I was born at three o'clock in the morning."

Milukoff is guiding her through a chronological progression from birth, and she is trying to be cooperative. So cooperative that Milukoff laughs, realizing she could not possibly remember the time of day she was born. But she proudly repeats, "I was born at three o'clock in the morning."

As I had anticipated, much of their talk was inconsequential. Even twenty-five years before, she had easily lost track of her thoughts. To make matters worse, Milukoff was hardly a skilled interviewer, and he often interrupted her, sometimes just as she was about to reveal a particularly intimate thought or opinion. "Not interrupting," she often told him. "Not to interrupt me or I lose where I am thinking."

But when Milukoff allowed her to speak freely and to organize her ideas, she had important things to say about what had happened to her, from the day she was born. She obviously felt comfortable during the taping sessions, but sometimes became angry. When this happened, she would fall silent or concoct some fabulous tale about her life and urge Milukoff to go investigate it for himself.

I found it odd that a woman whose whole life had revolved around a controversy over her identity would want to create greater confusion by telling such transparent lies. Eventually, I began to realize that she used these fabrications for a reason. They were often so outrageous that interviewers would become overwhelmed with the thrill of discovering whether they were true. Meanwhile, the interviewers left her alone. Once they learned they had been duped, they never returned to plague her.

Perhaps the reason they initially accepted her fictitious tales was that the true stories about her life were equally outrageous. By listening closely for her special phrases or intonations, however, I had learned how to tell whether she was more likely to be reciting fact than to be creating fiction. After hearing some of these tales, I would check my source material and often found that what she had said was true. Sometimes my research showed that the historical literature had established certain facts years after she had first told them to Milukoff. Sometimes what she said turned out to be untrue, but when she spoke in a particular manner, I knew that she fervently believed what she was saying.

On Tape Five, for example, Anastasia insisted to Milukoff that she was not the last daughter born to Czar Nicholas and Czarina Alexandra. She told him about her mother's supposed false pregnancy in 1903 and said that Alexandra had actually given birth to a fifth daughter. In adamant tones, she related the story of a birth kept secret from the world and asserted that she had met this unknown sister as an adult. The story of the fifth daughter was perhaps the greatest of the many unsolved mysteries that Anastasia posed throughout her life, and one that I eventually felt compelled to investigate on my own.

THE Milukoff recordings have been invaluable to me, as Anastasia's authorized biographer. The tapes provide many more details about dates, events, and people than have ever been chronicled before. This information has proved indispensable in helping me sort out what had become a confused and abbreviated chronology of her life.

The tapes' greatest contribution, however, was to reveal her understanding of all that had happened to her. Anastasia was very forthcoming with Milukoff. She often spoke openly of her reactions to events, providing insights about her own and others' motivations and expressing her feelings about the life she led. She had told me some of these things before, but her extensive talks with Milukoff filled in the shadows to complete her portrait.

In short, her dialogue with Milukoff revealed Anastasia as a person who was completely aware of what had happened to her and how it had changed her life forever. She spoke of people and developments with an immediacy and discernment uniquely her own.

After listening to the Milukoff tapes, I realized that Anastasia had provided the key to understanding her, without which a biographer could never hope to write her story as she had wanted it told. At last, I could faithfully and reliably convey how a Russian imperial princess had made the long journey from St. Petersburg to rural Virginia.

NOTE

The titles *czar* and *emperor* are interchangeable, as are *czarina* and *empress*. Although emperor was a higher distinction, Nicholas II preferred the more traditional czar. His wife Alexandra preferred to be called empress.

The titles *grand duke* and *grand duchess* were given to the sons, daughters, and grandchildren of a czar. Anastasia's title, Grand Duchess of Russia, was the equivalent of a European princess.

Stylists vary on the issue of capitalization of the word czar and its derivative forms, czarina and czarevitch. These words are capitalized herein when they refer to a specific member of Anastasia's family and otherwise only when they appear as a part of an appellation, e.g. Czar Nicholas II. It is the method commonly accepted in Romanov literature.

All spellings of names, places, and titles appearing in this text are those commonly used in the United States.

Russian patronymics are not used in this text, with one exception. In some quotations, the initials A. N. appear, indicating that Anastasia was Nicholas's daughter: Anastasia Nicolaievna.

Anastasia

BOOK ONE

The Court of the Double Eagle

There is a deep symbolic meaning to the massacre of the ex-Czar, his family and staff. Just as liberty has its great historic days—the battles of Lexington and Concord, the storming of Bastille—so does totalitarianism. The manner in which the massacre was prepared and carried out, at first denied and then justified, has something uniquely odious about it, something that radically distinguishes it from the previous acts of regicide and brands it as a prelude to 20th-century mass murder.

— RICHARD PIPES

I.

The Imperial Dynasty

AN ANCIENT RUSSIAN LEGEND, which begins on "a dark,
stormy night," tells the story of a hunting party of young nobles
forced to take refuge in a small hunting lodge on a hill near the River
Yauza, a tributary of the Moskva River.

As the sun rose the next morning, one member of the party, a
young aristocrat named Stephen, woke to the sound of horns announcing the beginning of a boar hunt. The youths quickly dressed
for the hunt and stepped outside the lodge, just as a mammoth wild
boar dashed into the clearing near the door. The hunters were about
to flee, when they heard a loud cry from above. Looking up, they
were astonished to see a huge, black bird soaring down toward them
through the clouds.

The creature had two heads and four fiery red eyes focused in
anger. Transfixed, the men began to fear the bird more than the boar,
which had also stopped in its tracks and stared skyward. In an
instant, the bird swooped down and seized the screaming boar with
giant, vice-like talons, then tossed it over the side of a nearby hill.
After the two-headed bird had flown off, Stephen and his friends
ventured down the hill, where they found only the boar's mangled
remains.

This strange occurrence proved a good omen for the day's hunt. In
fact, so successful were the young nobles in their sport that Stephen's
servants balked at laying out the game, fearful that the predators of
the forest might steal the hunters' spoils during the night. Upon
hearing this, Stephen ordered them to dig a trench around the
hunting lodge in order to protect the trophies. As he surveyed their
handiwork later, he realized that the natural barricade created by the
excavation had transformed the hill into an easily defended summit.

3

That night, the young hunter dreamed of a large city built on the site of the lodge. At its center was a fortress with gold-domed churches.

To commemorate these fantastic events, Stephen later built a hunting village on the hill and named it Kuchov. Stephen's small hamlet—located almost exactly at the geographical center of European Russia—grew into the Kremlin, the fortified, golden city of his dream. And the strange two-headed bird that saved his life became the Imperial Double Eagle, forever the symbol of the Romanov Empire.

THE Romanov reign formally began in March 1613, when the leaders of the Russian Empire traveled to the city of Kostrona to ask the sixteen-year-old Michael Romanov to become their new czar. Finding him sequestered with his mother in the crumbling Ipatiev Monastery, they offered him the crown. He returned to Moscow and founded a dynasty which would, over the course of the next three centuries, acquire a vast empire through war, intimidation, and diplomatic maneuvering.

By the late seventeenth century, Russia under the Romanovs had finally realized its imperial ambitions, by expanding its territory in all directions to become the single largest nation in Europe. In the early nineteenth century, Russian sovereigns were the most financially and politically secure of all the royal houses. After the defeat of Napoleon in 1812, Russia remained at relative peace. Despite participating in the few minor wars that erupted on the European continent in the period between the Congress of Vienna and the Franco-Prussian War, Russia faced no serious threat to its borders from foreign rivals. The Romanov czars had long fought to establish Russia as a major world power, and their successors now set out to fully enjoy the vast influence and wealth afforded by their control over the empire.

NEITHER Russia nor its rulers, however, could remain immune from the outside world. As the nineteenth century progressed, the nation was clearly developing into an anachronism. Like the czars, the

Russian nobility wanted to enjoy its newly secured prosperity to the utmost, but a great menace was rising from the new concepts of democracy and liberalism, which stemmed directly from the French Revolution. Sown across the continent during Napoleon's conquests, the seeds of reform grew into powerful movements that, in turn, fostered efforts to deny monarchs their hereditary powers.

For the most part, such revolutionary ideas were championed by adherents in England and France, and Russians viewed liberalism and democratic reform as Western notions. The ruling classes in Russia had always maintained an odd mix of anti-Western xenophobia and admiration for Western culture. Peter the Great had to force his nobles to accept the ideas and practices he brought home from his travels to the West. Once appreciation for the trends and tastes of France and Italy took root, however, the Russian nobility did not hesitate to mimic them. This was especially true in the arts, and the imperial capital of St. Petersburg was the showcase for such efforts.

Yet suspicion about other Western ideas and practices, particularly about methods of governing, had never abated. Indeed, it had grown all the more entrenched after Napoleon invaded Russia. In one regard, the defeat of Napoleon only reinforced the sense of security established by the empire's completion. As revolutionary activity grew in the years following the Congress of Vienna, however, many members of the Russian aristocracy believed that the nation could best survive by strengthening the autocracy. In order to do so, they shunned Western thought, particularly such radical and dangerous notions as the overthrow of monarchial rule.

Nonetheless, these new ideas spread rapidly elsewhere and encouraged rebellious activities that would change the face of Europe during the latter half of the nineteenth century. The widespread revolutionary movements of 1848 had most clearly signaled these new trends. By the time the Franco-Prussian War began in 1870, most of southern Europe had to some degree succumbed to these beliefs. Even the old autocratic dynasties of central Europe had begun to heed the concept of restricted monarchy. In other nations, liberalism and democracy increasingly challenged the underpinnings of absolute rule on which Romanov power and glory were based.

5

In Russia, however, the nobles became more determined to maintain their prominence within the empire. They even developed a particular wariness of other European royal houses, viewing them as increasingly prone to yielding to the forces of dangerous reform. Although the Russian nobility continued to copy Western fashions and build upon Western art forms, the nobles largely ignored or suppressed political changes and reveled in power and wealth.

By the mid-nineteenth century, the Romanov czars ruled virtually unchallenged over Europe's largest landmass. Their authority was grounded in nearly three centuries of supreme rule and perpetuated a tradition of completely autocratic emperors, whose ranks included the non-Romanov xenophobe, Ivan the Terrible, and the enlightened despot, Peter the Great. Yet the Romanovs were more than mere sovereigns. They embodied Mother Russia and maintained inseparable ties with the Orthodox church. To their subjects, particularly the peasant class, they were demigods.

The center of such a dynastical empire could only be a capital like St. Petersburg. Known chiefly for its material opulence and moral decadence, it was a place of legend and mystery to outsiders. Tales of St. Petersburg's excesses compared easily with the legends of China that Marco Polo brought back to Venice.

Much has been said of the countless treasures and baubles that have survived from the Romanov era. But the numerous pictures, books, and exhibitions of these objects portray only a small portion of the magnificent splendor of that era. Crowns and jewels, incredible arrays of art objects, and playthings filled the palaces of the nobility. All were intricately fashioned from the most precious metals and stones, often only for ceremonial use or impressive display in rooms that were themselves designed to resemble elaborate jewelry boxes. Marble, exotic woods, priceless carpets, and tapestries from around the world adorned the magnificent palaces and mansions where Russian nobility lived and entertained.

The Romanovs were not alone in enjoying the riches afforded by the empire in the nineteenth century. Greater and lesser nobles among the Russian aristocracy at St. Petersburg soon copied any astounding acquisition of the czar and czarina. Exquisite collections of art and archaeology were displayed in open competition throughout the capital. Fashion was no less important. There were endless parties, official ceremonies, and balls, where gowns of the finest cloth and jewelry of extraordinary workmanship—perhaps worn only once—could be modeled and compared.

Among the czars' best-known competitors in wealth and ostentation were the Youssoupovs. Many noble families possessed enormous estates throughout Russia, but the Youssoupovs—who owned mines, mills, and factories—were among the few to use their land for productive purposes. By the late nineteenth century, the Youssoupovs had amassed "a fortune that by today's standards would be reckoned in the billions." The family owned private rail cars and yachts and traveled often within Russia and overseas, dividing their time among the many palaces they owned.

One of their most extraordinary residences, a gift from Catherine the Great, was located by one of the canals in St. Petersburg. The Youssoupovs spared no expense in transforming the building into one of the capital's most glorious mansions. The main vestibule was designed by an Italian architect and featured a double staircase of white marble. Ceilings and walls throughout the enormous mansion were painted by Italian artists, and many of the furnishings were purchased in France. One room was set aside for receiving members of the imperial family. Another was built and decorated to resemble a Moorish palace chamber, complete with inlaid marble, a fountain, and an onyx chimney.

Most spectacular, however, was the private theater built in 1899, for which the Youssoupovs employed their own full-time musical director and orchestra. For one performance, "the chairs were removed from the orchestra and the space filled with hundreds upon hundreds of tea roses." This was only one of the Youssoupovs' houses, and much of what it contained has been lost or destroyed. Yet even in its current restoration, the palace on the canal gives some idea of the grandeur that became commonplace for Russia's nobility in the nineteenth century.

Once the Romanovs and their adherents had created a magnificent physical environment, sparing no cost or effort in providing aesthetic pleasure, their quest for self-satisfaction extended into the moral atmosphere of court life at every level. Leading the pursuit for personal pleasure were those closest to the czar and his family.

Imperial court society was stratified, with rigid gradations of rank and precedence. Immediately beneath the czar, his wife, and children, came the grand dukes, who were the sons and grandsons of czars. Standing just heartbeats away from the throne, these men made up the extended imperial family. Their lifestyles were often exotically extravagant, and their wild escapades filled European courts and drawing rooms with a never-ending source of gossip. Rich, dashing, usually impeccably clad in tailored uniforms, they were romantic, almost legendary figures of their time. As Prince David Chavchavadze wrote, "the Grand Dukes roamed Europe in their private trains, sailed the world in battleships, bought great art, collected jewels, and gambled millions on the turn of a wheel at Monte Carlo. . . ."

The grand dukes also competed in matters of the heart. They often had mistresses, and brothers and cousins had been known to marry these women after their original imperial sponsors had dismissed them or died. As in other aspects of court behavior, the lesser nobles not only imitated trends set by the Romanov hierarchy, but made every effort to excel.

Nineteenth-century Russian writers, as well as chroniclers of the court, have given us detailed portrayals of the elaborate intrigues and deceits perpetrated by noble families which reveal characters wholly different from the godlike image the czars sought to project. Competing endlessly for power and position within the imperial sphere, the courtiers employed flattery, snobbery, and vicious—but verifiable—rumor about the loose morals of fellow aristocrats.

A paragon of moral indifference and decay was Prince Felix Youssoupov, who would eventually marry the niece of Czar Nicholas II. The Prince devoted his time solely and uninhibitedly to the pursuit of pleasure. "Tall, slender, androgynous, he became at an early age a committed transvestite who, decked out in his mother's magnificent furs, jewels and gowns, would pose convincingly as a demi-mondaine in the most fashionable venues of St. Petersburg and Paris." Although often the object of virulent gossip and poorly disguised snickers among the courtiers, Felix Youssoupov was nevertheless an imposing figure in the Russian capital. His wealth and his ties to the imperial family accorded him the greatest protection, and he did not hesitate to use either to punish his enemies.

The lavish lifestyle of the court circle increasingly isolated the aristocracy from the world outside St. Petersburg. This purposeful and studied remoteness would prove to be little more than a magnificently crafted facade that only partially obscured an outdated and crumbling social and political foundation.

The gulf between the Russian rulers and their subjects first became apparent during the mid-nineteenth century, when small revolutionary reform groups sprang up in Russia, as they had already done elsewhere in Europe. Although reformers within the noble circles and among the citizenry attempted to make the nobility responsible to those it governed, the imperial rulers' attitudes and traditions remained largely unchanged. Violent and tragic conflict was inevitable.

II.
"Never forget who is Czar"

AS THE MOST PROGRESSIVE autocrat in recent Russian history, Alexander II became known as the Czar Liberator. His attempts to bring some degree of representative government to his nation, however, had only encouraged radicals to push their demands even further. In the twenty-six years of his reign, there had been many unsuccessful attempts on his life, and the police had foiled other assassination plots in the planning stages. On a Sunday afternoon in 1881, as Czar Alexander left his palace to attend a weekly parade, his wife Catherine begged him not to go, because two of the streets his procession normally passed through had reportedly been mined by terrorists.

As was customary, the Czar's return route that day was announced only minutes before he was to pass. Contrary to their usual practice, the police had neglected to bar the public from one of the main thoroughfares he was to travel. As Alexander's carriage passed the crowd, someone threw a bomb at him. The Czar was unhurt, but the explosion wounded several of his Cossack outriders. Concerned about the injured soldiers, and refusing admonitions to leave the scene at once, Alexander insisted that the procession stop so he could personally attend to his men.

As the Czar stepped out of his carriage, he looked around. Seeing that there had been no fatalities, he crossed himself and said, "Thanks to God." At that moment, an assassin screamed, "Is it thanks to God yet?" and tossed a bomb at his feet. A wall of fire engulfed the Czar, as the explosion tore off both legs and ripped open his abdomen. His brother, the Grand Duke Michael, ran to his aid and was surprised to find Alexander still alive and whispering, "Home to the palace—to die there." Michael picked up his brother's broken body and shielded it with his own as the procession rushed through the streets of St. Petersburg to the imperial residence.

Deeply disturbed by the increasing revolutionary activity, and her husband's apparent lack of concern for his personal safety, Catherine had waited at the Winter Palace, then decided to meet his carriage and insist that they take a walk through the gardens together. There she could finally persuade him to leave St. Petersburg until the political situation calmed.

When the imperial servants announced the hurried approach of the Czar's procession, the Czarina rushed toward the main portico of the palace. Before Catherine arrived, Grand Duke Michael stepped from his carriage, cradling his maimed brother. The palace servants watched as the Czar, barely alive, was carried into a nearby room, which was hastily prepared to receive his shattered body.

Word of the tragedy spread quickly, and before long the most benevolent ruler in Russian history was surrounded by his grieving family. The Czar's physician, Professor Sergius Botkin, was notified immediately and hurried to the chamber where his sovereign awaited death. He could do nothing for the Czar except try to alleviate the pain of the massive wounds. When Catherine entered the room and saw the extent of her husband's injuries, she fainted.

Her stepson, the Czarevitch Alexander, heir to the throne, so disliked Catherine that he ordered those present not to touch her. But Professor Botkin's sense of duty as a doctor overrode the command, and he left the Czar's bedside to assist the stricken woman.

The Czar's grandson Nicholas observed the scene from the periphery of the family's circle around the dying man. As he watched his grandfather slip from life, Nicholas swore silently that if he ever became Czar of all The Russias, he would never allow such horrors to be inflicted upon him—or any of his successors.

THE new Czar, Alexander III, was nearly thirty-six when he inherited the throne. He brought with him clearly established methods and ideas, which he employed to quickly gain control over Russia. His simple dress and enormous stature set him apart from most of his predecessors. He would not hesitate to use his commanding physical appearance to intimidate and impress his ministers and subjects. A favorite story told of him was that during a meeting of his ministers, one of them threatened to resign. Alexander picked the man up by his lapels and threw him to the floor saying, "You will resign when I allow it. Never forget who is Czar!"

The new Czar completely rescinded the reforms initiated by his father. Undoubtedly, his policies were motivated by the circumstances of his father's death, but the harsh manner in which he imposed them was wholly of his own design. After gaining the throne, Alexander III ruled Russia with the iron fist his father had lacked.

Alexander had married a petite and elegant Danish princess, Dagmar, who took the Russian name Marie. They had been married for nearly sixteen years, and Marie felt completely at home in Russia. She was everything her husband was not. She gave luxurious parties and gowned herself in expensive materials festooned with diamonds, emeralds, and pearls. She used her talent for interior decoration to refurbish many of the imperial palaces, and introduced a period of unparalleled opulence into the life of imperial Russia. Anastasia described her grandmother as

a happy, active, outspoken and impulsive person. Right away she was comfortable with the traditions as they had always been and that feeling never changed. And she knew how to fill the role of the top representative of the family with skill and bearing. She enjoyed a universal admiration . . . [and] during my grandfather's reign she . . . led a great number of public charities and cultural institutes.

Despite physical and temperamental differences between Alexander and Marie, theirs was a true love match. When Marie mentioned a small decorated egg displayed in the royal palace of her native Denmark, Alexander—contrary to his simple ways but always eager to please the wife he adored—ordered the creation of the first Fabergé egg. It became an Easter tradition that would last until the end of the dynasty.

The Fabergé eggs became the best-known example of the fantastic indulgences of the court and, perhaps, justifiably so. Each one captured—in a small piece of masterful handiwork—the self-contained fantasy that more and more had come to characterize St. Petersburg. Envisioned as curiosities or toys, they often froze scenes from dynastical history. They were designed exclusively for the aristocracy by the master craftsmen of Peter Carl Fabergé. Each one was specially commissioned and took months to create. Hundreds of hours of delicate assembly and hand decoration went into their manufacture, in order to disguise the latest technological wizardry within a flawless glitter of priceless jewels, the finest enamels, and gold and silver. Only after such painstaking construction were they suitable for presentation—each an amusing illusionary world where the beholders could become lost in fantasy.

The flamboyant Marie gave birth to three sons, Nicholas, George, and Michael, and two daughters, Xenia and Olga. The Czarina personally supervised her children's education and training, and established an especially close relationship with her oldest son and heir to the throne, the Czarevitch Nicholas.

DESPITE the stern measures the Czar instituted to crush political dissention, he was unable to eliminate the revolutionary movement, and in October 1888, an anarchist's bomb derailed the train in which the imperial family was traveling. As the bomb exploded, the roof caved in on the dining car in which they sat. Alexander held the roof in place until his wife and children could escape. Nicholas, who had always been intimidated by his father's robust health and looming physical presence, wondered how he could ever follow such an imposing czar.

III.

"A misunderstood and unloved Czarina"

IN 1884, Nicholas's uncle, the Grand Duke Serge, married Princess Elizabeth of Hesse, one of the most beautiful women on the continent. Nicholas attended the wedding in Russia, where he made the acquaintance of Elizabeth's sister, Princess Alix. Their mother, the late Grand Duchess Alice of Hesse, was the daughter of Queen Victoria, and had been considered psychic by some members of the British aristocracy. In 1878, the six-year-old Alix had been summoned to Windsor Castle where her royal grandmother supervised her education for the next six years.

Czarevitch Nicholas was a very attractive young man—almost the twin of his cousin, Prince George of England. His melancholy blue eyes set in a handsome face made him the classic figure of a prince and one of the most eligible bachelors in the royal houses of Europe.

Nicholas was attracted to Alix immediately. Although not nearly the beauty her sister was, Alix's bright disposition and gay nature had earned her the name Princess Sunshine. Each time he saw her, Nicholas's attraction grew stronger. His family, however, opposed his interest in her because of religious differences. As the relationship became more serious and Nicholas appeared to want to marry Alix, many of the Russian courtiers opposed the union on other grounds. Not only was Russia on unfriendly terms with Germany, but Alix's upbringing at the liberal English court was frowned upon. Perhaps most important from a dynastical viewpoint, descendants of

Queen Victoria had begun to manifest symptoms of the "bleeding disease," which could be passed on to any potential heir to the throne. Nevertheless, an increasingly serious courtship ensued over the next ten years.

Not long after the wedding of his daughter Xenia to the Russian Grand Duke Alexander in July 1894, Czar Alexander III's health began to decline drastically, and his weight plummeted. His doctors believed that the strain of holding up the roof of the bomb-damaged dining car had permanently weakened his kidneys. The imperial physicians realized they could do little to improve his health.

As the Czar's condition deteriorated, the courtiers anticipated the worst and muffled their criticism of the Czarevitch's interest in Alix. The young prince was allowed to proceed to Germany to make his proposal, but Alix's initial reaction was negative. Although she saw in Nicholas many of the qualities she admired in a potential husband, she maintained one serious reservation. A devout Protestant, Alix could not conceive of converting to the Russian Orthodox faith. Kaiser Wilhelm II of Germany intervened and convinced her that she would not have to give up or significantly alter her basic religious beliefs by converting.

Nicholas described this time as "long and very difficult" and his "quest" for her hand in marriage as "desperate." When she finally consented to his proposal, he wrote, "I cried like a child and she did too; but her expression had changed; her face was lit by a quiet content." It was the start of a life-long, unshakable devotion between them.

DESPITE the romantic ardor that bound her to Nicholas, Alix's decision to marry into the Romanov family and enter the world of St. Petersburg seemed marked by misfortune from the outset. She and Nicholas were not yet married when her prospective father-in-law, Alexander III, died. She was derided throughout Russia as the "funeral bride" and the "German bitch."

Within a few weeks, however, Nicholas and Alix were wed. As was customary, she took a Russian name and thereafter was known as Czarina Alexandra. Her entrance to court was difficult, because unlike her mother-in-law, Marie, Alexandra had little time between marriage and coronation to acquaint herself with the court's intricate customs and traditions. She came to the throne still viewed as very much an outsider.

Her own background had scarcely prepared the new Czarina for the court of St. Petersburg. Having fully assimilated the ideas and strict rules of behavior of her grandmother, Queen Victoria, Alexandra was every inch a foreigner. As one English observer noted, "Her whole morale was English. English was the language which she always spoke and wrote to the Emperor . . . and the Empress always thought of herself as an English woman." Nonetheless Alexandra made every effort to become a responsible and concerned consort. She had begun immediately to prepare herself for her new role in an effort to compensate for knowing little of Russian life. She plunged into language lessons and went through a fervent conversion from Protestantism to the Russian Orthodox faith. Ironically, the Orthodoxy she had once eschewed now allowed her to more freely express her already pronounced tendency towards mysticism, which she had inherited from her mother. The St. Petersburg court viewed her embrace of the occult as further evidence of her ties to her German and Victorian heritages.

For her part, she disliked the licentious behavior of some members of the imperial family, the Russian nobility, and St. Petersburg society in general. In her view, such loose morals could seriously undermine her husband's authority. Her disdain for the Russian court caused physical as well as emotional discomfort. According to Anastasia, Alexandra

> was a misunderstood and unloved czarina, she who had such a deep feeling for the true essence of Russia. For what surrounded her—the world of Grand Dukes, the world of palace officials—was that other Russia, that Parisian, elegant, superficial Russia, with its enormous extravagance, its love of the good life and its lack of morals. I remember very well the looks that the Czarina gave, as she saw the behavior of these people, and the red flecks of agitation which would then rise from her neck up to her cheeks.

ALEXANDRA'S difficulties at court were exacerbated by her relationship with her mother-in-law, Marie, who was now the Dowager

Czarina. From the beginning, Marie openly treated the new Czarina as an unwelcome addition to the family and resented the time Nicholas spent with his bride. Pleading grief and loneliness, Marie had insisted that Nicholas and Alexandra occupy a small suite of uncomfortable rooms in her St. Petersburg palace for the first year of their marriage.

Tradition called for the Dowager Czarina to retire from her active social life and turn over ceremonial responsibility to Alexandra, but Marie pointedly refused to do so. She also resisted passing on to Alexandra the jewelry traditionally worn by the reigning czarina. Quite the contrary, Marie insisted on taking precedence over Alexandra at public ceremonies. As Anastasia recalled, the motivation was simple:

> The Dowager Czarina Marie . . . hated my mother most. My grandmother knew that her son held her in the highest regard and that he would never contradict her. I'm sorry to say she used this knowledge to so strongly promote her position as Dowager Czarina in contrast to the passive, unassuming daughter-in-law, that without contest she seized the primary place . . . during the entire reign of her son. . . .

The pattern had been established early. When the period of official mourning expired, the Dowager Czarina—still elegant and beautiful—returned with vigor to the life of glittering balls and spectacles she had always loved. Alexandra would attend such events more as another courtier than as wife to the Czar.

Her mother-in-law's dismissive attitude only fed Alexandra's growing insecurity. The longer Marie continued to reign as *de facto* Czarina, the more Alexandra began to chafe under the pressure. Even after moving to a separate residence, she could not escape the Dowager Czarina's shadow.

Alexandra's attitude about the lifestyle at court, her ignorance of custom and tradition, and her growing devotion to the Russian Orthodox faith set her ever further apart. She lacked friends of her own in St. Petersburg and had no one in whom she could confide or seek counsel. The growing isolation and negative comparisons with her mother-in-law sharpened her feelings of alienation and inadequacy.

ALEXANDRA began to feel, quite justifiably, that she was being denied her rights as the reigning Czar's wife. Anastasia's recollections from her childhood are filled with repeated references to her mother's attempts to exert herself, even though she had become very reserved and mistrustful of the court. Two aspects of Alexandra's life helped to nurture her tenuous self-assuredness, which she needed in order to assert herself as Czarina.

The first was her relationship with her husband. Despite continually trying conditions, it remained conjugally sublime. Nicholas and Alexandra enjoyed a genuine love match, rare among royal circles. Their diaries and letters candidly attested to a satisfactory sexual relationship throughout the marriage. The morning after their wedding night, for example, she wrote, "Never did I believe that there could be such utter happiness in this world, such a feeling of unity between two mortal beings."

The Czarina's second solace was in her role as potential mother to Nicholas's heirs. Her most fervent desire was to deliver a male successor to the Romanov dynasty. Within four months of her marriage, she discovered that she was expecting. She spent her time planning and decorating her family's future apartment in the Alexander Palace at Czarskoe Selo (The Czar's Village), the imperial compound fifteen miles from St. Petersburg and the Winter Palace, which historically served as the primary official residence for the sovereigns.

By November 1895, a year after the death of Alexander III, the new Czarina's pregnancy was causing her continuous pain. Despite concern over her health, the Russian Empire eagerly awaited news of the birth. As tradition prescribed, huge cannons were rolled into place in St. Petersburg. Three hundred rounds would be fired to announce the birth of a future czar, one hundred one rounds would announce the birth of a daughter. Late in the year, the cannonade began. For miles around the people counted, waiting in vain for the hundred and second round to be fired. Grand Duchess Olga was born.

Two years later, in 1897, another daughter, Tatiana, was delivered. Almost exactly two years after that, the third Grand Duchess, Marie, came into the world.

Although the Czar and Czarina delighted in their children, the three successive female births proved unpopular with the court and with the Russian people. Alexandra was now scorned for not fulfilling her dynastical duty. The nation demanded a male heir. The Russian laws of succession—known as The Pauline Law—dictated that only a male could inherit the throne, and Alexandra felt pressured by the requirements of the dynasty. Worse was the vindictive gossip at court.

IV.

"Even the roses were mauve"

BY 1900, Alexandra had become somewhat more confident in her role as Czarina. Nevertheless, she continued to despair over her inability to give the empire a male heir and began seeking advice from all quarters on this most personal matter, which had begun to create political problems. One of the friends whose counsel she sought was the Grand Duchess Militsa, married to the Czar's uncle, the Grand Duke Nicholas. Militsa and her sister Anastasia were former Montenegrin princesses who had made advantageous marriages into the Romanov family. Widely known as exotic beauties, they dabbled in psychic phenomena and sponsored a salon devoted to promoting their esoteric beliefs.

After Alexandra confessed her fears to Militsa, the Montenegrin held the Czarina spellbound with the story of a "holy man" named Philippe Vachot from Lyon, France. Vachot had convinced Militsa that when he wore a certain hat, he and anyone accompanying him were invisible. Militsa assured Alexandra that she had often been invisible when in Vachot's company. Moreover, she regaled Alexandra with stories of the other fantastical powers of this French mystic, faith healer, and "psychic doctor"—particularly with stories of his ability to determine and control the gender of an unborn child. Alexandra decided that if all else failed, she would consult Philippe Vachot.

For Militsa to propound such views, or for Alexandra—ever the converted zealot—to so readily accept their validity, was not as unlikely as it might appear. The Russian Orthodox faith embraced mysticism of many varieties. Seers, holy men, martyrs, and living saints were accepted as easily as visions, miracles, and speaking in tongues. The sanctioning of the supernatural by the established church was partly the result of the far-flung empire's incorporating vastly disparate peoples and cultures, some of which clung to medieval ways. Alexandra, once so fearful of changing her religion, now reveled in a faith that allowed her greater spiritual freedom.

Alexandra's penchant for the religiously bizarre explained her fascination with Mitia Koliaba, a deformed peasant who was believed to possess "the special gift of direct communication with God." Koliaba had stumps instead of arms, which he flailed wildly during violent epileptic seizures, "accompanied by horrible sounds uttered in painful gasps and a terrifying howling and spitting." Religious zealots believed Koliaba received divine inspiration during his seizures.

The Czarina attended these performances regularly. She would listen with rapt attention to the epileptic's babbling, and would strain to glean the holy revelations she thought they contained. The experience was exhausting. As a witness to Koliaba's demonstrations said, "One had to have extremely strong nerves to endure the presence of this imbecile."

In 1901, when the Czar and Czarina were scheduled to make a state visit to France, Alexandra recalled her conversation with Militsa about the French mystic Vachot. At the Czarina's request her friend arranged a meeting with him for the imperial couple. At the appointed hour, Nicholas and Alexandra met the strange-looking Vachot, a sinister man with sharp, penetrating eyes and a full, black moustache. Although the Czarina was already pregnant at the time, Vachot confidently announced that by practicing "astral medicine," he could promise that she would give birth to a boy. So impressed—or desperate—was the imperial couple, they hired the mystic to return with them and minister to Alexandra. Once back in Russia, Alexandra followed Vachot's instructions faithfully, "bathing" in moonlight on astrologically auspicious nights, drinking herbal concoctions, and fervently praying for the heir the nation demanded.

In the early hours of June 5, 1901, Alexandra delivered her fourth child. To her bitter disappointment, it was another daughter. As the cannons in St. Petersburg rumbled and once again stopped at a hundred and one, the Russian people feared that they would never be blessed with a czarevitch. The new Grand Duchess was named Anastasia, meaning "reborn," after the sister of the friend who had first told the Czarina about the French mystic.

Vachot was undeterred by the failure of astral medicine to accomplish what he had predicted. Her Imperial Majesty, he explained, had already been expecting when he began his ministrations. If allowed to continue working with her, he promised, he would surely fulfill his prophecy the next time. Alexandra continued to believe in his powers, and Vachot remained at court.

OUTSIDE the private family quarters, the imperial couple's failure to produce a male heir was blamed entirely upon the already widely unpopular Czarina. Alexandra's nerves began to fray and, following her recovery from Anastasia's birth, she withdrew from court activities and public functions.

As she grew more isolated from members of the court, criticism of her mounted. The courtiers continued to compare her unfavorably to her predecessor, the Dowager Czarina. Alexandra reacted by drawing even further away from imperial duties and ceased attending public events almost altogether. She concentrated her energies on her daughters and, still hoping to be blessed with a son, became more devoted to the study of religion. Anastasia's memories of her mother's attitude come from the earliest days of her childhood and provide a unique perspective on the Czarina's preoccupations:

> [I]t had become the fashion [at court] to talk a lot about the Russian people and to praise simple Russians to heaven. My mother had

nothing at all to do with this. . . . Her relationship [to the people] came from the heart. . . . [She felt] it was destiny, and . . . she held to her plain and simple lifestyle and her rigid moral tenets. Because of this, she made many enemies among those who surrounded her. She wanted no part of the general moral decay or the frenzy for enjoying life. Her view of life remained deeply religious and earnest. She was very much tied to the spiritual, the other-worldly, to fate.

Alexandra's dependence on Vachot and her pursuit of other bizarre mystics and thinly veiled charlatans proved to be a serious error in her relations with the court. As much as she wished to avoid ceremonial functions, the Czarina could not shun all official responsibilities. Yet when she went to the court, the enmity of her courtiers was evident. She became convinced that the entire nobility and aristocracy were plotting against her. She ignored all criticism of her actions and activities, no matter how justified or from what quarter. Her self-alienation evolved into a "siege mentality" and eventually into paranoia.

The Czarina's biographers chronicle the progression of her emotional decline through innumerable hysterical outbursts and incidents of uncontrollable weeping. These scenes inevitably culminated in her withdrawing into her boudoir in the family apartments in the Alexander Palace at Czarskoe Selo. Outsiders were seldom allowed into these private chambers, and only a few trusted servants attended the family there.

These rooms were in the west wing of the palace, and Alexandra's taste in Victorian furnishings predominated. They were full of English chintzes, potted plants, and portraits of the British royal family. Prince Felix Youssoupov later wrote:

In spite of its modest size, the Alexander Palace would not have lacked charm had it not been for the young Empress's 'improvements.' She replaced most of the paintings, stucco ornaments, and bas-reliefs by mahogany woodwork and cozy-corners in the worst possible taste. New furniture by Maples was sent from England, and the old furniture was banished to storerooms.

Biographer Greg King noted that, "[i]nstead of using the exquisite French and English antique pieces at her disposal from the collection of Catherine the Great, she furnished her home by mail order, with machine-made assembly-line couches, tables, and chairs."

More than any other, Alexandra's own room became her sanctuary from the world. Greg King characterized this room as "Alexandra's obsession. Everything, carpets, draperies, furniture, even the roses, lilacs, and orchids decorating its tables, were mauve. She loved this room, and lay on a flowered chaise looking onto her private balcony for hours." Filled with family photographs and icons of her favorite saints, the mauve boudoir became famous in history as the center of activity of the ill-fated Romanov family.

She claimed these furnishings reminded her of her happy years with her grandmother in England, but they only served, in the eyes of outsiders, to underscore the fact that the Czarina was a foreigner.

ALEXANDRA took pains to severely restrict her social circle. Anastasia recalled that her mother characterized the obligatory retinue of noblewomen assigned to her as "rodents." She never viewed most of the courtiers and members of St. Petersburg society as friends, but there were a few, including the Montenegrin princesses, in whom she could confide. Her most intimate friend was undoubtedly Anna Viroubova. For three generations, Anna's family had served as directors of the Private Chancellery of the Emperor. As a result, she had grown up at court, although she did not become close to Alexandra until about 1900, when the Czarina accepted her as a member of the small coterie of intimates outside the official retinue.

Historians accurately described Anna as a plain, frumpy, rather stupid woman, whose sole function was to play the role of Alexandra's lapdog, or sycophant. Anastasia said that her mother "sensed Russia in Anna Viroubova, that Russia which . . . [mother] sought and that she felt so near in her heart but so far away in her life."

Indeed, Anna had no outside interests beyond the life of her Czarina, who treated her like a younger, simple-minded sister. They would spend hours together sewing and painting, all the while gossiping about members of the court and ministers of the government. For by this time, the Czarina had developed a condescending attitude toward the courtiers and ministers. She disliked them intensely but loved to hear of their mistakes, intrigues, and secrets. She and Anna also shared an interest in mysticism and psychic phenomena, and the Czarina found Anna to be a willing and unquestioning adherent to her views.

Anna became so indispensable that she was given a small house adjacent to the palace on the grounds of Czarskoe Selo. She filled her residence with the styles of furniture favored by the Czarina, and covered the walls with portraits and snapshots of the imperial family. As the years passed, she came to spend all of her time with her mistress, and her devotion to Alexandra was complete.

Although historians have derided Anna Viroubova for decades, her two books of reminiscences, written while living in exile in Finland in the early 1920s, provide invaluable insight into the daily life and psychology of Czarina Alexandra.

Part of Anna's value as a chronicler comes from her love of photography, in which she also mimicked the Romanovs. One of the favorite pastimes she enjoyed with Alexandra was to place the family's private photographs into oversized albums. When Anna went into exile after the revolution, the photo albums were sent to her. They have since found their way to the Houghton Library at Harvard, where they still reside, mute evidence of the lifestyle and activities of the family that all but adopted her as one of their own. Her memoirs and albums stand as singular contributions to what we know today about the intimate life of the imperial family.

The few friendships that Alexandra cultivated—even those as intimate as that with Anna—were not enough to dispel the Czarina's sense of isolation and detachment from the world around her. As it became more pronounced, her contemplations within the sanctuary of her mauve boudoir would continually lead her to seek further guidance from God. Anastasia recalled that her mother spent much time in the private chapel at the Alexander Palace:

> Especially in her own chapel, which she had built at Czarskoe Selo, we often saw her in deep prayer. This chapel was a complete expression of her being . . . we would see her in her chair withdrawn into herself, sitting almost lifeless. . . . We stayed here mostly without priests. No daylight forced its way in, only many candles, which were reflected in the gold mosaic of the walls.

The Czarina would also seek understanding from a wide range of mystics; as with her friendships, however, there was always only one spiritual adviser in which Alexandra placed utmost trust. During this period, Vachot remained the chosen guide.

V.

"Incomparable as a mother"

IN THE FIRST QUARTER of 1903, nearly two years after the birth of Anastasia, Alexandra again believed herself to be pregnant. Although it was widely accepted at the time that the Czarina was enceinte, and Vachot apparently confirmed that she had conceived, no official announcement was made. Those who knew of or suspected the pregnancy felt that the imperial couple did not wish to be embarrassed should the child be yet another daughter.

By all accounts, Alexandra showed every sign of a normal pregnancy until September, when she complained of "a pain" and fainted. She was ill for a long time afterward but refused to see the court-appointed medical doctors. When she finally consented to an examination, the doctors announced that she was not pregnant. The news circulated that she had suffered a false or hysterical pregnancy.

TEN months later, in July 1904, Alexandra at last gave birth to the long-awaited son, named Alexis. When the cannons roared three hundred times that day, the Russian people rejoiced. Their reclusive Czarina had finally delivered a czarevitch and assured the continuation of the Romanov dynasty. Even the nobility, who had long despised their Empress, could not help but be pleased that the dynasty that protected them would continue.

His mission at last complete, Vachot was showered with imperial honors and endowments and sent back to France, where he died a year later. At his last audience with Alexandra, he presented her with a silver bell and told her to ring it to ward off evil spirits. He also predicted the coming of another mystical friend who would speak to her of God.

Nicholas and Alexandra focused nearly all their attention on their young children. The family circle was now complete: the Russian imperial house boasted four daughters and an heir, whose parents provided a loving but carefully fashioned upbringing. The official residence remained the Winter Palace in St. Petersburg, although the Czarina preferred the remoteness of the Alexander Palace at Czarskoe Selo. There she established what she considered the perfect routine for her children.

Public appearances of the entire family were rare. Nonetheless, every event in the lives of royalty was chronicled in detail. The public viewed supreme rulers like the Czar as celebrities, and following the birth of Alexis, the Romanovs were idealized as a family. Each member seemed to play a stereotypical role: the handsome father, the stern but elegant mother, the beautiful daughters, and the baby brother. Their every public movement or statement appeared in illustrated magazines, newspapers, and newsreels. Their portraits on postcards, plaques, and dishes were best-sellers around the world. They came to be viewed almost as fairy-tale figures.

LIFE for the Romanov children was enviable in many ways. Anastasia's remembrances, which have remained largely unpublished until now, provide the most intimate account. They show clearly that despite whatever reluctance Alexandra may have felt about exerting herself at court, she dominated family life:

> The Czarina was incomparable as a mother . . . [and] we knew that when she had a moment free she would come to us. As a result, each time together was like a gift. Never was there among us the short, daily ceremonial meetings that were common in other princely houses.

After the Czar moved his wife and children permanently to Czarskoe Selo in 1905, to guard against assassination, the pattern only intensified.

Alexandra lived isolated with the Grand Duchesses and the Czarevitch in the private quarters of the palace. She still had to attend to some ceremonial duties, but for the most part she could concentrate all her energies on the children. She showered them with love and affection, and even when she could not be with them, they were constantly attended. A small army of governesses and liveried servants, all trained in the English manner, served the imperial daughters. The same was true for the Czarevitch, who was accorded his own retinue. The children's lives centered around their doting parents. Alexandra was a kind and compassionate mother; the facade of cold reserve she showed to members of the court was seldom apparent to her children.

Determined that her son and daughters have the same type of upbringing she had enjoyed at her grandmother's court in England, Alexandra saw to it that the imperial family spoke English at home, and the children learned English first, then French, and finally Russian.

Although clearly loved and spoiled, the Romanov children led controlled lives. Their days were regimented by their governesses and tutors, carefully chosen to educate them in languages, the classics, and history. The girls also studied the "feminine arts" of needlework, painting, poetry, and posture. They were the "daughters of the empire," and were being prepared for marriage to foreign kings and princes.

Like most young children, Anastasia and her siblings disliked attending lessons:

> The classrooms were set aside for that special purpose and we did not like to go there. More than anyone else, I had the greatest aversion to them. I hated this cold learning, the dead, abstract manner in which we were taught. But I excelled at composition. I must say that all my poems were satires, lampoons, from which no one was safe. Private tutors divided the lessons among themselves and foreign men supplemented their efforts in specialized subjects. They always appeared in black robes, which made us furious because it gave to the lessons a particular stiffness. Otherwise we had a nanny and a governess. . . .

Of all the children's many caretakers, their favorite was Anastasia's nursemaid, Shura, who spent time with all the Grand Duchesses. Anastasia developed a particular closeness to Shura and often reminisced about her:

> She had our total confidence and knew all our little secrets and wishes. . . . One imagines usually that a nanny is an old, stout woman, but this picture in no way describes Shura. She was . . . the youngest of all the people who cared for us. But she was motherly and evoked absolute trust. My brother and I had fights over her, even though he was not at all under her care. . . . It was our greatest joy to see her turn beet red when we played a trick on her.

One of brother Alexis's most influential attendants was Pierre Gilliard. He was Swiss-French and had previously been tutor to the Leuchtenberg family in Germany. The Leuchtenbergs were related by marriage to the Romanovs and had established close ties to Russia. Part of the family lived in St. Petersburg and were accorded all rights as part of the court nobility.

Their former tutor Gilliard proved a success with the Czarevitch, as well as with the Grand Duchesses. He taught all of them French and traveled as part of the imperial entourage. Gilliard fell in love with Anastasia's "beloved nursemaid" Shura and married her years later. Their romance provided the girls with endless opportunities to poke fun: "How we teased her when we discovered this tender relationship between the two of them! And how happily she reacted to our goading!"

THE imperial children at Czarskoe Selo had many diversions from the daily routine. An enormous park was part of the imperial compound, and Anastasia loved to play there with her sisters and brother. She adored animals of any kind. The government of France had once given her a cow, which now resided at the park along with a menagerie of other creatures:

> Tame black swans . . . came and sailed there . . . stooping to let us feed them from our hands. I also think of the other animals—our dogs and Shetland ponies, which we loved and on which we rode through the

park. Alexis . . . had a particular favorite, which no other child like
him had: a small elephant.

One of Anastasia's favorite animals was Jemmy, a King Charles
spaniel that belonged to her sister Tatiana. Anastasia often played
with him and came to care for him as if he were her own.

The children enjoyed teasing the guards and causing other mis-
chief. In an attempt to instill a degree of discipline, their parents
assigned each of them a little garden plot in the park. They enjoyed
gardening, for the Czar had built them a small cottage nearby and
would come to oversee the progress of their labors, then allow them
to serve him tea in the cottage. Anastasia was quite proud of the fact
that "we had to do all the handiwork ourselves: digging, sowing,
watering, weeding, and later harvesting. No one was allowed to
help us."

Although the imperial couple kept their children as isolated as
possible, they did allow them to have a few playmates. Anastasia and
her siblings did not roam the palace and grounds freely romping
with the children of court nobles, but neither were they entirely
without friends. For example, when she was very young, Anastasia
played with her Romanov cousins. She would particularly remember Princesses Nina and Xenia, who were about her age.

As she grew older, Anastasia also spent time with Gleb and
Tatiana Botkin, whose father, Eugene, was the court physician.
Their grandfather, Sergius Botkin, had attended Alexander II and
was present at his side when he died. Although the Botkins were not
of imperial rank, Anastasia bonded with them strongly and considered them "my special friends." Tatiana Botkin was allowed to visit
the Romanov daughters, but was at first more of a companion to the
other Grand Duchesses. Still, as she spent more time with the
family, Tatiana Botkin also became friends with Anastasia, who
called her Tanya.

Gleb Botkin, a year older than Anastasia, became her closest
friend. He was a quiet, serious boy with a talent for painting and
caricature. Gleb was especially adept at rendering detailed water-
color scenes of animals assuming human guise. There were foxes in
hunting garb and boots, for example, and turtles in top hats and
tails. Anastasia, with her passion for animals and her skill at compo-

sition, eagerly waited for her friend to finish a picture so that she could write a story to explain it. The two youngsters amused themselves for hours with this activity, and years later Anastasia recalled her times with Gleb as "the most happy of my childhood."

Aside from having a few playmates their own age, the imperial children were largely sequestered within their parents' private world. Other adult role models were few. Anna Viroubova lived across the park in the house that Nicholas and Alexandra had built for her, and it became a special haven for the family:

> This simple but cozy house, where human imperfections were always accepted, became more and more of a refuge for us. We always took something to eat for tea, which [Anna] herself prepared. My parents carried these packets [of tea] themselves, for they never allowed their servants to accompany them [to Anna's house].

Anna was also one of the few adults allowed access to the family's private quarters at the Alexander Palace.

Although a constant stream of visitors came to the large imperial compound at Czarskoe Selo, few of them felt welcome at the palace. This was the case even with relatives. The Romanovs, led by Dowager Czarina Marie, had long shunned Alexandra, and they did not approve of the manner in which she raised her children or lived her life. Alexandra was equally disdainful of their gregarious lifestyles. She certainly did not complain that her mother-in-law preferred to remain in St. Petersburg to take part in the extravagant social life of the capital. The Grand Duchess Xenia, sister to the Czar, was of much the same mind as her mother and was seldom seen at Czarskoe Selo. Nicholas's brothers, the Grand Dukes George and Michael, almost never came to the Alexander Palace. The entire clan gathered rarely and, then, only for the most important state and religious ceremonies, when public scrutiny demanded a show of solidarity.

The Grand Duchess Olga, youngest sister to the Czar, was more sympathetic to the Czarina and closer to the family than the other Russian relations. Anastasia recalled her fondly as someone "who was very similar to [my mother] in her modest and simple ways. I remember her as an affectionate person who was always particularly delightful to us children."

For the most part, however, the imperial family formed its own close-knit unit. They made room in their lives for a few special friends and servants, including the Botkins, Anna Viroubova, Shura, and Gilliard, but Nicholas and Alexandra remained intent on keeping their children away from the corrupting influences of court life.

SOME of Anastasia's favorite memories of her family involve their travels together. Often they would take official trips to England or Germany to visit her mother's relatives. There were opportunities to relax and enjoy one another's company in these surroundings. Her mother was fond of visiting Cowes in England, where the imperial family used a residence. The German branch of Alexandra's family included Anastasia's uncle, the Grand Duke of Hesse, who maintained an enormous hunting lodge at Wolfsgarten. The entire family would go to the lodge when the Grand Duke and the Czar got together for sport. Otherwise they seldom went to Alexandra's homeland. Perhaps, as Anastasia recalled, it was because they "always felt somewhat strange around [the] German relatives." Their two favorite retreats—Livadia in the Crimea and Spala in Poland—offered more privacy. But wherever they journeyed, they always did so in complete comfort.

The Romanovs were indisputably one of the wealthiest families in the history of the world. Despite Alexandra's relatively simple taste in the Victorian furnishings of their private apartments, no expense was spared in the construction and decoration of the imperial trains and yacht.

Two identical trains, painted imperial blue, were constructed for the exclusive, private use of Nicholas and his family. According to Romanov expert Robert K. Massie, each was "a traveling miniature palace . . . [consisting] of a string of luxurious royal-blue salon cars with the double-eagle crest emblazoned in gold on their sides, pulled by a gleaming black locomotive."

The private car of the imperial couple contained a bedroom "the size of three normal compartments." The Czarina had a sitting room decorated in mauve, like her palace boudoir. The dining car was equipped with a full kitchen containing three stoves, and the dining salon seated twenty at table. The family ate from silver and gold plates and serving dishes. Anastasia remembered with fondness that, when the train stopped in snowy locales, she would grab the solid silver trays from the dining car and use them as toboggans on the snowbanks outside.

Even more, she liked to travel by train to the Crimea. Each spring, the family would travel to Livadia at the Black Sea, which Anastasia recalled that "we especially loved. It was our earthly paradise filled with southern beauty, a sun that shined forever and the blue sea, where we were allowed to swim. We all swam like fish and it was a joy. . . ." The children's rooms looked out over the sea. The landscape was much different from that of northern Russia, and the flowers and animals fascinated the youngest Grand Duchess. "Among my special memories of Livadia belongs a beautiful birdhouse. There lived all kinds of colorful birds. In one part of the birdhouse we children had a great number of canaries, which sang beautifully."

In addition to the trains, the imperial yacht *Standart* was a favorite means of traveling together as a family. The 4,500-ton black-hulled steamer featured such luxurious appointments as gold-leaf fixtures and varnished decks and masts. The staterooms were decorated with crystal chandeliers, mahogany paneling, and velvet drapes. The furniture in the Czarina's personal quarters was covered in mauve chintz, and she had a private chapel.

The Czar and his family spent some of their happiest hours aboard the *Standart* sailing the Finnish waters in summer. They swam in the ocean and often went ashore for picnics or excursions in search of wild mushrooms. Anastasia and her father became the family experts on the discovery of the proper mushrooms to pick. She developed her talent into an exact science and could tell at a glance which fungi were poisonous.

VI.

"I was named the 'Clown'"

AS THE YOUNGEST daughter of the Czar, Anastasia was considered by the court to be the least "important" of the imperial
children. She was expected to marry last and probably not as well as
her three sisters. The press and nobility scrutinized the other Grand
Duchesses as they matured into beautiful young women. Anastasia
received scant attention, except when her high-jinks caused laughter,
or worse, embarrassment. Because she was not as well-chronicled as
her parents or her siblings, the recollections of those people who
survived the revolution provide the only glimpse of Anastasia's nature as she grew up at court. Invariably, they describe the Grand
Duchess as a precocious child.

Gleb Botkin later recalled that there was something about Anastasia that gave her "a particular fascination." He continued:

> This was not due to her beauty, for Anastasia was less beautiful than
> her sisters. She was small in size and her features were irregular. Her
> nose was rather long and her mouth quite wide. She had a small,
> straight chin which lacked almost entirely the usual curve below the
> lower lip. But her eyes—blue, luminous eyes, always sparkling with
> humor—were truly beautiful. It was from her father that she inher-
> ited those eyes. I have never met a person who was introduced to the
> Emperor for the first time who did not comment on the beauty of his
> eyes.

Throughout her life, it would be those eyes that people would
remember. Their unique color would set her apart and stamp her as
a Romanov.

Gleb befriended her early, and their relationship endured. He recorded his impressions of her in three books and hundreds of letters:

> At first glance she impressed one as a picture of innocence and model behavior. Very straightlaced and prim she appeared when she entered the room, holding herself as erect as all her sisters did, her head slightly bent forward, a very grave expression in her blue eyes. But usually, the more serious she looked, the more certain it was that some mischievous idea was brewing in her head, and in a few minutes the fun would begin.

Anastasia herself was almost proud of her reputation. Recalling her childhood, she would say:

> I was named the "Clown"—which I'm sorry to say was often the case. Aunt Olga, the youngest of the Czar's sisters, called me . . . quicksilver. . . . I believe that . . . really was a good name for me. . . . I loved any joke or nonsense, which I also promoted along with Aunt Olga. For example, I would lie right across the floor when she was expected, so that she had to step around me. Anything stiff or unmoving was against my nature and I had to fidget and churn in order to set things in motion.

Others would remember her as a talented mimic, a tomboy, an imp whose hat was often askew as she trailed out of step behind her sisters during official processions.

Anastasia was not, however, without any serious interests. She always seemed to carry her box camera around with her. More than likely, her devotion to photography reflected the influence of her parents. Inveterate photographers, Nicholas and Alexandra recorded family holidays and private parties. The Czarina published a book of her own family photographs, and Nicholas was one of the first to sponsor successful experiments in color photography. Anastasia, however, was the one who excelled at the art. The technology interested her from an early age, and the images she created became favorite mementos. Many of the pictures she took survive to this day, providing unique insight into the private world of her family.

Never easily controlled, the young Grand Duchess did not like to adhere to the many demands made on her and her siblings. Anastasia could prove particularly problematic for her elders, and the tutors were favorite targets of her pranks. The children's French teacher, Pierre Gilliard, recalled Anastasia as

> very roguish and almost a wag. She had a very strong sense of humor, and the darts of her wit often found sensitive spots. She was rather an *enfant terrible*, though this fault tended to correct itself with age. She was also extremely idle, though with the idleness of a gifted child. Her French accent was excellent, and she acted scenes from comedy with remarkable talent. She was so lively, and her gaiety so infectious. . . .

Alexandra's best friend, Anna Viroubova, thought Anastasia "a sharp and clever child, [who] was a very monkey for jokes, some of them almost too practical for the enjoyment of others." Although the Czar's sister Olga would call her niece "my favorite god-daughter," she also knew her to be "a fearful tomboy. . . . Anastasia, even when quite small, was a desperate tease and everybody in her world came in for their share of it. . . . The child was brimming with vitality."

MORE than anything, Anastasia hated to attend obligatory functions, and she would participate in formal ceremonies only when forced.

> From the age of seven we were used to standing in line in order to give a word or if possible say something personal to complete strangers. You can imagine how difficult this was for children. Each person who was presented to us waited to be addressed—always you had to find just the right word to say or the right question to ask. You were not allowed to notice any embarrassment and had to maintain proper bearing. It required a lot of self-control. . . .

But even on these occasions, the young Grand Duchess managed to have fun and often enlisted the help of her sisters.

> Nevertheless, we allowed ourselves little escapades. For example, there were some people who had the habit of bowing ridiculously low

before us in order to show their devotion. We found this foolish and rid ourselves of it by curtseying improperly low in order to make fun of them. Naturally, we didn't do this in the presence of our parents.

As Anastasia grew older, her independent spirit became even more pronounced. She chafed at having to dress for formal occasions; her attire was more casual than that of her stylish older sisters, and she exhibited flashes of a quick temper. When angered, she broke out in red blotches on her face and arms, just as her mother did.

One of the rare, but unavoidable, occasions when the entire imperial family appeared in public was a concert in 1911. Also in attendance were Post Wheeler, a professional diplomat, and his wife, the popular novelist Hallie Erminie Rives, both of whom were assigned to the American legation in St. Petersburg at the time. They enjoyed circulating in aristocratic society and had readily accepted the imperial invitation to attend the annual Military Concert at the St. Petersburg Opera House. The event was of the utmost social importance that season, for the Czar himself had not attended the concert for six years. Moreover, he would be appearing in public with the Czarevitch Alexis for the first time.

Hallie Erminie Rives later described the evening:

> The Opera House was a superb building, its horseshoe larger by a third than the Metropolitan in New York, a splendid site, packed as it was with the court, the *Corps Diplomatique* and the high officers of the various services, all *en grande tenue* and the women's white arms and shoulders decked with jewels. The imperial box was high in the center back, draped in Gobelin-blue velvet, with golden cupids at the top pelting one another with roses.

The Wheelers were delighted to find themselves seated in a box that not only afforded a clear view of the Czar and Czarevitch, but adjoined the box of other members of the imperial family—the Dowager Czarina and all four of the Czar's daughters. Such proximity was due to the fact that the Czar's police considered Americans, in contrast to Europeans, unlikely to assassinate the Romanovs.

Ten-year-old Anastasia carried with her a box of chocolates in silver wrapping paper. As she sat down near the railing separating her from Rives, she smiled and set the chocolates between them.

During the concert, Rives secretly studied the Czar's loge. She was fascinated by "what Russia had never seen before"—Nicholas and his son together. "Very few of that great audience, outside of the court functionaries, had ever seen [Alexis], he had been only a fable."

At the intermission, Rives stayed in her seat observing Anastasia. "She was not a beautiful child, but there was something frank and winning about her. Her hair was drawn back in a one-sided whorl, perhaps to hide a small scar whose edge I fancied I saw under its dark loop." The child was eating the chocolates in the silver-wrapped box, without having removed her white gloves, which were now "sadly smudged."

"She shyly held out the box to me," Rives wrote, "and I took one." From behind the curtain came music and Anastasia began to softly hum the song. Rives thought it "a haunting air suggestive of the Volga Boat Song" and asked Anastasia its name.

"Oh," she replied, "it is an old song about a little girl who had lost her doll."

"There were many more songs to come . . . but the odd little strain went weaving through them all," Rives wrote. "When I went to sleep that night it was humming away tantalizingly in my head."

Anastasia, however, preferred Czarskoe Selo or anywhere else she could be alone with her family. Lacking contact with most outsiders and having only one another for diversion, she and her siblings grew up with a naive, proscribed view of the world. Several foreign diplomats who met them noted that the insularity of their existence made them seem immature for their age. To the children, it mattered not, for only with their parents did they truly feel that peace and comfort ruled.

ALTHOUGH Nicholas and Alexandra loved all their children immensely, the Czarevitch Alexis was their central focus. The Czarina had waited a long time to provide an heir, and from the moment he appeared in the world, Alexis was accorded a special place in the hearts of the family and the nation.

One day, as young Alexis played outside, he fell and bruised his knee. The bruise grew dark and ominous, and the boy complained of excruciating pain. Examined by doctors, he was diagnosed as having the dreaded bleeding disease that affected some of Queen Victoria's descendants.

Alexandra could not accept the notion that she carried hemophilia. After years of derision and repeated failure to give birth to a son, this news devastated her, and she did everything she could to deny it. But the doctors were certain of their diagnosis and told her that medical science knew little about the disease, and even less about treating it. Hemophilia was then viewed as a slow death sentence. The doctors could offer only one bit of advice for prolonging Alexis's life: he would have to be watched and attended every minute; he could never be left alone. They told the parents that the slightest bump or scrape could cause fatal bleeding.

The Czarina still refused to believe the diagnosis. She was sure that the medical men had made a mistake or had blundered during the boy's birth. The doctors' inability to treat or cure his illness was their fault, not hers, she said. Desperate, she ordered that any treatment, any theory, any hope be fully explored. The immense resources of the Romanov fortune and the Russian Empire were to be put at the disposal of those who could provide a cure.

Neither the court nor the Russian people were told of Alexis's condition. Rumors circulated among the nobility that something was wrong with the boy, but nothing was confirmed. Nicholas and Alexandra remained vigilant about not allowing their son to be seen by anyone other than the close family circle. The Czarevitch was photographed under rigidly controlled circumstances, and his public appearances were kept to an absolute minimum.

ALEXIS naturally wanted to play, and hemophilia did not affect his rambunctious spirits. Despite being carefully watched, he fell or scraped himself several times even as an infant. What might appear at first to be a minor incident would often result in a frightening injury. He would remain bedridden for weeks with swelling from internal bleeding. As he lay in excruciating pain, the doctors could only shake their heads in resignation.

As was her wont, Alexandra reacted to her son's illness and repeated convalescences by withdrawing even further into her mysticism and religion. She spent hours communing with God, begging that her son's health be restored. She blamed herself. She constantly railed at doctors and science. Her despair was total, as was her denial to others of the full consequences of Alexis's hemophilia. She began keeping other members of the Romanov family at an even greater distance from the children. Those few who were allowed even nominal access to Alexandra began to whisper that she must be losing her mind. Photographs of the period show her sullen and withdrawn, rarely smiling.

In desperation, the Czarina again turned to her mystic friend, the Grand Duchess Militsa. She had willingly advised Alexandra to seek out Vachot years before, and the Czarina believed that only through his intervention had she been able to conceive a son. Although Militsa did not know the exact nature of Alexis's disease, she knew that something was terribly wrong. She recommended her newest protege, another "holy man" named Gregory Rasputin.

VII.
"God's gift to Russia"

THE RASPUTIN WE KNOW from history is a caricature, not a real man. Many volumes have been written analyzing his actions and personality, but none has captured all his facets. He has been described variously as the Mad Monk, as Father Gregory, as one of the greatest villains in history, and as a saint. His complex character and contradictory psychology have perplexed historians throughout the twentieth century.

Militsa and her sister, Anastasia, had been the first to welcome the so-called holy man into court circles. He became part of their salon of mystics and psychics. Just as they had told the Czarina about the Frenchman, Philippe Vachot, they now regaled their visitors with tales of Rasputin's psychic healing abilities. He did not, however, make any particular impression on Alexandra at their first meeting, on All Saints' Day in 1905. Indeed, Rasputin struck her initially as little more than a simple peasant.

The imperial couple, although purposely isolated from court and the aristocracy, fancied themselves in touch with the lower classes, especially the peasantry. As Anastasia would later recall, her mother thought herself to have a particular attachment to the Russian people:

> Charitable causes were of the most heartfelt concern. During the entire reign of my parents, my mother had long, serious conversations, often in the presence of my father, with . . . representatives of spiritual Russia. She did this in order to find out how progress and spiritual cultivation could be brought in the most splendid manner to the . . . simple classes of the Russian people.

The Czarina's friend Anna Viroubova shared her fascination with mysticism and developed an interest in Rasputin. The imperial couple came to know this strange man better when they visited Anna's house at Czarskoe Selo. According to Anastasia, "my parents frequently met Rasputin there. It was the 'dangerous center of secrets.' "

As he began to insinuate himself in the court circles, the imperial couple heard even more of him. Then, when the Czarevitch Alexis suffered massive hemorrhaging from another fall, and the doctors gave up hope, Rasputin was called. No one knows exactly what he did or how he did it, but Rasputin relieved the boy's pain and swelling, and finally managed to slow the internal bleeding.

The guilt-ridden and despairing Alexandra became convinced that Rasputin could work miracles. Whether by a genuine psychic gift or hypnosis, Rasputin always succeeded in putting the boy's symptoms into remission. But the treatment was temporary, a stopgap measure until the next bump or the next fall brought on the painful bleeding again. As a result, Rasputin was summoned more and more frequently to minister to the Czarevitch at the Alexander Palace.

SLOWLY, Rasputin gained influence over the grateful and devout Alexandra. With his piercing eyes and deep voice, he would come to the Czarina and speak of God. Philippe Vachot had told Alexandra that another friend would follow him and speak to her of God, and the Czarina accepted the Mad Monk as that person. She and the rest of the family began referring to him as Our Friend. To court observers, Alexandra's reliance on Rasputin was the worst manifestation of her obsession with esoteric religious beliefs. His growing influence was reported widely and with distress.

Just as disturbing was the imperial couple's growing and blithe use of drugs. Alexandra was careful about her diet, as Anastasia remembered from her early childhood days:

> My mother avoided all stimulants, because she had a sensitive stomach and preferred a light regimen, above all white bread. She liked to eat fruit most. . . . Occasionally she would like to drink coffee but not regularly. She drank wine only for medicinal purposes, sometimes on an impulse, but that was seldom.

Nonetheless, Alexandra and her husband enjoyed some very harsh substances. The Czar and Czarina themselves chronicled the effects. "I woke up with a shocking cold in the left nostril, so that I am thinking of spraying it with cocaine," Nicholas confided to his diary. Alexandra also made meticulous records in her journals of the use of opium to relieve the pain of minor ailments and discomforts.

Diaries and memoirs of foreign diplomats and former members of the court who came into frequent contact with the Czar and Czarina also document the frequent and open abuse of opium and cocaine. Rasputin reputedly bragged to Felix Youssoupov that he regularly supplied Nicholas with an herbal-tea concoction that produced an effect of supreme euphoria.

Historian Bruce Lincoln wrote, "there is . . . circumstantial evidence that Nicholas may . . . have developed a dependence upon drugs." He further surmised that "hallucinogens . . . morphine . . .

opium . . . cocaine . . . all of these singly or in combination, could produce the disorientation, dull gaze, vacant smiles, inability to concentrate, and the apparent unconcern with impending crises that people noted in Nicholas. . . ."

In later years, Anastasia railed against the use of prescription drugs. Like her mother, she was vegetarian and made an effort to eat only fresh foods. She evinced a life-long concern with the food and drugs she ingested and would often throw hysterical tantrums if forced to take medication. "I have seen what these poisons did to my parents," she would later recall. "Perhaps this was the only mistake he [Rasputin] made, because it is deadly to take such poisons." Anastasia did make an occasional exception, however: "Cocaine is a natural plant and can be very good for one. I have nothing but good to say [about it]. Everyone should take this."

OF greater concern to the court and the nation were the growing rumors of war. The first decade of the twentieth century had seen increasing international conflicts. Russia itself had suffered a major setback in the Russo-Japanese War, and only with the good offices of America's President Theodore Roosevelt had the Czar been able to prevent complete humiliation. Other minor conflicts had arisen between Germany, France, and England, but they had been mostly confined to overseas territories. Thus far, rivalries had been settled without any of the major powers bringing the battle to Europe, but the general peace on the continent would probably be shattered before long.

Russia had become more closely allied with England and France, in an effort to counter the increasingly expansionist tendencies of its sister empire, Germany, and the suppression of Slavic minorities by Austria. Many at court did not approve of this policy and cautioned the Czar to avoid becoming involved in what would surely be a major conflagration.

When the rumblings of war began, Rasputin implored the Czar to do whatever was in his power to avoid armed conflict. The Mad Monk accurately predicted that, if Russia entered into hostilities, she would emerge a radically changed nation. And he added what many thought was an implied threat: if he lost his life, the Romanovs would also lose theirs. Threat or not, by linking his fate to theirs in this manner, he solidified his relationship with Alexandra, who was terrified of the possibility of war.

The First World War finally began in 1914, and the Czar left home to personally command his troops. Before departing, however, he let it be known that he had turned over the helm of state to his wife. Although she had never been taken seriously by the court or the imperial ministers, the Czarina began to exert her influence as a reigning consort. Because she trusted no one, however, she treated her husband's advisers in a manner that only made matters worse. For example, she turned to Anna Viroubova as her general factotum and message-bearer. The Czarina was not above using her friend to gain petty advantages, and she personally insulted cabinet members, military leaders, and high government officials by communicating with them only through Anna. Their memoirs contain passages expressing their indignation at the Czarina's refusal to receive them and her use of a semi-literate lackey to transmit her messages or commands.

Anna's unwitting participation in these types of palace rivalries fueled the controversy over the relationship of these two women. Some writers have speculated that they shared a lesbian relationship, but nothing could have been further from the truth. Anna filled a void in Alexandra's life by playing the role of mindless playmate, a follower who never questioned the opinions or orders of the woman to whom she devoted her life. Whereas almost everyone else was critical, even spiteful, toward Alexandra, Anna remained faithful.

The Czarina's other loyal supporter was Rasputin. In trying to decide how best to advise Nicholas on events in Russia, she began to consult Rasputin on all manner of subjects. With his advice, she made incredibly bad political decisions, judgments that certainly hastened the downfall of the Romanov dynasty.

Rumors and scandalous stories of Rasputin's conduct in St. Petersburg circulated as fast as those about Alexandra and Anna, and were of a similar nature. Gossips reported that he had seduced the Empress and that she and her daughters engaged in wild orgies with the Holy Man. Subversive groups pasted posters on public streets, caricaturing the Czar and Czarina as Rasputin's puppets. "He never touched us," Anastasia vehemently remarked to Milukoff. "I saw him maybe once during the war." "These terrible stories that you hear," she recalled, "are the work of creators. He was a saint. He was God's gift to Russia."

RASPUTIN was without doubt of the greatest importance to the Czarina. He served as the focus for her extremely fervent religious devotion. In the midst of the horrors of war, Russian Orthodoxy would remain Alexandra's source of strength and her one true passion. Thus, it was not surprising that both she and the Czar paid close attention to reports in 1916 that a Russian pilot had spotted what appeared to be the remains of an ancient ship on an upper slope of Mount Ararat. This first visual evidence of what had long been believed to be the landing site of Noah's Ark prompted a quick response from Nicholas. He sent an expeditionary force of scientists and ecclesiastics, accompanied by expert photographers, to investigate.

The team located the site and photographed it thoroughly. In addition, they gathered physical evidence and compiled a lengthy report of their findings. Everything was sent ahead to the Czar. Most historians believe that the report and its accompanying evidentiary material never reached the imperial household, because of the war and the growing revolutionary activity that had begun to erupt by late 1916. Anastasia, however, recalled that her parents had, indeed, received the report and read it, and that she had seen some of the photographs and found them fascinating. The Czarina was presented with a piece of petrified wood, purportedly one of the timbers from Noah's Ark. She had pieces taken from the relic and made into crosses for herself and the Grand Duchesses, to wear for protection.

ANOTHER sign of the Czarina's Christian principles was her sponsorship of a number of hospitals during the war. They were established also as a patriotic duty, for their main purpose was to treat the wounded. Alexandra often attended the patients herself, dressed in a white nun's outfit. Marie and Anastasia also sponsored a hospital in a converted mansion on the grounds of Czarskoe Selo. A large sign on the facade designated it "the Hospital of the Grand Duchesses Marie and Anastasia." The girls were so proud of their work that they took photographs of the patients and spent time talking with them. Marie compiled an album of photographs of the family and hospital patients and presented it to Tatiana Botkin, who also worked there as a nurse. The pictures in the album show the imperial daughters dressed in white nuns' costumes, like their mother, tending to the medical needs of soldiers wounded at the front.

Despite the grueling work, Anastasia and her sister enjoyed their time at the hospital:

> We had to take care of all manner of things: cutting material for bandages, preparing gift packages, thinking of small distractions for the wounded, making visits. Since the building was within the park, we were allowed to go there alone. On the ground floor were the soldiers; upstairs, the officers. And it was an incredible experience to be so suddenly among a group of officers. Sometimes we also did nonsense things. . . . It was very funny when someone helped us on with our coats and we couldn't get our arms through because the sleeves had been sewn together.

As the war progressed, pressures increased from all sides. Alexis's health continued to deteriorate, and most members of the Romanov family suspected that the boy suffered from what was considered a fatal disease. After a particularly bad incident, the Czarina could no longer hide the truth from the family. Upon discovering that the Czarevitch suffered from a life-threatening illness, various Romanovs began to plot for succession to the throne. Because one of the Czar's brothers had died and the other had been disqualified for marrying below his station, Anastasia's male cousins were prime candidates to become the next czar. She recalled one especially troubling plot: "This time it was even worse, because the relatives—here I mean in particular Grand Duchess Vladimir, Aunt Mischa—spoke up and said that we should exclude my brother from the line of succession. The next paternal relative [who could inherit the throne] would have been her son, Grand Duke Cyril. . . ."

The rivalries among the Romanovs for control in Nicholas's absence continued to grow. Many felt that the best means of gaining the upper hand would be to eliminate Rasputin, who had become the Czarina's closest advisor.

The effeminate, cross-dressing Prince Felix Youssoupov, who had married the Czar's niece Irina a few years earlier, traveled in some of the same circles as Rasputin. One night in December 1916, the Prince lured the mystic to the Youssoupov family's fabulous palace on the St. Petersburg canal. As fellow conspirators waited nearby, the Prince reportedly served Rasputin wine and cake that had been laced with cyanide. When his guest did not succumb, Youssoupov and the other assassins shot him and bludgeoned the body before finally throwing him into the river.

Alexandra was devastated and wanted Youssoupov arrested, but, because of his close relationship with the Romanovs and his family's tremendous wealth and influence, the Czar instead ordered Felix to be sent into exile. This posed only a minor hardship for the Prince, because his destination was one of his family's grand estates in central Russia, where they went annually on hunting trips.

The Czarina, however, went into a period of deep mourning and arranged for Rasputin's body to be buried in greatest secrecy in a far corner of the park at Czarskoe Selo. She attended the burial service herself, as did her daughters, all of them dressed in black and wearing locket necklaces with Rasputin's picture inside. "Mama said the end was near when Father Gregory went to Heaven," Anastasia remembered.

VIII.
"The old Russia was no more"

AS RASPUTIN HAD PREDICTED, the Romanov dynasty began to break apart months after his death. Like other nations, Russia had suffered enormous losses during the war. The economy was shattered, and the Czar's absence from the capital had left an enormous vacuum of power and authority. Alexandra had never been an effective substitute for her husband as ruler, and she had been unable to counter the growing revolutionary forces that demanded democratic government and peace for Russia.

CALLS for peace came from other quarters as well. Sometime in 1916, the Czarina's brother—Grand Duke Ernest Ludwig of Hesse—arrived at Czarskoe Selo. Having traveled by a circuitous route through Sweden and Finnish Russia, he brought with him a secret offer for a separate peace between Germany and her sister empire. Kaiser Wilhelm II was searching for a way to end the war with Russia while preserving the Romanov dynasty. His government had already begun plans to send the revolutionary Vladimir Lenin across the border in an attempt to foment revolution and thereby effectively end Russia's participation on the battlefield. But rather than wreak such havoc on his cousins, the Kaiser was willing to circumvent his own military and political advisers and seek another solution.

Given the nature of this secret mission and its lack of success, the Grand Duke never acknowledged having traveled to the capital of an enemy nation during the war. No documents have ever surfaced to contradict his denials, but many eyewitness accounts and other reports from those close to both the Kaiser and the House of Hesse have confirmed that the Czarina's brother did, indeed, attempt to bring the war to a close in a clandestine manner. Although the Dowager Czarina's diaries remain unavailable in a Soviet archive, one report says that in November 1916 she recorded that "GDE [Grand Duke Ernest] has arrived unannounced!" Anastasia's memories provide a personal account of the visit:

The Grand Duke of Hesse, brother of the Czarina, put out peace feelers. Today it is known that he went on such a mission to Sweden. Then it was kept the greatest secret. Even the German General Staff knew nothing. It was known that General Ludendorff was against a separate peace. And what no one knew or was supposed to learn was the trip that the Grand Duke made from Sweden to Czarskoe Selo. He traveled incognito and the greatest precautions were taken. But I saw him there and it was a big event to have one of our German relatives with us for a few hours in the middle of the war.

IN March 1917, the monarchical government was finally overthrown, and the worst fears of the nobility seemed to be coming true. Nicholas had no choice but to return from the war and was shocked to find the Grand Duke Cyril parading through the streets of St. Petersburg, leading a large contingent of deserters and Bolsheviks in support of the new revolutionary government. The Czar had been forced to abdicate the throne while still on the train from his military headquarters. To avoid putting the ailing Alexis under the strain that a contentious regency would bring, Nicholas also abdicated the throne for the Czarevitch.

Anastasia recalled the remarkable change in their lives:

> The old Russia was no more. They brought the Czar to Czarskoe Selo as a prisoner. The Czar and Czarina were kept separated, they were not allowed to share the same bedroom nor to talk to one another. We [children] were also watched and allowed to go into the park only when accompanied by the police. . . . Anna Viroubova, who had recently lived in the palace because we did not want her to be left alone in her little house for fear of persecution, was taken away and put under confinement, so that mother was completely isolated. We children were severely ill with measles. During this time, the Czarina became an old, white-haired woman.

THE Romanovs remained under house arrest at Czarskoe Selo for some time. The Provisional Government was trying to consolidate its power, but leader Alexander Kerensky found himself in repeated political conflict with the hard-line Bolsheviks. Russia's continued involvement in the First World War and the internal conflict, which was threatening to erupt into civil war, became too much for the Provisional Government. With St. Petersburg facing anarchy, Kerensky could no longer assure the imperial family's safety so near the capital, and he had them moved to the Siberian city of Tobolsk.

The trip was long but bearable, and upon their arrival, they were installed in the local governor's mansion. Dr. Botkin and the Czarina's lady-in-waiting, Baroness Sophie Buxhoeveden, were among those who accompanied them. The family was also allowed to bring some valued personal possessions and mementos. Happily for Anastasia, they were even granted permission to bring along her favorite dog, Jemmy.

Gleb and Tatiana Botkin followed their father and the imperial family to Tobolsk. Although they were not allowed to visit the house where the Romanovs were held, Gleb continued painting his fanciful watercolor animals and sent them to Anastasia by messenger. When it was learned that the family was to be moved again, Gleb walked around the block on which the Tobolsk governor's mansion was located. Seeing Anastasia alone in a window, Gleb waved. She smiled and returned the gesture.

FROM the few existing letters of this period, we know that the imperial family had been advised, perhaps in carefully coded messages, to expect a rescue attempt. For more than seventy years, rumors and stories have circulated about the various plots—real and imaginary—to rescue the Romanovs. The civil war was worsening. Kerensky had lost power and then been forced to flee to America. Fierce battles between the White monarchist forces and the Red revolutionary factions were tearing the empire asunder. Yet even as Russian soil was being stained with the blood of hundreds of thousands, the world's attention focused more on the fate of the imperial family.

Having been raised, in her own words, "as an English woman," Alexandra believed that her family would be offered sanctuary in England, if necessary. She commented often to her ladies-in-waiting that if they had to go to England, they would live in comfort because the Czar had significant funds on deposit in British banks. However, other events overshadowed these hopes.

The Bolsheviks, led by Lenin, came to power after Kerensky's Provisional Government fell on October 25, 1917. When the reports of the Soviet takeover reached Tobolsk, the conditions of the Romanovs' imprisonment worsened. With no liberal forces to mediate on their behalf, they were subjected to harassment and mistreatment by their jailers. No longer could they draw on their own bank accounts or correspond with anyone. Severe food rationing was imposed, and Christmas was a somber occasion that year.

In late March 1918, the imperial family received news that they might be moved to a new and harsher environment. Alexandra immediately began to take precautions. Between March 28 and April 10, she and her daughters sewed their jewelry into the linings of their clothing in preparation for their uncertain future. The Romanovs learned that they would not be able to take their full compliment of servants and attendants with them, and Dr. Botkin was told that his own children—Gleb and Tatiana—would not be allowed to follow him this time. Alexandra was extremely distressed by the possibility that her family would be separated, but her captors left her no choice. On April 26, she and her husband, together with their daughter Marie, Dr. Botkin, and a few servants, were forced to begin a four-day trip to their new exile in the Urals. Alexis was too ill to travel, and arrangements were made for him to follow later with his sisters under the care of Baroness Sophie Buxhoeveden, who had volunteered for the task, despite the fact that she had recently seemed uncomfortable around the family. The Czarina had remarked on the Baroness's unaccountable behavior, but Anastasia had more important things on her mind: she and her sister Tatiana were successful in their insistence that Jemmy accompany them on the long trip.

IX.

"That I cannot forget"

REUNITED IN EKATERINBURG, a rich mining community and site of one of the royal mints, the family moved into the requisitioned house of a wealthy, retired army engineer named Nicholas Ipatiev. By the standards of a city as remote as Ekaterinburg, the house was unusually lavish, with hot running water and electric lights. To provide maximum security for their captives, the Bolsheviks constructed a tall, wooden palisade around the house, blocking it from the street. The windows were sealed and covered with white paint, and the building was renamed The House of Special Purpose.

The irony of their placement in the Ipatiev residence was not lost on the imperial family. "Mama said the dynasty began in the Ipatiev Monastery and she feared what this house was called was a sign from God that the end was coming," Anastasia remembered years later.

The treatment of the Romanovs in their Ipatiev prison was harsh in the extreme. The Czarina, suffering from severe arthritis, was confined to her wheelchair most of the time. When members of the family used the lavatory, a Bolshevik guard always came along to watch and jeer from the doorway. Their belongings were plundered before their very eyes, but the family dared not complain. French newspapers recounted tales of violent sexual abuse of the family. Their meals were sometimes restricted to bread and water. The guards were said to have been intoxicated twenty-four hours a day, taunting the family, slapping the Czar, jeering him as Bloody Nicholas. Cleaning people, maintenance crews, and nuns delivering bread from a local convent often came in contact with members of the family, but the Romanovs were not allowed to speak to them.

Stories of planned attempts to rescue the imperial family circulated throughout the Ural region, and the Czar himself was aware of them. Perhaps this is one explanation for the reports emanating from the Ipatiev House that the family remained happy, despite their confinement. Before the Romanovs left Tobolsk they felt confident that they would be rescued on the way to Ekaterinburg, or at least not long after their arrival. The family began to suspect that the plans had gone awry when the Bolsheviks gave the Baroness Buxhoeveden her freedom upon her arrival in Ekaterinburg with the children.

Anastasia bitterly recalled:

> That there had been a betrayal was clear to us. We spoke of it often in prison. I must always think how Papa and Mama sat there in Ekaterinburg and said that they could not understand why Isa [Buxhoeveden] had changed so during the last time in Tobolsk. We knew that we were supposed to be freed, and when nothing came, no rescue came, Papa and Mama said that they must connect Isa's changed behavior with the unsuccessful rescue. They believed that Isa had betrayed the rescue plans [in exchange for her freedom]. That I cannot forget.

Nonetheless, the family could still hope for rescue, because large battles were raging nearby, and the White Army was anxious to find the Czar and help restore his authority.

IN the first week of July 1918, the Bolsheviks allowed a priest to visit the Romanovs and conduct a religious service. As he left, the entire Russian imperial family fell to their knees in unison, praying. Later, the priest recalled that, although he did not know what had gone on in the Ipatiev House, it must have been terrible.

On July 4, the drunkenness and lewd conduct of the guards had become so notorious that they were replaced by an efficient cadre of ten members of the Bolshevik Secret Police. Their leader, Jacob Yurovsky, was a former dealer of photographic supplies in Ekaterinburg. Nicholas confided to his diary, "This specimen we like least of all." In the words of historian Massie, "From the moment of Yurovsky's appearance, the fate of the Imperial family was sealed. The . . . squad were not guards, but executioners."

The captain of Yurovsky's guard, P. Medvedev, was as harsh and cold-blooded as his superior. Both men wrote official reports of their activities months later and submitted them to higher authorities in Moscow.

By mid-July, the family was beginning to worry that the end was approaching. They were surrounded by a tall fence, supervised at every moment by Yurovsky's men, and attended by only Dr. Botkin, a butler named Aleksei Trup, a maid named Anna Demidova, and a cook named Kharitonov. This small group, all that was left of the once-proud Romanov dynasty, waited.

"IT still surprises people to learn that the popular story of the murder of the Romanovs—that is, the story of their mass execution in the cellar of the Ipatiev House—is, in reality, only a theory of history."

These words of a Romanov scholar best describe the historical conundrum surrounding the disappearance of the imperial family. Seven decades have passed since the summer night in 1918 when history recorded the murder of the Czar, his family, Dr. Botkin, and three servants. A small library of volumes, in more than six languages, comprises the writings that have attempted to explain and interpret the events of that night. No version is definitive. All of the participants in whatever occurred inside the Ipatiev House on the night of July 16 and the early hours of July 17, are dead. The testimony they left, of which there is very little, consists of conflicting and contradictory observations.

The version that has found its way into history books and encyclopedias the world over is that a firing squad shot the family and its entourage in a sub-basement room, loaded the bodies onto a truck, and removed them to an abandoned mine outside Ekaterinburg. In the commonly accepted story, the bodies were dismembered, burned, and thrown into one of the mineshafts.

There is, however, no conclusive forensic evidence, and the inability to establish hard facts has opened the way for rumors, speculation, and even nonsense. Some people went so far as to submit that the Romanovs were miraculously rescued and made their way to safety through China in a covered wagon; others claimed that the family escaped the Ipatiev House via a secret tunnel connected to the nearby British legation.

GIVEN the lack of clear evidence or supportable facts, we will never know exactly what happened on that July night in 1918. The best we can do is to reconstruct the most plausible conjecture of what might have occurred during those hours, according to the statements of participants, as reported by the most reliable investigators.

Some of the following narrative is based on the report Yurovsky prepared for his superiors. Perhaps the most thorough recounting of the events in Ekaterinburg, this report, which was published recently in the West, "may or may not be entirely true, but only time will tell." Upon reading it, Dr. Botkin's granddaughter, Marina Botkin Schweitzer, asked, "Can we really believe the words of the cold-blooded murderer of innocent people?" It is a question that will probably never be answered.

ACCORDING to Czarina Alexandra's diary, July 16 passed as another monotonous day for the prisoners. The final entry she made, just before retiring at 11 p.m., reflects no premonition of what was about to happen.

An hour or so after Alexandra retired, Yurovsky began fretting that the Fiat truck he had requisitioned to haul the bodies away had failed to show up at the appointed time of midnight. When the truck finally arrived, an hour and a half late, the driver was ordered to keep the engine running to muffle the sounds of the executioners' gunfire.

At 1:30 A.M., Yurovsky "went to fetch them personally and had them go downstairs. . . ." He awakened Dr. Botkin and told him to inform the family that unrest in the city required that they immediately dress and prepare to be moved to the safety of the sub-basement.

Anastasia remembered:

Everything was so sudden. It all happened at once. It came so quick nobody could think . . . it was late in the evening. We were all in bed.

53

They just came and told us to get ready. We had to dress and follow them. We knew nothing—were just ordered to come along. . . . I do not know what they told my father. We were just ordered to go—to follow the soldiers.

Yurovsky did not unduly hurry the family, allowing them thirty minutes to wash and dress. When all were prepared, he led the group downstairs. Directly behind him walked Nicholas, holding Alexis in his arms. Alexandra, limping with her cane, followed with the girls. Anastasia carried Jemmy in her arms. Years later, she would recall that it was "a clear starry night." Dr. Botkin and the maid Demidova followed, carrying pillows for Alexis. Bringing up the rear were the valet Trup and the cook Kharitonov.

All was apparently normal—at least as normal as their captive circumstance could allow. Anastasia remembered, "We weren't supposed to be going anywhere, just into another room. . . ." Medvedev confirmed that the family "appeared calm as if expecting no danger." Yurovsky wrote that "the Romanovs suspected nothing. . . . The room chosen had plastered walls (so that the bullets would not ricochet). . . . The firing squad was ready and waiting in the room next door."

The imperial family was taken into a room previously used as a guard barrack. All the furniture had been removed. Centered high on one wall was a barred, arched window. On another wall was the locked door to a small storage room. The room's dimensions were fourteen by seventeen feet. As Summers and Mangold commented, "These would be cramped conditions for a cocktail party, let alone a mass execution."

Yurovsky wrote, "When they entered the empty room Alexandra asked, 'How can this be? Not even a chair? Can't we at least sit down?'

"[I] ordered two chairs to be brought in. Nicholas had Alexandra sit in one and Alexis in the other. [I] then told the others to line up and called in the firing squad."

Anastasia remembered Yurovsky taking her father outside the room, where they spoke for a moment. When they returned, the Czar's face was ashen, and he was speechless.

Yurovsky: "When the [firing squad] entered, [I] told the Romanovs that in view of the fact that their relatives continued their offensive against Soviet Russia, the Executive Committee of the Urals Soviet had decided to shoot them. Nicholas turned his back to the detachment and faced his family."

Some witnesses remembered Nicholas making the sign of the cross.

Yurovsky: "Then, he asked [me], 'What? What?'

"[I] quickly repeated what [I] had said and ordered the firing squad to get ready. Each one already knew who he was supposed to shoot, and they had been told to fire directly at the heart in order to avoid great spilling of blood and to finish the task as soon as possible.

"Nicholas said nothing more and turned to face his family again. The others made a few disconnected exclamations. All this lasted a few seconds."

Anastasia would recall later, "Nobody could believe what was going to happen. . . . There was nobody there to do anything to help us."

Yurovsky: "[I] killed Nicholas on the spot," apparently with a bullet through the temple.

Some reports indicate that at the last second, Dr. Botkin jumped in front of Nicholas to shield him, and took the first bullet himself. Others say the doctor moved to protect Alexandra.

The Czarina began to cross herself, but before she could complete this last gesture of her adopted faith, "the firing began and went on for two or three minutes . . . the bullets ricocheted around the room like hailstones," according to Yurovsky. Residents of the neighborhood surrounding the Ipatiev House later reported having heard gunfire in the early morning hours.

Most accounts agree that Nicholas and Alexandra died first—and instantly, as did at least one of their daughters. The others were screaming. One of the bullets knocked Alexis from his chair. Kharitonov was hit so hard that he "sat down and died."

Anastasia was standing slightly behind Tatiana, who took a direct hit. The impact knocked her backward against Anastasia, and as they fell to the floor Tatiana's body shielded her younger sister from the fusillade of death pouring down on them. Anastasia recalled that Jemmy fell from her arms. "I fainted, everything was blue, and I saw stars dancing, and there was a great roar."

Although each executioner had been ordered to aim for the heart, not everyone died instantly. Some accounts say that as many as six were still alive when the initial firing ceased. An acrid mist of smoke and gunpowder filled the room, as did the pungent odor of the fresh carnage.

Alexis, the hemophiliac, lay moaning in a pool of his family's blood. Yurovsky stepped up to him, put the barrel of his gun to the boy's ear, and fired.

He later reported that Dr. Botkin and some of the daughters had to be shot again or bayoneted as they lay wounded and helpless.

Anna Demidova, the maid, suffering from only superficial wounds, backed up against the wall. When the executioners closed in on her with bayonets, she shielded herself with the pillow she had carried from upstairs. Shrieking like a trapped animal, she ran back and forth along the wall, as the executioners continued to jab at her with their bayonets. The first blows may have been deflected by a metal box containing the Czarina's jewelry hidden deep within the feather pillow. All accounts agree that Demidova fought furiously and was stabbed at least thirty times before she died.

In almost every retelling of these events, Anastasia is the last to die. Some say a bayonet was driven through her face. Robert K. Massie, in *Nicholas and Alexandra*, wrote that Anastasia "only fainted, regained consciousness and screamed. With bayonets and rifle butts, the entire band turned on her."

Lord Louis Mountbatten claimed that Anastasia was stabbed eighteen times.

Gleb Botkin wrote, "Anastasia suddenly screamed, and tried to get back to her feet. The soldiers hit her with their rifles, and one of them pierced her foot with his bayonet, pinning her down to the floor."

Not one of these commentators, however, was there.

Anastasia: "I really had no idea whether I was still alive. . . . Why were my dresses all bloody? Everything was full of blood. . . ."

Eleven bodies lay on the floor, and the room was quiet. Someone noticed that Jemmy had avoided injury when he fell from Anastasia's arms. Frightened by the noise of the bullets and the screams, he crouched among the bodies, whimpering. A member of the firing squad walked over to the terrified animal and, swinging his rifle butt like a golf club, smashed Jemmy's head.

The other soldiers were ordered to make sure there were no survivors. They began to methodically plunge bayonets into their victims. Yurovsky complained that the women's corsets withstood the bayonet thrusts. He finally was so sure of the success of the "procedure" that he ordered the soldiers to stop. Medvedev later described the scene before him: "They had several gun wounds on various parts of their bodies; their faces were covered with blood, their clothes too were blood-soaked."

X.
"To destroy all traces"

YUROVSKY SENT the men upstairs to strip the sheets from the imperial family's beds. When they had reassembled in the execution room, the men lifted the bodies onto the sheets and carried them out to the waiting truck. Streams of blood marked the path.

As soon as the executioners were out of Yurovsky's sight, they began plundering the corpses, searching for valuables. We can imagine the lifeless limbs hanging from sheets saturated with blood; children's faces frozen in grimaces of terror, their bodies riddled with wounds and now violated by furtively searching hands; the once aloof Czarina groped by peasants. The last reigning members of the proud three-hundred-year-old dynasty were pillaged by common strangers.

But the men were not out of Yurovsky's sight for long, and when he noticed them pocketing a gold watch, a diamond cigarette case, and other loot from the family's clothes, he demanded the return of the items under threat of death. Later he forwarded the plunder to Moscow.

A tarpaulin lined the floor of the idling truck. The soldiers lifted the bodies, piled them one on top of the other, and covered them with another tarp. Yurovsky climbed up into the cab with the driver, and they left the grounds of the Ipatiev House. The structure had served its "special purpose."

A group from the local soviet met the truck a few miles out of Ekaterinburg and transferred the corpses onto carts. They proceeded ten miles north of the town to a wooded area "full of swamps, peat bogs, and abandoned mineshafts." When they arrived at an abandoned gold mine, they unloaded the bodies.

HISTORIAN Richard Pipes probably best captured the Bolsheviks' fears that night when he wrote: "Aware that the Russian people assigned miraculous powers to the remains of martyrs, and anxious to prevent a cult of the Romanovs, the Ekaterinburg Bolsheviks went to great pains to destroy all traces of their bodies."

The obliteration of the Romanovs' remains was extremely gruesome. According to Yurovsky:

> When they began to undress one of the girls, they saw a corset partly torn by bullets: in the gash showed diamonds. The eyes of the fellows really lit up. [I] had to dismiss the whole band. . . . The detachment proceeded to strip and burn the bodies. Alexandra . . . turned out to wear a pearl belt made of several necklaces sewn into linen. (Each girl carried on her neck an amulet with Rasputin's picture and the text of his prayer.) The diamonds were collected; they weighed about half a pud [about 18 pounds]. . . . Having placed all the valuables in satchels, other items found on the bodies were burned. . . .

Historian Pipes adds to this account of the scene a horrifying remark: "What indignities were perpetrated on the bodies of the . . . women must be left to the . . . imagination: suffice it to say that one of the guards who took part in this work later boasted that he could 'die in peace because he had squeezed the Empress's _____ .' "

Some reports relate in vivid detail how the Bolsheviks, after stripping the bodies, hacked them into small pieces and threw the remains onto huge bonfires. As the last flames flickered away, acid was poured on the remaining bones and ashes. Whatever was left was thrown into a mineshaft. This process reportedly took three days. Finally, hand grenades were tossed into the shaft. Only Jemmy's body was not mutilated or cremated; he was tossed in, almost as an afterthought, once the grenades had exploded.

Another theory, advanced by Soviet detective-writer Geli Ryabov, indicates that Yurovsky thought the mine was too shallow to completely conceal his work, so he ordered the bodies, after they had been stripped, reloaded onto the Fiat truck in search of another site to hide them. They had driven just a short distance when the truck became mired in a bog. Frantic now to complete his assignment, Yurovsky ordered a shallow grave dug. The soldiers then dumped the Romanov bodies on the ground, poured sulfuric acid over them, and hurriedly covered the imperial family with the soil of their native Russia.

ANASTASIA maintained for years that she was left wounded and unconscious. As a result, she explained, she could never remember the events leading to her rescue from the macabre disposal of her family's remains. All we can speculate is that someone whom she called Alexander Tschaikovsky—perhaps one of the guards at the Ipatiev House, perhaps one of the members of the group from the local soviet who met the truck later—noticed that she was not dead. In the confusion of these horror-filled hours, he managed to pull her into some underbrush, where she remained hidden from view until he and his brother Serge could come back for her later.

It was neither improbable nor impossible that Anastasia could have been overlooked in the chaos and panic. Even Yurovsky miscounted the number of bodies as they lay before him on the floor of the Ipatiev House. The Bolshevik executioners, nervous and excited, were well-fortified with quantities of vodka, and may have been reluctant to examine their work closely. However it came to pass, someone risked his life and his family's welfare that night to rescue the youngest daughter of the Czar.

*   *   *

MANY have speculated why nothing came of various, rumored attempts made to rescue the Czar and his family before the events of Ekaterinburg. It has long been known, for example, that negotiations between the Russian Provisional Government and the British government over the possibility of saving the Romanovs had been underway. The true story has long been clouded in mystery and contradiction. One of the chief perpetrators of the confusion was the late Lord Mountbatten. Years afterward, he castigated Prime Minister Lloyd George for abandoning the family to certain death, claiming that the actions of this prime minister aided in their bloody destruction. This statement, like so many made about the Romanovs by Lord Mountbatten, has been proved false. The true culprit was the King of England.

Historian Kenneth Rose has conducted the most extensive research on the shameful machinations of the British royal family regarding the fate of the Romanovs. Rose has thoroughly documented the perfidy of King George V, as he vacillated and obfuscated before finally consigning his cousins to death.

According to Rose, the Foreign Minister of the Russian Provisional Government, Pavel Milyukov, contacted the British ambassador, Sir George Buchanan, in St. Petersburg on March 19, 1917. The Minister at first "suggested" that the imperial family go to England. Ambassador Buchanan immediately transmitted this information to the Foreign Office in London.

The next day, Milyukov filed a formal request for the British to grant asylum to the Czar and his family. The Foreign Office hesitated and suggested that the Romanovs might find a "more suitable place of residence" in Denmark or Switzerland. Milyukov responded with a more urgent request that the British take immediate action, fearing that extremists might try to kill the Czar. Ambassador Buchanan reported to London: "I earnestly trust that, in spite of the obvious objections, I may be authorized without delay to offer His Majesty asylum in England and at the same time assure the Russian government that he will remain there during the war."

On March 22, the Prime Minister invited King George's private secretary, Sir Arthur Stamfordham, to a meeting at 10 Downing Street. In consultation with others, the two men agreed that because the request for asylum had originated with the Russian government, it could hardly be refused. The King's secretary, however, raised some questions: Could the Czar financially support his family in exile? Where would they live? On behalf of King George, Stamfordham even argued that Balmoral Castle in Scotland, one of the suggested refuges, was not "a suitable residence at this time of year."

Finally, the meeting adjourned with the agreement that Ambassador Buchanan should offer formal British asylum to the Czar but should stipulate that the Russian government was to provide adequate funds to maintain the imperial lifestyle in England. In other words, the fabulously wealthy royal family demanded that the beleaguered and impoverished Russian government bestow a fortune on the English King's wealthy Russian relatives.

As Rose indicates, this was an obvious delaying tactic designed to make the Provisional Government reconsider its request. It gave the Bolsheviks, who were hungry for Nicholas's blood, time to consolidate their efforts to destabilize the government, and it gave King George time to re-think his position.

On March 30, Stamfordham wrote another letter to the Foreign Secretary saying that the fate of the Romanovs had been much on the King's mind. He explained that although the King felt "a strong personal friendship for the Emperor and therefore would be glad to do anything to help him in this crisis," His Majesty was suddenly apprehensive about "the dangers" of the sea voyage that would be necessary to transport the Romanovs from Russia.

The Foreign Secretary waited three days before answering. "His Majesty's Ministers quite realize the difficulties to which you refer in your letter, but do not think . . . that it is now possible to withdraw the invitation which has been sent . . . on the advice of His Majesty's Ministers."

Within the next few days, Stamfordham sent the Foreign Secretary a flurry of nearly hysterical communications, which reflected the King's state of mind. Using all manner of paltry excuses, George V was doing his best to convince the British government to withdraw the offer of asylum. Foremost in the King's mind was his evident fear that "the presence of the Imperial Family (especially of the Empress) in this country would raise all sorts of difficulties." The King's message by proxy mentioned that he was receiving a tremendous amount of mail written by citizens "in all classes of life, known or unknown to him . . . expressing adverse opinions to the proposal."

As historian Rose writes, "Under such sustained bombardment, the Foreign Secretary's resolution faltered." Sensing that he had finally gained the upper hand, King George ordered Stamfordham to pay a call on the Prime Minister and demand that the invitation of asylum be rescinded. Rose characterizes King George's activities as a "campaign to deny asylum to his cousin," because he "particularly feared the consequences of inviting the Czar's wife to England. . . ." George V, in his own words, held her "largely responsible for the . . . state of chaos that exist[ed] in Russia." The British ambassador to Paris, Sir Francis Bertie, who also closely followed events in St. Petersburg, echoed the King's views about the Czarina: "She is regarded as a criminal or a criminal lunatic and the ex-Emperor as a criminal from his weakness and submission to her promptings."

No one will ever know how King George really felt about the fate of the Russian imperial family. According to historian Rose, "There is no record of his having expressed sorrow, much less contrition, at his own role in the tragedy."

In addition to the negotiations at official levels, there were rumors afoot that the British Secret Service was setting into motion several plans to rescue the Romanovs from their Bolshevik captors. In the end, none of these plans reached fruition, much less success. To be fair to King George, however, he may have had some knowledge of the rescue plans. Perhaps he hoped that they would succeed and absolve him from direct public responsibility for his cousins' fate.

IN a matter of weeks, the whispers about shots being fired inside the Ipatiev House in the early hours of July 17 would begin to spread, and before long the alleged assassination of the Czar became international news. The Soviet government at first refused all comment on the reports but, several weeks later, issued a statement confirming only that Nicholas had been executed. The statement contained no mention of the rest of the family, Dr. Botkin, or the servants.

Many historians have reported that during the daylight hours of July 17—and continuing for a couple of weeks thereafter—the Bolsheviks conducted a house-to-house search of Ekaterinburg and the surrounding villages. The men were reportedly searching for one of the missing grand duchesses. Bounty posters demanding her return and threatening death to anyone harboring her, were allegedly quickly printed and distributed throughout the territories held by Bolsheviks. To the outside world, however, officials in Moscow remained mute.

Despite the dissimilation by Lenin's government, word began to spread quickly that the entire Russian imperial family had been gunned down at Ekaterinburg. This news brought forth a new rash of headlines, which captured the attention of a horrified public. Editorial writers on every continent condemned the execution.

Independent confirmation of the deaths of the family was impossible, even though the story of the purported assassinations was one of the major news events of its time. Under the best circumstances, communications within Russia were primitive, and the violence and disruption brought on by the revolution only exacerbated the problem of transmitting information accurately.

The White Army had reached Ekaterinburg just eight days after the murders. Not until six months later, however, did the White government in Siberia decide to undertake an investigation of the event. Nicholas Sokolov, a legal investigator, examined the grounds of the Ipatiev House and the area around the mineshaft where the disposal of the bodies had reportedly taken place. He took months to reach his conclusions, which were not made public until after his escape from the Bolsheviks in 1922. The report indicated that the entire family had been killed in the house and the bodies removed to the mine, although Sokolov found almost no traces of human remains. Despite its many flaws, for years his report was accepted as the most accurate official account of the events at Ekaterinburg.

Meanwhile, the rest of Europe was engaged in the final months of the First World War, and no nation was willing to approach the fledgling Bolshevik government with inquiries. As a result, no unbiased and thorough accounting of the truth was possible. What had been done in secrecy would remain for many years unknown and unknowable.

In this atmosphere, innumerable rumors were spawned and widely reported. The thought of the assassination itself was too appalling for many to believe. This was especially true in royal circles. Among the stories reported and accepted—at least for a time—were that the entire family had escaped to freedom; that only the Czar had been shot; and that one or some of the children had escaped. This last rumor was among the most readily believed, perhaps because the world could not imagine that even the dreaded Bolsheviks would murder innocent children.

Within months, several teenage boys and girls showed up in various parts of Russian and Europe, claiming to be one or the other of the Romanov children. Most were quickly and easily disproved. But the suspicion that there might have been a survivor of the horror of the Ipatiev House lingered.

BOOK TWO

The Lost Princess

Some persons seem endowed with a peculiar and semitragic gift. They live out their lives and die, only to provide drama for the playwright or novelist. Theirs is not the stuff of life but the stuff of fiction. Such a woman was Anastasia, daughter of the last Russian Tsars, supposedly massacred at Ekaterinburg in July, 1918. She lived her life like a princess in a fairy tale, with her bumbling, bourgeois Emperor father the only false note in the royal symphony. Anastasia laughed and played and worked through the hours of her young life, touched with the magic of unreality, carrying a thousand years of august tradition upon her frail shoulders.

In the fairy tales, the princesses lived happily ever after. Anastasia lived in an all-too real world.

Officially, her life was snuffed out by Bolshevist guns in the Ekaterinburg cellar. If it was, she fell—I am sure—with dignity and grace, her silken skirts weighted with the jewels that would have bought her way to freedom.

The historical Anastasia vanishes here, reduced to a grotesque, red-stained doll lying limply across a sack of potatoes; and the infinitely more satisfying Anastasia of the legend rises, phoenix-like, from her body.

It is this Anastasia who was spirited out of that dark place of death, to wander through Central Europe, beaten, starved and half-mad, to end at the Berlin canal . . . whence she was rescued.

—EDWIN FADIMAN, JR.
From the introduction
to the Signet edition of *Anastasia*
by Marcelle Maurette, 1956

I.

The Escape

AS UNCERTAIN as are the details of the events at Ekaterinburg, even less can be verified in the recounting of Anastasia's escape
from Bolshevik Russia. One of her biographers has termed this
period of her life as "The Story," which probably best characterizes
the scattered remembrances she supplied in bits and pieces over the
years. Anastasia never willingly talked about her flight to the West.
What she did relay came in the form of extremely emotional and
vividly disturbing flashes emanating from her partial and disjointed
memory. The Story, therefore, comprises little more than fragments
pieced together by historians and friends. Because no individual
ever heard all its parts, the tale naturally contains many inaccuracies,
third-hand repetitions, and a good deal of guesswork. Still, the
highlights are worth recounting for an understanding of the events
that shaped her life.

Alexander Tschaikovsky, accompanied by his brother Serge and
perhaps their mother and sister, reportedly concealed Anastasia in a
cart and proceeded west, trying to escape the chaos of revolutionary
Russia. From Siberia, they traveled among the thousands of displaced and war-weary refugees. With Russia in tatters even a person
as well-known as a Romanov could have been secreted out of the
country in this manner. The central government in Moscow was
having too much trouble sustaining its own existence to question for
very long whether a member of the Czar's family had survived the
massacre, or to pursue her among the masses of displaced souls
crossing vast expanses of territory.

The two brothers hauled the crudely made cart over rutted back
roads and rough terrain. Inside the cart, the teenage girl lay delirious, feverish, slipping in and out of consciousness. She had suffered

severe trauma to the head, as well as stab wounds, and would remember the journey only as a nightmare of excruciating pain.

How much time the Tschaikovskys spent crossing the country is uncertain, but the trip was probably long and arduous. They would have been forced to take extra precautions for their own sake as well as for that of the hidden Grand Duchess. They undoubtedly had to avoid many checkpoints in occupied territory, and some researchers have theorized that they might have had to bribe border guards in order to pass. Many wealthy nobles bribed their way out of Russia by selling the valuables they carried with them as they fled. Some of the Romanov jewels and gold secreted in Anastasia's clothing may have been overlooked by the executioners and would have enabled the Tschaikovsky brothers to barter for the party's safety.

Their flight finally ended that winter in Bucharest, Romania. No one knows whether this was a planned destination, and there is no documentation proving that Anastasia or the Tschaikovskys were ever there. The Romanian capital teemed with tens of thousands of refugees from all countries and classes, however, and one more war-shocked young noblewoman would hardly have garnered special attention. Many people apparently suspected that one of the Czar's daughters had escaped from Ekaterinburg and found refuge somewhere in the city. One investigator has reported that Heinrich Dietz, a German military officer assigned to Bucharest at the time, said that it was "quite generally known" that Anastasia was living in the Romanian capital "under the protection of the Germans." The Grand Duchess, herself, could recall only that she lived with the Tschaikovskys in a gardener's cottage on Svienti Voyevoda, a street named for a saint. This seemingly inconsequential detail stuck in her mind because it reminded her of "another saint who had been murdered in Russia," Rasputin. She never pinpointed the street's location, but the name resembles that of Sfintii Voyevozi, a Bucharest street with a side entrance to the German embassy.

Anastasia, severely ill, continued to drift in and out of consciousness. She also turned out to be pregnant. Despite her continued severe health problems, she gave birth to a boy, which was taken from her and put up for adoption.

Her rescuer, Alexander Tschaikovsky, decided to marry her. No record of any wedding ceremony has ever been found, but Anastasia dimly recalled taking part in a Roman Catholic service. In any event, she would use the name Mrs. Tschaikovsky for years afterward.

The family continued to live in fear of being discovered. Anastasia reported that she never left the cottage. Apparently, Alexander dealt with the outside world and procured the food and supplies they needed. One day he did not return, and his wife learned that he had been shot in the street. He lived a few days then died of his wounds. No record of his death has ever been found, but Anastasia retained a clear image of his body in a coffin.

She suspected that the Bolsheviks had attempted to assassinate Alexander because he was protecting her. When his brother Serge disappeared, she assumed that he had gone into hiding to avoid sharing Alexander's fate. Now that her protectors were gone, the ailing Grand Duchess had to face her terror alone.

WHILE Anastasia struggled to survive in Bucharest, arrangements were underway to help other members of the Romanov family circle to escape from Russia. Anastasia's grandmother, the Dowager Czarina Marie, and a large contingent of courtiers had taken refuge on a group of imperial estates in the Crimea, but the Bolshevik forces were rapidly advancing on the area. The British sent a battleship, the *HMS Marlborough*, complete with a letter from Queen Alexandra—widow of King Edward VII—imploring her sister, Marie, to take advantage of what might be the last opportunity to save herself. At first, the old woman was determined to stay, but the rest of the family soon convinced her of the folly of remaining on Russian soil.

As the Red soldiers continued to advance, the Romanovs began hurried preparations to depart, making quick decisions as to which jewels and other valuables to take into exile and which trusted servants they would save from the certain revenge of the Bolsheviks. On April 7, 1919, the party of eighty-one refugees boarded the ship. In addition to the Dowager Czarina, the group included the Czar's sister Xenia and her sons; the Czar's uncles, Nicholas and Peter and their wives, the Montenegrin sisters Militsa and Anastasia; Felix and Irina Youssoupov; other family members and aristocrats; and a large contingent of servants. The possessions they had deemed crucial to their survival outside Russia comprised two hundred tons of baggage. The embarkation required an entire day.

As the ship prepared to sail away, a British sloop steamed by in tribute. On her decks crowded hundreds of Russian officers, loyal to the monarchy, singing *God Save the Czar*. With the help denied Nicholas, Alexandra, and their children, surviving members of the Romanov family voyaged in safety and comfort to their new lives in the West.

ALTHOUGH Serge had returned, Anastasia continued to live a precarious existence and felt that Bucharest provided an inadequate haven for her. She decided that she must try to contact her mother's sister, Princess Irene of Prussia, who lived in Berlin. Serge arranged the sale of Anastasia's few remaining jewels and agreed to accompany her on the trip north.

In the beginning, they traveled at night on trains crowded with other refugees, but Anastasia, still fearing discovery, insisted that they abandon this mode of transportation, because soldiers and police officials often came on board. They ended up walking for miles, always at night, with Serge carrying her when she became too exhausted to continue on her own. Although they did not have identification papers, they managed to sneak around the border crossings, which served as their only points of reference in an otherwise bleak and monotonous landscape. At some point, they boarded another train and proceeded to their final destination.

II.

"I was still alive"

Berlin, 18 February, 1920. Unknown girl's attempted suicide. Yesterday evening at 9 P.M., a girl of about 20 jumped off the Bendler Bridge into the Landwehr Canal with the intention of taking her own life. She was saved by a police sergeant and admitted to the Elizabeth Hospital in Lutzowstrasse. No papers or valuables of any kind were found in her possession, and she refused to make any statements about herself or her motives for attempting suicide.

—Official Police Report

It was certainly the stupidest thing I could have done, and all the developments which followed, all the misery that faced me, come back to this one step.

—I Am Anastasia

"WHERE NOW?" Serge asked, when their train finally stopped at the Berlin station. To Anastasia, this day was "the most dreadful of all." She had endured the trip in a dark, frozen blur, unaware of how many days, or even weeks, it had taken. As she and Serge alighted from the train, they had no idea where to go. After only a short walk through the station, she was impressed by the contrast between Berlin and Bucharest. The station was bright and bustling with activity. Out on the streets, car lights brightened the whiteness of melting snow.

Serge couldn't speak German, and they had difficulty finding someone who could direct them to a hotel. Finally, they learned the name of a hotel supposedly not far from the station and hailed a cab. As their cab drove on, the streets seemed to darken and activity lessened, until they reached the hotel, which was located in one of the poorer parts of the city. They took two rooms on the same floor, separated by what seemed to her a great distance. After helping Anastasia settle into her room, Serge left.

"I tried to go to sleep, but could not do so in this awful room. I walked restlessly up and down. My nerves were all churned up, and I was once more in pain. *I must get out of here*, was my only thought." She left her room in search of Serge, but his room was empty. At first, she thought he must have gone out on an errand, perhaps to get food. But he did not return, and she grew frantic.

She wandered around the hotel, looking in vain for Serge, hoping to find him in one of the corridors or in the lobby. She walked out onto the street and began searching for him, drifting aimlessly, fearfully, until she knew she was lost. In her state of exhaustion, she had not noted the name of the hotel or the street. How would she get back? Had Serge abandoned her? After all the perilous months of flight and pain, the unremitting terror about being recognized or discovered, she had finally reached relative safety in a city and a country where she felt less afraid, only to be left alone.

THIS night was pivotal to the Anastasia story. It has been recreated on stage, on film, and in numerous books, always told differently and, to Anastasia's mind, inaccurately. Some of the depictions dramatize her trudging through deep snow or fighting horrendous winds, as she makes her way through darkened winter streets.

The weather that February night was not particularly cold. A high-pressure center had moved in from the west during the day, melting the existing snow cover. The skies were clear, and the lack of cloud cover caused radiational cooling as night approached, but there was no heavy wind. The temperature was about thirty-five degrees Fahrenheit at 9 P.M.

"Now I wondered even more what on earth was going to happen to me," she remembered. "I was wholly without help. From a park I came to a canal, with a road on each side of it, joined by a bridge. There were trees along the canal banks, which were quiet and deserted." She saw no one about; no boats were on that part of the canal.

I leaned over the side of the bridge and looked into the water, which was black and had a slight mist drifting over it. The sight of this water disturbed me greatly. I never thought about it being cold if I jumped in, I thought instead that it would completely envelop me with its white mist and then everything would be over: the pain in my head, my despair and my loneliness. Then I should no longer need Tschaikovsky, nor Aunt Irene; and after death I should meet my parents again, meet again my sisters and little brother. I don't know how long I stood like this, nor do I remember whether I dropped from the bridge or one of the canal banks. I believe I was no longer in this world when I glided into the water.

As she jumped, Sergeant Hallman of the Berlin city police rounded a corner near one end of the bridge. He saw a figure fall into the canal and heard a loud splash. He dashed down the bank of the canal, pulling off his overcoat as he ran, and dove into the water. He grabbed hold of the young woman dressed in heavy winter clothing and, despite their combined weight, was able to drag her through the water to the bank. He pulled her semiconscious body back onto the bridge. She offered no resistance as he tried to perform artificial resuscitation. A passerby had noticed the commotion and called for assistance, and a police vehicle arrived.

"WHEN I came round, there were a lot of people standing round me. I must have been still lying near the canal . . . but I was almost numb with cold. I simply could not grasp that I was still alive."

Sergeant Hallman escorted her to a nearby police station, where she was offered warm blankets and a hot drink. As she began to warm up, the police began interrogating her. Attempted suicide was a crime, and they demanded to know her name, where she lived, why she was alone, and why she had tried to kill herself. They had already discovered that she did not have a handbag. The pockets of her clothing were empty, and there were no labels in her clothing. *They must take me for the worst type of woman*, she thought, and as the policemen shouted questions, she wondered what to say. "I have asked for nothing," she said defiantly, in what the police described as "a completely foreign accent."

She said nothing more, and the frustrated police assumed that she was a mental case. They transported her to the Elizabeth Hospital, where she was admitted for the night. There, after being examined by the nurses and put into a coarse hospital gown, she was led into an open ward for indigent women. Not surprisingly, after the exhaustion and tension of the preceding months, culminating in the dramatic events of that evening, she slept.

She awoke the next morning surrounded by doctors and nurses. The questioning began anew. They wanted to know who she was, where she came from, what her occupation was, and why she had jumped. The doctors noted on their records that she seemed stronger than the night before, but fearful. She shut her eyes, covered her face with the bedsheet, and turned toward the wall, silent and unresponsive.

"I recognized the danger threatening me. As soon as I opened my eyes again, the questioning would start. If I told them the truth, they would not believe I was the daughter of the Czar. But if they found out I was a Russian, they would hand me over to the Bolsheviks. After all the terrible ordeals I had been through during the last years, had I come to Berlin for that?"

She made a decision to remain silent and reveal nothing about her identity. There were half a million foreign emigres in Germany at the time, one hundred thousand Russians in Berlin alone. Overburdened by the influx of foreign nationals, the German government was attempting to repatriate them as quickly as possible. She knew that if she could be identified as a Russian, she would be sent back to certain death in the country now controlled by the government that had slaughtered her family.

III.

"A time of appalling suffering"

AFTER SIX WEEKS of almost continuous questioning at the Elizabeth Hospital, Anastasia was transferred to the Dalldorf Asylum outside Berlin during the last week of March. The diagnosis was "mental illness of a depressive character." Because she had hardly spoken, the police and hospital authorities could not identify her, and she was admitted to Dalldorf as Miss Unknown. Assigned to a ward for "quiet" patients, she had a bed in a room with fourteen other women.

On March 30, 1920, she underwent the first physical examination for which a record exists. Her weight was recorded at one hundred ten pounds and her height at five-feet two-inches. Under persistent questioning, she began to speak, but her answers were brief and belligerent. The doctor's report noted that her body was covered with scars and lacerations. A prolonged examination revealed that she was not a virgin. We can only imagine the indignity the daughter of a Russian czar must have felt while being probed and prodded by strange doctors in a foreign country. She continued to answer questions reluctantly and only after sustaining long barrages by examiners.

By the end of May, the Dalldorf doctors reported to the Berlin police that they had learned nothing more about Miss Unknown. On June 17 she was fingerprinted and photographed from various angles at the hospital, and the police prepared an information sheet labeled "Unknown Female Person" for circulation around Germany. The Dalldorf staff had no expectation that the information sheet would yield any new clues, because Miss Unknown was obviously one of thousands of stateless foreigners who roamed Germany after the war. Her German was imprecise, and the nurses noticed that, when she suffered nightmares, she spoke Russian and English in her sleep.

Her medical charts indicated that she was a "suffering person," consumed by melancholia. She did not interact with the other patients and stayed in her bed most of the time. She kept her face turned to the wall, as if she no longer wanted to be part of the world. When she did rise, she remained withdrawn. Often, she refused to eat and was forcibly fed.

The nurses began to remark to each other that Miss Unknown was an unusual personage. Her posture and demeanor, they thought, were not those of a working woman. Her hands were delicate and fine. The aloofness with which she carried herself seemed distinct and natural. Her self-imposed isolation made her stand out. The staff took particular note of her aristocratic bearing, which they felt indicated she must have been "born to a high station."

"In Dalldorf, a time of appalling suffering began for me. When-

75

ever I look back on it today, I am still amazed that I did not really go mad. Nobody who had not been through it can imagine what it is like to be . . . confined with . . . lunatics in an asylum for two-and-a-half years. I shall never forget the shattering things I saw there. Such things stay with one for a lifetime. . . ."

Ward B of House Four at Dalldorf had barred windows to keep the patients inside, but although she felt trapped, Miss Unknown had no desire to leave. The other patients in the large open room were "pathetic creatures" who babbled constantly, so she stayed in bed and built a barricade of pillows around herself: "I felt I had to guard against becoming like my neighbors."

Her complaints of an almost constant toothache prompted the Dalldorf dentist to remove several of her front teeth. Some of the nurses noticed her plucking hair from her forehead in an apparent attempt to alter her hairline. Whoever Miss Unknown was, they surmised, she was trying to change her looks.

IN old age, Anastasia would reflect on the Dalldorf years only reluctantly. It was a time she wished to forget, yet her stay there provided a refuge when she had nowhere else to live. The world outside the barred windows of Ward B was quickly changing. The Bolsheviks had gained a firmer grip on Russia, and the embryonic National Socialist movement in Germany characterized the Bolshevik threat as one that could soon consume the Fatherland. But for Anastasia, time seemed to stand still. The only news she received came from out-of-date newspapers and magazines left in the ward by families of the other patients.

Days passed slowly, and weeks became months. Inevitably, an orderly routine was established, and Anastasia felt more secure in her surroundings. The familiar faces of the nurses and staff calmed her, and she began to feel that she could trust some of them.

As the deliberate suppression of her identity and personality took its toll, something of her natural self began to emerge. Once she became accustomed to Dalldorf, she allowed the staff small glimpses through her facade of anonymity. Some evenings after the other patients went to sleep, she would walk to the nurses' desk and sit and talk. Her knowledge of the political and military events preceding the Great War, especially of Russia and monarchial affairs, impressed them. She spoke of members of various royal and imperial families in a tone so familiar that the nurses wondered whether she had known them personally.

No one knows to whom she first admitted that she was Anastasia. After a while even she could not recall exactly when she "betrayed" herself. The strain of her physical ailments and the burdens of her memories, combined with daily life in an insane asylum, blurred her senses. After she became famous, several of the nurses at Dalldorf took credit for having been the first one taken into her confidence.

NEAR the end of 1921, as Anastasia was growing stronger and better able to face unfolding events, Clara Peuthert was admitted to Dalldorf. One of the more improbable characters to enter Anastasia's life, Clara Peuthert had been diagnosed with a nervous breakdown. At age fifty-two, she was a big, bony, boisterous woman who liked to drink and claimed to have worked as a governess in imperial Russia. From the first day of her admission to Ward B, Clara was drawn to the quiet girl the staff continued to call Miss Unknown.

"This . . . was a strange woman," Anastasia later recalled. "There was something good-natured about her. She too . . . was sane, and only in Dalldorf because of her fits of temper . . . so her neighbors got a doctor to send her to the asylum. I felt a certain bond with her because of this, and as she was the only person in our ward you could talk to sensibly, we got into conversation." Clara herself would later claim that she was not mad, "only pathological," and that she had never belonged in an asylum.

As she began to form a bond with Miss Unknown, Clara was struck by something in the girl's features. "Your face is familiar to me. You do not come from ordinary circles." Then one day, not long after being committed, Clara had a revelation while leafing through an edition of the *Berliner Illustrierte Zeitung*. The magazine featured a cover story, "The Truth About the Murder of the Czar," illustrated with pictures of the Russian imperial family.

She studied the photographs carefully, glancing from the pages to Miss Unknown across the room. "I know you!" she screamed, pointing and waving the magazine in the air. "You are the Grand Duchess Tatiana!"

The whole ward witnessed this outburst, but in an insane asylum where much stranger activities occurred, the other patients paid little heed to Clara. Miss Unknown, however, took Clara's outburst seriously. There is no evidence that the girl tried to correct the misidentification, but before Clara was dismissed from Dalldorf on January 20, 1922, she promised to write letters to the Czar's mother in Denmark and to the Czarina Alexandra's sister, Princess Irene of Prussia, informing them that their relative was alive.

THE surviving members of the Russian imperial family had received the news of the massacre at Ekaterinburg stoically. The threat of assassination was a daily peril in revolutionary Russia, and the murder of kings was an occupational hazard. Regicide was not new, but the brutal extermination of the entire family, including the innocent children, was even then a horrendous event. The assassination of Nicholas, Alexandra, and their family stunned the world. Then the conspiracy theorists set to work, variously blaming the revolution in general and the family's death in particular on the "universal Jewish conspiracy," the Freemasons, and the Gypsies.

Rumors abounded: the imperial family had not been murdered; all had survived and found refuge on a Pacific island; or they had escaped on an ocean liner consigned to sail the globe forever. There seemed to be no end to the variations of these bizarre stories and, of course, the surviving Romanovs found them deeply distressing.

One of the most persistent rumors was that one of the Romanov children had escaped the firing squad. Several pretenders to the identities of each of the daughters and the son emerged in various locations in Europe; all were quickly exposed as frauds. Yet refugees flooding Western Europe from the east continued to bring with them tales of a surviving Romanov daughter. Whether based on fact or wishful thinking, these stories flourished. By the early 1920s, the Romanovs in exile had become accustomed to hearing them, and tabloid newspapers made tidy profits from fueling the flame of hope in the displaced Russians' hearts.

* * *

WHEN Clara Peuthert left Dalldorf, she was confident she had discovered the Grand Duchess Tatiana. She lost little time in circulating the story among Russian-emigre circles in Berlin. Although Clara was hardly perceived as a credible individual, she persisted in her campaign to have "Tatiana" recognized in monarchist circles. The Supreme Monarchist Council, made up of exiled loyalists, appointed Zinaida Tolstoy, a friend of the murdered Czarina, to interview the newly discovered Grand Duchess at Dalldorf. She, the council decided, would be able to judge the young woman's authenticity.

Madame Tolstoy and a small delegation visited the asylum at the beginning of the second week of March 1922. Miss Unknown hid under the covers most of the time, but was finally cajoled into showing herself when one of the doctors assured her that nothing bad would happen. Slowly the doctor lowered the bedsheet covering her head. At first, only Miss Unknown's hair was visible. She was still whimpering as the doctor exposed her eyes, which stared tearfully back at the interrogators. Madame Tolstoy realized she was looking into the eyes of the Czar—the unique shade of blue was unmistakable. As were the red blotches that covered the young girl's face—so like the blotches Madame Tolstoy had noticed on the Czarina when she was under stress.

Surely Miss Unknown must be Tatiana.

Based on the positive report Madame Tolstoy presented to the council, they decided further investigations were in order. Council members debated the matter of who should interview the alleged Grand Duchess. Sensitive to the need for a person familiar with the imperial family but concerned about being too precipitate, in case this Tatiana was a hoax, the council chose to invite Baroness Sophie Buxhoeveden. They could not have known that their choice was one of the worst selections possible, or that Anastasia would remember the Baroness's betrayal of her family at Ekaterinburg.

Life in exile was far removed from the one the Baroness had enjoyed at the Russian imperial court. She lacked funds and had lived for many years on the generosity of various members of German and Russian nobility. Over time, she had become a loud, demanding woman who crassly traded upon her friendship with the dead Czarina.

When she arrived at Dalldorf with Madame Tolstoy, the Baroness demanded that Miss Unknown be brought to meet her in the reception room. After waiting for several minutes, she stormed into Ward B with Madame Tolstoy in tow. Miss Unknown had been forewarned by Clara Peuthert that she should expect a distinguished but unnamed visitor. When she saw the Baroness enter the room, she hid under the covers of her bed and refused to come out. As images of Ekaterinburg flooded Anastasia's memory, the Baroness spoke to her in several languages, calling her "darling," and displaying items she said had belonged to "Mama." But "no persuasion could move her [Miss Unknown] to appear again," the Baroness reported later.

Feeling that her time was being wasted, the Baroness stepped up to the bed, tore off the covers, and pulled the young woman to a standing position. "She's too short for Tatiana," the Baroness bellowed as she left the room. Miss Unknown climbed back into bed and pulled the covers over herself again. Just outside the ward, the Baroness told Madame Tolstoy that the girl was not Tatiana, despite "some resemblance."

News of the encounter with the Baroness spread quickly. The Supreme Monarchist Council lost all interest in Miss Unknown, and Clara found the efforts to help her thwarted at every turn. The stalwart Clara continued to regularly visit Dalldorf, bringing food and magazines to her friend, and her resolve to confirm the girl's true identity did not weaken.

Clara did find a chief ally in Captain Nicholas Schwabe, a former member of the Dowager Czarina's personal guard who lived in Berlin and managed *The Double Eagle*, a fascistic, anti-Semitic publication of the Supreme Monarchist Council. At Clara's request, he had witnessed Madame Tolstoy's visit and stood by horrified as Baroness Buxhoeveden "interviewed" Miss Unknown. Convinced that the young woman was an imperial Grand Duchess, he worked with Clara to solicit interest in Miss Unknown's welfare and continued to visit her in Dalldorf.

He wrote a note to Miss Unknown on the flyleaf of a Russian Bible, asking her to trust him and promising to serve her. She tore the page from the book and ripped it to shreds, but eventually began to trust the captain.

"I did not say I was Tatiana," she meekly informed Schwabe one day. She had become nervous and withdrawn again after the visit of the Baroness, so Schwabe carefully refrained from questioning her. Instead, he handed her a piece of paper on which he had written the names of the four daughters of Nicholas and Alexandra, and asked her to strike through the names that were not hers. When she handed back the pen and paper, the only name that remained was Anastasia.

IV.
"And Anna I remained"

CAPTAIN SCHWABE WAS INTENT upon fulfilling his promise of support. Knowing Baroness Buxhoeveden had a reputation for boorish behavior, he was undeterred by her caustic visit. If Anastasia were to have a genuine chance of being recognized, she needed to get out of Dalldorf, because being there undermined her credibility. He began searching the Russian emigre community for someone who could sponsor her. Very few emigres had much money, and most lived in greatly reduced circumstances, so the captain's task was not easy. Finally, he made contact with Baron Arthur von Kleist, who was relatively well-off and had a spacious apartment in Berlin. Despite daily visits and frequent gifts from the Kleists—all part of a courtship-like campaign to convince her to leave—Anastasia resisted leaving Dalldorf for two months. She did not know that the Kleists were aware of her identity: "I believe they did not know who I was, but were trying to help me out of pure kindness."

She finally relented, but only because most of the patients in Ward B were scheduled to be moved into an institution in Brandenburg, much further from Berlin than she already was. She feared the isolation of Brandenburg, and felt certain that the Bolsheviks would find her there.

By the time she was ready to leave Dalldorf, the story that an alleged Grand Duchess of Russia was a patient at the asylum had spread throughout the emigre community. As she looked through the bars of a window in her ward, she saw that the streets outside were full of "curious spectators."

"I found this so distressing that I asked a nurse to put a thick, black veil over my face," she later recalled. "I wanted nobody to see me and not to see myself."

She moved into the Kleists' apartment May 30, 1922, and was immediately depressed to learn that it was located near the canal she was pulled from two years before. The family gave her a room of her own and treated her quite well in those first days, buying her new clothing and other gifts and pampering her extensively. But as time passed, Anastasia realized that Baron Kleist had ulterior motives.

As always, she was careful to guard her identity. When Baroness Kleist asked how she wished to be addressed publicly, Anastasia "asked her to call me Anna, after the first part of my name—and Anna I remained." But despite their promise to guard her obsessive anonymity, the Kleists quickly spread the word that the Czar's daughter Anastasia was their house guest.

Almost from the hour of her arrival, their home became the most popular gathering place for Russian emigres in Berlin. In fact, there was rarely a time when there were not visitors. This left Anastasia very little privacy, and although she made it clear that the Russian language was one she would not speak—because of the memories it brought back—the visitors continually insisted on speaking Russian to her.

Madame Tolstoy visited frequently during this time, and Anastasia began to feel comfortable with her—eventually more comfortable than she felt with the Kleists. Clara Peuthert also attempted to visit, but her coarse manners and blunt, direct speech did not ingratiate her to the pretentious monarchists who filled the Kleists' drawing room. Soon, Baroness Kleist suggested to Anastasia that Clara be prohibited from returning.

Anastasia's health began to deteriorate after she moved in with the Kleists. She still suffered intense headaches and blurred vision from her ordeal in Ekaterinburg, and her thought processes and memory were distorted.

Many of the visitors wanted to discuss the old days in imperial

Russia, and some criticized the actions of the Czar and Czarina, as well as those of Rasputin.

> Also it happened more than once that the refugees dared to tell lies about Father Gregory . . . and his family, declaring that he had exerted a fatal influence on Russia. They also spread malicious stories about the Grand Dukes. At first I pretended not to hear, although my heart was thumping with indignation and I had to fight to keep back the tears. But then I found it too much to bear and I could just not control myself any longer, so I got up and went out of the room. . . .

With the strain of living in the Kleists' house, Anastasia's health continued to worsen, and her anxiety increased. On the few occasions when she went out with the Kleists to visit parks and museums, she expressed tremendous fear of being followed by Bolshevik agents.

Gradually, Anastasia realized that Baron Kleist hoped to benefit from having harbored the Czar's daughter, in the event of a restored Russian monarchy. He even asked her to sign a document guaranteeing him payment of a certain sum, if she were ever officially recognized. Once, she claimed, he made an indecent overture to her.

Finally, she became so sick that the Kleist family physician began to make regular house calls. The doctor noted that she seemed to be in great pain resulting from an old head injury. Just as in the asylum, however, she refused to answer even the simplest questions and would not give him so much as her age.

On June 30, after just one month with the Kleists, she collapsed. The doctor returned and began to treat the pain with injections of morphine. Worried about Anastasia's health, Madame Tolstoy moved in with the Kleists and stayed with Anastasia almost constantly, sometimes sleeping on the floor beside her bed. Only now, under the influence of the drug, did she admit to Madame Tolstoy that she was the Grand Duchess Anastasia, and she began to disjointedly recount her memories of Ekaterinburg and the flight from Russia.

"In normal circumstances I should not have told them, but then I thought my last hour had come, and besides I was under the influence of the drug. . . ."

This was the first time anyone had heard the details of her escape or of her rescuers, Alexander and Serge Tschaikovsky. The most shocking part was the revelation that she had given birth to a child. Dazed by morphine, Anastasia told Madame Tolstoy that the father of the child was Alexander Tschaikovsky, and that she had given the baby up for adoption. Such conduct was so alien to the concept of monarchy that when Baron Kleist began to repeat the story, many Russian emigres could no longer accept that this woman could be the daughter of their Czar.

The Kleists had attempted to hide from her the fact that they were sharing her newly revealed tales with their friends, but during the worst part of her illness, Baron Kleist escorted visitors into her sickroom for a final look at what he described as the dying Anastasia. Realizing that her innermost secrets were now being bandied about in public, discussed and debated by strangers, she became unbearably ill at ease with the Kleists. She began wishing that she had never left Dalldorf and began seriously considering Clara's recent offer to share her home with Anastasia.

On August 12, 1922, Anastasia disappeared from the Kleists' apartment. Knowing that she had a special fondness for Clara, the Kleists began their search for Anastasia at her dingy, one-room flat, but Anastasia was not there. The Kleists called the police, who then mounted a search. Two days later, she was found at the Berlin Zoo. She had been wandering the streets and sleeping in parks, and said that she would rather sleep with the animals than return to the Kleists'.

BERLIN in the mid-1920s was a city far removed from its glorious past as the capital of the Imperial Second Reich. Although Berliners had always taken pride in the efficiency of Prussian authority, they had also maintained an irreverent love for life. Now that they had been humbled by the devastating defeat of the war, that irreverence served as a shield against the grim reality of a city filled with the unemployed and the stateless. In a time of unreconciled extremes—political, artistic, and cultural—the once charming city had descended into wild and unrestrained decadence.

Nothing was too bizarre. Transvestites promenaded down the tree-lined avenues in broad daylight. Magnus Hirschfeld opened his

Institute for Sexual Science. Christopher Isherwood walked hand-in-hand with the woman he would later fictionalize as Sally Bowles. Cafe life—in this city of night-people and fantasts—provided a twenty-four-hour arena for the *outre*.

At the crossroads of the cataclysmic changes rocking Europe after the First World War, Berlin became a center for a myriad of political refugees and their crusades. Former nobles, sometimes working as taxi drivers or maitres d'hotel, argued politics and upheld lost causes with factory workers who now had the power to elect their own governments. A topsy-turvy world where no cause was too obscure and no outcome too improbable. A place for lost souls to survive.

It was through this city that Anastasia wandered after escaping from the Kleists. The world she had known was gone forever, and she wondered whether she was as mad as the city—and its people—appeared to be.

A friend of Captain Schwabe arranged for her to be lodged at the home of a wealthy police inspector and historian, Franz Grünberg, who was a sympathizer of the then-embryonic Nazi party. His country home at Funkenmühle was in a pastoral setting. Anastasia recalled:

> At first I had no regrets. It was really lovely out there in the country and [they] did everything they could to make my stay pleasant. His wife especially took great care to see that I had peace and was well fed. . . .
> I felt in heaven. I sat a lot in the garden, which was well-kept. After a long time I again took up a drawing-block and drew the animals which leapt around in the meadow. I found myself thinking of Gleb Botkin, who could do it so much better than I, and whom I had last seen at Tobolsk; I wondered where on earth he was now. Sometimes Doctor Grünberg sat near me and watched me, and then he would talk.

Grünberg later wrote: "Feeling that there was a historical mystery here comparable to that of the Man in the Iron Mask, I decided to take the young lady for three weeks to my estate. . . . Staying two years at Dalldorf had completely shattered her nerves. Moreover, she had been wounded in the head (skull battered by blows from a rifle) which led to a certain mental derangement; and in addition there was a mental instability in the family on her mother's side."

In talking with Grünberg, Anastasia set aside whatever reluctance she had felt with the Kleists and other emigres about discussing Ekaterinburg and the escape. "I did not get this narrative from her," he wrote, "in [a] coherent form, but only in rather disconnected fragments; and even then I had to proceed very gently, because recalling these horrible experiences made her tremendously excited, until she would completely collapse."

The inspector had no doubt that his guest was the Grand Duchess Anastasia and began to work earnestly toward effecting a reunion with members of her family. Using his contacts in the law-enforcement community, he approached Princess Irene of Prussia—her mother's sister—and asked her to visit his estate for the purpose of identifying Anastasia. After all, finding "Aunt Nini" was the reason Anastasia and Serge had come to Berlin.

Inspector Grünberg gave Anastasia no indication that she was about to receive a visitor. Instead, he invited the Princess to come incognito, and she arrived with a lady-in-waiting. The Princess had told Grünberg that she did not think she could recognize Anastasia, because ten years had passed since she last saw the Czar's family.

"The day Aunt Irene came to Funkenmühle," Anastasia said later, "is one of the most painful memories I have of that period." Although she had not mentioned it to the Grünbergs, Anastasia was feeling ill again and had noticed a swelling on her chest. She had taken a walk alone through the countryside, where she found wild mushrooms growing. "Not having brought a knife or a basket, I dug them up with my hands, even carrying them home in my arms. Unsuspecting and dirty, I entered the house with these mushrooms."

"I showed [Grünberg] my mushrooms and explained that before supper I would just like to go to my room to wash and do my hair." The lights had been dimmed, so when the inspector escorted two ladies into the dining room, she "could not distinguish them properly." When he introduced the women to Anastasia, he did not give her their real names. "I took them for friends or relatives of his."

Sitting at the dinner table, Anastasia recognized her aunt's voice and, realizing she had been tricked, got up and ran to her room. The Princess followed, begging her to talk, but Anastasia turned her back and stared out the window. She felt betrayed and full of indignation. This was her mother's sister, "Aunt Nini," with whom she had spent so many happy weeks as a child. This was the woman she and Serge Tschaikovsky had risked their lives to travel to Berlin to find. She had asked Clara and a doctor at Dalldorf to write to this favored relative, only to have those letters ignored. It was this same relative who had hosted Baroness Buxhoeveden at the time of her hostile visit to Anastasia at Dalldorf. Now, instead of enjoying the imagined happy reunion with her beloved aunt, Anastasia found herself being tested by a woman who had presented herself as a stranger.

NOT long after this episode, Anastasia grudgingly returned to the Kleists. She had been there barely three weeks when she was diagnosed with "incipient tuberculosis of the breastbone" and admitted to the Westend Hospital at Charlottenburg. She remained there through the end of the year and during most of 1923. She was occasionally discharged from the hospital for brief periods and chose to spend her time with Clara Peuthert. Even though a friend of the Kleists was paying her bills, she said she would rather stay in Clara's dirty apartment—where at least she was treated well—than endure the Kleists and the constant parade of gawking visitors.

As Anastasia's behavior grew increasingly more erratic, her relationship with Clara became strained. Eventually, Clara became abusive. Their friendship ended when Clara threw Anastasia out of her apartment in the middle of the night.

By the end of 1924, Anastasia had been in and out of the hospital many times. When not institutionalized, she often wandered alone, feeding the animals at the zoo and sometimes sleeping on park benches. The once-rambunctious imp who kept a menagerie and loved playing practical jokes had become but another lost soul aimlessly walking the streets of a former imperial capital.

When her plight came to the attention of the Berlin welfare office, they asked inspector Grünberg to make inquiries. He found her living with an impoverished family of coal carriers who had taken her in not knowing or caring that she was a grand duchess. "They shared their last bit of bread with me and cared for me as best they could," she later said. "If I ever have any money my greatest desire is to help these people who sheltered me only through generosity, without asking me who I was or if they would be paid for doing it."

Grünberg took her back to Funkenmühle for several weeks, but not even the country air and wholesome food could restore her health. She had developed a tubercular lesion on her left elbow. A doctor called in to treat her noticed "deepenings in the skull," which he took to be the result of "an act of violence."

The Grünbergs provided her with care, but the inspector showed little sensitivity for her weakened physical and mental state, and even less for her dignity. During the height of her illness, he invited the former German Crown Princess, Cecilie of Prussia, to visit, with the hope that she would recognize Anastasia. "I was struck at first glance by the young person's resemblance to the Czar's mother and to the Czar himself, but I could see nothing of the Czarina in her. There proved no opportunity of establishing her identity."

"How was she supposed to recognize me in a few minutes?" Anastasia later said to a friend. "I have grown so old, the missing teeth in front make me look so strange."

After this second unsuccessful attempt to have his guest recognized by a fellow royal, Grünberg announced that Anastasia must prepare to leave his home again.

Once more, Anastasia seemed to be on the brink of total destitution. By this time, however, her case had received a good deal of publicity. Dr. Karl Sonnenschein, a wealthy philanthropist, had followed her story with interest and now set out to help her.

V.

"We change our shell"

ON THE MORNING of June 19, 1925, Dr. Sonnenschein telephoned Harriet von Rathlef-Keilmann, a thirty-seven-year-old divorced Russian emigre who supported her four children by working as a sculptor and a writer of children's books. The doctor asked her to call upon him, and said he thought she could help him deal with the case of a Russian woman who was seriously ill and needed accommodations.

"Have you heard anything about a daughter of the Czar of Russia being still alive?" he asked. Harriet "was more than surprised."

That afternoon, she drove to the Grünbergs' house and met Anastasia:

> She was small, very thin, and appeared to be ill. She was shabbily dressed, like an old woman of the poor. When we approached to shake hands, I observed that she had lost practically all her front teeth, which made her look older than she really was.
>
> Her movements and her bearing were those of a lady of the highest social rank in Russia. That was the impression which she created at the first glance. I was, however, particularly struck by her resemblance to the Dowager Empress. She spoke German, but with a typically Russian accent. When I addressed her in Russian, I noticed that she understood everything I said, for, although she answered in German, her reply was perfectly accurate.

Harriet noticed the open wound on Anastasia's left arm and advised her to check into a hospital. Dr. Sonnenschein had arranged for her to have a bed in St. Mary's Hospital in Berlin, and Harriet returned to the Grünbergs' the next day to escort Anastasia there:

> When [she] appeared, her eyes were swollen with weeping, and she was in an excited state. She timidly held out her hand to her former protector [Grünberg], but . . . he angrily refused to take it.
>
> I took the modest parcel containing the worldly belongings of the patient, and conveyed her to the hospital.
>
> Now, a hospital is certainly not the place in which a person under the influence of sad memories and suffering from bodily afflictions can be expected to make satisfactory progress, no matter how devoted the care which is lavished on the patient. . . . The funds at our disposal were extremely limited, and I had to be content with . . . a third-class public hospital ward for this young girl, who might be a daughter of the Czar of all the Russias. . . . The five patients who shared the ward with her were . . . working class women. . . .

* * *

HARRIET Rathlef probably saved Anastasia's life by giving her friendship, counsel, and the motivation to live. Harriet left detailed and articulate records of her friendship with Anastasia and began the first exhaustive investigation into her identity and past. Harriet's notes and files have become primary material for all subsequent biographers, and her book, *Anastasia: A Woman's Fate as a Mirror of the World Catastrophe*, is a mine of precious information and insight upon which all subsequent researchers have depended. Without Harriet's selfless devotion, Anastasia would likely have disappeared into the twilight world of Berlin's nameless and homeless, never to be heard of again.

Harriet Rathlef also introduced Anastasia to the Anthroposophical movement, which was based on the writings and lectures of Dr. Rudolf Steiner, an Austrian philosopher who had died earlier that year. Steiner's teachings were a distillation of ancient Christianity and other Eastern and esoteric philosophies. He embraced the theories of karma, reincarnation, the lost continent of Atlantis, "spirit groups," and dance therapy (which he called "Eurythmy"), melding them all into "spiritual science."

Anthroposophy was in particular vogue among Russian emigres in the Western Europe of the mid-1920s, largely because Steiner's Russian wife, Marie Steiner-von Sivers, believed that her native land had undergone a psychic upheaval unlike any in world history. Steiner's philosophy meshed with the Russian mystical tradition. As millions of displaced immigrants sought to understand their collective misfortune, they gravitated to his wildly unorthodox teachings.

Not surprisingly, given her upbringing, Anastasia listened with interest as Harriet explained Steiner's teachings. Although Anastasia herself never became an Anthroposophist—what she called an "Anthrosop"—she did adhere to some of the movement's peripheral canons.

As she explained to Milukoff:

> God they don't mention, but Christ. Always Christ. God is not mentioned by them, but always Christ. And all is in Christ. It is renewing of Christianity. . . . The Roman Catholics don't like this . . . at all. But it is, in fact, a renewing of the oldest religion, so as the religion first was taught, this is the meaning of it. . . . This society was founded by Doctor Steiner, an Austrian, and his wife, a Russian, before the First War. And in the First War it was worked out more and more.

One never knows how the soul is running, you know? That [is what] the Anthrosops would tell [you]. You see, that is because the soul is wandering . . . which is the truth. . . . The soul is wandering. We change our shell, but our soul stays our soul . . . always.

THERE were many reasons Anastasia might have been attracted to a set of beliefs as far from the mainstream as Anthroposophy was. By this time—1925—Anastasia was twenty-four, and seven years had passed since Ekaterinburg. For the past five years, she had slept alternately on park benches and in fine country estates, when not confined to hospitals and asylums. Her life now was not even a faint shadow of her childhood at Czarskoe Selo, and the world around her was wholly alien. The armistice ending the First World War had brought with it a new world order. The Russian Empire was fading into history, national boundaries had been redrawn, and socialism and the rights of workers dominated European political considerations. The foundations of her youth had been swept away, replaced with a more proletarian—even vulgar, to her—reality.

In later years, she would speak of these days only with the greatest reluctance. The shock of realizing that her innocent view of the world no longer comported with reality must have been considerable. That she had often been cared for by someone—the Kleists, Clara Peuthert, various hospital nurses—never alleviated her sense of insurmountable isolation.

Jungian psychiatry, still in its infancy, would have found Anastasia a fascinating case study. The universe of her youth had been cast with archetypes in classic molds—kings, princes, obsequious servants, and the Mad Monk, all orbiting around a supreme emperor who was accepted as God's personal representative by the millions who populated his empire. Suddenly her universe was gone, cast into disrepute. Her value system and beliefs were shattered.

Anastasia was never a deep thinker, and the mystical foundations of Anthroposophy must have seemed comfortably familiar, offering her a hope of understanding where she stood in relation to the world around her.

* * *

AFTER visiting Anastasia at St. Mary's every day and supervising almost every aspect of her care, Harriet Rathlef had no doubt that this girl was the Russian princess she claimed to be. But some disturbing problems were apparent. Although she clearly understood her visitor when spoken to in Russian, Anastasia would never reply in Russian, resorting instead to her halting German. She had forgotten how to count. She couldn't tell time; the numerals on clocks were incomprehensible to her. She found even the simplest written material impossible to master. Mrs. Rathlef felt instinctively that something horrible must have happened to this well-educated young noblewoman to cause her mind to forget the most basic learned skills.

Compounding these problems were two other pressing concerns, her mental condition and her physical health. The events of recent years, whatever they were, had obviously left her fearful and paranoid. She was very high-strung, and her memory of her life before Berlin seemed as tattered and frayed as the state of her nerves. Recalling the past, she told Harriet, was like straining to see distant images through dense fog.

The more immediate worry was her physical health. The tuberculosis of the bone in her left arm and elbow had developed a staph infection, which had broken open, causing almost constant pain. She also suffered from recurring fevers, severe anemia, and occasional blinding headaches. The doctors at St. Mary's told Harriet frankly that they were not sure their patient would live.

Anastasia's overall condition was so precarious that an outside physician was called in. Dr. Serge Rudnev was Russian-born and one of the outstanding medical practitioners of his day; he knew who his patient was reputed to be and recalled a curious incident, one that had always seemed too trivial to discuss with anyone before. On the day war was declared in 1914, he had been walking by the palace in Moscow with a friend when Anastasia and her sister Tatiana pelted them with paper balls from above. When observed, the two girls quickly disappeared back inside. Now as he examined his new patient, Rudnev asked whether she remembered what she was doing on that historic day nine years before. "Shame, shame!" she replied. "My sister and I were playing the fool, and were pelting the passersby with little paper balls."

One of Dr. Rudnev's first orders was that she be given a thorough examination, with every facet of her physicality documented. His analysis of the evidence would determine not only the extent of the numerous wounds that had precipitated the present crisis but would also provide points of possible identification.

Even before Dr. Rudnev was called in on the case, Harriet had been researching the life of the Grand Duchess Anastasia, and had found a wealth of material. After the initial shock of the Russian revolution had passed, the public became fascinated with the Romanovs, particularly with Nicholas's reign. The fall of the Czarist Empire invited analysis and study, and bookstores and magazine racks were full of stories about even the most personal aspects of the imperial family. It didn't take Harriet long to compile a checklist of the identifying marks possessed by the teenaged Anastasia. When Dr. Rudnev compared the notes of his report with Harriet's list, neither was surprised at what they found.

The Grand Duchess Anastasia and her sisters had suffered from a congenital malformation of the feet called *hallux valgus*. So did the patient. In his report, Rudnev noted, "On the right foot I observed a severe deformity, apparently congenital in nature, in that the big toe bends right in over the middle, forming a bunion." This condition was not highly unusual, and was often found in women who had worn ill-fitting shoes for many years. But in the case of his patient, the *hallux valgus* was so extreme that it could only have been present since birth.

Then there was the matter of the scars. Harriet had documented that the Grand Duchess Anastasia had a small scar on her right shoulder blade as a result of the cauterization of a mole. So did the patient. Another scar surrounded the base of the middle finger of the left hand of the Russian princess, as a result of a footman's having accidentally closed a carriage door on it. The patient had a scar in the same location. The young Anastasia had a small, indistinct scar on her forehead, which was usually concealed by her bangs. (This was the scar Hallie Erminie Rives had noticed in 1911, as she observed Anastasia in a St. Petersburg theater.) The patient also had such a scar.

Other comparisons were made, photographs of the youngest Romanov daughter were carefully studied, and as the number of similarities increased, the conclusion was clear to the two examiners. Dr. Rudnev and Mrs. Rathlef were convinced that the woman lying in the hospital bed before them was the Grand Duchess Anastasia, even if her famous rebellious spirit had been completely altered.

VI.
"This is Anastasia's body"

EVENTUALLY, news that the young woman in a bed at St. Mary's Hospital might really be Anastasia reached the ears of the small court surrounding the Dowager Czarina. Following her escape from Russia, she had returned to her native Copenhagen to take up residence at the Danish court. Anastasia's grandmother had never accepted as fact the death of Nicholas and his family. Quite the contrary, she insisted that she *knew* her son, his wife, and their children to be alive and safe. The old Empress remained so steadfast in her conviction that she had never expressed much concern about their fate.

She was accompanied in exile by one of the Czar's sisters, Grand Duchess Olga. Olga had been the plain one—in fact, most people considered her ugly. She had married twice and fled Russia without money or assets with her second husband, whom her mother had never liked. Olga had nowhere else to turn for support, and the Dowager Czarina treated her as little more than a lackey. Although embittered by such treatment, Olga attributed her mother's behavior to senility and did not want to risk disturbing the old woman's equanimity. Upon hearing the rumors about the alleged Grand Duchess in Berlin, Olga asked her uncle, Prince Valdemar of Denmark, to investigate the matter first.

They decided to ask Herluf Zahle, the Danish ambassador in

Berlin, to look into the case of the alleged Anastasia. Zahle was a consummate career diplomat with the added stature of having been President of the League of Nations, which was at that time regarded as the most important international organization in the history of man. By virtue of his service, then, Zahle was one of the most eminent European statesmen of his generation and was considered unimpeachable.

Prince Valdemar wrote to Zahle, charging him with the task of conducting a "private" investigation and agreeing to underwrite the patient's medical expenses until a final determination of her identity could be made. The instructions were hand-delivered by Alexis Volkov, the former Groom of the Chamber of Czarina Alexandra and one of her closest personal servants. He was among the few members of the imperial staff who had had daily contact with the Czarina and her children and had accompanied the family to Ekaterinburg before being separated from them. Even in exile, Volkov maintained a deep loyalty to the Romanovs. Now an elderly man, he had been taken in by the Dowager Czarina and depended upon her favor, as well as the good graces of her Danish relatives, for his livelihood.

Prince Valdemar instructed the old servant to accompany Ambassador Zahle to the hospital and to observe the alleged Anastasia. Once he returned to Copenhagen, Volkov was to deliver his own personal report to the family.

ZAHLE and Volkov arranged to meet Harriet Rathlef at St. Mary's on the afternoon of July 3, 1925. Once there, they observed Anastasia through a window as she strolled in the hospital garden. Even though the visit was brief, Volkov's initial reaction encouraged Harriet. As he watched the young woman pass by the window, he thought she "did indeed resemble Grand Duchess Anastasia."

The two men returned the next day and met the patient. "Volkov was disappointed," Harriet said. On closer inspection, he concluded that the young woman did not look like the girl he remembered. For her part, Anastasia did not seem to be able to remember him, either, and seemed pained and concerned that she could not recognize the man who had been so much a part of her childhood. When told that he had come from Denmark, she seemed confused as to how this might be. "But he belonged to our court," she said. Harriet reported that it was an uncomfortable meeting for the both of them.

Still, charged with a grave responsibility, the old courtier paid two more visits to the hospital. On each occasion, he asked Anastasia several questions that only a member of the imperial family would have been able to answer accurately. Her responses were correct and detailed, and Volkov was eventually moved to the point of tears. "He was deeply upset." Harriet reported. "He was crying and he kissed her hand several times. . . .".

But Volkov left without acknowledging that the patient really was Anastasia. When Harriet pressed him on the matter, he responded that he feared for his job.

After Volkov returned to Copenhagen, he made his report to his employers, but even today it remains sealed by order of the Queen of Denmark. We do not know what he said to the Danish royal family or whether the Dowager Czarina ever saw his report.

THE Volkov visit was not the only disappointment Harriet faced in these early days. She did not bother to ask Anastasia direct questions, mindful that her fragile mental state and the inquiries she had already endured made her resistant to being interrogated. Instead, they would talk about whatever seemed to interest Anastasia. Undoubtedly, they gossiped about royalty, a subject Anastasia always found interesting. During one of these talks, the topic may have turned to the marriage of Prince Philip of Hesse to Mafalda, the daughter of the King of Italy. The event was of such importance to Anastasia that she recalled its details to Milukoff more than thirty years afterward: "[It] . . . was in '25, when I was so ill with this arm. . . . This wedding was a big sensation. Mussolini was at this wedding . . . it was a *big* sensation at that time. She was a daughter of Elena of Montenegro. . . ."

Mafalda was the niece of the Montenegrin princess for whom Anastasia was named, and Prince Philip was distantly related to the Czarina. It may have been during a discussion of the Hesse family that Anastasia revealed her relation to the Grand Duke Ernest Ludwig of Hesse. We do know Anastasia mentioned that she had last seen him "in the war, with us at home."

Harriet was puzzled. Surely a German grand duke could not have traveled to Russia at a time when the two countries had been bitterest enemies, locked in mortal combat. She suggested that Anastasia must be mistaken. But Anastasia's recollection of the circumstances of the meeting was exact, and she insisted that she was not in error. She explained that her Uncle Ernie had undertaken a secret mission to Russia in 1916, in an effort to convince his sister and the Czar to either leave Russia or negotiate a separate peace with Germany. Despite the fact that the trip was of the utmost diplomatic importance and had been cloaked in the greatest secrecy, the Grand Duke had taken the time to see Anastasia and other members of the family while he was there.

This subject made Anastasia nostalgic, as she drifted between her memories and the unreal haze of her drug-induced confusion. So overcome was the young woman by this happy memory that she asked Harriet to contact her uncle and invite him to visit her immediately. Harriet wrote a long letter to the Grand Duke of Hesse, describing the desperate state of his niece and outlining for him as much of Anastasia's story as she knew. She relayed Anastasia's wish to see him as soon as possible and asked him to take an interest in the young woman who lay dying in a bed at St. Mary's. He never answered.

Although disappointed, Harriet was not surprised. She had learned of Princess Irene's disastrous visit and had witnessed first-hand Volkov's equivocation. Other Romanov claimants had come forward, and Harriet could imagine that the family found it difficult to deal with people posing as their murdered relatives. Growing ever more convinced of Anastasia's authenticity, however, she was not ready to give up on the Grand Duke.

Harriet decided to ask her friend Amy Smith, whose grandfather was a well-known German political figure, to travel to Darmstadt and intercede with Anastasia's uncle. With her credentials, Miss Smith not only could gain access to the nobleman but would also bring to the case the air of legitimacy that a letter from a complete stranger would lack. Anastasia found out about this trip and was excited, certain that her troubles would be over once Uncle Ernie had seen her.

When Miss Smith arrived at the Grand Duke's castle, he was away hunting, and she was received instead by Count Kuno Hardenberg, Grand Marshal of the court of Hesse-Darmstadt. At first, the Count listened with interest, but when Harriet's friend revealed that Anastasia had spoken of the Grand Duke's secret mission to Russia, he exhibited "extraordinary agitation." Reporting back to St. Mary's, Miss Smith said he began "pacing around the room, and I had the impression that he felt it was a catastrophe. . . ."

Although the Count's response might seem like an overreaction, it reflected his concern for the Grand Duke's position and ambitions— chiefly political—during this period. At the end of the World War, Kaiser Wilhelm II had gone into voluntary exile in the small Dutch town of Doorn. The German revolution, which had driven him out of his kingdom, had also usurped the power of the rest of the nobility, including the once-mighty Grand Duke of Hesse-Darmstadt. But in 1925, despite the rising tide of democratic fervor, the new Weimar Republic was already viewed as unstable and, like other nobles, the Grand Duke considered the restoration of the German monarchy—and consequently, his own power—a very real possibility. The revelation that he had made a secret journey to Russia during the last war would have been, for him, "a catastrophe," leading to accusations that he had traded with the enemy, and branding him and his peers as unworthy of being trusted with the fate of the German nation again.

FOR the time being, Harriet had other concerns. Almost immediately following Volkov's departure, Anastasia's health suffered a precipitous decline. The pain from the inflammation in her left elbow had become so debilitating that the doctor prescribed an injection of morphine every three hours. The drug made her delirious and brought about hallucinations. As Anastasia's emaciated body grew ever weaker and her mind clouded over, Harriet never left her side, spending the night in a chair by the hospital bed.

Zahle, still under instructions from Prince Valdemar, had remained in close contact with Harriet. He also visited St. Mary's every day and notified the Danish royal family of the patient's worsening condition. Fearing that the alleged Anastasia would die before a final determination could be made, the Grand Duchess Olga wrote to Anastasia's former nursemaid, Alexandra Tegleva, known in the Romanov family as Shura. The nursemaid now lived in Switzerland with her husband, Pierre Gilliard, who had been the Romanov children's French tutor and had become a professor at the University of Lausanne. In 1921, he had published a book on the Romanov family, which helped establish him as an expert among the Russian emigres in Europe. Moreover, he had successfully unmasked a Russian boy posing as the Czarevitch. Olga requested that the couple—who had last seen Anastasia as a plump, active young princess—visit the woman at St. Mary's to determine whether she was genuine: "If it really is she, please send me a wire and I will come to Berlin to meet you."

The Gilliards traveled to Berlin almost at once, and on July 27, they accompanied Ambassador Zahle to the hospital. Anastasia was experiencing severe hallucinations that day, which caused her to see the ambassador's face as a pattern of red, blue, and green stripes. The visitors saw that she was in no condition to receive them and would not be able to recognize them, let alone hold a coherent conversation. The Gilliards told Zahle that they would return when she had improved. Before leaving, however, Shura managed to remove the bed covers from Anastasia's malformed feet. "The feet look like the Grand Duchess's," she said. "With her it was the same as here, the right foot was worse than the left."

Once the small group of visitors left the room, Pierre Gilliard became upset at the condition in which they had found "the Grand Duchess." He berated the doctor and demanded explanations from Zahle as to why she had not been placed in better surroundings. He gave everyone concerned the distinct impression that he would do everything in his power to assist in the recovery of "Her Imperial Highness." Finally, he insisted that she be moved to a more suitable facility, where proper monitoring and care could be administered.

The next day, on Zahle's orders, Anastasia was transported by ambulance to the exclusive Mommsen Nursing Home where Dr. Rudnev elected to perform surgery on her arm, fearing that he might have to amputate it. Although that proved unnecessary, the extent of the infection was so great that the procedure was long and exhausting, and the elbow joint had to be removed. Her recovery was extremely painful, and the morphine injections continued to be given in dosages that hampered her ability to recall her past or reason with her present.

PERHAPS at no time since her escape from her Bolshevik captors had Anastasia faced such a critical juncture in her lifelong effort to survive. As she lay in the hospital room unaware of her surroundings, she became the object of intense efforts to secure her safety and well-being. In pursuing this goal, both Ambassador Zahle and Harriet Rathlef took steps that inadvertently set the stage for decades of controversy and speculation. As the years passed and individual perspectives altered with age, spite, or remorse, much of the truth about the deeds, words, and motivations of those surrounding the Grand Duchess would become blurred, deliberately or not. As a result, we are left to carefully sift through the conflicting stories and the confused chronology in order to piece together the most logical explanation of how and why Anastasia's life after 1925 continued to take such odd twists and turns.

Following her transfer to Mommsen and the surgery on her infected arm, Anastasia was assured of better care, which pleased both Ambassador Zahle and Harriet Rathlef. Nevertheless, they still viewed her situation as precarious. In addition to enduring numerous wounds and requiring a lengthy recovery from surgery, her body had withered from the tuberculosis and her mind seldom seemed capable of coherent thought. The morphine she needed for pain exaggerated her natural unwillingness to talk about the horrors of her past, unlike her reaction to the drug at the Kleist's. Moreover, the drug increased her fear of strangers. The poking, prodding, and ceaseless questions from a phalanx of nurses, psychiatrists, and investigators must have exacerbated the wild images and fantasies brought on by the opiate.

One of the patient's few comforts was a small white Angora cat, which Harriet brought her following the surgery. Anastasia named the pet Kiki and always wanted it by her side. In fact, she seemed to respond immediately to the animal without the reluctance she showed toward her human visitors. Whether Mrs. Rathlef was aware at this point that the young Grand Duchess had been renowned for her passion for all types of pets is unknown.

When Anastasia's medical situation failed to improve within the first few days of her confinement at Mommsen, her two protectors took drastic measures to assure that she had some peace of mind. Zahle had guards placed at her door to give her a sense of security, and Mrs. Rathlef took over the duties of an assistant nurse, cooking the patient's meals and even administering some of the massive doses of sedative.

Apparently, these precautionary measures were not designed solely to ease and comfort a paranoid, irrational patient, but to protect her from life-threatening dangers beyond the very real concerns about her health. The only detailed and objective analysis of this period appeared in March 1926, in Bella Cohen's article for *The New York Times* entitled " 'Anastasia' is Europe's Deepest Mystery." Among the many aspects the story covered was the fear that the patient was being monitored by her old enemies. Cohen noted that those caring for the patient were undertaking extreme measures: "[A]ll gifts of sweets are analyzed; all flowers brought by strangers thrown away—so great is the fear of Soviet conspiracy." As proof that the concerns might be genuine, Cohen noted that "agents of the Soviet Government make long reports to Moscow" about the condition of the alleged Anastasia. The Soviets would probably have paid no attention to this woman, unless they felt that there was a possibility of her being genuine.

The Soviets were not the only ones compiling reports on Anastasia. Harriet Rathlef had already combed the existing literature on the imperial family and was aided in her cause by Dr. Rudnev and Ambassador Zahle. She also began making extensive notes about everything Anastasia said and did. With her practical experience as a writer and her compassionate sensibility as an artist, Harriet was ideally suited for the task. She wrote letters to follow up leads about Anastasia's activities since leaving Russia, and asked questions of visitors, probing their impressions and their memories. Harriet remained cautious about examining Anastasia directly but developed methods of nudging their conversations in directions that provided useful information. Soon, she was devoting her life to proving Anastasia's identity.

For his part, Ambassador Zahle continued his investigations on behalf of the Danish royal family, compiling a dossier—which quickly grew from a single file folder into a small archive. He had already come to intuitively believe that Anastasia was the genuine Grand Duchess. He speculated that perhaps he believed in her authenticity because of the manner in which she conducted herself. Even when gravely ill, she had a certain bearing that he found unmistakably royal. The compelling evidence he gathered only served to confirm his instincts.

As the ambassador and the sculptor became more intimately involved with the patient and grew unalterably convinced of her identity, they began to feel that her chances of recovery would be considerably improved by the acceptance and nurturing of what was left of her family. The Romanovs were related by marriage to most of the royal houses of Europe, so Anastasia had innumerable cousins in nearly every continental nation. But the Czarina Alexandra's efforts to wall her husband and children off from outsiders meant that most of these relations had not seen the Romanov children for over a decade. Even those who had remained in relatively close contact with the imperial family had not visited with the Czar, his wife, or their children for years. In addition to the great geographic distance separating the Russian court from Western Europe, the First World War and the Russian revolution had made family gatherings virtually impossible.

Harriet was determined to avoid repetitions of Anastasia's disastrous meeting with her aunt, Princess Irene, and the abortive contact with her uncle, Grand Duke Ernest Ludwig. Still, Mrs. Rathlef felt a pressing need to reunite Anastasia with close members of her family, people who had known her intimately during her childhood. Harriet and Zahle agreed that the obvious choices were the Czar and Czarina's remaining brothers and sisters, including those in Denmark who themselves had not yet come to see Anastasia in person. They also agreed that, in order not to raise false hopes or to risk further shocks to Anastasia's already tenuous mental balance, they would try to shield her by keeping their plans closely guarded.

VII.

"We shall not abandon you"

NO ONE KNOWS precisely what Shura and Pierre Gilliard reported back to Denmark, but in October, while Anastasia was still at Mommsen recovering from the surgery on her arm, they returned, accompanied by Anastasia's Aunt Olga.

The group spent three days with Anastasia. Almost immediately afterward, these meetings sparked controversy within the Romanov family. Some members stated that Olga instantly realized she was facing an impostor; others believed that Anastasia's emaciated body was so changed that it was impossible for her aunt to recognize her.

As happened so often in Anastasia's history, conflicting stories from third-hand sources were embraced as truth. In the resulting confusion, the actual reports from eyewitnesses were overshadowed to the point that they were almost forgotten.

Both Harriet and Ambassador Zahle, who were in the room most of the time that Anastasia was visiting with her aunt and the Gilliards, made copious notes about what transpired. Harriet wrote, "[Olga] went straight to the invalid's bed, and smiling, offered her hand. We saw how the thin, pale face changed and became suffused with a glowing red. Her eyes, which were generally tired and dull, sparkled. She looked happy."

Grand Duchess Olga spent two hours with Anastasia that first day, and although, in Harriet's words, "the conversation did not turn on events which had convulsed the world," it was obvious to her and to Zahle that Anastasia had immediately recognized her aunt. It was equally apparent that Olga did not think she was in the company of an impostor.

Over the course of the next two days, Olga and the Gilliards returned to Mommsen several times to visit Anastasia. Their conversations were simple but compassionate. According to Harriet, "The whole room was full of . . . a spirit of happy excitement. . . ." Harriet noted that Anastasia seemed more excited about visiting with her beloved former nursemaid than with her aunt. Shura had cared for Anastasia since birth and had been considered almost a member of the family. When she walked into the room, Anastasia "could not take her eyes from her. Then she grasped her bottle of eau de cologne and poured some into Shura's hand. She begged her to moisten her forehead. Shura laughed with tears in her eyes" at the repetition of a little ritual the two of them had enjoyed in Anastasia's childhood. This time, the nursemaid thoroughly inspected the patient, checking for identifying marks she remembered from the Grand Duchess's childhood. Her conclusion: "This is Anastasia's body." Harriet was pleased to notice that, while all this was taking place, Grand Duchess Olga was "beaming with happiness."

The reunion of the lost princess with her aunt, nursemaid, and French tutor seemed to signal the end of her long ordeal. Harriet went out into the hallway and found Dr. Rudnev there. "I have the impression," she said, "that this affair is approaching a happy conclusion." The doctor was so overcome by emotion that "tears ran down his cheeks, and in his excitement he could only repeat: 'Oh dear, oh dear . . . !' "

ANASTASIA'S account of the meetings never varied. She said that Olga recognized her, and that during a private conversation her aunt despaired of the fact that the Russian revolution had deprived them of most of their money and possessions. Anastasia urged Olga not to worry about money, saying that not long before "the end" the Czar had gathered his daughters together and told them that if the family were separated, ample funds for their support were on deposit in an English bank.

Anastasia went on to explain that at the beginning of the First World War, the Czar had withdrawn most of his funds from foreign banks both as a nationalistic gesture and in order to buy armaments and war material. But the money in one particular English account was earmarked for his daughters' dowries and, therefore, had not been touched. Unfortunately, Anastasia could recall few other details, although she did state that the money had been placed in an account under a name other than Romanov. To her best recollection, the name was a short Germanic word that contained the letter "a" and related to trees. At this point Anastasia sensed that her aunt became slightly, but perceptibly, distant.

We will never know exactly what transpired between the two women as they sat talking, but Harriet also thought she noticed a slight change in Olga's attitude when she emerged from Anastasia's room. Olga's earlier open acceptance of Anastasia seemed to have been transformed into general compassion for an invalid woman:

> My intelligence will not allow me to accept her as Anastasia; but my heart tells me that it is she. And since I have grown up in a religion which taught me to follow the dictates of the heart rather than those of the mind, I am unable to leave this unfortunate child.

FROM all outward appearances Olga remained warmly affectionate. Harriet witnessed the aunt's departure: "The Grand Duchess . . . kissed the patient affectionately on both cheeks, and said: 'Don't be downhearted, I will write. . . .' " A few days later, Anastasia did receive a card from her with the message, "You are not alone now and we shall not abandon you." The note confirmed Anastasia's belief that her aunt's visit laid to rest any controversy about her actual identity.

Four more cards from her aunt arrived between October 31 and Christmas Day. They read, in part:

> October 31, 1925
>
> My thoughts are with you—I am remembering the times we were together, when you stuffed me full of chocolates, tea and cocoa. . . . I hope you will soon be quite well. Am waiting for your letter.
>
> Olga

> November 4, 1925
>
> I am sending to my little patient my own silk shawl which is very warm. I hope that you will wrap this shawl around your shoulders and your arms and that it will keep you warm during the cold of winter. I bought this shawl in Japan before the war. . . . Thinking of you all the time. . . .
>
> Love from Olga

December 25, 1925

Am longing to see you. . . . I had already packed one of my "sweaters" for you which I wore myself and like very much, but cannot make use of it now. . . . So I hope you will not mind wearing it—please do. . . . We shall still keep our Russian Christmas. In the meantime everyone is celebrating the Danish Christmas. Best wishes. . . .

Olga

Early the following year, Harriet collated her notes about Anastasia into a series of articles for publication in Germany. She sent an advance copy of the manuscript to Olga for confirmation and criticism. In a letter to Zahle, Olga said that Harriet's manuscript was "correct." Zahle wrote to Harriet that the manuscript "agrees with my memories and my notes."

But the Christmas card was the last message Anastasia received from her aunt. The woman who had promised "we shall not abandon you," abandoned her niece.

What caused this sudden about-face? It is difficult to believe that a Russian imperial grand duchess, sister of the Czar, would travel all the way from Denmark to meet Anastasia, behave in the affectionate manner recorded by Harriet Rathlef and Ambassador Zahle, and send cards and presents to a woman she truly believed was "a stranger" posing as her niece.

Anastasia surmised that when Olga returned to Copenhagen and her unhappy life with the Dowager Czarina, she began to think about the money in the English bank. Perhaps she thought that if she denied Anastasia's identity, she and her equally impoverished sister Xenia could inherit it.

Over the years, Olga told contradictory stories to the various reporters and researchers who interviewed her and in sworn testimony used in German courts. The gist of most versions, however, was that the woman who claimed to be Anastasia was not her niece.

Olga reportedly told her authorized biographer in the late 1950s:

As soon as I sat down by that bed in Mommsen Nursing Home, I knew I was looking at a stranger. The spiritual bond between my dear Anastasia and myself was so strong that neither time nor ghastly experience could have interfered with it. I don't really know what

name to give to that feeling—but I do know that it was wholly absent.
I had left Denmark with something of a hope in my heart. I left Berlin
with all hope extinguished.

Whatever her motivations, Olga's denial of her niece and the
doubts it spawned in others hurt Anastasia in a deeply personal
manner and cast a cloud over all future efforts to prove her case.
Anastasia's aunt could not have failed to realize the damage that her
reversal had caused.

OLGA'S rejection was but the first of many attempts by family
members and their associates to try to discredit Anastasia. Unbe-
knownst to Harriet and Ambassador Zahle, after the visit by Amy
Smith, the Grand Duke Ernest Ludwig had contacted tutor Pierre
Gilliard and apparently hired him as an investigator before his
return to Mommsen with the Grand Duchess Olga.

While Olga was endorsing her niece at the hospital, Pierre Gilliard followed the Grand Duke's instructions and began tracing
every lead about her activities since arriving in Berlin. The Grand
Duke remained deeply concerned about Anastasia's revelation that
he had secretly visited Russia during the First World War. He could
have simply ignored what many considered the ramblings of an
invalid or he could have visited her and asked her not to discuss his
wartime trip. Instead, he determined to work behind the scenes and
take the offensive against her. His main weapon in this battle was
Pierre Gilliard.

Although Gilliard's efforts to uncover damaging evidence from his
researches into Anastasia's activities proved fruitless, he knew he had
to discredit her for the good of his benefactor. Abandoning a factual
inquiry, he began trying to establish himself as the sole, best authority on his former pupil and her supposed reincarnation as an invalid
in a German hospital. He would tell anyone who would listen that
she did "not bear the slightest resemblance to Anastasia—apart from
the color of the eyes—neither in the features nor in the facial expres-
sions." He also reported that she could not answer any of his questions about the private lives of the imperial family, and that what she
had recounted to others obviously had been culled from the nu-

merous books that would have been readily at her disposal. As his final condemnation, the language professor stated categorically that the young woman at Mommsen could speak only German—a tongue foreign to the Grand Duchess—and did not understand or speak any English, French, or Russian. He called her two major supporters, Ambassador Zahle and Harriet Rathlef, fools. In short, Gilliard did everything possible to completely discredit Anastasia and her supporters, spreading his lies in numerous articles and lectures.

Although Gilliard was clearly trying to dampen interest in Anastasia, his constant carping instead revived public interest in the debate. Zahle and Harriet worried that the controversy about her identity would inevitably force the unstable, recovering invalid into a harsher, more public light, undoubtedly with dire consequences for her health.

Ambassador Zahle noticed that the imperial family, including those in Denmark who had charged him with his present duties, were starting to equivocate. Despite Olga's fond parting words and her sympathetic postcards and gifts, she wrote to the ambassador shortly after returning to Denmark and refused to acknowledge that Anastasia was genuine. The Dowager Czarina had finally become aware of Anastasia's existence but, rather than look into the matter more closely, clung to her conviction that her son and his family remained intact. To her mind, anyone in Germany claiming to be a daughter of the Czar had to be an impostor.

Instead of resolving the issue within the family, the matriarch's adamancy further polarized the relatives outside Denmark. One of the Dowager Czarina's nephews, the Grand Duke Andrew, who had trained at the Military Law Academy in St. Petersburg, determined to begin his own investigation into the matter. As one of the last of the Romanovs to see the children, he would be best able to recognize any of them as adults. Fiercely loyal to the family, he was concerned that the increasingly public efforts by Ernest Ludwig and Olga to discredit Anastasia would be interpreted as a callous dismissal of the helpless young woman. He asked Olga for permission to undertake his own inquiry and she agreed, believing that she could influence him and assure that his "objective" analysis endorsed her denial of Anastasia. Ernest Ludwig, however, warned Andrew that any further investigation of the case could prove to be "dangerous."

Overshadowing the family bickering about Anastasia was a raging controversy as to who was the rightful successor to Czar Nicholas II. Grand Duke Cyril, Andrew's brother and Nicholas's first cousin, had broken his oath of allegiance to the Czar by leading a band of revolutionaries through the streets of St. Petersburg. Now safely out of Russia, he had declared himself Czar-in-Exile. He was perhaps trying to finally fulfill the wishes of his parents, who had first proposed him as a candidate to replace the Czarevitch while the boy lay suffering from hemophilia. His actions incensed the Dowager Czarina, who was herself titular head of the House of Romanov, and as such commanded respect from a sizable number of family members. Cyril, already aware that his claim to the throne would be at best tenuous so long as he was opposed by a powerful branch of the family, was adamantly opposed to recognition of Anastasia. As a woman, she would not be able to inherit the throne, but if she were to be accepted by the rest of the family, her authority in matters of imperial succession would be unquestioned. Cyril could not risk the consequences of such a turn in events, and he, too, wrote to Andrew, urging him to drop his investigation.

The growing controversy among the Romanovs, coupled with the increased public attention focused on Anastasia, raised alarms with Mrs. Rathlef and Ambassador Zahle. Up to now, the family in Denmark had continued to supply funds for Anastasia's care. Valdemar's agreement with Zahle was that he would underwrite her medical expenses until a final determination of the case could be made. Zahle and Harriet had kept this fact hidden from the patient and had tried to shield her from knowledge about the bickering among the family members. But as the Romanovs' arguments over her became more public, Anastasia was bound to learn of them on her own, and that knowledge would likely be the final blow to her fragile psyche. They determined that the best course of action would be to remove the patient from the center of the controversy.

IN March 1926, Zahle made arrangements for Anastasia and Harriet to stay at the Hotel Tivoli in Lugano, Switzerland. Her convalescence began successfully. Pictures from this trip show her happy and smiling, often dressed in white. Some of the photos were taken by Anastasia herself, the skilled amateur photographer returning to the hobby she had so loved as a child. Harriet involved her in many activities and concentrated particularly on probing to see whether Anastasia would speak English and Russian with her. Her letters reporting the patient's progress to Ambassador Zahle in Berlin were very optimistic.

Then, quite unexpectedly, Anastasia's depression returned. Harriet had experienced these mood swings before, but this time she could find no way to combat the development. She told Zahle that the young woman said the mountains "hemmed her in." Anastasia began picking fights with her friend, blaming all her problems on Harriet. The Grand Duchess treated the selfless companion as a mere servant and complained to the hotel staff about having to sleep in the same room with a domestic.

Harriet could not understand why Anastasia had suddenly turned on her, of all people, and could find no way to alter Anastasia's attitude. After a few weeks of such treatment, Harriet wrote to Zahle demanding that he send money for her passage home, even if it meant traveling fourth class. In short order, she was preparing to return to Berlin, and Anastasia faced the possibility of losing the kind of support she needed most.

This was not the last time Anastasia would inexplicably dismiss a fervent champion. Throughout her life, Anastasia depended on the support of people who, after sacrificing various amounts of time, effort, and money for her benefit, would suddenly feel the scorn and wrath of the Grand Duchess. Like Harriet Rathlef, some of those Anastasia shut out remained loyal to her. Others exerted the same amount of effort in denouncing their onetime friend as they had previously exerted in defending her. Nonetheless, someone else would invariably arrive on the scene and undertake new efforts to care for her.

WHEN Zahle realized that Harriet was intent on leaving, he sent Baron Vassili Osten-Sacken, the secretary of the Berlin Russian Refugee Office, to assess the situation in Lugano. The Baron, who had met Anastasia in Berlin and was familiar with the particulars of her case, was greatly dismayed by what he found when he arrived at the hotel. It became quickly apparent that Harriet's departure would be in the best interest of both women. Zahle had already investigated the possibilities of housing Anastasia elsewhere, and the Baron now followed up on those plans, arranging for her transfer to the Stillachhaus Sanitorium in the Bavarian Alps.

When Anastasia learned that Zahle intended to send her to a sanitorium, she became furious and refused to leave Switzerland. Remembering her confinement at Dalldorf, she feared being consigned again to "an asylum." The Baron assured her that the Stillachhaus facility was more of a clinic or spa where the wealthy found respite from the world. In the end, he prevailed and accompanied Anastasia by train back to Germany.

Once she arrived in Bavaria, the young woman was overjoyed by her surroundings. The Stillachhaus sat majestically among the snowcapped mountains of southern Bavaria. The air was crisp and pure, which was crucial for her continued recovery from tuberculosis, and the towering peaks lent a certain peace to every vista, which perhaps helped to calm her. She also felt reassured by the director of the sanitorium, Dr. H. Saathof, who welcomed her and took special care to let her know that he would oversee her treatment and that Dr. Theodor Eitel would be her primary physician.

From the beginning of her stay, Anastasia received excellent care and she responded almost immediately. Within a few days, she was obviously delighted with her new environment.

One of the first tasks the doctors at Stillachhaus undertook was to thoroughly review and examine Anastasia's physical and mental state. They observed her in different settings, noting her reactions and mannerisms. Her medical records had been sent from Berlin, and both Dr. Saathof and Dr. Eitel made careful comparisons of the diagnoses formulated there. They concluded that the young patient was not an impostor. "I maintain," said Saathof, "that it is absolutely out of the question that this woman is deliberately playing the part of another. . . . One must, without knowing anything at all about her origins, recognize her as the off-spring of an old, highly cultured and, in my opinion, extremely decadent family. . . ."

The authorities at the sanitorium realized that Anastasia was in such poor health that at least a year of treatment would be necessary. In addition to helping her recover from tuberculosis, they needed time to combat the damage that the prolonged use and massive doses of morphine had inflicted on her body and mind.

In her later conversations with Milukoff, she would recall this as one of the happiest periods of her life. She spoke of her affection for the two doctors: "I wouldn't change Dr. Eitel for nobody. Dr. Saathof was very kind and very friendly. They were both very kind; they were gentlemen."

As her treatment progressed, Anastasia began to take part in organized activities at the sanitorium. For the first time, she abandoned her self-imposed isolation and interacted with the people around her, including the other patients whom she would later remember as "very interesting." To all appearances, she seemed finally to be interacting with others in a normal, everyday manner.

But Anastasia herself never felt entirely confident of her psychological recovery. Having endured years of examinations, lectures, and analyses of her mental instability, she questioned even her most insignificant lapses. Misstatements that might appear normal and unimportant to anyone else greatly distressed her. Once, for example, she mistook somebody for Dr. Saathof and greeted him accordingly. Upon learning that the man was not Dr. Saathof, she went into a confused flurry of activity, trying to sort out what had really happened. "When I at last found Dr. Eitel in one of his rooms there downstairs, I at once told him what had happened to me. When he told me that Dr. Saathof . . . had just left again, then I have told I have seen then maybe his spirit, and surely he will die soon. Surely Dr. Saathof will die soon."

Dr. Eitel must have realized that despite her progress, his patient was likely at any moment to slip back into her groundless presumptions. Neither time nor treatment could erase her mysticism, her need to blame every aberration on forces beyond her control, and her fear that the specter of death would forever haunt her and those around her.

VIII.

"I immediately recognized Grand Duchess Anastasia"

WHILE ANASTASIA WAS being treated at Stillachhaus, several people who had taken an interest in her case from the Berlin days continued to follow her story. One of these was the Czarina's friend Madame Tolstoy, who had visited at Dalldorf at the behest of the Supreme Monarchist Council. Having mistakenly identified Anastasia as her sister Tatiana, Madame Tolstoy was now filled with remorse. She believed that her error had contributed to the confusion, and was particularly concerned that the White Russian community remained grossly unaware of the facts, thanks in part to the lies that Gilliard was busy spreading to discredit the Grand Duchess.

In August 1926, Madame Tolstoy chanced to meet Tatiana Botkin Melnik, the daughter of the court physician who disappeared with the imperial family. It was her older brother Gleb who had waved at the young Grand Duchess from the street in Tobolsk, before the Romanovs were removed to Ekaterinburg. Tatiana was widely regarded as an expert on the imperial family, not only because she had known them intimately, but also because in 1921 she had published one of the first authoritative biographies of the Romanovs. Madame Tolstoy felt that if anyone could positively identify Anastasia and have that recognition acknowledged as authoritative, it would be Tatiana Botkin.

Tatiana agreed to travel to Bavaria to see the recovering patient with a sense of "duty . . . to recognize the Grand Duchess or to expose the fraud." She went in the company of her aunt and Baron Osten-Sacken, who had taken Anastasia from Lugano to the Stillachhaus Sanitorium. They obtained Ambassador Zahle's consent for their trip but kept their plans secret from everyone else—even the authorities at the sanitorium. Above all, Anastasia was not to be told anything.

When the group arrived at Stillachhaus, the Baron went to see Anastasia and told her that she had visitors. Even before leaving Berlin, she had grown tired of being suddenly presented with strangers and asked to speak with them, to identify them, and to remember her most personal history. Demanding an end to such shenanigans, she insisted that the Baron tell her the visitors' names. He firmly refused to comply, and Anastasia finally agreed to grant them an audience on the following day.

The visitors had taken rooms at the sanitorium, and Tatiana Botkin saw the young woman in the dining room that evening. The glimpse was brief, but the impression was striking. "The way she turned her head, the movement of her body when she got up to leave, the gesture she used when she offered her hand [to the manager], her bearing, her walk, were the same as the Grand Duchess's."

They met the next day and took a walk on the sanatorium's grounds. Tatiana was at once convinced of the patient's identity:

> When I first saw her face close up, and especially her eyes, so blue and so full of light, I immediately recognized Grand Duchess Anastasia. . . . I had known Anastasia when she was an adolescent, lively, rough, mischievous, a real tomboy. . . . I found myself now before a wraithlike young woman, sickly, very sad, much more mature and much more feminine. . . .

> And when we were strolling along together . . . which lasted barely ten minutes, I noticed more and more the resemblance to what she had been before all the tragedies and all the experiences. . . .

> The height, the form, the color of the hair are exactly hers. In her face I discovered signs from before . . . the eyes, the eyebrows, and the ears are fully the same. Her unforgettable eyes and the look in them have remained exactly the same as in the days of her youth.

Although Tatiana's recognition was instantaneous, Anastasia remained somewhat uncertain about the identity of her new visitor.

Later that same day, when the visitors went to the patient's room for tea, Anastasia seemed particularly nervous. She turned the conversation toward a harmless discussion of the local area and, at one point, brought out picture postcards depicting a local festival. Seizing the opportunity to discuss the Romanovs, Tatiana brought out a photo album that had been a gift from Anastasia's sister, the Grand Duchess Marie. On the front cover was a picture of the hospital the two sisters had sponsored for soldiers wounded in the First World War. On their visits to the infirmary, the sisters would see Tatiana as she carried on her duties as a nurse. Inside the cover were more photos of the hospital and its patients, as well as other more personal photos of the imperial family, many of which had been taken by the Czar. When Anastasia began to look through the album, she immediately closed the cover and said, "This I must see alone." She ran to an adjoining room, where Tatiana—at the urging of Baron Osten-Sacken—followed. She found the young woman sitting on a chaise lounge with the album open before her and "could see that she was extremely moved; her eyes were brimming with tears." Anastasia asked if there were other pictures, and Tatiana left the room briefly before returning with additional photographs of the imperial family. "Anyone who had seen her bent over these photographs, trembling and crying, 'My mother! My mother!' would not have been able to doubt any longer. . . ."

Understandably, Anastasia was filled with mixed emotions. For the first time since Ekaterinburg, she held in her hands items that had once been touched by her family. Tempering the joy of reestablishing such a direct connection to her happier youth was the sad knowledge that it had all been destroyed forever. She remained visibly upset as the two women began to reminisce. Tatiana was uncertain how her revelations were affecting the troubled woman. Finally, that night the answer became clear: "Through her tears, her eyes were shining with joy. Coming up to me, she laid her head trustingly on my shoulder and stayed like that for a long time. Then she sat down, but still said nothing and gazed off somewhere in the distance, as though she could see something beyond the walls of the room."

Anastasia would always cherish the photo album and the spirit of support it embodied. Unlike the many Romanovs who had refused to accept her, Tatiana Botkin had given her instant, total, and un-wavering acknowledgment. Whatever else she might provide the Grand Duchess in the future, the gift of unquestioned loyalty and friendship offered that day would remain priceless to Anastasia.

THE party stayed at the Stillachhaus for two weeks. The change in Anastasia's attitude was remarkable. "She was radiant. She started beaming whenever she saw . . . [Tatiana] approaching from the distance, wanted to have her continually at her side, never wanted to part with her, and was always tender in a way I had never seen her be before," Baron Osten-Sacken reported back to Ambassador Zahle in Berlin. Tatiana seemed equally joyful over the reunion. They talked and reminisced for hours.

As a former nurse, Tatiana was concerned about Anastasia's condition. Despite the obvious signs of improvement in her demeanor, the continuing psychological effects of her physical trauma were alarming:

> The defect obviously lies in her memory and in eye trouble. She says that after her illness, she had forgotten how to tell the time, so she had to relearn it laboriously. She still has to practice doing it every day. She adds that without constant practice she forgets nearly everything. Each time she has to force herself to get dressed, to wash, to sew, so that she won't forget how.

Knowing that she must return to her home in France and could not remain to care for Anastasia, Tatiana did what she could to protect the Grand Duchess from vilification by the people who did not—or would not—believe her. In a letter to an uncle, Tatiana promised "to write to anyone I have to—to entreat, to swear, and to demand."

She addressed her first letters toward those she felt had wronged Anastasia the most—Olga and the Gilliards. Anastasia, who always kept important mementos with her wherever she was, undoubtedly had shown Tatiana the four short notes her aunt had written following the Mommsen visit. Tatiana knew that since promising not to abandon Anastasia, Olga had recanted ever recognizing her niece and, indeed, seemed bent on a campaign that would leave her utterly forsaken. Thus, when the nearly immediate response arrived from Denmark, its lie was not unexpected: "However hard we tried to recognize this patient as my niece . . . Anastasia, we all came away quite convinced of the reverse."

The Gilliards took a good deal longer to reply. After nearly two months, Pierre Gilliard, who had been in the room when his wife, the cherished nursemaid Shura, had exclaimed, "This is Anastasia's body," responded with another lie: "Neither Grand Duchess Olga, my wife, nor I could find the slightest resemblance between the invalid and Anastasia. . . ."

Gilliard's motivation was financial: Ernest Ludwig, the Grand Duke of Hesse, had paid him to discredit Anastasia. Olga's actions could have been influenced by the possibility of her gaining access to the funds in England, although she asserted that she was acting to protect her mother, the Dowager Czarina, from certain death at the shock of being confronted with the patient in Germany. Tatiana could make little headway with Gilliard or Olga, but once back in France, she went about trying to enlist the aid of the sizeable Russian emigre community there.

Great divisions of opinion were already developing among the noble and imperial Russians who had fled their native land. None really expected the Soviet government to last, but the death of the Czar and Czarevitch made succession an open question, and the identity of the next Czar would affect the emigres' chances of regaining their fortunes. Nicholas's sister, the Grand Duchess Xenia, was attempting to have her son recognized as the logical successor to the throne. Grand Duke Cyril had already proclaimed himself Czar-in-Exile. Marie in Denmark remained the titular head of the Romanovs and refused to even address the issue, because of her belief that the Czar and his family still lived.

Given these and other rifts, it is not surprising that Tatiana found the emigres in France splintered as well. She met with anyone and everyone she felt might be helpful, but she soon learned that she couldn't take anyone's support for granted. "Even if she is Anastasia," one of Tatiana's relatives counseled, "this affair must be defeated in the interest of the Russian monarchy."

*　*　*

As Tatiana continued to work within the relatively private world of the Russian emigre community in France, Ambassador Zahle maintained his efforts among the same close-knit groups in Germany and Denmark. Although the people who had sponsored his investigation and continued to pay for Anastasia's care were pulling away from him, he shielded the patient from knowledge of these developments.

In the autumn of 1926, as Anastasia continued recuperating at the Stillachhaus, a reporter from a German tabloid, the *Berliner Nachtausgabe* (the *Berlin Evening Edition*), arrived and asked to interview her in connection with a book Harriet Rathlef planned to publish. The memory would remain vivid even forty years later, when Anastasia spoke to Milukoff:

> I had not the slightest idea that she was writing it. I didn't know anything, that she was publishing a book . . . then suddenly from the *Nachtausgabe* a reporter coming there to Dr. Eitel with the not-finished book of [Mrs.] Rathlef. And Dr. Eitel threw this man out. . . . He was furious at [Mrs.] Rathlef that she dared to send a reporter from the *Nachtausgabe*. At that time she was still great friends with the *Nachtausgabe*. And the fact is that [Mrs.] Rathlef was it who was first with the *Nachtausgabe*.

Harriet had made no secret of her plans to publish the notes she compiled through all those long months of companionship; she had even sent her manuscript to Olga. Zahle had counseled Harriet not to publish the manuscript because he feared that any publicity criticizing the Romanov family for knowingly abandoning the Grand Duchess would only widen the chasm between Anastasia and the family whose help she would need in order to fully recover.

Anastasia, however, knew nothing of the project until the reporter turned up at the sanitorium. Dr. Eitel threw the man out, but not before Anastasia learned about the book. She was livid at Harriet for being such an "idiot." Anastasia understood that the imperial family had always scorned publicity. A book about her, published in serialized form by a German tabloid, was bound to be sensational. All the tentative—but, to her mind, still hopeful—efforts she had made to rejoin her family would be destroyed, because the Romanovs could not help but reject someone whose story had become so garishly public.

Ambassador Zahle asked those around Anastasia to help minimize, as best they could, the controversy that was sure to come following the book's publication. He was laboring under a handicap, in that the Danish family had been relying on him less and less, ever since Grand Duke Andrew had won the agreement of Olga and the Dowager Czarina to pursue the case. Sensing that the family was about to withdraw its endorsement of his own work, Zahle had begun making overtures to many people in an effort to find a refuge for Anastasia. One of the people he approached was George, the Duke of Leuchtenberg, a distant Romanov cousin, who lived at Castle Seeon only an hour's drive from Munich.

By early February 1927, Zahle's worst expectations came to pass. In a letter to Tatiana Botkin's uncle, just days before the first installment in the *Nachtausgabe*, he wrote:

> I hope you can understand my position. I am now left hanging in the air. The commission which I received from the Danish (Russian) family a good year and a half ago has now been *de facto* withdrawn. . . . On the other hand, Grand Duke Andrew now has received the authority of . . . [the Dowager Czarina] and the Grand Duchess Olga to take matters into his own hands, and all I can do now is assist in the transition. The letters, which I now get almost daily from Dr. Eitel, are considerably alarming. It is impossible for my wife or me to travel to her, because a collapse and complete depression would be a natural outcome, if we had to tell her that the . . . family no longer stands behind me. Should it become evident that neither Grand Duke Andrew nor the Duke of Leuchtenberg really wants to become effectively involved in this matter, I have no idea what will happen. Your niece once offered to let her live with her. I am prepared, if it should come to that, to assume the costs of her trip, if need be with escort, as well as the costs of the incidentals necessary to outfit her.

The Berlin paper took advantage of every opportunity to profit from the controversial story. Posters went up all over the city announcing its publication, and as more installments appeared, the mysterious lost princess became the subject of cabaret songs. The name *Anastasia* appeared on candy and cigarettes. Within weeks, the former Miss Unknown was sensationalized into a commercial product.

Harriet's intentions in pursuing the project had always been honorable. She felt that by publishing the story—including the duplicity of Anastasia's Aunt Olga, Grand Duke Ernest Ludwig, and the Gilliards—the Romanovs would have no choice but to acknowledge the daughter of the last Russian czar. Despite the way Anastasia had treated her at Lugano, Harriet fully expected that the book would be published in a respectable manner and that its success would help provide money for Anastasia. When the publishing house instead serialized the book, the trouble began, and each installment only exacerbated it. The family filed lawsuits. Anastasia received death threats. Officials at the Stillachhaus were pressured to get rid of the patient.

The story fast became international news, and the family's reaction was as expected. Those Romanovs who were already intent on abandoning Anastasia used the excuse of Harriet's book to further isolate her. Grand Duke Ernest Ludwig augmented his reliance on Pierre Gilliard, who had commissioned an anthropological study of evidence relating to Anastasia. Performed by one of Gilliard's colleagues at the University of Lausanne, the study included a comparison of photographs taken by the Berlin police when Anastasia was at Dalldorf with pictures of the Grand Duchess as a young girl. The anthropologist concluded that the facial features, including certain aspects of the women's ears, did not match. Gilliard had the report published in the spring of 1927.

Almost immediately, Harriet Rathlef challenged the credibility of the study, noting that the Lausanne professor had compared only six photographs, and that the methods used to make the anatomical comparisons were unscientific. She also accused Gilliard of knowingly providing the anthropologist not with a picture of the young Anastasia but rather with one of her sister, the Grand Duchess Olga.

The Grand Duke of Hesse decided to have another study done, this time by the police in Darmstadt, the ancestral home of the Hesse family. This study confirmed the anthropologist's report, and the Grand Duke publicly denounced his niece. In a further attempt to prove himself correct, he had samples of her handwriting, still in his possession from the pre-war years, compared with samples by the patient at the Stillachhaus. The handwriting expert concluded that the specimens were written by the same person, a result that apparently displeased the Grand Duke. The expert's report disappeared and was not seen again until thirty years later, after the Grand Duke died.

THE Grand Duke Andrew made no effort to continue caring for Anastasia after Zahle had been dismissed from the case, and the Danish family also ceased supporting her. Zahle's efforts to enlist the aid of Duke George of Leuchtenberg, however, succeeded. Duke George had heard of Anastasia's case through the monarchist community in Berlin, but he had doubted her authenticity—until he spoke with General Max Hoffman. Although the general had never met the Grand Duchess, he had been on the Russian front during the First World War and had later headed the German delegation that negotiated the peace with Russia at Brest-Litovsk. At the time, Germany had showed great interest in the fate of the Romanovs and had made repeated inquiries about the family's welfare. Duke George assumed that, as a former intelligence officer, the general had special knowledge—probably secret information—regarding the fate of the Romanovs. The Duke's doubts evaporated when the general stated without reservation that the woman was Anastasia: "I don't need to see her. I know." He and Zahle quickly arranged for the patient to be transferred from the sanitorium to Castle Seeon.

The process was not easy. First, Zahle wrote to Anastasia and implored her to continue to trust his judgment. "The best thing you could do at the moment is to move to Castle Seeon. . . ." Knowing that she could not travel alone, he wanted to ensure that she was accompanied by someone she could trust. He turned to Tatiana Botkin and used his considerable influence to quickly resolve a visa problem so that Tatiana could travel at once from France to the Stillachhaus for the move.

THE two women arrived at Castle Seeon within two weeks of the publication of Harriet's story. The site must have seemed familiar to Anastasia, for it was reminiscent of the area around the Stillachhaus. The grounds and the furnishings, moreover, were Russian. The castle had been refurbished in the 1840s by the Leuchtenberg family and had been a welcome respite for the Russian nobility and officers of the czarist army traveling in that part of the world since before the First World War.

The Leuchtenbergs were intimately connected with Russia. The first duke had been the stepson of Napoleon and had been given the title after the fall of the French Empire. His second son had eventually inherited the title and wed the daughter of Nicholas I in 1839. Following the marriage, the couple traveled often to Russia and eventually established homes in both countries, a practice continued by their successors. Even though the Romanovs considered the Leuchtenbergs only distant cousins by this time, the Leuchtenbergs' loyalty to the imperial family had never abated.

Ambassador Zahle had hoped that Anastasia would find peace and comfort in surroundings so closely tied to Russia. At first, however, the Grand Duchess kept to herself, seldom leaving her suite of rooms on the second floor and communicating with no one from the Leuchtenberg family other than Duke George. She reportedly "lost ground psychologically." Her fear of strangers increased, she became easily disoriented, and the terrible headaches resumed. Anastasia blamed her new misfortunes on Harriet Rathlef, and her anger against the woman grew so intense that Ambassador Zahle dared not tell the Grand Duchess that Harriet was providing money for her care from the royalty payments for the book.

Still unaware of the actions Aunt Olga and Uncle Ernie had taken against her, Anastasia continued to believe that, if she could be reunited with her family, especially her grandmother in Denmark, her problems would be over. It was a theme repeated as constantly as her anger against Harriet. Tatiana knew differently, however, and decided that Anastasia should realize the gravity of her situation. In a long conversation, Tatiana spoke bluntly, telling her friend that her Aunt Olga had denounced her and that her grandmother would never agree to meet her. Anastasia was at first disbelieving; she knew that she could convince her relatives, given the chance. Tatiana continued to argue, trying to explain logically that there was no proof of Anastasia's identity. Finally, she pointed out, the family would never accept Anastasia for fear that if the throne were restored, the Grand Duchess might be named the new ruler and the son she had abandoned in Bucharest would be eligible to become the czar. At this, Anastasia grew angry: "What madness! I have not seen my child since he was three months old. I would not know how to recognize him. Do you think I would allow any little bastard to proclaim himself the grandson of the Czar and Emperor of Russia? It is *I* that will not receive *her* [Olga]." Shortly after this conversation, Tatiana had to return to France. Her caretaker duties were assumed by one of the nurses who had attended Anastasia at the Stillachhaus.

Over the course of the next few weeks, a change came over Anastasia. Perhaps realizing that she had nowhere else to turn, she became accustomed to her new home. Gradually, she relaxed and interacted a bit more with the family. At Easter, they attended the Russian Orthodox ceremonies at the chapel on the castle grounds. Afterward, while thanking the Duchess of Leuchtenberg for arranging the festivities, Anastasia spoke, almost nonchalantly, in Russian. Although earlier encounters had clearly demonstrated that she understood the language, this was the first time since her arrival in Berlin that she conversed so easily in her native tongue. She began using Russian more and more, but only when she was relaxed or happy and always in an offhand manner, as if she herself were unaware that she had reverted back to the language of her homeland.

IX.
"We will have you out of the way"

NEARLY SIX WEEKS had elapsed since Anastasia's arrival at Castle Seeon, and her enemies had not remained idle. In early April, the *Berliner Nachtausgabe* again went to press with startling news about the Grand Duchess. It reported that, following the publication of Harriet's book, further investigations had been made. The truth of the matter, the *Nachtausgabe* now stated, was that the woman who had been rescued from the Landwehr Canal was actually a missing Polish factory worker named Franziska Schanz-kowska, and that witnesses had been found to corroborate the new evidence. The story created an immediate, worldwide sensation.

What the paper failed to disclose, however, was that the evidence was concocted at the behest of the Grand Duke Ernest Ludwig. Having failed in his effort to disprove Anastasia's story by an analysis of her handwriting, he had come up with a new plan for silencing his niece. In collusion with his old conspirator Gilliard, and with the full knowledge of the self-proclaimed Czar-in-Exile Cyril, the Grand Duke had decided to fabricate a story that would be hard to verify but credible enough to gain public acceptance. He hired a private detective, Martin Knopf, who quickly put together the tale of Franziska Schanzkowska, bribed witnesses to back him up, and then contacted the newspaper. The gist of the legend was that a demented Polish factory worker—one who had, in fact, disappeared in Berlin in 1922—was the same woman who had been rescued from the Landwehr Canal. Some of Knopf's "witnesses," including a prostitute, swore that they had seen Anastasia during the short period in August 1922 when she had run away from the home of Baron Kleist to avoid being humiliated and exploited by them. The Kleists, whom Knopf had also bribed, said that she had simply been missing and portrayed themselves as concerned hosts. They spun other stories to corroborate the article the Grand Duke of Hesse had planted through his agent Knopf. The *Nachtausgabe* knew of Knopf's connections to the Grand Duke but reported that the detective was in employ of the newspaper itself.

Once the story broke, Anastasia's allies became alarmed, but it was Harriet Rathlef who took steps to discover the truth. She began her own investigation of Franziska Schanzkowska, hiring private detectives and enlisting friends in the cause. She eventually managed to locate the Schanzkowska family and persuaded one of Franziska's brothers to go to Bavaria to meet Anastasia. At first glance, the brother said that Anastasia was indeed his missing sister, but when asked to swear to his identification in a legal document, he quickly recanted and testified instead that she could not possibly be Franziska.

Despite Harriet's successful efforts to expose the story of Franziska Schanzkowska as a hoax, the myth had already been widely reported and was not easily overcome. Those who sought to discredit the Grand Duchess would continue to repeat and promote the lie, even after Anastasia's death more than fifty years later. They completely ignored such facts as detective Knopf's offering to sell the story of his own culpability in the hoax for the sum of five thousand dollars.

The Franziska Schanzkowska story forced Anastasia to recognize that her family had indeed abandoned her. Having been savagely separated from her parents and siblings at a young age, she had now been savagely rejected by her remaining relatives. Not only had they failed to welcome her into their lives, but they had done everything in their power to make her unwelcome on any doorstep. She must have been plagued by horrendous loneliness and desolation.

But no doubt because the enormity of her family's duplicity was too painful to accept, Anastasia continued to believe that she could somehow win them over and find the peace she craved. She persisted in her belief that—if only Anastasia could see her—the Dowager Czarina would magically set things right. And for the rest of her life, Anastasia continued to defend the Romanovs by going to extreme lengths to justify their actions to herself and the world.

WHEN the Bolsheviks had hauled Czar Nicholas and his family off to Ekaterinburg, Anastasia's childhood friend Gleb Botkin had remained in Tobolsk and gathered as much news of his father and the imperial family as those troubled times allowed. He eventually heard reports of the assassination and rushed to Ekaterinburg as soon as the White Russian forces had retaken the town. There he met a Persian prince, formerly a colonel of the Czar's personal convoy, who showed him several secret reports indicating that some members of the family had been sent to a monastery in Perm. Gleb discounted these stories but could not bring himself to enter the Ipatiev House to personally inspect the scene of the murders.

Although he found no trace of his father or the Romanovs, he remained in the area and spent the summer at a nearby Russian Orthodox monastery. He considered becoming a priest but decided against devoting his life to Orthodoxy. As the Bolsheviks began to secure their hold on the country, he fled to Japan via Vladivostok.

Once out of Russia, Gleb became active in emigre circles, where he met Nadine Konshin, the daughter of the former President of the Russian Bank of State under the Czar Nicholas. Gleb and Nadine married and lived for a short time in Japan before going to the United States in 1922. Gleb managed to obtain employment as a photo engraver and attended art classes at the Pratt Institute in New York City. Continuing to follow stories about the imperial family, including the many impostors that came forth and were eventually uncovered as frauds, he became convinced that no one had survived the massacre at Ekaterinburg.

Then in 1926, he read Bella Cohen's *New York Times* article describing the visit of Grand Duchess Olga and the Gilliards at Mommsen. He had been aware that a woman in Berlin was claiming to be Anastasia, but he had dismissed her as "a maniac, a fraud or both." Upon learning that the Grand Duchess's aunt and former nursemaid had both recognized her body as Anastasia's, however, Gleb was intrigued.

The North American Newspaper Alliance offered him the opportunity to travel to Europe and try to interview her, but Gleb was reluctant to undertake such a task without further investigation. He was aware that almost immediately after Bella Cohen's piece appeared, the Grand Duchess Olga and the Gilliards had publicly recanted their identification of the patient in Berlin. Although Gleb no longer blindly accepted the opinions and decisions of members of the imperial family, he still paid them the greatest respect. He wrote to Olga in Denmark, asking her true feelings about Anastasia, but received no response. Gleb also contacted Gilliard, who vehemently urged him to drop the matter completely or risk becoming the victim of an elaborate Bolshevik ruse to place a puppet impostor on the throne.

Gleb felt that something significant must lie behind the wide discrepancy between the public and private statements Olga and the Gilliards had made about the patient in Germany. Olga's retraction had come reportedly after her sister, the Grand Duchess Xenia, had sent a cable from England mentioning that the two of them could inherit the dowry money deposited in the English banks if Anastasia's claim were denied. Gleb was also curious about the wild accusations and adamant denunciations coming from all quarters of the Romanov family. Whereas the family members had simply dismissed or ignored other impostors, they had issued endorsements of Anastasia, then went to great lengths to discredit her. He determined that the only way to resolve the matter was to travel to Germany. He accepted the newspaper assignment.

Before leaving New York in April 1927, Gleb had received two letters from his sister Tatiana confirming her belief that the woman at Seeon was Anastasia. He stopped in Paris to discuss her reports that Anastasia's "nearest relatives have conspired against her and that something must be done to save her. . . ." Even though he also got word of the Franziska Schanzkowska story, he had become so skeptical of rumor and third-hand evidence that he felt he must make his own determination. He proceeded on to Bavaria.

THE Duke and Duchess of Leuchtenberg met Gleb in Munich that May and, during the short drive to Castle Seeon, talked of nothing but Anastasia. When they arrived, however, she refused to see her old friend. After several days of repeated attempts to arrange a meeting, he had accumulated many interesting facts about her behavior. For instance, when Duke George described her tantrums and hysterics, he mentioned that when she was angry, her face was covered with red blotches. Such details caused Gleb to pause:

> The more of such stories I heard, the more I recognized in . . . [her] a striking resemblance, not only to Anastasia, but even more to her mother . . . even to the presence of red spots on her face, which were caused by some peculiar nervous affliction from which Empress Alexandra was known to have suffered.

Nonetheless, Gleb remained torn about finally seeing the woman. Having worshipped the Romanovs, he was loath to believe that the remaining relatives in Denmark would callously and pettily refuse to acknowledge the Czar's daughter. He had already accepted the deaths of the imperial family and knew that, if the recovering invalid at Seeon were indeed the lost princess, both their lives would change. He would be honor bound to help her regain her health and her identity, and she would need someone to shield her from the Romanovs' hatred and vilification, which was sure to increase if he challenged their behavior.

The Duke had arranged for Gleb to be present one day when Anastasia would be leaving the castle. Gleb waited in a corridor outside her suite of rooms, full of contradictory feelings: "The more I thought of it, the more I hoped that . . . [she] would prove to be an impostor. As these . . . thoughts were whirling through my brain, the door opened, and on the threshold stood—Anastasia!" She was older and seemed particularly frail and emaciated, but he knew without doubt who she was. As Anastasia passed by, she nodded to him with a casual, familiar greeting, "Oh, how do you do?" The Duke escorted her out of the castle without any further conversation.

Later that day, while discussing the incident with Duke George, Gleb stated immediately that "my impression—knowledge, rather—is that she is Anastasia." Afterward, he went out to the garden to collect his thoughts. As he stood there, he noticed that he was being observed from one of the castle windows. Looking up, he saw his old friend smiling and looking down at him. "Exactly thus had she stood at the window and smiled and waved to me the last time I saw her in Tobolsk. . . ."

Although Anastasia recognized Gleb, she stubbornly refused to see him. She remained upset over the Franziska Schanzkowska affair and did not want to face any further questions or encounters with visitors or investigators, or even with close friends, who might want to write about her. Gleb's appearance, however, had evoked certain happy memories of their carefree days together at Czarskoe Selo, and one day she asked a member of the Leuchtenberg family whether "he has his animals with him." By now they were used to her strange and seemingly random requests and remarks, but this one was particularly odd. Her listener could not imagine why the Grand Duchess would expect an old friend to bring animals all the way from America, but she relayed the question to Gleb.

Gleb immediately knew that she was referring to the pictures he had drawn as a child in Russia, pictures that had inspired the young princess to invent stories for their amusement. Gleb had, indeed, brought some of these drawings with him, and Anastasia agreed to see him, if he would show them to her.

The next day he met the Grand Duchess with one of her attendants. Anastasia leafed through the small portfolio and began to recount the stories she had created years earlier. She insisted on speaking only German with Gleb, a request with which he complied, although he continued to address the attendant in Russian. He later remarked that the Grand Duchess followed all his comments in both languages and even answered a simple question in her native tongue. Much had been made of her refusal to speak Russian, but this incident only confirmed Gleb's feeling that, if she were an impostor, she would have made every effort to convince those around her that she understood the language of her youth. The manner in which she reacted could not have been more natural.

The culmination of the day's events came as a violent storm broke over Seeon in the afternoon. Sitting in the room with the Grand Duchess, while thunder and lightning shook the castle, Gleb was mesmerized by the scene:

> The gold of her hair shimmered softly against the background of the dark, bluish clouds. Her finely carved features acquired an ephemeral quality in the weird glow of the almost uninterrupted lightning. And her blue eyes stared in the distance, with an expression wherein profound sadness blended strangely with a sort of solemn joy. What thoughts, what emotions did that magnificent display of nature's noble anger provoke in her? What did she perceive in those heavy clouds? What messages did she hear in that thunder which scattered through the mountains in a thousand echoes?
>
> One thing I could see clearly—the storm did give her some deep emotional relief. And something truly regal there was in the utter fearlessness, indeed pleasure of that frail young woman—a child almost—in the face of that violent tempest. . . .

Through the many years ahead, Gleb would remain Anastasia's unwavering "best friend" as she faced repeated controversy and duplicity.

Gleb's efforts on her behalf began immediately. Now that he knew that she really was Anastasia, he became even more suspicious of the Romanov family. He believed without doubt that her Aunt Olga and Grand Duke Ernest Ludwig would go to any lengths to deny her identity. Their motivations—grounded in money and reputation—seemed clear to him, and he knew well from his days at the imperial court that such motivations had often led to intrigues with deadly results. Gleb decided that the safest place for Anastasia would be America, where she would at least be physically removed from the grasp of the imperial family. When he approached her with this idea, she agreed readily but said that, with her lack of money and legal status as an immigrant, she doubted the U.S. authorities would allow her into the country. Nevertheless, he promised to make every effort to aid her.

WHILE Anastasia struggled with her emotions following the Franziska Schanzkowska affair and the reunion with Gleb, she once again encountered intrigue and trickery from an unexpected quarter. Prince Felix Youssoupov, who had married the Czar's niece Irina and later led the conspiracy to kill Rasputin, had made several attempts to see Anastasia after her move to Seeon. Because of his role in the murder of Father Gregory, Anastasia hated her cousin by marriage and refused his entreaties. The Prince's persistence was remarkable. He tried to use Duke George of Leuchtenberg as an intermediary and even went so far as to request a meeting on the pretext of having the Grand Duchess fitted for dresses from Paris, where he now lived. When Anastasia still refused him an interview, he simply hopped into a chauffeured car in Paris and appeared at Castle Seeon one day in May. After first refusing to receive the Prince, Anastasia agreed to meet him in the open garden, where they could be seen from the windows in case he exhibited his murderous tendencies. She donned a cape to conceal her healing arm and went outside.

There are various versions of what happened next, but Anastasia maintained that as she entered the garden, Youssoupov approached, recognized her, and acknowledged that she was Anastasia. He then began berating her for abandoning her family. She stopped him short by reminding him that he was addressing "the daughter of [his] Emperor." Concluding the brief interview, she swept past him back into the castle and retired to her room upstairs.

Standing in front of her dressing mirror a few minutes later, Anastasia caught the Prince's reflection as he quietly entered her room. She spun around and demanded to know what he was doing in her private chamber. Stepping toward her with his arms outstretched and hands trembling, Youssoupov said, "I killed Rasputin, and I will kill you for what your mother did to my country. We will have you out of the way."

Overcome with fright, she stood frozen for a minute, then ran past him, circling around the room before reaching a door that led into the hallway. The Prince pursued her down the corridor. She managed to reach the staircase and almost fell trying to run down it.

At the bottom of the stairs she encountered a party in progress, one of the Duchess of Leuchtenberg's many luncheons, and managed to lose herself in the crowd. As Youssoupov followed her down the stairs moments later, he could do no more than look around, grab his coat from a butler, and storm out of the castle to his waiting car.

The incident left Anastasia deeply shaken. What the murder attempt demonstrated more clearly than anything else was that she could never again rely on others for protection. Her only means of defending herself from this harsh reality was to retreat again into herself, where she was safe with her selective memories.

ANASTASIA'S determination to seek seclusion did not stop others from taking an active interest in her life. There were many visitors, some of whom she refused to see, as she lay suffering with blinding headaches in her darkened room. When she did venture into the company of the major and minor nobility who came and went at regular intervals, she often became hysterical over petty affronts. Slowly she became more withdrawn and, upon learning of threats against her life from Bolshevik quarters or agents of her Uncle Ernie, readily acceded to the Duke's request that she not go outside. Arguments erupted continually, and Anastasia's isolation and self-absorption only intensified within this atmosphere.

Among the people most insistent on seeing the troubled young woman at Seeon was Captain Felix Dassel, a former patient at The Hospital of the Grand Duchesses Marie and Anastasia at Czarskoe Selo. He had escaped Soviet Russia and settled in Berlin, where he had since earned his living as a writer. He had heard the stories circulating through the Russian emigre community there for the past four years, heard how the alleged Grand Duchess Anastasia had been seen wandering the streets of Berlin, shying away from people like a frightened animal and sleeping on park benches. Already skeptical that such a person could be the daughter of the Czar, Dassel had dismissed her credibility outright upon learning who was sheltering her: "I knew that circle. I had no confidence whatever in Baron . . . Kleist."

When Dassel heard that the supposed princess was now living with the Leuchtenbergs at Seeon, his interest was piqued again. He had clear memories of the Grand Duchess from his stay at the hospital. As a dedicated monarchist, he continued to revere the imperial family and mourned the tragedy of their murder. If an impostor was violating the memory of the Grand Duchess Anastasia—and doing so under the protection of a family as distinguished as the Leuchtenbergs—Dassel felt a duty to unmask her.

He decided to travel to Seeon in mid-September. Before his departure, he wrote a detailed account of his experiences at the imperial hospital, planning to interview the supposed Grand Duchess and try to catch her in a lie. When he arrived at the castle, he asked the Duke to lock the journal in a safe so there would be no doubt later about his estimation of the young woman.

As with the majority of visitors to Seeon at this time, Dassel was at first refused an interview with Anastasia. She had tired of the constant stream of visitors, each testing her memory. Not only did these people bring up subjects and topics she would rather forget, but they doubted the very memories that had come to serve as her major source of comfort. In this case, however, the Duke of Leuchtenberg himself intervened, saying that she must see an officer who had been treated at her and Marie's hospital in Russia and had remained loyal to the family's memory for the past ten years. Anastasia agreed to a short interview.

When Dassel entered the room, he saluted the Grand Duchess in a formal military greeting. She offered her hand in return but said little and kept her mouth covered with a handkerchief. Dassel left the room with no clear impression that the woman was genuine, although some of her gestures had seemed faintly reminiscent of the young Anastasia.

As Dassel sat that evening in a nearby tavern with a traveling companion, Anastasia's attendant rushed in alarmed. She told him that the Grand Duchess insisted on knowing whether he had brought the medallion that the two princesses had always given to officers released from the hospital to return to the front. At first, he could not imagine what she was referring to, but then remembered the custom. He, however, had not been released for battle duty. Having remained to serve as an aide to the two grand duchesses, he had never been awarded the commemorative. That the young woman in the castle would even know of such medals seemed to prove that she at the very least had an intimate knowledge of the habits of the imperial family. Knowing that he must see her again, he ended the first day feeling "very troubled."

Over the next two days, Dassel and Anastasia would have several encounters, always with Duke George and an attendant present. Dassel had begun to feel that the reclusive woman was the Grand Duchess. Observing her gestures and her deportment more closely, he noticed unmistakable similarities. Having thoroughly recorded details from the days at Czarskoe Selo and safely stored them with the Duke, he proceeded to test her recollection of the slightest details by introducing falsehoods into their casual conversation. At every turn, Anastasia immediately and abruptly corrected him. He said that he had seen the grand duchesses every day at the hospital—as Tatiana Botkin had published in her book on the imperial family. Anastasia corrected him. Not every day, but often. He reminisced about the Christmas presents of sabers and watches the two girls had given the officer patients. The Grand Duchess remembered the watches but knew that they had never given sabers. As Dassel had recorded in his journal, the other presents had been cigarette boxes. The billiard room in the hospital had been upstairs. No, she replied with assurance, it had been downstairs. Dassel remained skeptical, convinced that, if the woman was not Anastasia, she was an unmatchable impostor.

Then, as they sat with the Duke, viewing photographs of the hospital and its patients, a question arose about the name of an officer in one of the pictures. Anastasia immediately referred to him as The Man With The Pockets—a nickname that the Grand Duchess alone had ascribed to the officer, who had breached etiquette by keeping his hands in his pockets when addressing her.

Knowing that only the real Anastasia could have been aware of this fact, the stunned Dassel endorsed her immediately and wholeheartedly.

He remained at Seeon only a short time longer, but he and Anastasia corresponded, and he returned for another meeting in late October. They spent a good deal of time together, reminiscing and walking around the castle grounds. That Duke George permitted him to accompany her was a testament to the former officer's loyalty. She herself felt so secure in his presence that she again partook of small pleasures, including buying a new Kodak camera. She always treasured the photographs she took with this camera and, years later, proudly told Milukoff, "I photographed Castle Seeon . . . myself. I have a photograph [in] which I am sitting in a room which is done with my camera, with my Kodak, quite nicely big, in a fur cloak sitting in Castle Seeon. [But now] it's all so far away."

X .
"I have seen Nicky's daughter"

WHILE ANASTASIA REMAINED in Seeon during the summer and fall of 1927, Gleb was busy in New York trying to fulfill his promise to bring her to the United States. Upon his return from Germany, he had written several articles and made entreaties among the large Russian emigre community. One of those who took an interest in Anastasia's story was Mrs. William Leeds, the former Princess Xenia of Russia and the Grand Duchess's second cousin, whose husband was heir to an enormous tin fortune. They moved in the highest social circles in New York and lived on Long Island's famed Gold Coast, where lifestyles matched those found in F. Scott Fitzgerald novels.

Xenia Leeds had played with Anastasia as a child, before fleeing

Russia with her mother and sister Nina prior to the First World War. Xenia knew that Gleb was attempting to have the newspaper syndicate that had sponsored his trip to Germany also finance her cousin's trip to America. Worried that such a highly publicized visit could prove embarrassing to the Romanov family, Xenia told Gleb that she would take in the woman from Germany. If she proved to be an impostor, as many in the imperial family claimed, Xenia could easily expose her. If she were genuine, however, Xenia found it "ghastly to think that nothing was being done for her." Determined to make amends, Xenia decided to send the family governess, Agnes Gallagher, to fetch Anastasia from Seeon.

Although the Grand Duchess had welcomed Gleb's original offer to bring her to America, she grew anxious about the trip. She complained that her family was driving her from Europe and repeated her intention of trying to see her aging grandmother, the Dowager Czarina Marie. After all the months of recriminations and ill-treatment at the hands of the Romanovs and their agents, she still clung to the hope that Marie's endorsement would bring the acceptance of the Romanov family. Anastasia complained loudly and openly to her hosts that she might lose her only chance for reconciliation if she left Germany.

Miss Gallagher arrived at the castle and found the Leuchtenbergs quite ready to see their guest leave. They had suffered through nearly a year of Anastasia's mood swings—the histrionics, the paranoia, and the haughty self-absorption—and had endured her open disdain for them and their company. They were weary of the death threats, the endless streams of curiosity seekers, and the countless demands for interviews from the press. "There is a universal feeling of compassion here for poor little Princess Xenia, who has no idea what she has landed herself in for." Despite some last-minute problems, the American consul—after being pressured by the Secretary of Labor, who was a close friend of Mr. Leeds, and after being assured that the Leedses would underwrite the costs of her stay— granted Anastasia a six-month visa for the United States.

Miss Gallagher and Anastasia left the castle in the company of Duke George on January 29, 1928. They were to be in Cherbourg, France, for embarkation on the luxury liner *Berengaria* on February 1, but had decided to take the train and stay for a few days in

Paris, where the Duke kept an apartment. Their arrival was kept secret, both to avoid more press exposure and because Duke George had arranged a special meeting between Anastasia and Grand Duke Andrew, who had replaced Zahle as the family's representative in determining her authenticity.

The Grand Duchess was not eager to meet Andrew. He was not only the brother of the self-appointed Czar-in-Exile Cyril, but also the embodiment of all the suffering that her family had caused her. "Ten years they have let me suffer like this," she said. The Duke of Leuchtenberg remained adamant, however, and the meeting took place. According to Agnes Gallagher, who witnessed the encounter, "Anastasia looked at him and sobbed but refused to talk to him. The Grand Duke himself was very much upset and looked as if he might be seeing a ghost." The interview lasted only minutes before he rushed from the room and slumped into a chair, saying "I have seen Nicky's daughter, I have seen Nicky's daughter."

Unlike Olga and the Gilliards, Grand Duke Andrew's belief in Anastasia would remain unshaken. Quickly he wrote to Gleb and Tatiana Botkin's uncle:

> For two days I had occasion to observe the invalid, and I can tell you that no doubt remains in my mind: She is Grand Duchess Anastasia. It is impossible not to recognize her. Naturally, years and suffering have marked her, but not as much as I would have imagined. Her face is striking in its profound sadness, but when she smiles, it is she, it is Anastasia, without a doubt.

But not even Andrew's endorsement could alter the need for Anastasia to leave Europe. The plans were firmly set, and the party left by train for Cherbourg.

Before Miss Gallagher and the Grand Duchess boarded the ship to America, Duke George assured his former guest that she would always be welcome at Castle Seeon, should things not work out in America. Anastasia did not reply and seemed bitter about being torn away from whatever tenuous security she had found in Bavaria. Once again she was compelled to travel in the company of a stranger to an unknown land. "I am afraid; I am afraid," she muttered as she took leave of Europe.

BOOK THREE

"That I Have Passed Through"

Penetrating so many secrets, we cease to believe in the unknowable. But there it sits nevertheless, calmly licking its chops.

—H. L. MENCKEN

I .
"What thoughts are going to haunt her"

THE *Berengaria*, named for the wife of Richard the Lion-Hearted, was one of the most luxurious ships of the Cunard line during the heyday of trans-Atlantic ocean travel. Decorated with "a few acres of gold leaf," its opulence inspired a well-known expression of the time, "Berengaria Baroque." A social history of the era described it as "a gleaming and bejewelled ferry boat for the rich and titled. . . . Everybody . . . even the dogs, were 'socially prominent.' "

Anastasia had been registered as Miss Gallagher's niece because of concerns about security. The false identity now provided an additional benefit in that none of the other passengers—the wealthy social elite of both continents—had the slightest idea who she was. Anastasia and Miss Gallagher rarely left their cabin, and the young woman seemed quite happy to take advantage of this first opportunity in years to avoid gossip and questions. One of the consequences of spending so much time alone with her companion from America was that Anastasia began speaking English again. It had been the language of her childhood, but from the time she first surfaced in Berlin, Anastasia had insisted on conversing only in her own broken and poorly pronounced version of German. Beginning with this voyage, English again became her language of preference.

A liner like the *Berengaria* provided many diversions for its passengers during the seven-day crossing, but only one enticed Anastasia from her cabin. The motion pictures that were screened onboard fascinated her. Her knowledge of photography gave her an immediate understanding of the power and beauty of moving pictures. And the larger-than-life dramas that they portrayed must have struck a special chord within the young woman who had created her own fantasy tales to accompany Gleb's paintings at Czarskoe Selo.

For the rest of her life she would have a special appreciation of film from a technical standpoint as well as a childlike wonder at the stories portrayed.

The *Berengaria* ploughed through rough, stormy seas for most of the voyage. The ship had been constructed with extravagance, not nautical engineering, in mind and was known to pitch and roll violently in rough weather.

Gleb had promised Anastasia that when she came to America, she would finally be able to escape the turmoil and controversy that had surrounded her in Germany. She looked forward to the chance to rest, to be out of the public eye which had focused so unwaveringly on her since the *Nachtausgabe* stories first appeared. Although her father had a special affection for President Theodore Roosevelt, who had won the Nobel Peace Prize for his arbitration of the Russo-Japanese War, Anastasia knew very little about the United States. She had followed the life of the late President's daughter Alice, and must have been overjoyed that Kenwood, the Leedses' estate where Gleb had arranged for her to stay, was so close to the Roosevelt compound at Oyster Bay. She was curious about two facets of America: one was the form of constitutional government, which must have seemed alien to the daughter of a czar; the other was Prohibition, a law that she had heard few people obeyed.

Her voyage in many ways simply continued the flight from Russia she had begun nearly ten years ago. She had suffered excruciating physical and psychological hardships from which she would never fully recover. Her faith in her fellow man, if not shattered by her treatment at the hands of the Bolsheviks, would probably never be fully restored. The conduct of her Romanov relatives, particularly because she felt they had purposely kept her from her grandmother, the Dowager Czarina, had only exacerbated Anastasia's distress in this regard.

GLEB Botkin awaited the arrival of the Grand Duchess in New York. His life had changed dramatically during the six months since he had been at Seeon. Having been reared as a devoted follower of the Romanovs, his loyalties still lay with Nicholas and his family. As for the other Romanovs, in particular those who had escaped to

Denmark, they warranted only his rage. He was shocked to discover that they would willingly abandon the Czar's daughter for such petty reasons. He was determined to make her life better in the United States.

Gleb's work as a newspaper reporter had exposed him to every aspect of American life in the 1920s. He was aware that Anastasia's story was familiar to most Americans because of the Bella Cohen article and the others that followed. He also knew, from the developments in Europe, that public curiosity could quickly lead to scandal. Gleb intended to avoid that on his side of the Atlantic. He had already taken the offensive by publishing articles presenting the evidence he had gathered to support her. His plan was to allow Anastasia to regain her health while he continued to build the case by collecting and making public the incontrovertible proof of her authenticity. It was the intractable promise he had made to his old friend.

Gleb's careful strategy was thwarted even before the *Berengaria* entered New York harbor. On February 6, 1928, the day before the ship was scheduled to berth, the New York papers were full of the news of Anastasia's pending arrival. Neither Gleb nor Anastasia ever knew who leaked the story to the press, but once it became public, there was no stopping the reporters' pursuit of her. On February 7, the fog was so thick that the ship had to lay anchor in the harbor. Port authorities refused to allow even a cutter to travel out to the ship, so Gleb had to wait on shore all that day. Sometime the next day the authorities finally allowed a cutter to go out to the ship, which was still waiting for the heavy fog to lift.

Much to Gleb's surprise, when he boarded the cutter for the trip to the *Berengaria*, he encountered more than thirty reporters, all intent on interviewing the mysterious Grand Duchess. They rushed onto the luxury liner and Gleb could not stop them before they reached Anastasia. Her reaction was immediate: "[I]t was a frightful mess. They were [sur]rounding the cabin. . . . Nobody could leave anymore the cabin. When somebody open[ed] the door, or got in, they were with the flashlights. It was hell on earth!"

The party remained captive on the ship because the fog continued to prevent berthing. All through the night the reporters badgered anyone who attempted to enter or leave the cabin. Their efforts did not abate even the next morning when the passengers were finally allowed to disembark. They were greeted on deck by photographers whose flashbulbs exploded in a manner that Gleb feared would evoke terrible memories in Anastasia. The press was aggressive, shouting questions, challenging the Grand Duchess. She became overwrought and shrank away, trembling. She remembered later being

> fetched by my friends. They were at each side, in front and behind, that I was [sur]rounded . . . and then we got . . . in the elevator. It was impossible! The reporters wanted to get in as well. And then was suddenly a British officer I fell right away in love with. And he took the reporters . . . and he drove them away, one after another. And he looked at me and smiled at me.

Anastasia and her companions finally escaped their pursuers by getting into a waiting car, which drove off hurriedly.

Xenia Leeds—Anastasia's cousin, hostess, and sponsor in the United States—was not at the ship to greet her. In fact, Princess Xenia was not even in New York, having inexplicably sailed with her husband to the West Indies before her guest had left Castle Seeon. The Princess did not return for nearly three weeks after her cousin's arrival. In the meantime, therefore, Gleb could not take Anastasia to the Kenwood estate on Long Island, so they drove to the Park Avenue home of a Leeds family friend and elderly socialite, Annie Burr Jennings.

Miss Jennings had never married. She was a descendant of Aaron Burr, Thomas Jefferson's vice-president, and her father had been one of the original investors in Standard Oil. With this background, she had made a name for herself in conservative circles, including the Union League Club and the Daughters of the American Revolution. She used part of her wealth to benefit the Republican party, and her opinions—if not always viewed as orthodox—were heeded. Miss Jennings was certain of her place in the world, styling herself as the nearest thing to American royalty, to the point of imitating the fashions of Queen Mary of England.

Annie Jennings greeted the still frightened and distraught Anastasia and managed to make her feel comfortable in the new surroundings. With the reporters left behind, the Grand Duchess began to feel secure in the company of Gleb. That night she had recovered enough to ask him to take her to the movies, where they relaxed and enjoyed themselves.

As Anastasia's life in America commenced, the scandal that had engulfed the Romanov family in Europe worsened. It began anew with a letter written by her visitor in Paris, the Grand Duke Andrew, to her Aunt Olga on February 4. The letter served two important purposes—to confirm his recognition of the Grand Duchess and to chastise her enemies within the imperial family:

> I went . . . to see her at last and to form a personal opinion about this woman, to find out who she really is, about whom such bitter controversy has arisen, such legends have been born and whose name inspires endless discussions of rights and family misunderstandings. . . . I recognized her at once, and further observation only confirmed my first impression. There is for me no doubt: she is Anastasia.
>
> Now she is already far away, in America. We shall not soon see her again, if we ever do see her again. What thoughts are going to haunt her in that distant country? God alone knows, but they will certainly be terrible, and a sorrowful question will obsess her, a question no one can answer for her. Will Anastasia survive these new ordeals? Who knows? But I am going to pray to God that she does survive, that she recovers her health and comes back to us from that distant land, not, this time, as a hunted and persecuted creature, but with her head high and with the strength of spirit to pardon those who have brought her so much misfortune.

The Grand Duke's letter was never even acknowledged, much less answered, but it showed for the first time a clear split among the most senior members of the imperial family. It was one that would continue unabated—at times in private and at times in the full glare of the public—from this point on.

At about the same time that the Grand Duke Andrew made his feelings known to Olga, her brother-in-law Grand Duke Alexander weighed in with his opinion. He had published a number of books on the occult and now used these methods to try to discredit Anastasia. His argument was that the woman who claimed to be the Grand Duchess was simply possessed by "her spirit [which] has returned to this world and incorporated itself in another body. She knows so much about the intimate life of the Czar and his family that there is simply no other explanation for it, and of course, it wouldn't be the first time that a spirit has returned to earth in a new physical form." Certainly, other than a small circle within the imperial family, few people would ever accept this explanation as anything but the ramblings of a self-styled mystic. Alexander was the husband of Grand Duchess Xenia, who had wired her sister Olga to urge that she deny any recognition of Anastasia after Xenia learned of the young woman's statement that czarist funds were deposited in a London bank. Until then, no one in the family was aware that any of the Czar's money was safely hidden outside Russia. Olga and Xenia both lacked their own means of support: Olga lived under her mother's roof in Denmark; Xenia in a grace-and-favor mansion provided by King George V and Queen Mary. Understandably, neither woman relished drawing public attention to this money before the controversy over Anastasia's identity was settled, and each had continued to deny that any funds of this nature could exist.

Now, however, they became desperate. Gleb had succeeded in removing Anastasia from their immediate control and appeared to have won the aid of a prominent Romanov in America. If Andrew's recent endorsement became public, Gleb's efforts would be unstoppable. They had to disparage his reputation somehow.

The tactic they chose, however, only raised the stakes. Shortly after Anastasia's arrival in America, Grand Duke Alexander wired *The New York Times* with the family's new theory. They accused Gleb of organizing a conspiracy to win control of the fortune that the Grand Duchess Xenia was trying to inherit in England. This was the first public acknowledgment by any Romanov that there was money in a London bank and that the family intended to lay claim to it. What had heretofore been dismissed as the fantasy of a befuddled impostor suddenly became of the utmost importance to the Romanovs as they sought to undermine Anastasia's search for simple recognition of her heritage.

II.

"Somehow not a home"

ANASTASIA REMAINED unscathed by these developments during her first few weeks in America, most likely because her new friends kept unpleasant information to themselves so as not to upset her. She had begun to feel quite at home with Miss Jennings and seemed to enjoy the busy social pace. The press had not tired of her story, but neither did they pursue her with the fervor shown at the ship. Anastasia was able to accompany Miss Jennings to numerous parties and balls, and from all reports, seemed happy in her new life although she remained anxious to see her cousin, Xenia Leeds.

Unknown to Anastasia, Mrs. Leeds and her husband had returned from their voyage to the West Indies and decided to attend a party at Miss Jennings's home in order to see the Grand Duchess for themselves. Fourteen years had elapsed since they had last been together in Russia and Xenia Leeds knew that any physical similarity between the young playmate she remembered and the woman who was now in her twenties would be hard to ascertain. From across the room, she noted that the young woman's comportment certainly appeared to be that of a royal personage, although whether she was Anastasia remained to be seen.

Mrs. Leeds felt that there was a good possibility that the young woman was the Grand Duchess. Having always intended to make her own determination away from the influence of others, she took her guest out to the fifty-four-acre estate on Oyster Bay. She quickly became convinced of Anastasia's authenticity and treated her in every manner as the imperial princess she was. Mrs. Leeds gave Anastasia her own suite of rooms and presented her with a special gift from the West Indies—a pair of parrots. The Grand Duchess, always fond of pets, took to them immediately and often spoke to them in Russian.

At first, Anastasia was comfortable at Kenwood and enjoyed strolling the spacious compound or spending time in her room with her birds. She had little contact with people outside the Leeds family. Gleb remained in New York City, and Mrs. Leeds was happy that he stayed away because she blamed him for the publicity that had greeted the Grand Duchess upon her arrival in America. Xenia and Anastasia would talk for hours, reminiscing about their days at the Russian court. The more they talked, the more Xenia—like so many others—found herself being reminded of stories and events that she had long forgotten. She intentionally did not press her guest for details, but simply allowed her memories to arise naturally. Xenia wanted to avoid upsetting the young woman, quite aware of the troubled and sometimes hysterical outbursts for which Anastasia had become known during her treatment in Germany. She understood that although the recovery was progressing, Anastasia was not "normal." The two women also discussed plans for the future, and Mrs. Leeds promised to do everything possible to reunite Anastasia with her grandmother in Denmark. For a while at least, Anastasia felt the joy of being under the protection of a fellow Romanov who did not question her identity.

Still, the lifestyle followed by Mr. and Mrs. Leeds of Oyster Bay was not something of which Anastasia always approved. She had been raised by her mother in an isolated, strict Victorian atmosphere. She had the Czarina's penchant for gossip, which combined wild fascination about the loose morals practiced by the rich and noble with an utter disdain for any human being—particularly those of the highest social rank—who behaved so shamefully. The Leeds family certainly provided a wealth of material for the Grand Duchess's sharp tongue.

Within a few weeks of her stay at Kenwood, Anastasia began to realize that Mr. and Mrs. Leeds did not enjoy the happiest of marriages. Thirty years later, she recalled to Milukoff the comings and goings at Kenwood:

> The estate was [at] Oyster Bay, at the ocean, where I was living. Xenia Leeds, nicely tall, well groomed, and . . . William Leeds, a tiny creature—like a little dwarf with brown eyes. And William Leeds

[went] with this dancing girl [Adele Astaire] on a boat, they went on a boat and then the boat exploded. And the dancing girl was heavy injured . . . and he almost lost his eyesight. He had not only one dancing girl but all the secretaries. . . . He was traveling with these secretaries and who knows what.

Despite her awareness of these events, Anastasia remained somewhat aloof, finding enjoyment in her own world and the small pleasures she could find. She had brought her Kodak camera from Seeon and "took thousands of photographs. Nobody was safe from me and my Kodak."

Guests were constantly arriving for varying lengths of time to partake of the hospitality at Kenwood. Often they were Russian emigres, including Anastasia's cousins, the sons of Grand Duchess Xenia and Grand Duke Alexander who continued their campaign against her in England. Despite other reports of her reaction to their presence, Anastasia never indicated in later conversations that she was at all upset that the two young men were at Kenwood. She never equated their activities with those of their parents, even after she had learned that the Grand Duke and Duchess were plotting to destroy her. She reported to Milukoff simply that the young men "were always about Xenia Leeds's. And I had photographed them from my window when they played tennis. They were living at the boats house [on the estate]."

She was equally unaware that the Grand Duchesses Xenia and Olga had been in contact with her hostess. Gleb first learned of their plans during a private conversation with Mr. and Mrs. Leeds in the boathouse on the estate. The only written record of this meeting came in his later book, *The Woman Who Rose Again*. Mrs. Leeds indicated that she had been corresponding with the Grand Duchess Xenia and that she and her husband wanted to convey an offer from Anastasia's two aunts. At her husband's prompting, she told Gleb that if he did not stand in the way of the family's attempts to inherit the Czar's fortune, and if he dropped his insistence that they formally acknowledge Anastasia, the Grand Duchesses Xenia and Olga would be willing to give their niece "something out of that money" and take care of her quietly in Europe. "You personally will also be taken care of," Mrs. Leeds reportedly told him.

A long argument ensued, and Xenia Leeds admitted that Anastasia's Aunt Xenia knew that the woman staying at Kenwood was indeed the surviving daughter of the last reigning czar. Gleb asked why either he or Anastasia should accept such a ridiculous arrangement—and how her family could be so callous. Mrs. Leeds replied that they had every faith in the eventual restoration of the Romanovs to the Russian throne, but not in the fitness of Anastasia to rule. Gleb rejected the offer out of hand, a decision he later confirmed with Anastasia. Despite the fact that Gleb published this story ten years later, neither of the Leedses ever challenged his account of the duplicity of Anastasia's aunts or their own role in relaying the offer.

As Anastasia's health improved and she became comfortable with members of the Leeds family, her fear of strangers began to subside. Many important and wealthy friends of the family would visit the estate, but rather than treating the Grand Duchess as an oddity, they readily accepted her as Mrs. Leeds's cousin. One of those she would always remember fondly was Hugh D. Auchincloss, who one day brought his new baby boy "Yusha" to visit his friends. Anastasia enjoyed the chance to hold the child but later told Xenia that the experience also evoked a certain sadness about her own son, whom she had given up in Bucharest years before.

Anastasia's physical and mental condition improved remarkably in the peaceful environment at the Long Island estate, but she still exhibited moments of inexplicable terror. These occurred most often when she was confronted unexpectedly by strangers. One day, as she sat by herself under a tree near the edge of the estate grounds, a couple looking for property to purchase happened to walk past Anastasia and overheard her humming a tune that seemed strangely familiar. When the woman, Hallie Erminie Rives, stopped to ask the name of the song, Anastasia averted her gaze, got up quickly, and ran away. Rives was surprised by the reaction to her simple question and remained curious about the encounter. In a later conversation with a local real estate agent, she learned that the woman was "a Russian duchess or something." Only then was she able to make the connection. The "duchess or something" was the very girl she had sat next to at a concert in St. Petersburg seventeen years earlier when she and her husband had been part of the American legation. The song was the one about a little girl who had lost her doll, and Anastasia had sung it while eating chocolates in the imperial box.

GLEB had remained largely absent from Kenwood during the first weeks of Anastasia's stay but kept busy on her behalf. The press maintained an interest in the story of the lost princess who had suddenly arrived in America and was in seclusion at a Long Island estate owned by one of America's wealthiest industrialists. Gleb was contacted again and again with offers for interviews, books, and movies. Often these proposals involved enormous sums of money, but he refused to profit at the expense of his old friend.

His more immediate concern was to battle the imperial family in Europe. As they continued their maneuvers to discredit Anastasia and to gain access to the money in the London bank, he became convinced that Anastasia must take the offensive or risk losing everything. He knew that the matter of inheritance would have to be settled soon. More than ten years had elapsed since the deaths of Nicholas and Alexandra, and if Anastasia did not claim this vast fortune, her aunts, the Grand Duchesses Xenia and Olga, would succeed in their attempt to acquire it all. Moreover, if she failed to establish her rights as the legitimate heir at this juncture, she would forever remain a legal nonentity. He could not allow Anastasia to remain a Miss Unknown without citizenship or what was rightfully hers.

Gleb began to visit Long Island to speak with Anastasia about these matters but soon ran into problems with Xenia Leeds. She informed him that she was unalterably opposed to anything that might cause further divisions within the Romanov family. She dismissed his new idea of trying to bring suit against the relatives. Even Anastasia wondered if this plan might not be "obscene."

Nevertheless, in order to better understand the legal situation, they agreed to talk with an attorney. Gleb sought the advice of Edward Huntington Fallows, a New York lawyer who was reportedly a cousin of Montague Norman, head of the Bank of England, where the czarist millions presumably had been deposited. The attorney agreed to conduct an initial investigation of the case and to talk to the Grand Duchess.

Xenia Leeds became furious when she discovered that Gleb had done more than simply discuss the case with the lawyer. Several screaming matches erupted between Xenia and Gleb, and Anastasia worried that if the situation worsened, her hostess might never fulfill her promise to take her to see her grandmother in Denmark. Unknown to her, Mrs. Leeds had already been forbidden by the two Romanov aunts in Europe to make such a trip.

Xenia was facing other problems as well. Anastasia recalled them years later in a conversation with Alexis Milukoff:

> Xenia Leeds wanted to take her life. Two years before I arrived in America, she had tried to kill herself. She had gone with a boat to a rock in the ocean and wanted to jump in the ocean because her husband was always traveling on steamers with . . . girls. . . . And then one night, he arrived at Oyster Bay with thirty boys, with thirty boys, with thirty boys. Thirty. Thirty boys! Xenia Leeds told at once 'That is the end!'

> And shortly later she crashed with her horse down. The horse fell on her, she was under the horse, and her backbone was heavy injured. She had a big operation and there he told her through the telephone when she did wake up that he would divorce her. . . . Alas, so all was at an end. [Kenwood] was somehow not a home. It was somehow not a home.

Now that her temporary refuge was crumbling around her, Anastasia became distraught and argued with Xenia Leeds. Her still fragile mind could not cope with such strains and she had no choice but to leave. Gleb hastily arranged for other quarters. She took a few belongings with her, including important mementos, her photograph albums, the letters from her Aunt Olga, her Kodak, and her pet parrots. Once she was ready, they drove to the exclusive Garden City Hotel on Long Island, where she was to stay temporarily and where friends of Gleb would pay her bills.

III.

"That malicious nonsense"

EVEN BEFORE Anastasia was safely settled in the hotel, Gleb resumed the role of protector. He was well aware of the continued interest in her story, particularly among the press, whose determination to pursue Anastasia had become only more dogged during her months incommunicado at Kenwood. Despite some physical improvement, she was still emotionally fragile, and the recent conflicts within the Leeds family made her fearful of strangers again. Gleb had therefore determined that she should register under a false name at the hotel.

She registered as Mrs. Eugene Anderson—Eugene being chosen in honor of Gleb's father. Anderson had no real significance, despite later stories that Anastasia chose it in memory of the shipbuilder who designed the Czar's yacht *Standart*. More likely it was a common name that could be easily remembered. Whatever the reason, the pseudonym gave her protection from the press, who would surely have found her quickly in such luxurious surroundings under the easily recognized names of Tschaikovsky and Romanov.

Gleb visited her every day and made certain she felt comfortable there. His family would later remember that he devoted all his time to Anastasia during this period. He would stay with her at the hotel and talk for hours about all sorts of matters, both mundane and practical. Of greatest concern to him remained the activities of the imperial family in Europe and how they would affect her future, and he gradually began to explain to her the necessity of taking some action on her own behalf. He expanded on his recommendation of legal maneuvers and bluntly told her that the family, including her grandmother, had no interest in her as a Romanov. Gleb also made her understand that certain members of the family would stop at nothing to discredit her, and might even do her physical harm, so great a threat did they perceive her to be.

Anastasia realized that she had been relying on the help and protection of others ever since her escape from the Bolsheviks. Moreover, she was tiring of the constant fear and uncertainty at every turn. In her confused state, she must have felt sometimes that there was no hope of finding a permanent refuge.

Although she became terribly depressed over her plight, at least she had her old friend with her. She would always think of Gleb—at least in part—as a playmate, and his visits allowed her to again recapture her youth. Like the young imperial princess she was, Anastasia disdained public opinion, and she argued with Gleb about his plan and whether it would have any real meaning to her. She was concerned only with what her family thought, and despite being told that her aunts and uncle had conspired against her, she clung relentlessly to the notion that if she could only see the Dowager Czarina, everything would be resolved. Slowly, however, she gave her trust to Gleb and welcomed him as a defender of her rights, perhaps the one person who had only her best interests in mind.

Much has been made of Gleb's motivations for helping Anastasia and the tactics he employed on her behalf. The Romanovs and their allies accused him of being interested only in the money in the London bank. They also implied that he sought to profit personally from her story, whether through selling interviews to the press— which he never did—or seeing an endless supply of royalties from books and movies. Given the personalities and potential fortunes involved, such innuendo could easily be taken as truth in many circles, but those who accepted it ignored Gleb's devotion to the memory of the Czar and the Czarina and to the happiness of their daughter, the Grand Duchess.

In truth, Gleb was spending nearly all his waking hours with Anastasia, patiently tolerating her mood changes, trying to help her avoid the recurring depressions, working tirelessly to garner the legal and public support that he knew were essential to her cause. Gleb had no time to pursue his own career, and his family seldom saw him. They accepted his absences, however, for they understood that in helping Anastasia, he was righting a terrible wrong. One of Gleb's daughters, Marina Botkin Schweitzer, described the first time that she realized the extent of her father's commitment and what precisely it meant:

> I must have been four or five years old when one evening past my bedtime I was standing on the stairs, hanging onto a newel post. I overheard my father speaking to someone about soldiers standing around a bonfire, destroying bodies. Although I didn't understand it all at the time, I know now that he was talking about the assassination of the imperial family and of my own grandfather.
>
> This is my first memory of Father's involvement [in the Anastasia case]. He was always trying to explain the story to people and was totally devoted to helping Anastasia gain legal recognition of her identity. He did not care about the money. The thing that people misunderstood most about him were his intentions. He had lost his own father because of the revolution, and all he was ever interested in was seeing Anastasia returned to her family, recognized by them. The actions of the Romanovs were deplorable to Father, and he had already become thoroughly disgusted with royal and imperial persons. Somehow I gained these impressions even as a sleepy child, and as our lives became more entwined with Anastasia, they were made permanent and unassailable.

Gleb had numerous conversations like the one Marina overheard. He continued to seek support from all possible sources by trying to expose the tragic injustice of Anastasia's situation. He investigated every aspect of her life since her arrival in Germany. He tried to cajole and convince potential allies. The more he learned about what Anastasia's family had done to her, the more he became convinced that without drastic steps, they would succeed in their attempts to discredit her, sentencing her to the life of an abandoned child.

ANASTASIA had been at the Garden City Hotel about two months when she received news of her grandmother's death. The Dowager Czarina Marie died on October 13, 1928, in her native Denmark, still believing that her son and his family had escaped Russia and lived in secret safety somewhere. Marie's death was the most tragic blow for the Grand Duchess since the events at Ekaterinburg, and she sat silent and depressed for hours, refusing to speak to anyone.

Her sadness lasted for days, and Gleb became concerned about how long she was taking to recover from the shock.

Marie's children, on the other hand, wasted no time in mourning her before they resumed their vendetta against Anastasia with renewed fervor. Within a day of the Dowager Czarina's death, some members of the family issued a document that would come to be known as the "Copenhagen Statement," although it was first issued in Germany and had been written by Grand Duke Alexander, the husband of Grand Duchess Xenia. He had failed in his attempts to convince others that Mrs. Tschaikovsky was "possessed" by the spirit of Anastasia, or that Gleb was leading a conspiracy to perpetuate a fraud on the world. The "Copenhagen Statement" formally recognized the assassination of the entire imperial family and denounced Anastasia as an impostor. The statement falsely claimed to represent the opinions and conclusions of the entire Romanov family, although only one of the signatories had ever even seen her. The court of Grand Duke Ernest Ludwig of Hesse in Germany had released the document to the Associated Press, which could be counted on to carry the news to America.

Gleb immediately recognized the statement as a declaration of war and knew that he must respond publicly to the assault on Anastasia by her relatives. With the aid of attorney Edward Huntington Fallows, Gleb intensified his activities on behalf of his old friend. The two men decided that Gleb, himself, should issue a rejoinder that, once and for all, would expose the deception being practiced by the Romanovs. Four days after the release of the "Copenhagen Statement," he threw down the gauntlet in a lengthy, public letter to Anastasia's aunt, Grand Duchess Xenia.

Gleb's letter clearly shows that he saw it as an opportunity to accomplish many purposes that had been too long untended. He first needed to make certain that the record was clear as to who was behind a denunciation that had been made in the name of the entire Romanov family:

Twenty-four hours did not pass after the death of your mother . . . when you hastened to take another step in your conspiracy to defraud your own niece. . . . You obviously knew that her late Majesty would not have permitted the issuance by you of such a statement and only waited for her Majesty's death to make it public. It makes a gruesome impression that even at your mother's death-bed your foremost worry must have been the desire to defraud your niece, and it is appalling to see that you did not have even the common decency of waiting if only a few days after your mother's death before publicly resuming your ignoble fight. . . .

The manner in which your statement was published is obviously calculated to mislead the public. It bears eleven signatures, which creates the impression that almost all members of the Russian imperial family have signed it. But of these eleven signatures three belong respectively to yourself, your husband and your sister, six to your children and only two not to the members of your immediate family, but to your first cousins. Further your statement is accompanied by the usual absurd lies so characteristic of the whole campaign of vile slander which you are leading against your unfortunate niece. . . .

Having exposed the individuals purporting to represent the entire family with the "Copenhagen Statement," Anastasia's defender next had to expose the real reason behind Xenia and Olga's vehemence in denying her claim: the money in England.

No matter what other monies or properties existed, Gleb never doubted that the deposits specifically designated for the Czar's daughters would prove of the utmost importance to Anastasia. He was certain the Grand Duchesses Xenia and Olga were of a similar opinion about its value to them.

Gleb had discovered that certain conditions had been placed on the dispersal of the funds, conditions that had been divulged a few years earlier to Ambassador Zahle. According to Anastasia, when she had revealed her knowledge about the dowry money to her Aunt Olga, she had also given the same information to the Danish ambassador. He in turn had made his own inquiries and had been informed by the Bank of England that the money was indeed there. Moreover, the ambassador had led Anastasia to believe that, unless one of the Czar's daughters laid claim to the funds within ten years of the imperial family's reported deaths at Ekaterinburg, the money would be given to the Czar's other heirs, including Anastasia's two aunts. With this understanding, Gleb had already sent a telegram to officials of various British banks, including the Bank of England, on July 13, 1928, four days before the tenth anniversary of the Ekaterinburg massacre. The telegram's purpose was to formally advise the bank officials that Grand Duchess Anastasia was still alive.

The document had been signed and authorized by her, and the family must certainly have been aware of its import. The official notice was intended to effectively freeze any of the assets in the English banks until Anastasia's claim could be adjudicated. In the past, Gleb had refrained from bringing up the issue of the relatives' greed as the primary motive for their opposition to Anastasia. Now, his public letter bluntly stated the charge:

> But permit me for the moment to disregard that malicious nonsense and come down to facts well known to [you]. These facts in short are—that there exists a considerable fortune in both money and real estate belonging to the late Emperor and his heirs, including personal funds of Grand Duchess Anastasia . . . all of which should now rightfully belong to her; . . . that you are trying for years by fraudulent methods to gain possession of that fortune . . . ; that much of the information concerning the Emperor's fortune came into your possession only after it had been disclosed by Grand Duchess Anastasia . . .; that your sister Grand Duchess Olga . . . practically acknowledged Grand Duchess Anastasia . . . in 1925 upon the assurance of physicians that she could not live longer than for one month and finally that as soon as Grand Duchess Anastasia began to recover and you could no longer hope for her immediate death, you and your sister began to denounce her as an imposter.

Gleb also saw the opportunity to review for the public—and potentially for the courts—the evidence supporting Anastasia's claim. He did not hesitate to repeat the most telling points, ones that he knew Grand Duchess Xenia herself must have read in Ambassador Zahle's reports:

> I refuse to believe that you are actually convinced that . . . Mrs. Tschaikovsky is not Grand Duchess Anastasia. You know very well that [she] remembers the slightest details of her childhood, that she possesses all her physical signs including birth-marks, that her handwriting is at present the same as it had been in her youth. . . . You also know that [she] has been fully acknowledged by many people of unquestionable truthfulness that had known her in her childhood, as well as by several members of the Russian Imperial Family. You

further know that all physicians who had ever treated [her] unanimously agree that it would be a scientific impossibility for her to be anybody but who she claims to be. Finally you know that all the so-called 'evidence' pretending to disprove [her] identity . . . consists of nothing but fabrications, falsifications, perjured statements of bribed witnesses and malicious and stupid fiction.

As a final judgment of the family, Gleb cast their duplicity in the most pernicious light:

That you are personally convinced of [her] real identity . . . is evident enough from the fact, that in the course of your whole fight against her you have never made a truthful statement nor mentioned a single fact, but resort exclusively to the vilest slander and most preposterous lies.

Before the wrong which [you] are committing pales the even [more] gruesome murder of the Emperor, his family and my father by the Bolsheviks. It is easier to understand a crime committed by a gang of crazed and drunken savages than the calm, systematic, endless persecution of one of your own family—an unfortunate, suffering and perfectly innocent young woman—the Grand Duchess Anastasia . . . whose only thought is that, being the only rightful heir of the late Emperor, she stands in the way of her greedy and unscrupulous relatives.

In some ways, the letter was an act of desperation and, like all such deeds, not without consequences. To many people at the time, disparaging the character and behavior of royalty was unthinkable. For those emigre Russians who were still fiercely loyal to the Romanovs, the very tone of Gleb's letter was enough to shock and disgust them. Even the people who had come to Anastasia's defense and aid, and who knew that Gleb's letter spoke the truth, could not sanction such an attempt to publicly embarrass the imperial family. Although many of these allies would continue to make discreet efforts to help Anastasia, they felt compelled to remove themselves from active involvement in her case so long as Gleb used such tactics.

A few people did not abandon Gleb and Anastasia. One who had already assisted her was Serge Rachmaninov, the Russian composer. He had been among the emigres in Paris who had first heard of Anastasia from Tatiana Botkin, and he had maintained a great interest in the Grand Duchess ever since. Rachmaninov knew the imperial family well and decided to go to Grand Duchess Xenia and discuss the controversy with her personally. As he later reported to Gleb, the trip was unsuccessful: "I was quite frank with her . . . and told her . . . that . . . [there] is a tremendous quantity of very weighty evidence. But Xenia kept staring past me at the wall and repeating like a wound-up mechanism: 'I simply know that she is not Anastasia.'" Despite his persistent attempts to draw her out, she would only repeat her conviction and offer no evidence to substantiate her view. Rachmaninov left feeling that despite knowing in her heart that Anastasia was her niece, the Grand Duchess Xenia would never acknowledge her. The Russian composer pledged his financial support for Anastasia in America "for as long a time as she might remain without any other source of income."

IV.
"Those jewels are mine"

THE MOST DAMNING ACCUSATION that Gleb's letter had made public was the attempt by Xenia and her cohorts in the family to gain control over the dowry money that Anastasia had said her father had left untouched in an English bank. Although their relative poverty could have easily motivated Anastasia's aunts to steal her dowry, many outsiders found it inconceivable that persons of imperial birth would yield to such a common temptation. Had these defenders of the Romanovs—many of them defamers of Gleb and Anastasia—known the extent of the avarice, they might have been more willing to accept Gleb's apparently rash actions and to support Anastasia's cause.

The Dowager Czarina had escaped from Russia with millions of dollars in precious stones and jewelry, which she kept in a large leather trunk that had been used to transport the treasure. Ever suspicious of governments and banks, she refused to allow the jewels to be deposited anywhere for safekeeping. Instead, she kept them under her bed and reportedly never let the key to the trunk out of her sight. As the Dowager Czarina grew weaker in her last months, she realized that the disposition of the jewels could cause a rift among the family, and she let it be known that she wanted them to be divided equally between her two daughters, Olga and Xenia. Immediately upon her death in October 1928, the two Grand Duchesses became concerned about their legacy. The Danish King Christian X demanded part of the jewels as compensation for the care he had provided to the Dowager Czarina and her entourage after their escape from Russia. The Bolshevik government was reportedly planning to claim the gems as state property and demand their return to Moscow, while international jewel thieves were supposedly waiting for the right opportunity to steal these riches.

Xenia had continued to live in the grace-and-favor mansion at Windsor, dependent on her cousin King George V and his wife Queen Mary. Although the king had refused entreaties to save the Russian imperial family from certain death, he had later shown an interest in helping the surviving Romanovs. He had provided financial support not only for Xenia but also—begrudgingly—for the Dowager Czarina and her household in Denmark. Perhaps that was why the British king felt he had a right to intervene in the disposition of Marie's estate. For whatever reason, he sent a representative to Copenhagen at about the time of the Dowager Czarina's death. With the aid of Xenia and Olga, the trunk containing the fortune was sent by diplomatic pouch back to London, where the king had it locked away in the vault at Buckingham Palace for safekeeping.

The king planned to personally oversee the valuation and sale of the treasure and to establish a trust for Xenia and her sister Olga, who had by this time also moved to England. More than likely, George V took these presumptuous steps in order to protect the two women from unscrupulous dealers, one of whom had already swindled Xenia out of her own small fortune of pearls. When the king became ill shortly after the transfer of Marie's fortune to Buckingham Palace, however, the plans began to go awry.

George V turned to his wife and two respected financiers to handle the matter for him. Queen Mary has been described as "predatory as any shark . . . using all manner of persuasion to net her catch" when it came to her passion for collecting rare objects. She had already acquired a good deal of the bounty of Russian imperial treasures that had flooded the market following the fall of the Romanov empire. One of the financiers chosen by the king was the Keeper of the Privy Purse, Sir Frederick Ponsonby, who retained complete allegiance to his two regents. The other was Peter Bark, the former Minister of Finance under Nicholas II, who had fled Russia and now served as the director of the largest subsidiary of the Bank of England. Ponsonby acted as the king's agent, and Bark was appointed trustee of the Dowager Czarina's estate in England by George V. Hennell & Sons, London jewelers who were known to have a special relationship with the British royal family, were selected to handle the task of valuing the treasure.

The division of the spoils took place in February 1929. The trunk was opened and its contents verified in the presence of Grand Duchess Xenia, Queen Mary, Ponsonby, and a representative of the London jewelers. Xenia and Olga later took a few pieces for themselves. The queen chose some of the more valuable objects, which one author described as "the choicest items," offering only half the appraisal price set by Hennell & Sons. The rest of the jewels were to be sold on the open market to establish the trust. Dependent on the charity of the British family for survival, and incapable of handling their own financial affairs, Xenia and Olga agreed to this arrangement.

What happened to the money from the sale of the treasure, other than the pieces taken by Queen Mary, remains unknown. Following Olga's death, information surfaced showing that neither she nor her sister Xenia were ever paid the full price that Queen Mary had set for the objects she had acquired. Olga's biography, published posthumously, stated that she had never received all the money promised by her cousin's wife, a fact confirmed by a former head of the Bank of England. After Olga's surviving sons demanded that Buckingham Palace investigate the matter, Queen Elizabeth's solicitors determined that her grandmother had indeed cheated the two Grand Duchesses. They discovered documents showing that Queen Mary had delayed payment until 1933, at the height of the Great Depression. She finally offered to settle accounts with her husband's cousins, but at the then-current market price, which was only a fraction of their value five years earlier. The present royal family settled with Olga's sons, but it was too late for either their mother or their Aunt Xenia to personally reap the harvest of their complicity to gain the bulk of Marie's wealth.

Anastasia's right to claim a portion of this treasure was completely ignored, perhaps intentionally so. Her only comment on the matter came late in life: "As the daughter of the last reigning emperor of Russia, those jewels were mine. Queen Mary of England stole them. They belonged to me! Such things I would never wear, but I could have used some of the money." Her right to the jewelry was unassailable, for both tradition and the laws of inheritance would have provided that the Czar's last female survivor be given some of the pieces. But this was to be only one instance of many where cupidity displaced custom.

EVEN though the intrigues involving Marie's jewelry were not public knowledge, it was clear that certain members of the Romanov family were intent on denying Anastasia everything. Gleb had hoped to embarrass the relatives into admitting their conspiracy before it went too far, but his attack caused Xenia, Olga, and the others to become even more stubborn. As the uproar over the public exchange of statements grew into an international event, the Romanovs stepped up their efforts to neutralize Gleb and to disparage the Grand Duchess. This time, Gleb could not keep the news from Anastasia, and he knew that her predicament was becoming desperate.

His immediate concerns, as always, were her present safety and her future well-being. The severe depression brought on by the Dowager Czarina's death did not abate. She tried to retreat into isolation again, but Gleb knew that she must face her problems. He held back little from her in an attempt to shake her from her inability to deal with reality. He undoubtedly repeated the litany of deceit practiced by her aunts, the Gilliards, and Grand Duke Ernest Ludwig. For the first time, he told her of death threats that had been made since her arrival in New York. Not unexpectedly, this woman who had always been fearful of assassination began to see conspiracy everywhere. She had felt relatively comfortable at the Garden City Hotel, but now she doubted the safety of such a public place. She told Gleb that she slept lightly, because she feared that she was under surveillance, possibly by Bolshevik agents or by spies from the British Secret Service conspiring with her aunts in England.

Her mental state deteriorated to the point that she herself began to recognize the consequences. Since leaving the Leeds estate, she had found comfort in her talks with Gleb, had joked with him and played the kinds of pranks that others who had not shared her childhood would find strange. Now, however, the stress of dealing with her grandmother's death, the undeniable rejection by her family, and the resulting depression threatened to overwhelm her. She became conscious of her inability to cope with events and feared another outbreak of the hysterics she had suffered at Castle Seeon.

Gleb must have been particularly alarmed when Anastasia began warning him that the time might come when she would cause a breach between them. They both knew that it had happened before, that she had forced herself back into abandonment by driving away those who had cared for her most. This time, however, she must have feared losing her last chance to be understood and accepted, for she implored him not to turn against her, not to deny her identity.

Gleb knew that in order to save Anastasia, he must find a way to give her mental peace and to assure her physical comfort and security. He saw no means of accomplishing these goals other than the public sanctioning of her claim as the sole legitimate heir to Nicholas and Alexandra. Such a practical victory would provide an endorsement of her true self and open the way for an income—whether from the Czar's estate or from whatever profits could be made from the sale of her story. He knew instinctively that this was her only choice, but he also felt that she would not understand the necessity of giving her personal approval to such a bold and frankly bourgeois step.

But Anastasia was ready to face reality. No longer the protected imperial princess, she recognized that without the help of others— from Prince Valdemar and Ambassador Zahle through Harriet Rathlef and the Duke of Leuchtenberg—she would not have survived. Despite her depression and paranoia, she could now conceive of the practical problems that had to be solved in order to avoid sleeping on park benches or facing confinement in mental institutions. Anastasia more than understood when Gleb explained the need to assert herself.

V.

"Who can blame the Grand Duchess"

GLEB HAD FORMULATED a general plan, but he also knew his own limitations. He turned again to Fallows, the attorney who had been helpful before with Anastasia's case. Several decisions arose from their discussions, but most important was the agreement that Anastasia must make a legal claim to the Czar's money in England. This was crucial, not so much because a successful defense of the claim would provide Anastasia with wealth, but because a court ruling that she was entitled to even a portion of the dowry money would give legal sanction to her authenticity.

Once they reached this decision, Gleb and Fallows saw that they would have to raise funds for what would surely be a long and expensive legal battle. Anastasia had no access to this kind of money and was relying on the generosity of her supporters just to survive. Even though many of these individuals were wealthy, they could not be expected to cover attorney's fees and court costs to the extent anticipated. Moreover, arrangements had to be made to develop a regular income for Anastasia. Both men saw that her dependence on a stream of temporary donors only increased her feelings of helplessness. One method of ensuring financial stability would be a planned management of the various article, book, and movie offers that could be expected once the legal challenge was made public. Already a silent film, *Clothes Make the Woman*—starring Eve Southern and Walter Pidgeon—had used Anastasia's name and story without her consent or compensation.

Eventually, Gleb and Fallows agreed that a corporation should be formed. Its primary purpose was to oversee Anastasia's affairs. In establishing a legal business entity, Gleb and Fallows could raise money by selling shares in any future profits that could be gained from confirmation of the Grand Duchess's identity. Through the purchase of stock and their oversight authority, those sitting on the governing board would share the task of caring for Anastasia, who would herself enjoy a certain sense of independence and security. The terms of the charter and its bylaws were drawn so as to provide that she be given a stipend. In addition, she would have final say in any compromise reached with the imperial family about the disposition of the Czar's fortune. With Anastasia's agreement, they drew up the papers for what was to become the Grandanor Corporation, the name being an acronym for Grand Duchess Anastasia of Russia.

While undertaking their initial preparations for the corporate charter, Gleb and Fallows realized that even though most of the public controversy had centered on the dowry money, the Czar surely had left substantial holdings in other countries, probably disguised purchases not readily traceable back to him. He was, after all, perhaps the wealthiest man of his time. Despite the fact that he had used huge amounts of his personal fortune to finance the last years of the war effort, his international investments in railroads and real estate, possibly even bonds and certificates, must have been substantial. The charter, therefore, gave the corporation authority to pursue claims for any and all of this fortune on behalf of the Grand Duchess.

Fallows was given both added duties and suitable compensation under the terms of the charter. Since he was an attorney and had agreed to spearhead the legal challenges, he was charged with establishing the case for Anastasia. He was named president of the corporate board and the charter provided him an additional share of future profits to compensate for the travel and long hours of interviews and investigations. The attorney began preparing his case even before Grandanor was officially incorporated.

Fallows traveled to Germany late in the autumn of 1928 in order to speak with some of Anastasia's supporters in Berlin. One evening he went to the home of General Helmuth von Moltke, who had been the chief of the German general staff during the First World War. Although the general had died, his widow had remained a prominent, if bizarre, figure in Berlin. Mrs. von Moltke was an Anthroposophist and held seances, in which she used her spiritual powers to communicate with "the other side." That evening she had invited a number of interested people and fellow believers, including Harriet Rathlef and Dr. Rudnev, the two people who had worked so hard to first establish Anastasia's authenticity in Germany.

Anastasia must have experienced considerable trepidation upon learning that Fallows was to interview her friends overseas. She had never been able to escape her fear of abandonment and must have wondered whether anyone could be counted on to tell the truth. The meeting, however, went splendidly. As she told Milukoff,

> all these people, they had a special meeting in the house of the Moltkes in Berlin and there happened something strange, very strange. A spiritual meeting, a seance. Mrs. von Moltke . . . had the power to call spirits from the other side. . . . The American lawyer was at this, it was an enormous meeting, masses of important people were there. What happened at this meeting had the American lawyer all written down. He had his secretary with him who had written everything shorthand down.

Had she been there, Anastasia would have seen this event as a coalescing of all the forces who supported her. In particular, the independent confirmation of her story by her friends was crucial in helping Fallows strengthen her case.

WHILE Fallows began his investigations in order to prepare Anastasia's case, Gleb remained in New York. He concentrated his efforts on ensuring continued care for the Grand Duchess and on laying the groundwork for Grandanor. Anastasia remained relatively comfortable in the Garden City Hotel, but the isolation—which she herself craved—prevented her from experiencing or enjoying the world outside. Despite the occasional interest she would show in the efforts of Gleb and Fallows on her behalf, she usually seemed to be brooding. Often, this mood led to hysterics and wild accusations. But at other times, she would come out of her reveries and exhibit a childlike lightheartedness.

Gleb himself particularly enjoyed those times when Anastasia would joke and demonstrate the sense of irony that would be needed to persevere. He recalled one such moment later:

One day she approached me with a sly little smile and gave me a wooden paper knife with her mother's monogram encrusted on it in metal.

'Have you ever seen this paper knife before?' she asked.

'I am pretty sure I have,' I said, for, indeed, the paper knife looked very familiar. 'But I cannot remember where.'

'Oh, no,' Anastasia laughed. 'You are not going to convince me of your identity with any such evasive answers. If you are Gleb Botkin, you must know where you have seen this paper knife. Otherwise, I shall send you to Gilliard for identification.'

I looked at the paper knife again . . . but where I was unable to remember. . . . Finally, she burst into laughter and exclaimed:

'What a memory! This knife belonged to your father and was always lying on his desk. You saw it every day in the course of several years. It was your sister who gave it to me in Germany. I do hope, for your sake, that you will never have to establish your identity on the basis of your childhood recollections.'

As the weeks passed, there would be other such glimpses of her good humor, but they would be eclipsed by practical concerns.

ALWAYS, the paramount problem was money. Plans for Grandanor were continuing to progress, and as Anastasia became somewhat interested in the possibilities the new arrangement might entail, she dropped her disdain for "what some people in the street may think." She told Gleb that she wanted to write her memoirs. It seemed an odd and sudden departure from her prior lack of interest in her own case, but it reflected her growing realization that she needed income. In addition, she knew that the idea of a book was an acceptable means of raising money, for other displaced members of European royalty had successfully published their own versions of history.

Gleb was somewhat skeptical of the success her efforts would bring, but he dutifully contacted his friends in the publishing industry. They agreed to pay Anastasia a substantial advance, but the project was doomed from the start. She was not a writer, and even though she had regaled Gleb and others with memories and anecdotes, she had no talent for translating her feelings and emotions into prose. She had also been raised a Romanov grand duchess—fascinated by gossip within a closed circle of trusted companions, but formal and proper in a public role. Finally, her imperious nature would not allow anyone to change a word that she said. The dictation never yielded a publishable manuscript:

> Anastasia . . . proved . . . the dullest and most injudicious of authors. . . . Any kind of informality in print appeared abhorrent to her. . . . Far from trying to make the best of a dramatic situation, it was precisely every dramatic situation which she reduced to a few dry paragraphs written in the style of a Court calendar. . . . Thus her memoirs . . . turned out to be utterly valueless for purposes of publication.

Although this project failed, Gleb continued to do all he could to find other ways of assuring Anastasia's future well-being.

MANY people made inquiries about the Grand Duchess and offered assistance, in one form or another, through Gleb. The strain of nonstop activity and lobbying on her behalf was beginning to tell on him, and his financial resources were sorely limited. He also lacked the expertise to effectively handle her various needs —legal, practical, and financial—with or without the success of the Grandanor Corporation. He was torn between his desire to accept offers of help and his fear that once other individuals were subjected to Anastasia's unpredictable behavior, events would follow the familiar pattern. These erstwhile supporters would tire of her moods and abandon her, which in turn would send her into a downward spiral.

One of those who seemed particularly persistent in offering assistance was Annie Burr Jennings, who had first extended her hospitality to Anastasia after she arrived in New York. Miss Jennings had already convinced Gleb to agree to let her pay for Anastasia to be moved to a private residence on the grounds of the hotel resort, but the elderly socialite pressed him unrelentingly to let her do more. She announced her desire to care for Anastasia, to watch over her daily, and to personally supervise and finance her recovery. Gleb carefully explained to Miss Jennings his fear that she would not be able to endure Anastasia's hysterics and accusations, but, as Gleb would recount in detail later, she insisted otherwise:

> Do you suspect me of being the kind of hostess . . . Xenia [Leeds] proved to be? Who can blame the Grand Duchess for not being always able to control her nerves? The wonder is that she is merely temperamental instead of being stark mad. No, I can assure you that no matter what she does, I shall never turn against her. She can insult me as much as she likes, she can quarrel with me ten times a day. Never will I abandon her!

> . . . I do love her as if she were my own daughter. I will never abandon her. . . . I will leave my whole fortune to her.

Gleb finally agreed to take the offer to Anastasia, but he was reluctant to speak with the Grand Duchess about this matter. He knew that she had grown to trust him and rely on him as the one person who would accept her without equivocation. From their many conversations, he realized that her nervous condition had improved but that she still felt alone and abandoned. He worried that she might well view his relaying of Miss Jennings's offer as a sign that he, too, was now deserting her. But in all fairness, he knew that he had to let her know of the invitation and that it must be her decision whether to accept.

His suspicions could not have proven more accurate. "Even such . . . indirect suggestions on my part sufficed to make Anastasia suspicious of my true motives . . . and [she] even hinted that I was probably tired of her and wanted to get rid of her in order to devote myself wholly to my own work." Anastasia did not agree to the proposal, but neither did she give a definite no. The incident put a strain on their relationship. Having directly expressed her doubts and suspicions about his loyalty, she could not later disguise how she felt. Gleb was also growing weary from the physical strain of making daily trips to the hotel to care for the Grand Duchess, while trying to maintain his ties to his own life and family. His lack of patience with the now recalcitrant imperial princess became increasingly evident.

In December 1928, Gleb contracted a severe case of influenza and could not visit Anastasia as he had before. She could not abide the change. "The Grand Duchess suspected my illness was a diplomatic one, that I simply wanted to take a rest. She felt deeply hurt. . . ." Not long after this, she decided to accept the offer to go to Miss Jennings.

In January, Anastasia moved from the Garden City Hotel back to the Park Avenue house where she had first stayed after leaving the ship from Europe. She arrived as Anna Anderson, the name chosen when she left the Leeds estate and one that had proved a useful alias in public. She brought with her the few mementos with which she always traveled, and of course, her parrots. She would later report that she was never truly comfortable in the Park Avenue home, with its heavy Victorian decor, the rooms appointed with priceless art alongside obvious copies. She felt compelled, for example, to point out to her hostess that the *Mona Lisa* which was proudly displayed in the home was but one of the many frauds that had come on the market following the mysterious and unsolved theft of the painting from the Louvre years before.

Even so, Miss Jennings did all she could to treat Anastasia as the grand duchess she was. Only Miss Jennings and her personal secretary were allowed to attend the imperial princess, despite the legion of servants that could always be summoned. Miss Jennings apparently showed every deference, even writing letters dictated by her guest, and providing her with an unlimited account at B. Altman department store, which accorded Anastasia the same standard of service extended to the very wealthy. She was able to buy all manner of expensive clothing, always in white.

In addition to providing physical comfort, Miss Jennings included Anastasia in her hectic social life. Although well into her seventies, Miss Jennings remained one of the most prominent and active social figures in New York. There was a never-ending series of balls, parties, openings, and social gatherings where the best of society mingled with acceptably curious characters. As they traveled from New York to Sunnie-Holme, the lavish estate Miss Jennings maintained in exclusive Fairfield, Connecticut, Anastasia was swept up in a lifestyle that she had not seen since her days at the Romanov court. It was the Jazz Age, and the very wealthy had seldom been able to enjoy and display their excesses with such abandon, flouting the legal restrictions of Prohibition and delighting in the freewheeling mores of the lost generation.

It was not unusual for famous people to attend these gatherings. Cole Porter and John Vernou Bouvier, III, were among her escorts, and she attended the most prestigious events, as she would later recount to Milukoff:

> The new Waldorf-Astoria was built when I was in New York in '29. You see, all the corner was bought by Mr. Morgan . . . and shortly before the old Waldorf-Astoria was broken down, I had been there for . . . a big good-bye concert . . . with Miss Jennings. [It was a concert] for the hotel. The old hotel . . . and it was . . . a very exciting thing, all the people were excited. . . . All the old people who had there their dancing clothes, dancing when they were young girls and young boys. And [they] bought the chairs on which they had been sitting . . . at parties and such things. They bought all the chairs.

There were many such happenings, and Anastasia—always preferring the name Mrs. Anderson—was often the center of attention. Likewise, having been raised a Russian imperial grand duchess, she knew exactly how to charm her admirers. Her desire for anonymity by hiding behind the alias made her all the more intriguing. Everyone knew of her story, and she became so famous for a time that the singular color of her eyes was popularized in fashion as "Anastasia Blue."

At times, the attention became oppressive. People gawked as she sat next to Miss Jennings in her box at the opera. The curious were always making inquiries about her or asking her questions directly. Her last defense became her alias, which she mistakenly felt provided her with a means to lose herself in another persona. She insisted on using the name as a retreat from the speculation and controversy surrounding her other, true identity. As an additional protection, Anastasia took to covering her jaw with a handkerchief. The constant attention, the need always to be on guard in the most glaring public light, must have been a tremendous strain on such a fragile and reclusive individual.

Anastasia's one retreat from these activities was Sunnie-Holme in

Connecticut. It was a magnificent enclave, with sculptured gardens that ran for a mile from the mansion down to Long Island Sound. The atmosphere was entirely peaceful and protected, even more so since Miss Jennings was a force of unquestioned authority in the town of Fairfield. This grandiose refuge surrounded by the little Connecticut hamlet must have seemed as close to the security and tranquility of her environment at Czarskoe Selo as anything Anastasia had seen since childhood.

THE interest Miss Jennings and her friends showed in Anastasia went beyond providing creature comforts and bringing her into their exclusive social circles. Gleb had quietly removed himself from any direct contact with the Grand Duchess once she had moved into the Park Avenue home, but he had continued his efforts on her behalf and maintained contact with those who cared for her now. Early in his attempts to establish Grandanor, he had approached Miss Jennings as a possible shareholder, but she had declined the offer.

Her refusal to invest in the corporation lay not in her feelings that it might not succeed, but rather in her belief that she had a better plan for helping the Grand Duchess. Annie Burr Jennings had begun to devise a scheme whereby she would finance an armed mercenary force to invade Russia and overthrow the Bolshevik government, which could then be replaced with a restored Romanov dynasty. She felt that once a new czar was in place, Anastasia would surely be in a favored position, particularly if her protector in America had provided the funds that ushered in the new imperial age. For her part, Anastasia ardently supported the idea, and she apparently even entertained notions of trying to have the law of succession changed so that, as the sole surviving child of the last reigning czar, she could inherit the throne.

Such an idea seems preposterous today, but Miss Jennings's plans might not have been so far-fetched. The Soviet government was still in a state of flux, and most nations in the world did not even recognize its legitimacy. The nation constantly teetered on the edge of economic collapse, and after Lenin's death in 1924, no strong leadership had emerged. Miss Jennings also knew from personal experience that private means could accomplish a change in government, and that it had been done before for less money than she would have at her disposal. In 1920, her good friends, Mr. and Mrs. Leeds, had used their wealth to destabilize the nascent postwar government of Greece and ensured that one of their relatives ascended that country's throne. The possibility exists that Miss Jennings felt she would profit richly from whatever influence and control she would be able to gain in Russia. Her Standard Oil fortune would have been unmatchable if the company had gained a foothold in the enormous oil reserves that lay untapped in the Soviet Union. Although she took these plans seriously, they never came to fruition. Perhaps the cost proved to be too great, or perhaps Miss Jennings decided that she was too old to see the scheme through to the end. She eventually dropped the idea and sometime thereafter, she expressed a new interest in the Grandanor Corporation.

Gleb realized the value of Grandanor to Anastasia, for their recent estrangement convinced him that a structured, legal process would be needed to avoid the rash and unpredictable strategies that would ensue if Anastasia—alone with a few ardent supporters—took matters into her own hands. His role in the venture, however, was beginning to cause difficulties. The Romanov family had accused him of trying to profit from the presumed Grand Duchess through Grandanor, and he felt that his association with this endeavor might jeopardize its acceptance as a legitimate investment. Gleb had difficulty interesting potential investors, particularly after Anastasia came under the care of the wealthy Miss Jennings. Therefore, the older woman's offer to take a more active interest in the plans for Grandanor seemed particularly opportune.

Up to this point, the corporation had not been officially registered. Once Miss Jennings became involved, steps were quickly taken to legally incorporate Grandanor in order to raise money by selling shares of stock. On February 9, 1929, Grandanor Corporation was granted a charter by the State of Delaware. Neither the Secretary of State in Dover (where by law all such records had to be filed and archived) nor the Delaware Registration Trust Company in Wilmington (which provided the corporation with a headquarters address in the state) have been able to find any documents that indicate the corporation ever existed. From other sources, we know that not only Miss Jennings, but also her relatives from the Rockefeller and Auchincloss families, provided a substantial amount of funds toward the venture. Their money made it possible for Fallows to pursue a full-fledged investigation and hire numerous assistants to prepare the many documents and testimonies he was gathering.

ALL the while, public interest in Anastasia was growing. In addition to the notoriety she received in the society pages as the mysterious Mrs. Anderson, numerous articles appeared. Her old enemy, Pierre Gilliard, also published a book in Europe entitled *The False Anastasia*. It was little more than a retelling of his previously discredited stories about the Grand Duchess, and with European interest in her waning because she had moved to the United States, the book was not at all successful. Also in 1929, an American edition of a second book by Harriet Rathlef was issued. Although Harriet again supported the authenticity of the Grand Duchess, the book only added to speculation about her case in America. Anastasia knew of both works and viewed their publication derisively.

Even worse, to her mind, were the activities of others not at all connected to her or to her family's past. The American industrialist Armand Hammer had developed a particularly trusting and lucrative relationship with the Bolshevik government by 1928. As the economic troubles in Russia worsened and the government desperately needed foreign currency and vital goods, Hammer was able to buy priceless imperial treasures that had not been destroyed during the revolution. He brought these items back to the United States and offered them for sale. Among the articles made available were jewelry worn by the Czarina and the Grand Duchesses and books inscribed by members of the family that had been taken from their personal library. Furnishings from the Romanov's private apartments were displayed next to clothing made from the vestments worn by the imperial family on ceremonial occasions. Anastasia was forever sickened by what she saw as a crass attempt to make commercial gain from her family's tragedy.

Perhaps it was her anger over the two books and ventures like Hammer's, coupled with the new investments in Grandanor, that spurred her once again to attempt to write her memoirs. Her previous effort with Gleb had come to naught, but now she began dictating again and worked on the project for weeks on end. Anastasia was encouraged by a brother of Miss Jennings, who said that a book of her remembrances would "make millions." But this idea failed as miserably as the first one had. Anastasia grew more and more distraught, and her complaints multiplied.

She had become weary of the social life that she now felt had been forced upon her by Miss Jennings. Rather than enjoy these outings, Anastasia came to see them as opportunities for her hostess to put her on display, much as the Kleists had done following her release from the Dalldorf asylum. She was not entirely mistaken about being exploited. She sometimes felt subjected—intentionally or not—to humiliating and distressing circumstances at the hands of Miss Jennings and her social circle. Once, for example, they proudly took her to see a new home that had been built in the style of a Russian palace for a recently married nephew. When she arrived, Anastasia was appalled to realize that the entire house was modeled after one of the residences owned by Rasputin's assassin, Felix Youssoupov.

Feeling the outside world increasingly unfriendly, she retreated to her suite of rooms and was content to sit there alone with her two parrots, which she often allowed to fly about uncaged. Her isolation, predictably, led again to paranoia and accusations against her supporters.

By 1930, her state of mind had worsened dramatically. When Fallows returned from Europe that spring, Anastasia confronted him and complained that he was not providing her with information, even though he had dutifully sent her copies of his reports. Explaining that the case was a difficult one requiring a great deal of documentation and investigation, he told her that she might achieve recognition within a year but, to pursue the matter thoroughly, he would need to make frequent trips to Europe. Anastasia grew more impatient and demanded closer contact with him. She went so far as to accuse him of bilking the Grandanor investors so that he could travel overseas and visit his mistress.

Fallows finally assigned one of his associates to provide her with regular briefings about the case in his absence, but the new attorney could neither deal with her outbursts nor assuage her fantastic suspicions. Her refrain was unvarying: she had waited ten years since Ekaterinburg for justice and could wait no longer. If the case was not progressing as quickly as she felt it should, that could only be due to the incompetency or duplicity of her attorneys.

ANASTASIA'S erratic behavior was beginning to wear on Miss Jennings. Gleb had warned her how unpredictable Anastasia could be, and his words were proving prophetic. The Grand Duchess seldom emerged from her room and, if disturbed or pressed, would rail against anyone and everyone. Still, in certain moments she could appear perfectly normal, as evidenced by a series of photographs taken at this time of Anastasia alone in her room with her parrots. Exquisitely posed, dressed all in white, she appears as the elegant imperial princess who had been trained from birth to conceal all inner emotions before the camera. One of these portraits, showing her with the parrots perched on her fingers, was hand-tinted and remained her favorite photograph of herself for the rest of her life.

Miss Jennings finally became desperate about her inability to judge Anastasia's moods and to deal with them effectively. She attempted to find other accommodations for her guest, even contacting her friend Xenia Leeds and asking her to take Anastasia back. Mrs. Leeds declined. Anastasia began to complain that she was tired of charity and needed her own money to establish her independence so that she could live the way she wanted. In exasperation, one of Miss Jennings's brothers pushed Anastasia hard to return to the book project in order to earn money, reportedly telling her that "if you do not do what we want you to do, we shall send you to an asylum from which you will never get out for the rest of your life." Not surprisingly, the tension increased.

Anastasia began to see conspiracy all around her. She accused Miss Jennings, through her involvement in the Grandanor Corporation, of trying to steal the money that rightfully belonged to Anastasia. She retreated completely within her rooms and to her birds, and when her hostess tried to cajole her into traveling from New York back to Sunnie-Holme, the Grand Duchess refused to leave. Miss Jennings packed her own bags and left the house to Anastasia, who then began writing outrageous letters, threatening to expose her benefactress as a crook and accusing her of being a drunken gossip. She demanded that some of her personal property, which she had left at the estate in Connecticut, be returned; she wanted to see Miss Jennings and her friends and fellow investors all put away in jail.

Concern about her condition increased as her behavior grew ever more bizarre and erratic. She threw things from her window in an attempt to get the police to come and hear her accusations. She ran around the room screaming her plans for retribution. She appeared one day at B. Altman as Mrs. Anderson and stood on the sales floor, yelling her litany of charges against Annie Burr Jennings for all the world to hear. She threatened to kill herself rather than continue her present existence. It was clear to those who suffered these abuses and who witnessed her crazed behavior that desperate moves were in order. They began talking of the need to again commit her to a psychiatric institution.

ONE afternoon in July, she was in her rooms, hysterical about some matter long since forgotten, when she accidentally trod on one of her parrots. She must have realized instantly that she had killed the creature, and this sudden, inexplicable, senseless death brought on a shock from which she could not emerge. The servants reported that she remained in her room all night screaming and crying, unable to sleep. Her uncontrollable agony over the death of the bird went unchecked for days.

Finally, after a week and a half, Miss Jennings's brother submitted an application to have Anastasia committed. As part of the supporting documents, he provided the testimony of three doctors who had been paid by the Jennings family to falsely state that they had examined the woman before making their diagnosis of insanity. On July 24, 1930, Anastasia was judged to be legally insane, although she had yet to be examined by a psychiatrist. After the decision was handed down, medical orderlies appeared at the Jennings home and went up to Anastasia's rooms. They pounded on the door, and when she did not respond, they broke it down with fire axes. The orderlies found her crouching in the bathroom, and she refused to leave. They had no choice but to drag her from the house. When Fallows later learned what had happened, he said " . . . [B]reaking down the door of her room . . . does not seem humane, to say the least. That alone would have been enough to derange temporarily any sensitive, high-strung, ill woman."

We can only imagine what terror engulfed Anastasia as she was removed bodily from her rooms and transported to another sanitorium. No longer able to face the horrors of the unfamiliar world into which she was thrust after Ekaterinburg, she was admitted as Anna Anderson to Four Winds sanitorium in Westchester County, an exclusive facility whose care and treatment was available only to the wealthiest patients. The Great Depression was at its height, but Miss Jennings made certain that Anastasia was installed in a four-room suite and provided with a personal attendant. She was examined by doctors, who determined that "she isn't deranged . . . just in need of attention for her disordered nerves." Whatever treatment was prescribed and followed is unknown, as all records of her stay at Four Winds have been destroyed. Nor do we have any comment or record from Gleb or Fallows as to their activities during the year that Anastasia was confined to the institution. Miss Jennings reportedly spent more than twenty-five thousand dollars on her care, so the Jennings family probably controlled the treatment.

The growing expenses became a concern to other members of the Jennings family. They decided that Miss Jennings would continue to pay for Anastasia unless some other solution could be found, and eventually concluded that sending the Grand Duchess back to Europe would be the best course of action. The Jennings brothers arranged with the German consulate in New York to have a passport issued under the name of Anna Anderson, complete with the photograph of another woman. Anastasia was furious when she learned that they had made use of an impostor to manufacture the false documents, yet she remained totally at their mercy. One night, she found herself being taken from the sanitorium and driven to New York harbor. There she and her trunks were placed aboard the German ship *Deutschland*, which was preparing to sail for Europe, and given over to the care of a Finnish nurse.

Years later, Anastasia would characterize this stay in America as nothing other than "a terrible mess."

VI.

"Nothing without Botkin"

THE VOYAGE on the *Deutschland* proved another grueling ordeal for Anastasia. She was locked alone in her cabin for the duration of the trip, which lasted about a week. The Finnish nurse had taken away the key to her trunk, so Anastasia was forced to wear only her dressing gown and could not get at her soap, toothbrush, or comb.

Upon the ship's arrival in Germany, she was taken—still under the care of the Finnish nurse—to the Ilten Sanitorium outside Hanover. The doctors at this institution had been cabled to expect the arrival of Mrs. Anderson from America, but knew nothing more about her or her condition. They were surprised when they discovered that the nurse who had been with her since America did not have any medical papers on the patient and could not provide the physicians with any details about the case. The nurse explained only that she had been told before leaving the United States that Mrs. Anderson was crazy and might try to escape at any moment. The doctors felt they had little choice but to accept her word, and Anastasia was placed alone in a guarded room for the night. Sometime before the next morning, the Finnish nurse left and was never heard from again.

On Anastasia's first day in the sanitorium, one of the doctors began to interview her, asking questions about her condition and her past history. She reached into one of her bags and pulled out a German identification certificate, issued in 1927, showing her to be Anastasia Tschaikovsky. The physician said nothing and left the room to confer with the director of the facility, who returned with him to the patient's room. "The faces of these gentlemen I will never forget," Anastasia would later recall, as it dawned upon them who she was.

Certainly, any psychologist in Germany at this time would have recognized the name of Anastasia Tschaikovsky from the cases that had been discussed in the early 1920s, but by now the woman's story had gained a notoriety far beyond medical circles. The decade since her first examination at Dalldorf had been filled with newspaper articles and books discussing Anastasia's identity, and the efforts of the Grand Duchesses Olga and Xenia and the Grand Duke of Hesse to discredit and isolate her, had only made her even more famous in Europe and America. The sanitorium officials quickly understood that Anastasia's hospitalization in a German mental institution would not remain secret for long.

Her friends and supporters in America were unaware that Anastasia had left the United States, let alone that she had been sent off to a mental institution in Germany. When they discovered the truth, they were furious. Gleb wrote, "I was assured that I did not have to worry, that the Jenningses would continue to support Anastasia and keep her in safety for life." Anastasia herself was livid. On the second day of her confinement, the doctors at Ilten had informed her that she was not insane and not in need of institutional care. She wanted and demanded explanations, and she summoned her American attorney, Edward Fallows, to Ilten.

Anastasia clearly understood that Fallows had been hired to protect her against just such treacherous acts as had been perpetrated by the Jennings, and she was very angry with her attorney for what she saw as a complete failure to fulfill his prime duty to her. Fallows was in Europe when Anastasia was dragged onboard the *Deutschland*, but had continued to make inquiries about her well-being through the associate that he had assigned to see to her needs in his absence. However, this man had colluded with the Jenningses, and purposely misled Fallows into believing that all was well, even after Anastasia had arrived at Ilten.

The American attorney certainly understood why Anastasia was so upset. He had his own concerns about how she had been secreted out of New York. The false passport issued under the name of Anna Anderson could cause serious problems. Although signed only with an anonymous "X," here was another document of identification that gave not only a new name, but also falsified that she had been born in Berlin. Anyone could now charge that Anastasia was not a Russian born in 1901, which the passport for Anna Tschaikovsky had truthfully recorded. If nothing else, the false passport could severely jeopardize the favorable conclusion of a court case, which remained his primary concern.

Fallows had been busy building his case since 1928, and had explored many opportunities to bring suit on his client's behalf, always aware that it would be best for Anastasia and the successful conclusion of the legal challenge if she were involved as little as possible. He knew that she would not be able to endure lengthy sessions with attorneys taking depositions. Neither could she spend endless hours sitting in a courtroom as lawyers and judges tried to unravel the many claims and accusations that had been made since her reemergence in Germany after the First World War. Anastasia's enemies had already been very effective on the public front by spreading mistruths in order to confuse the issue, and they would be sure to continue such tactics even in the legal arena. With her return to Europe, her family would feel more directly threatened and would likely intensify their efforts to eliminate her so that they could gain control of the Czar's fortune. Despite these difficulties, Fallows persisted in believing that Anastasia's future could only be secured in a court of law. As a result, he left Ilten with the understanding that he should continue to pursue his legal strategy.

ALTHOUGH the doctors at the sanatorium had soon determined that their patient did not require their care, Anastasia remained there as long as possible. She felt she had no place else to go, and once the threatening aspects of confinement—the possibilities of renewed psychological examinations and endless questions about her life— were removed, she began to feel quite at home in the protective environment, being tended by nurses and visiting with other patients. Besides, as Anastasia discovered, Miss Jennings had already agreed to pay for six months' treatment at the facility.

As the presence of the Grand Duchess at the Ilten Sanatorium became known, the German press again took a great interest in her life. This time, however, in addition to the usual tabloid fabrications, a long and positive recounting of her story appeared in a Hanover newspaper, the *Hannoverscher Anzeiger*. It had the largest daily circulation of any newspaper outside Berlin and was owned by Paul and Gertrude Madsack. The Madsacks quickly took an interest in Anastasia, and became convinced of her identity. It was not long before they also befriended her.

As had always been the case, once her whereabouts were publicized, many visitors came to Ilten—whether out of curiosity or sympathy, or both. Among those who arrived at the sanitorium was Empress Hermine, the second wife of the deposed German Kaiser Wilhelm II. Following the war, the Kaiser had been forced into exile, where his first wife, Augusta Victoria, had died. The Kaiser had eventually settled in the Netherlands, and he took up residence on an estate at Doorn.

The Kaiser had left Germany with great reluctance after his abdication, but his advisers convinced him that he could not remain in his own country. The allies had wanted to try him for execution because of his role in starting the First World War. The Queen of the Netherlands had provided sanctuary, but with two conditions: travel was restricted to approved trips within the Netherlands; and he could not undertake any political activities. As a result, when he needed to conduct confidential business elsewhere, the Kaiser turned to his wife as his emissary.

Princess Hermine of Reuss had married the Kaiser in 1922, against the wishes of Wilhelm's family and the remaining German nobility, which Anastasia referred to as "first society." The Reuss family was one of the oldest in Germany; their lineage went back to medieval times and had two basic branches. Hermine was from the older branch, which was also fabulously rich, "swimming in gold," Anastasia once told Milukoff.

However, as Anastasia already knew, the marriage between the Kaiser and Hermine

was a scandal in society. It would have been better if the Emperor had not done this foolery. It was insane foolery. With the help of the Grand Duchess of Baden she married him. But it was foolery, nothing more. . . . All the family, the children of the Emperor, were shocked to death. The Crown Princess [Cecilie] . . . never went to Doorn when . . . Hermine was there. . . . She swore she would never enter Doorn when this woman was there. Never! Hermine had to leave Castle

Doorn when the Crown Princess had the intention to come. There was nothing to be done.

Anastasia probably could not help but sympathize with what she knew was the common view of the Empress: "This the people told: . . . she is trying to play the empress, she is not our Empress . . . as *Princess* Hermine, she's all right, but she is not our *Empress*." When Anastasia learned that the Empress was coming to see her at Ilten, she must have been filled with a mixture of curiosity and cautious anticipation.

Anastasia had long believed that the Germans knew of her rescue from Ekaterinburg, for she had been given shelter on the grounds of the German embassy in Bucharest. The Kaiser's interest in Anastasia perhaps reflected the high-level German involvement that she had always suspected, or simply resulted from the fact that he was related to the entire Russian imperial family. But the choice of his Empress as emissary is telling evidence of the significance he placed on making contact with the patient at Ilten. Hermine would have undoubtedly conveyed to Anastasia some explanation of the Kaiser's position during their meeting. Perhaps it was the same as the one that Gleb would receive later from one of the Kaiser's closest advisers, namely that her claim was "wholly valid" and that "were the Russian Imperial Family to arrive at the conviction that . . . Mrs. Tschaikovsky is . . . Grand Duchess Anastasia, His Majesty would naturally welcome such a development." Whatever occurred between the two women at Ilten, Hermine endorsed Anastasia wholeheartedly. It was the beginning of a special friendship that the Grand Duchess would remember forever after. The German nobility viewed Hermine's acknowledgment as a sanctioning of Anastasia's authenticity by the Kaiser. As a result, many doors opened to the Grand Duchess among that nation's considerable aristocracy.

EQUALLY important to Anastasia's future was the visit in October 1931 of Prince Frederick Ernest of Saxe-Altenburg, a member of another powerful and wealthy German noble family. His lineage was closely tied to the Romanovs, and his sister had married Prince Sigismund of Prussia. Sigismund was a son of Anastasia's Aunt

Irene, who had failed to recognize her at the Grünberg estate. Prince Frederick was also related to the Grand Duke of Hesse, Anastasia's most vehement enemy among her remaining family, and had heard the Grand Duke's ravings. As a result, the Prince had a natural interest in Anastasia and he had approached Harriet Rathlef, whose book on the Grand Duchess he had read previously, to discover more of her view of the story.

Prince Frederick had first come in contact with Anastasia's circle of German friends while she was still in America. He had continued to stay in contact with these people as he became more interested in their mystic philosophy. He had been present during the spiritual evening at the Moltke home when Edward Fallows had begun his investigations into Anastasia's case. Anastasia described to Milukoff her understanding of the seance:

> [B]y this big meeting there was for the first time Prince Frederick. He had got at Mrs. Rathlef and by this meeting the twenty-five-year-old prince was for the first time in this society [of Anthroposophists]. . . . He had read the book of Mrs. Rathlef [about me]. There he got for the first time at Mrs. Rathlef. And Mrs. Rathlef had brought him together with the American lawyer.

The Prince's active involvement in her life began at this point, but he had always been determined to keep an open mind about Anastasia unless and until her identity could be proven conclusively to him.

Before arriving at Ilten, Prince Frederick had conferred with his brother-in-law, Prince Sigismund. As a nephew of the Czarina, Sigismund had played with the imperial children at Czarskoe Selo, where he had fallen in love with Anastasia's older sister Olga. He had last seen the Romanov children just prior to the First World War, in a meeting that had remained private for nearly twenty years. His mother had not recognized Anastasia when they had met, but Sigismund wanted to prove to himself that Anastasia was not the Grand Duchess. He had, therefore, devised a set of eighteen questions about their last meeting in Russia and enlisted the aid of an already curious Prince Frederick to travel to Ilten and pose his queries.

Anastasia was initially unwilling to see the Prince. She asked how she could know that he was really a person of royalty and not a Polish factory worker, and wondered aloud why she should subject herself to another such ordeal. Prince Frederick thought her comment funny and realized that whoever she was, she had managed to maintain a sense of humor, despite her many travails. She agreed to speak with him and accurately answered all of Sigismund's questions. Prince Frederick often said that although he had felt intuitively that she was Anastasia and had heard a great deal of evidence to that effect before visiting Ilten, her correct responses wholly convinced him that she was, indeed, the Grand Duchess. He became one of her most ardent defenders and would seek to help her by gathering a cadre of fellow supporters over the next fifty years.

IN early 1932, Anastasia left the sanatorium at the urging of a German attorney who was trying to convince her to dismiss Edward Fallows and allow him to act on her behalf. She lived for a short time at a spa and then with a family before finally tiring of the situation. For reasons never explained, she walked out of her hosts' home one day, went to a public phone, called Harriet Rathlef, and told her to come and get her.

Anastasia went back to Berlin with the woman she once felt had betrayed her, and they quickly achieved a reconciliation. Harriet installed Anastasia in a small hotel, and, most likely because of Hermine's endorsement, the Grand Duchess soon became the toast of German society. In addition to receiving visitors in her room, Anastasia went to many parties and dinners and was treated as a welcome guest in the best homes. She also began traveling and met a wide variety of people, from Harriet's Anthroposophist friends to those interested in and supportive of her case.

One person she met at this time was Countess Astrid Bethusy-Huc, the stepdaughter of Mrs. von Moltke, who held seances in Berlin. The Countess had learned from her father's former military colleagues that the German government had played a role of some kind in assuring Anastasia's well-being after her escape from the Bolsheviks. The Countess was particularly kind to the Grand Duchess and took her home to a castle in Silesia. Anastasia was always very happy to spend time in this region, where Empress

Hermine also maintained a residence. Harriet would sometimes join Anastasia in Silesia, and they would often visit the large circle of Anthroposophists who had settled there. This group had come to believe that the Russian revolution was the manifestation of a major psychic upheaval and that Anastasia was a victim of what they termed this "karma." She felt comfortable among them, for their strong ties to Russian mysticism were not at all unfamiliar to the daughter of Czarina Alexandra.

THIS was one of the happiest times of Anastasia's life. She had no worries about money, for many of those she visited provided her discreetly with funds. Eventually, the newspaper publishers in Hanover, the Madsacks, paid for an apartment in that city and took over caring for her needs. And while she was in Hanover, Anastasia met the man who would come closest to being the one great love of her life.

Despite the many men who acted as her protectors—Gleb, Prince Frederick, and finally Jack Manahan—people have generally assumed that Anastasia never had the joy of knowing true love. But gossip about her love reached Milukoff, and his interest in the matter became so persistent that one day Anastasia reluctantly told him part of the story. Although she never gave him the "name of names," the conversation revealed some general information, including the facts that he had been a Thuringian prince a little bit older than she, that he had never married, and that he had long been dead. She provided other information to Milukoff, but he was never able to make the pieces fit.

Many years later, the Anastasia scholar Greg Rittenhouse took the time to review her clues in more detail and compared the information with facts contained in genealogical charts of the German noble houses. His careful research shows conclusively that Anastasia's love was Heinrich of Reuss, a cousin of Empress Hermine.

His full name was Heinrich XLV, Prince Reuss zu Schleiz, but little is known of his life. He was arrested by Soviet invaders in the eastern zone of Germany in 1945 and disappeared forever. Anastasia always treasured remembrances of the Reuss family and would fall uncharacteristically silent at the mention of Prince Heinrich's name.

It is but one more ironic tragedy of her life that she lost him at the hands of the successors of the Bolsheviks who had taken away her family.

IN 1934, two years after reconciling with Harriet Rathlef, Anastasia suffered another tragic loss, when the forty-four-year-old Harriet died of breast cancer. Anastasia suspected that the Grand Duke of Hesse had somehow induced Harriet's cancer by poisoning her. From this point on, the Grand Duchess would often suspect that the death of anyone close to her must be from other than natural causes.

She began to view her wealthy and socially prominent associates as exploitative. She felt once again that she was being turned into an object of curiosity, and her mental health began to deteriorate. In 1935, she suffered another nervous breakdown.

Anastasia did not withdraw as completely following this illness as she had under similar circumstances in the past. For one thing, the Madsacks continued to provide her an apartment in Hanover and oversaw her care. Unlike Miss Jennings, Mrs. Madsack thought no less of Anastasia because of her breakdown or her tendency toward paranoia and hysteria. Instead, she treated the younger woman as a member of the family, providing her with the same guidance and discipline that the Madsack children received. Anastasia always remembered the generosity and acceptance of the Madsacks and she emphasized repeatedly to Milukoff that they had played a very special role in her life.

The Madsacks' efforts must not have been easy, for it was at this time that Anastasia discovered what she thought might be a means of escaping the pervasive attention focused on her by the curiosity seekers who never stopped coming. To herself, she was Anastasia, a person who had suffered untold horrors and then been abandoned by her family. But she knew that to others she was only a public figure, a mysterious grand duchess, the daughter of the last Russian czar. She believed that they took no notice of her needs and desires as a human being. To avoid feeling like a hollow object among such people, she decided to redefine her own public image. She began to assume different names for brief periods when in public. Before permanently settling on the pseudonym Anna Anderson, the Grand

Duchess would call herself Frau Lange and Miss Brown. She seemed to be testing which of the many ways her personality had been interpreted by others would allow her to exist with the most freedom and the least scrutiny.

IN late 1937, the Grand Duke of Hesse died of cancer. Within one month, a fatal plane crash took the lives of most of his immediate heirs. As a result, Lord Louis Mountbatten—cousin to Anastasia and uncle to the future Prince Philip of England—effectively became the head of the Hesse family. Now that the man responsible for the Franziska Schanzkowska story was gone, many of Anastasia's supporters hoped that the torment the story had caused her would end. They did not know Lord Mountbatten.

WITHIN a very few months of the Grand Duke's death, the Nazi government in Berlin unexpectedly informed Anastasia that she must meet with the family of Franziska Schanzkowska. The Nazis had begun their own investigation of her case, and despite the flaws in the story of the missing Polish factory worker, some people still believed it. Perhaps the German officials felt that a direct confrontation between the two parties, under the auspices of an official investigation, would finally resolve the matter.

Anastasia refused to comply with the demand. Fallows, still in Europe, intervened on her behalf, but she insisted on having Gleb's help as well. Since her return to Germany, she and Gleb had remained in close contact through frequent correspondence. Their estrangement long forgotten, Anastasia had come to rely on him as her most trusted advisor and confidante, and she now declared that she would do "nothing without Botkin." Gleb did arrive from New York and, along with Fallows and Mrs. Madsack, accompanied a reluctant Anastasia to police headquarters to meet with the Schanzkowska family. The result was what they had expected: the Schanzkowskas did not recognize Anastasia as their sister. Still, Anastasia stormed from the room, angry at even having to endure such an indignity.

Gleb did not remain long in Hanover, but the visit must have given him and Anastasia a chance to review the course of their lives in the nine years since they had last seen one another. Gleb still did all he could to support Anastasia and had written a novel and two biographical works about her as a means of presenting her case to the public. His chief concern would always be to give Anastasia a sense of belonging and security in the face of the abandonment and helplessness imposed on her by her relatives. The battles against the Grand Duchesses Olga and Xenia and the Grand Duke of Hesse had sickened him. Reared to respect royal personages, he had seen firsthand their pettiness and selfishness, and the revelation shocked him. He felt the need to seek a new understanding of the world.

After searching for his father and the imperial family at Ekaterinburg, Gleb had considered becoming a Russian Orthodox priest. Within a few months, however, he abandoned the notion because he rejected that religion's insistence on a secondary and subservient role for women. Still, his deeply spiritual nature led him to investigate other beliefs, including the pagan religions that had preceded Christianity. He was particularly drawn to these ancient faiths precisely because their worship had centered around a supreme goddess, who symbolized the bounty of the earth and the giver of life. Gleb would eventually become devoted to this concept and see in it a means to retreat from disillusionment. He moved his family from New York to a cottage in an isolated rural setting in New Jersey where he founded his own church devoted to the ancient Greek goddess of love and beauty, Aphrodite.

VII.

"Entirely contrary to seeing the truth found out"

ALTHOUGH THERE HAD BEEN much talk of bringing Anastasia's battle for recognition to the legal arena, no significant action was taken on her behalf until 1938. Edward Fallows had given much thought to her case during the prior ten years, and he knew that a proper strategy would be key to his success. He had formulated a plan to put the onus on her relatives by making them explain why they had lied about their early acknowledgments of Anastasia. Exposing their cruel and self-serving machinations in the glare of public view, he felt, would convince any court that the victim of their intrigues must be telling the truth.

If his strategy failed, he would first have to prove that not all the imperial family had died at Ekaterinburg. Next, he would have to show that the sole survivor was the woman who had come to be known as Mrs. Anna Anderson. Fallows knew that all the evidence required to legally prove Anastasia's identity could never be gathered without the cooperation of her relatives. That was no more likely than the possibility of getting the Soviet government to tell the truth. The alternative was to allow the present and untenable situation to continue.

He was confident that his strategy would be successful and that the court case could be completed within a year's time. Yet no matter how long it took, it was certain to be a grueling process, albeit one that would assure her legal identity and her right to her murdered father's fortune. Fallows was very much aware that his client had little interest in lawsuits and even less understanding of what would be involved. She had once asked him if they were not "obscene."

Anastasia had never shown much enthusiasm for obtaining her rightful share of the monies and properties left by the Czar. Rather, it was her supporters, including Gleb, who had seen this plan as the best means of assuring her future independence and well-being. Nor had she ever had any long-standing interest in seeing her authenticity endorsed in a legal forum. Like her most loyal defenders, she never questioned her identity. But she was capable of taking actions to protect herself if she felt truly threatened or injured. The conduct of her relatives in these matters had finally spurred her to agree to the legal suit, and their further machinations could almost always be counted on to evoke a negative reaction from Anastasia.

One such incident occurred in May 1933, when Anastasia was asked to meet with a group of lawyers in Berlin. There she learned that the Romanovs were again thinking of offering her money to drop her claim to be the daughter of the Czar. This time, the conspirators were her Great-Uncle Cyril, the self-appointed Czar-in-Exile, and Felix Youssoupov, who had killed Rasputin and had later tried to kill her to keep her quiet and steal her dowry. This offer was similar to the one from Grand Duchesses Xenia and Olga that Mrs. Leeds had conveyed to Gleb at Oyster Bay. It infuriated Anastasia to learn that the family was still intent on denying her identity out of purely selfish motives, so she stormed from the room. Undoubtedly, she demanded of Fallows that he take action immediately, but at that point there seemed no legal means of defending her from these pernicious attacks. Anastasia never truly understood what her legal battles entailed, and when a quick resolution was not forthcoming, the matter ceased to interest her.

Indeed, this is the attitude that Anastasia always took during the nearly forty years that the court cases consumed. For the most part, she remained uninterested in and aloof from the proceedings. She took an active interest only when she felt that one of her detractors had egregiously libeled or slandered her. She paid no attention to the complicated maneuverings within the courts and wavered between demands for quick resolution and boredom when it was not forthcoming. She remained secure in her knowledge of her own self and in the support of those few who cared for her on a daily basis, and eventually the trials became nothing more than a nuisance. To her mind, they warranted little notice unless attention by the press or visits by lawyers and court officials forced her to acknowledge the proceedings.

In 1933, the Central District Court in Berlin ruled for the first time that the Czar and his family had all died at Ekaterinburg. The court, therefore, declared that because no other survivors existed, only the imperial couple's siblings and their descendants would be entitled to any wealth that remained in Germany. The decision came as a result of a legal action taken by the widow of the Czar's brother, Grand Duke Michael, and her impetus was clearly an attempt to gain control of the Czar's money. The Romanov relatives had long understood that once Anastasia was out of the picture—legally—as a potential heir, the fortune would be theirs for the taking. The widow's efforts were well rewarded. The court determined who held status in Germany as immediate surviving heirs and that their rights to the fortune could also be passed on to their own descendants. In addition to the woman who had originally brought suit, those named included the Grand Duchesses Xenia and Olga, the Grand Duke of Hesse (prior to his death), and the Czarina's sisters, Irene and Victoria.

ALTHOUGH technically the Berlin decision pertained only to whatever remained of the Czar's wealth in Germany, a determination of heirs in that country would certainly go a long way toward aiding claims to monies and properties elsewhere. Without doubt, one of the prime targets in the minds of the Grand Duchesses Xenia and Olga was the dowry money that Anastasia had said was deposited in the Bank of England. Gleb certainly did not hesitate to make this very assertion in his open letter to Grand Duchess Xenia, written in 1928; Edward Fallows believed the money had been deposited there; and in many conversations on the Milukoff tapes, Anastasia undeniably demonstrates her lifelong conviction that her father had put money in the Bank of England and that members of the British royal family had conspired to hide that fact.

Examining some of the details regarding the personalities and circumstantial evidence on this subject reveals why so many people held such strong views about it. The first two people to learn of the money were the Grand Duchesses Olga and Xenia. At the same time, they were aware that it had been set aside specifically for the daughters of the Czar, and therefore might not be considered his personal funds. Xenia was already living in England in the grace-and-favor mansion near Windsor Castle and was intimately involved with the British royal family. King George V and Queen Mary had been instrumental in helping her and Olga dispose of the Dowager Czarina's jewels early in 1929. In the course of that spurious transaction, they had employed the services of Sir Frederick Ponsonby—Keeper of the Privy Purse and private secretary to the king. Peter Bark, the former Finance Minister to Nicholas II and later founder and director of the Anglo-International Bank, was also connected with the transaction. He had been knighted shortly thereafter for his efforts.

Fallows would later subscribe to the theory that the Czar had deposited the funds in the Bank of England, just as Anastasia said, and that Bark—as his former Finance Minister—must have been well aware of the money and its special intended purpose. It was Anastasia who had originally made the connection to Bark, recalling that her father had deposited the money in a secret account at the Bank of England, where access could only be granted through the use of a password. The password, she had explained, was a man's name, and although she could never say for certain who the person was, she knew that his was a short, perhaps Germanic name with an "a" in the middle, and that it had "something to do with a tree." The American lawyer—after piecing together these clues—would go so far as to imply that Bark had used the money set aside by the Czar for his daughters to capitalize the Anglo-International Bank. It was not clear whether Fallows thought that Bark had taken this action in the belief that the imperial family had all died. But Fallows did think that the former minister to the Czar had lied about the deposits to deceive the Grand Duchesses Xenia and Olga.

Further suspicion about Bark's knowledge of and interest in the Czar's money arises from his involvement—along with the Bank of England's Sir Edward Peacock—in retaining counsel for Xenia and Olga once the court proceedings began. At first glance, the interest of the former imperial minister might seem easily explained. He had been entrusted with some of the family's financial affairs before 1917 and had been named trustee of the Dowager Czarina's estate in England by King George V.

Peacock's role might seem perfectly ordinary as well. He had close ties to the King, who continued to provide Xenia and possibly even Olga with money. Moreover, the Bank of England, which Peacock headed and which made the payments, could only benefit if the grand duchesses won the case in Germany and thereby established their rights to the other monies in Europe. This is certainly the story that the two men wanted told. Bark repeatedly asserted that the Czar had called in all his foreign investments to help fund the war effort, and Peacock stated that Nicholas II had never invested any funds in England. This argument, however, is rather easily dismissed. Although the Bank of England and the British royal family would have had a monetary interest in seeing the case settled, Xenia's expenses could hardly have been great enough to cause the level of concern that would continue for decades.

Moreover, there is the matter of the active and repeated involvement of members of the royal family in the efforts to discredit Anastasia, who saw Lord Louis Mountbatten as the prime instigator. He probably first developed an interest in Anastasia's case when he became the *de facto* leader of the Hesses in 1937. Lord Mountbatten quickly became more intensely involved and contributed money to the Romanov side in the German courts. In addition, he came to express—at first in private but later publicly—an almost personal virulence against Anastasia. He was eligible for a portion of the Czar's estate upon the death of his mother, Victoria, and therefore a more personal connection was to be expected. However, his mother lived until 1950. And in any event, he was already enormously wealthy by virtue of his marriage to the granddaughter of Sir Ernest Cassel, one of the wealthiest men in England. His attacks against Anastasia went far beyond what might have been expected from someone who could hope to inherit only a small amount from the German funds. Nor can his adamancy be attributed to a desire to maintain the secrecy of the Russian trip the Grand Duke of Hesse had made during the First World War. Particularly interesting is the fact that Lord Mountbatten's activities became much more public after his nephew, Prince Philip, had married Princess Elizabeth, the granddaughter of King George V. And that coincidence points to the possibility that Anastasia was correct in charging that members of the British royal family themselves had known about her dowry money and had acted in collusion with Grand Duchesses Xenia and Olga to keep it from her.

One document has recently surfaced that would seem to provide the first written evidence to support Anastasia's statements. Grand Duchess Xenia died in 1960, but her last will and testament was not made public. Among its provisions designating properties and interests to her heirs, there is a reference to "the property comprised in a Settlement dated Thirty first day of December One thousand nine hundred and twenty nine and made between myself of the one part and the Right Honourable Sir Frederick Ponsonby, . . . His Excellency Peter Bark, . . . and Edward Robert Peacock of the other part." In this one short phrase the man that Edward Fallows accused of stealing the dowry money is linked with both the director of the Bank of England and the Keeper of the Privy Purse for King George V. That some sort of special arrangement was made with Grand Duchess Xenia after the sale of her mother's jewels and after her sister Olga had returned to Denmark in 1929, is undeniable. That the arrangement involved the money deposited by the Czar in the Bank of England is not unlikely.

At the very least, this document raises some interesting possibilities. The Grand Duchess Xenia might have gone to her friends the King and Queen, or perhaps even directly to Peter Bark, upon learning of Anastasia's story about the money in the Bank of England. If so, she would soon have discovered that her niece was correct. If Fallows was right, Bark was intent on hiding from the surviving Romanovs the fact that he had used the dowry funds to establish the Anglo-International Bank. But he could not have concealed that fact from the British royal family. For a former Russian minister to suddenly be able to capitalize such a huge financial institution in England could hardly have escaped the notice of King George V and his closest advisers.

Thus not only Bark, but the British royal family itself would have had a personal stake in avoiding any controversy that would have hinted at collusion in appropriating the Czar's money. Consequently, they might have offered Grand Duchess Xenia a "Settlement" in exchange for her silence. Her muteness was probably total. Because the Grand Duchess Olga remained impoverished, Xenia probably never even told her sister that the money was, indeed, in

England. After all, even if the funds were discovered, they had been reserved for the Czar's daughters. Grand Duchess Xenia would not be entitled to them if Anastasia could prove her identity. If Xenia revealed her knowledge of the money, her niece's authenticity would have been almost automatically confirmed—for how else could her aunt have learned of the money's existence? At the same time, the British would have had no objection to the Grand Duchess's attempts to acquire a portion of the Czar's other investments. Thus, they could have offered a "Settlement" through their representatives—Ponsonby, Bark, and Peacock. This would have both assured Xenia's silence and guaranteed their continued alliance in her battle against Anastasia.

Among all the Romanov relatives, Grand Duchess Xenia was undeniably one of the most adamant in denying Anastasia's claim. Shortly after the 1929 "Settlement," Xenia's estranged husband, Grand Duke Alexander, wrote a book in which he tried to prove that the Czar had never been a rich man and that whatever money was left would be so little as to be negligible. All the time, Anastasia's aunt kept up a public and legal battle to lay claim to whatever "negligible" funds existed, and Bark and Peacock acted as her legal advisors.

For now, a description of the exact nature of any such arrangement can be no more than speculative. The British royal family continued to pay Grand Duchess Xenia until she died—a good deal longer than royal duty might require in caring for a first cousin. Despite the conventional wisdom that she had lived nearly impoverished, the grand duchess died leaving an estate of nearly $350,000 in 1960. It might be interesting to discover whether this money included any of these payments she received from the British. It would be more interesting to know whether the payments were made in lieu of what she could have expected to receive as a portion of the funds in England that Fallows had accused Bark of stealing, had Anastasia not survived.

Finally, it might be most intriguing—especially given Anastasia's strong and repeated accusations—to delve further into the motivations of Lord Mountbatten. He had worked diligently all his life to enhance the status of his family, including the House of Hesse; in 1947, he had successfully arranged the marriage of his nephew Philip to the future Queen Elizabeth II of England. Once the two families were merged so completely, he became a devoted and protective influence in the lives of the British royal couple and their children, especially Prince Charles. Thus, Lord Mountbatten might have felt an even greater need to completely discredit Anastasia. If her identity were legally confirmed, her attorneys might discover that the British royal family had perhaps colluded with Bark to keep the Czar's deposits hidden. Such a revelation, or even the hint of it, would be scandalous. Because the court cases centered on funds in Germany, it would have been highly suspect for a member of the British royal family to take an active part in challenging Anastasia's claim. In 1950, however, Lord Mountbatten became eligible for a portion of whatever monies might exist in Germany. Moreover, he had a strong and proven interest in safeguarding the reputation of the family. In the end, if members of the British royalty were intent on actively avoiding certain embarrassing revelations, they could turn only to Lord Mountbatten to serve that cause. This is one possible explanation for his actions. But no matter what his reasoning or motives, Anastasia would always view his activities as confirmation that he had willingly assumed the mantle of the Grand Duke of Hesse. Even more than his uncle before him, Lord Mountbatten became her most reviled enemy.

ALTHOUGH there was no immediate disposition of any money as a result of the Berlin court's ruling in 1933, Fallows was aware that there were deposits at the Mendelssohn Bank in Berlin and that eventually the Romanov relatives would try to obtain them. Germany was clearly the country in which the crucial legal suit on Anastasia's behalf would eventually need to be filed. Because he was not licensed to practice law in Germany, Fallows set about trying to find local counsel. During the next five years, Anastasia would constantly revoke the power of attorney granted to Fallows. At one point, she actually fired him and apparently sought to engage a German attorney of her own choosing.

In the end, however, she returned to Fallows as her most trusted advocate in these matters, and indeed his loyalty to her never abated. It is not known precisely who paid his bills, although there is some evidence that in the late 1920s, his efforts were subsidized by the

Jennings family and perhaps some of their friends who had planned to invest in Grandanor. The corporation apparently never issued shares to any investors, however, and eventually money from the venture must have stopped altogether. As Fallows doggedly pursued his cause, he ended up spending a great deal of his own funds and died before seeing any of the compensation that had been promised him under the terms of Grandanor's charter.

Prior to his death and with the aid of two German attorneys, Paul Leverkuehn and Kurt Vermehren, Fallows finally succeeded in bringing the suit to court in 1938. The previous year, the Berlin tribunal had issued a certificate of inheritance which authorized the payment of the money left deposited in the Mendelssohn Bank to the heirs that had been named in its 1933 action. Officials of the bank wrote to Anastasia as "Imperial Highness," telling her that the money had indeed been distributed and that she should protect her own interests by petitioning the very same court to withdraw the certificate of inheritance. A petition on her behalf was filed on August 17, 1938.

In 1941 the Central District Court in Berlin rejected Anastasia's petition, an action that finally set up the possibility for an appeal of the 1938 decision and a hearing on her case. Before going ahead with the formal legal process, Leverkuehn decided to attempt a compromise with the relatives opposing his client. He made approaches to the King of Denmark, among others, because the Danish government had forced Ambassador Zahle to remain silent all these years. Moreover, Zahle's findings had been suppressed at the direction of Dowager Czarina Marie's Danish relatives. Before Fallows died, Leverkuehn had reportedly discussed this strategy with him: "The Danish King has more than once expressed that the Danish royal family is entirely neutral and only wants the truth to be found out. If the Zahle papers are not produced . . . this would be entirely contrary to the intention of seeing . . . the truth found out." Leverkuehn's requests to the Danish were rejected, however, and the appeal went forward.

As the Second World War engulfed Europe, progress in the court slowed. Although Leverkuehn and Vermehren continued to file papers with the appeals panel, the court in 1942 halted all action on the case pending the end of wartime hostilities.

VIII.

"The burning streets"

ANASTASIA'S LIFE had remained largely unaffected by the rise
of the Nazis in Germany and the early war years in Europe. Apart
from forcing her to meet with the Schanzkowska family, the Nazi
government had not interfered with her activities. Like many others,
she remained untouched personally by the ruthlessness with which
the government assumed control over the country. She was largely
apolitical, reflecting the narrow and elitist views that had been part
of her imperial upbringing. Having been raised at a court where
Jews, Gypsies, and Freemasons were regarded as the root of all evil,
she remained unconcerned about the developments under Nazism.
She had long sought every means possible to isolate herself from a
world she believed had gone awry. To her mind, the Nazis had at
least exercised some control over the chaos that followed the First
World War. She certainly never subscribed to the hero worship that
surrounded Adolf Hitler, but she credited him with creating the new
Germany.

She was, therefore, pleased to receive an invitation one day to visit
the Führer in Berlin. Anastasia's usual excellent memory for dates
would fail her in her recollection of this event, but the meeting
probably took place in 1940 or early 1941. She remembered only
that one day a large black limousine took her to the Reichstag
Building, where she was led down a long hallway accompanied by
two tall, handsome guards. Everything in the building, she later
recalled, was built on a grandiose scale. They eventually arrived at a
set of massive double doors which opened into a large office. Perched
on the corner of a large desk was Adolf Hitler.

As she entered the room, he rose and bowed to her. They sat in
chairs facing one another as he began to explain why he had wanted

to meet with her. He said that his government had conducted a thorough investigation of her claim to be the Grand Duchess and that its indisputable conclusion was that she was Anastasia. He said that he knew the British royal family had betrayed first her family and then her, but that he would destroy them in this war. He would also soon invade the Soviet Union and annihilate the Bolshevik government that had murdered her parents. He promised that once this feat was accomplished, he would personally restore the Romanov monarchy. Anastasia said later that she was very impressed by the Führer's courtly manners. He acted always as a gentleman, referring to her as "Your Imperial Highness," and showed every deference to her station. She felt that she had finally been officially recognized by the German government, and she was forever proud that its supreme leader had taken the time to reassure her of this fact.

As the war progressed, the British and American bombing missions over German cities made living in Hanover increasingly precarious for Anastasia. She found temporary refuge outside the city with various people, often German nobility or Anthroposophists she had met through Harriet Rathlef and Prince Frederick. One of those who showed a particular interest in·her was Baroness Monica Miltitz, a leader in the Anthroposophical movement and a self-proclaimed authority on the German Romantic writer Novalis. The Baroness had been introduced to Anastasia in the 1930s by Prince Frederick, who had become more involved in Anastasia's life since their meeting at Ilten. He often accompanied her on her travels and was undoubtedly the reason that Baroness Miltitz had many times entertained the Grand Duchess at the Miltitz family's castle, Seven Oaks, near Meissen.

Baroness Miltitz's interest in Anastasia centered around her belief in the tenets of Anthroposophy. The Baroness fully subscribed to the ideas set down by the group's founder, Dr. Rudolf Steiner, whom she interpreted as having felt that "different cultural leaders are the impulse carriers of the intellectual world" by which "the people" would come to know of cosmic influences. The ability to relate to "the people" was, in turn, closely tied to an understanding of the forces of nature and the earth which peasants, and others who lived off the land, felt innately. Finally, the Anthroposophists believed that in each individual was a kind of special soul, an "ether body," which—although sometimes suppressed—bonded best with the "cosmic influence." Baroness Miltitz saw in the Grand Duchess "the child of Russia—completely the entity and destiny carried by these people. She had the controlled vitality, the Russian 'ether body,' and the connection with the land." The Baroness's later writings would show clearly how she came to believe that Anastasia symbolized the collective experience of the soul of Russia.

When it became necessary for Anastasia to flee from Hanover because of the war, the Baroness insisted that she come to Seven Oaks. Her guest arrived with two trunks filled with her most treasured possessions. Anastasia would always say they were worth "ten million dollars." Included among them were thousands of the photographs, documents, and medical records she had been able to compile; pieces of Romanov memorabilia she had been given over the years—including a gold chalice used by her brother; and the letters Grand Duchess Olga had written to her at Mommsen. The Baroness decided that in order to protect what Anastasia called her "precious goods," they should be placed in iron vaults and buried on the grounds of Seven Oaks.

Anastasia never felt comfortable under the Baroness's roof and stayed only sporadically at the Miltitz castle. In addition to espousing extreme views, the Baroness was sixteen years her senior and acted as a stern mother, protective but controlling. Anastasia resented such treatment and after only a short while at Seven Oaks, regretted having left Hanover. She insisted on returning to her apartment, but the Baroness and others knew how unsafe it would be for the Grand Duchess to leave. They became even more alarmed when her health began to fail once again.

During one of her visits to the Baroness, Anastasia collapsed from exhaustion and the effects of a new bout of tuberculosis. Her hostess remained constantly at her side. As Anastasia succumbed to fever, the Anthroposophist would overhear her "speak[ing] tenderly with her parents . . . and with eternal sadness, [she] spoke about her meetings with her siblings in a dream."

Undoubtedly, the Baroness cared for Anastasia as best she knew how. She would recall later what was for her a particularly moving scene with the Grand Duchess during this time:

[S]he . . . lay in bed by an open window which looked out onto a park. We had to black out the lights because of the war, but we left the windows open, and I groped my way in the dark to an armchair next to her bed. Then she said, 'Say something,' and I gave her the fundamentals of Anthroposophy . . . and spoke to her about the evolution of man in relationship to the cosmos. . . . We could not see each other, but I felt how she was literally drinking my words. Eventually she remembered her dead family, and then I said The Lord's Prayer in the following manner:

Our Father, who art in heaven!

Hallowed be thy name
in Germany, in Poland, in Russia, in China,
in Japan, in the United States of America,
in England, in France, in the Netherlands,
in Scandinavia, in Italy, in the Balkans.

Thy kingdom come,
to all countries in Europe,
to all countries in Asia,
to all countries in Australia,
to all countries in Africa,
to all countries in America.

Thy will be done, on earth as it is in heaven.
let it be done in Germany,
let it be done in Poland,
let it be done in Russia,
let it be done in Japan,
let it be done in the United States,
let it be done in England,
let it be done in France,
let it be done in the Netherlands,
let it be done in Scandinavia,
let it be done in Italy,
let it be done in the Balkans.

Give us this day our daily bread,
and give it to all men on earth as a banquet

of love
in the spiritual.

And forgive us our trespasses,
us in Germany,
as we forgive those who trespass against us.

And lead us not into temptation,
But deliver us from evil.

AMEN

Despite the Baroness's Anthroposophistic invocation, Anastasia's condition worsened. She refused to eat and treated her hostess "with the utmost sharpness and coldness."

As Anastasia eventually grew somewhat stronger, she became even more determined to leave Seven Oaks and return to Hanover. This time her insistence could not be overcome. The Baroness remembered the parting this way: "I knew that she was very worried about Hanover because of the attackers. She wouldn't let herself be held back. . . . I took her to the train station . . . away from this place which had up till now been so happy."

ANASTASIA was well aware of what might await her in Hanover, but so great was her distaste for the extreme control that Baroness Miltitz tried to impose on her that she was willing to risk returning to what she would later describe to Milukoff as "the burning streets." Her conversation with Milukoff about her experiences in Hanover during the Second World War provides the only documentation of this portion of her life, which, as she told him, "is never recorded by *nobody. That nobody is interested to hear*," as opposed to the questions endlessly asked about all other aspects of her life.

Her account is so gripping, however, that it can best be told only in her own words.

All Hanover washed away! And our little house was standing. . . . All was smashed, but our little house was standing. The large windows all was out, doors torn off, everything out, but the house was standing . . . it was standing. I had at once doors put in and at once were the windows put in, that was quickly done. And then I had done the mistake to stay there for a few days, I wanted to stay there.

[T]he lights all was put out, you see, because when the bombs were falling the lights went on alone. So all the lights were put out, everything was taken out, that this could not happen. . . . [I]t is ten o'clock in the evening and I went to bed. Had undressed, had put a nightgown on, and had gone to bed. And one had warned me, 'For God's sake, don't undress. Do not undress!' But I had undressed myself completely, and put a nightgown on.

I was terrible sleepy, and had gone to sleep and suddenly is the room lit white. White lit is the room. Snow *white* is the room lit. I am flying out of the bed, and the people are yelling, shrieking, 'Come out! Come out! In the cellar, in the cellar.' Shrieking and yelling. Frightful!

And I [got] out of the bed [and went] to the window, and there hangs a 'Christmas tree,' directly at the corner, hanging. They were called 'Christmas trees,' these signs which the Americans and the British throw down. They throw four such trees. . . . When they centered something out, where they wanted to throw the bombs in, then they made it with four such trees, such lighted trees that they were called 'Christmas trees.' And such a beast was hanging just at my corner, directly.

What Anastasia must have seen as she awoke was the piercing light from one of many parachute flares which the bomber pilots dropped to mark their nighttime targets. She understood immediately what it meant, for as she explained to Milukoff,

[A]lways . . . the bombs didn't go through, but exploded *over* the houses. That was a different type of bombs, you know? It was several types . . . that exploded over the houses. They exploded over the houses and the air pressure was so frightful that all went to ashes. Finite. All was pressed to ashes. . . . When somebody run somewhere out and was uncovered, their head was torn, their stomach was torn, and all was torn, the arms were torn, and whatnot all. That has happened, yes. 'X' times, 'X' times, and 'X' times it has happened. Almost happened to me, too.

She knew she had little time before the attack would begin.

And I, as quick as I could, somehow managed to put something on me . . . and the tiny bit [of my possessions] what I had, I snatched. And in the shock [I] had forgotten to open the window and shut the door behind me. I run [toward] the cellar and am still confused when I arrived down. And the people yelling and shrieking! All were shrieking, 'Come here! Come here! Come here!'

And I stand still near the chimney there . . . and I was thinking, 'Now, for God's sake, I have shut the doors, and the window is shut. All is shut. That will happen something dreadful, that [an explosion] will tear [it] all out. And I was taking my keys which was hanging around my neck, [thinking] 'Shall I run . . . up? Shall I not? For God's sake, shall I run? . . . .' I had already decided that I intended to fly up [the stairs] to open everything.

And in that second is this big explosion directly over the house. Directly over the house. And I had been standing near the chimney and the people yelling, and I standing like an idiot, paralyzed, unmovable. Standing on my feet. I didn't fall down, nothing. Just imagine, I didn't fall down. I was not sitting, nothing. . . . I just stood paralyzed.

But all the [soot] from the chimney, all this cloud of dust which came because it was breaking. . . . It had reached my lungs. . . . I had got too much from this dirt, this dust, on my lungs. And I was from that moment in a condition which was not very pleasant. I was coughing from that moment. It [continued] for several years, I got suffocating conditions from this terrible mess.

But . . . when I would have run up in that second, it would have just catched me on the stairs. The doors were torn out . . . the windows were torn out, all was torn out, *everything* was torn out. It would have torn my head off and opened my, torn my body up.

Then, a woman who had left the electric train, was driving the electric train, wanted to run to her children home quickly too. It catched her, this bomb, on the street, when she was running. Tore her head off, tore her stomach open. She was torn entirely open. And so this was, in the last second, prevented [to happen to me], that I am still as a poor idiot sitting here. Otherwise this would not have been the case.

The scene outside was "*Horrid!* It was black and all on fire. All the streets on fire . . . [and] I was running through the burning streets of Hanover. . . . Everywhere the houses were falling like nothing [held them] together, in fire. And in the black night behind, and smoke—the bombs were on my head almost falling. That I have passed through."

Anastasia would see even more devastation, as she tried to find safe haven in Hanover.

> Once the little house in which I was living went, too. And we were in the cellar. We had no other possibility, [the bombers] were suddenly there, it was in the midday, they were suddenly there. We had no possibility to run to the bunker, [so we] run in the cellar. And the bombs were raining in a dreadful way and this little house went so. And I saw how the walls were moving so. It went. And I just shut my eyes and put my face in my fur cloak . . . in the cellar of our house.

Her description of these events on the Milukoff tapes is detailed and vivid, but Anastasia's tone and manner in telling this story indicates the distance she placed between herself and the devastation of the bombings. Her entire world had been torn away by war and revolution when she was but a young girl, and she had been forced to relive that agony countless times in her own mind. As horrifying as she found the Second World War, she had by then developed an almost fatalistic attitude about the lengths to which men and nations would go to impose their will on one another, and she could view such events only with a sense of irony and dispassion.

WITH the few possessions she had managed to salvage, Anastasia left Hanover and went to stay for the duration of the war with yet another acquaintance who had a castle in the eastern part of Germany. As was her practice, she traveled under the name Anna Anderson, and her presence in the area was kept secret. She remained in relative safety there, until the Russian occupation troops began to solidify their position in 1946. One day, as she was standing in the kitchen, a Soviet soldier entered and demanded that she approach him. Fearing that he might rape her, she picked up a knife and pointed it at him, her eyes projecting utter hatred and scorn for this symbol of her family's Bolshevik assassins. He backed away.

Even though she survived this confrontation with a representative of a government that would surely want her dead, Anastasia's friends felt that her only hope for survival was to flee back toward the West. An appeal went out to Prince Frederick, who arrived to take Anastasia to his family's palatial estate at Altenburg. They stayed there only briefly before gathering a few possessions and heading toward the western occupied zones.

All that is known of their journey is that at one point they had to cross a river in a small rowboat, which began to take on water. The Prince, fearing that they would sink unless the load was lightened, picked up one of Anastasia's suitcases and tossed it overboard. She screamed, "No," and stood up, nearly capsizing the boat, but she managed to grab the bag before it was swept away. Anastasia quickly opened the case to check its contents—the few remaining mementos of her life—and was relieved to see that the photograph album from Tatiana Botkin, containing pictures from her childhood, was undamaged.

BOOK FOUR

"Who I Am and Who I Pretend to Be"

The last Russian czar [was] murdered with all his family except for Anastasia, who took refuge in Hollywood.

—WILLIAM F. BUCKLEY, JR.

I.

"They did not suspect who she was"

ANASTASIA AND PRINCE FREDERICK finally approached
the end of their journey, the border of the Soviet zone, only to find
that it had been sealed. Nevertheless, even this last barrier to her
escape from the Red soldiers was not insurmountable. She would
later hint to Milukoff that she and the Prince had been smuggled
across the border with the aid of the Red Cross and a black American
soldier. The Grand Duchess was quickly placed under medical
supervision at a clinic near the little village of Unterlengenhardt, an
Anthroposophist enclave at the edge of the Black Forest. Anastasia
must have been relieved to escape "the Bolsheviks" again and to win a
respite from her seemingly endless journeys.

While Anastasia rested, Prince Frederick sought a place that could
provide her shelter once she was released. He had lost all access to
his family's enormous wealth, but he had managed to escape with
some of his funds. He reportedly used this money to buy a former
military barrack and convert it into a small home for the Grand
Duchess.

The villagers in Unterlengenhardt did not know the true identity
of Mrs. Anderson, but the Anthroposophists who lived there
learned of her story from Prince Frederick. One of this group, Adele
Heydebrand, volunteered to live with Anastasia and oversee her
care. Prince Frederick was pleased to see the Grand Duchess in the
company of such a compassionate and understanding woman. Mrs.
Heydebrand had been a friend of one of the former nurses at Stillachhaus and, therefore, already knew how difficult Anastasia could
be. Moreover, Mrs. Heydebrand had cared for Rudolf Steiner during the First World War, and the Prince felt she could be entrusted to
oversee the needs of the Grand Duchess. Anastasia had already

become an important figure for many of the Anthroposophists, and she would later recount to Milukoff her own version of Adele Heydebrand's devotion to the movement's founder:

> Dr. Steiner was very ill with his lungs and [Mrs. Heydebrand] . . . had bought . . . a goat and had [it] in her garden during the war . . . One didn't get milk and whatnot all . . . and she ever herself was milking this goat and brought to Dr. Steiner this milk. She kept Dr. Steiner, in fact, alive with this goat what she had bought. [Mrs. Heydebrand] . . . was the footing in all this . . . [and] played a very big part in perfecting Dr. Steiner.

Adele Heydebrand, a descendant of a wealthy Dutch family, was twenty-two years older than Anastasia and seemed to understand exactly how to take care of her. In addition to calming her when she became excited or upset, Mrs. Heydebrand could ignore the imperious and demanding airs that Anastasia so often displayed. The two women quickly established a rapport and settled comfortably into a life in the small barrack, far removed from the outside world.

ONE of the first things Anastasia had done when she arrived at Unterlengenhardt was to write to her old friend Gleb Botkin in the United States. Although they had corresponded actively prior to the war, he had been without word of her for a long time. As the war intensified and the bombing raids destroyed more and more German cities, Gleb had been unable to find out what had happened to Anastasia. As far as he knew, she had continued to live in Hanover. His daughter, Marina Botkin Schweitzer, remembered listening to radio reports of the fighting in Europe and how her father would pace the floor, asking aloud, "What has happened to the Grand Duchess?" Gleb was overjoyed when he received the letter from Unterlengenhardt with the news that she was safe and protected.

The two friends quickly reestablished their correspondence and for the next twenty years would write one another often, as much as several times a week. Anastasia trusted Gleb's judgment implicitly and sought his advice and opinion about all manner of things, from the court trials and her lawyers to common gossip in the small

German village. Frequently, especially after Gleb moved with his wife to a cottage in rural New Jersey to pursue his studies relating to the Church of Aphrodite, his letters would end with descriptions of the forest in which he lived. Anastasia must have felt that their lives had become even more closely entwined, despite the great distance that separated them, as she read his accounts of the birds and flowers, for one of the things she enjoyed most about Unterlengenhardt was the beauty of its rural setting.

Gleb also corresponded with her attorneys, Prince Frederick, and others who had the responsibility for overseeing the Grand Duchess's affairs in Germany. He would then comment on these exchanges when writing to Anastasia. Gleb's correspondence, much of which has been saved by his daughter and remains unpublished, provides new insight into his relationship with Anastasia, as well as their views of events that unfolded over the next two decades.

One of the themes developed early in the letters was Anastasia's growing concern about money. She had never before expressed much interest in the wealth left by her father and, in general, had few concerns about income. This had been the case particularly after her return to Germany, when the Madsacks and her other friends had paid all her expenses. Now, however, she saw how the war had changed everything. Even royalty had not escaped its devastating effects. As she later told Milukoff, the fate of the Princess of Italy made a lasting impression on her:

> Because the King of Italy had gone over to the Americans, had the Americans to come into Italy, and they had taken Mussolini as a prisoner . . . they [the Nazis] had taken the daughter . . . and put [her] in a concentration camp where she had under some different name been kept. It's so horrid! I could die!

Anastasia had followed Princess Mafalda's story since her marriage to Anastasia's distant relative, Prince Philip of Hesse. The Princess's demise must have increased Anastasia's fear that "everything was lost."

Further evidence of the need to secure her own resources was closer at hand. Because of the war, Prince Frederick had lost his great wealth and Baroness Miltitz had been forced to flee from eastern

Germany, leaving behind her magnificent estate, Seven Oaks. She had lived in severely reduced circumstances somewhere in the western zone before finally arriving in Unterlengenhardt. Anastasia realized for the first time in her life that the people who were looking after her might not have enough means to continue doing so for very long. She would have to find her own way of making money. Not long after settling in the German village, the Grand Duchess wrote to Gleb seeking his assistance once again to write her autobiography.

Apparently, Prince Frederick had also written to Gleb about the possibility of an autobiography and had inquired about the legal concerns such a project might entail. Gleb's response indicated that he had sought the advice of an American attorney and had been assured that Anastasia was "not legally obligated to anybody" in the United States. The reference could only have referred to the Grandanor Corporation, whose plans for overseeing all legal and monetary issues for Anastasia had never been activated, even though it remained a properly chartered business operation.

In addition to seeking legal advice, Gleb spoke with Isaac Don Levine, a New York magazine editor and writer of Russian descent. As a young reporter, Levine had accompanied a group of American senators on a tour of the Soviet Union, including a visit to the Ipatiev House in Ekaterinburg. After that journey, he had maintained a strong interest in the Romanov family and had already become known as an expert on the imperial couple and their children. In his letters to Anastasia, Gleb described Levine as a dispassionate and trustworthy person who might be able to help them find a publisher. The only record of Anastasia's attempt to engage in the new book project is a fifty-page memoir of her youth dictated to Baroness Miltitz, who had recently resettled in Unterlengenhardt. The memoir was never published as part of any book, and despite Levine's attempts to contact publishers on her behalf, the project never went any further.

Levine did provide another, more important service to the Grand Duchess. In the late 1940s, Anastasia became desperately ill at Unterlengenhardt and needed penicillin. Whether supplies of the medicine were short or her friends simply could not afford to buy it is unknown, but an appeal went out to Gleb in America. He turned to Isaac Don Levine, who arranged for a shipment of the antibiotic to be sent to Germany. Anastasia would always believe that Levine's intervention had saved her life, and she held him in the highest regard during the years to come.

ALTHOUGH Anastasia's life settled into a routine rather quickly, she was not unaffected by the war's destruction of Germany. By 1947, the court system had been restored in the newly emerging West Germany, and her case—which had begun in 1938—was now reactivated. The records and evidence compiled by her attorneys, however, had been destroyed when Kurt Leverkuehn's offices in Berlin were bombed. The files of the former Berlin Central District Court, where the case had been heard before the war, were now in the Soviet zone of the divided city. As they prepared to go to trial, her attorneys faced the daunting task of reconstructing documentation, depositions, and internal memoranda. They had hoped for some assistance from Annette Fallows, the daughter of Anastasia's American attorney, but Miss Fallows remained bitter, attributing her father's early death to his relentless pursuit of Anastasia's case and the fact that he had never been paid for his efforts. She refused to accede to the German attorneys' request for cooperation.

Nevertheless, Leverkuehn and Paul Vermehren filed their official appeal of the 1938 decision releasing the Czar's monies from the Berlin bank to Anastasia's relatives. The attorneys continued to reconstruct evidence and gather new information to present to the appeals panel, but another ten years would pass before the case progressed far enough for the court to complete its consideration.

DESPITE her concerns about money, Anastasia's life during the first few years in Unterlengenhardt was generally peaceful and happy. The people of the village, long used to the colony of Anthroposophists Dr. Steiner had established there, seemed to readily accept Mrs. Anderson. According to Baroness Miltitz, "they did not suspect who she was. . . . But when later it became known . . . it caused no sensation. . . . They had come to know her as a kind lady who lived among them and was interested in their lives. . . ."

Anastasia lived very much like everyone else who had survived the war. The barrack she shared with Mrs. Heydebrand was no larger than fourteen by eighteen feet, a spartan but comfortable structure. Anastasia had no money and "went to the forest to gather timber for her fire, to pick berries and mushrooms." She would also go to the nearby village when other supplies were needed, but generally preferred to remain close to her home in Unterlengenhardt. There she could rely on Mrs. Heydebrand to prepare the vegetarian meals she now preferred. Her companion was a devoted and understanding caretaker who successfully shielded her from the intrusions of the outside world.

In addition, for the first time, Anastasia was the center of a close-knit group of women who seemed interested only in ensuring her well-being. This growing circle of acquaintances began with Adele Heydebrand's sister, Annemarie Mutius, and Baroness Miltitz. Together with Anastasia's companion, they formed a core group of English speakers who ran errands, monitored the mail, and wrote letters that Anastasia dictated. Most important, they sought to ease the strain and anxiety of trying to survive in postwar Germany. As the Baroness recalled later, "in the first years . . . she lived like all the other fugitives. . . . She was desperately poor all the time. . . . Finally, it was arranged that she got a small sum out of the social funds of the state treasury." While these women handled the day-to-day chores of caring for Anastasia, Prince Frederick managed other matters. He had been granted her power of attorney and followed the court trials closely. In addition, he had assumed the role of her spokesman, and others began to look to him for an interpretation of the Grand Duchess's lifestyle and character. For a time, then, Anastasia remained happy and purposely ignorant of the world outside.

By the early 1950s, however, her situation became well known beyond Unterlengenhardt, especially after the Prince began to more actively champion her cause. One result was that Annaliese Thomasius, a former governess of Empress Hermine's family—the House of Reuss—also settled nearby and quickly became one of Anastasia's most trusted companions among the older women who already surrounded her. Knowledge of her whereabouts also raised the interest and concern of many of her distant relatives, the great majority of whom were related to Anastasia through her mother. They began to visit Unterlengenhardt and invited her and Mrs.

Heydebrand to stay in their villas and castles. In addition to the recognition and acceptance they accorded Anastasia as a member of the family, often calling her "aunt" or "cousin," they sent her valuable and rare Romanov artifacts. The little barrack soon overflowed with priceless paintings, silver, photographs, and furniture—including a bed once slept in by her great-grandmother, Queen Victoria.

Among the growing number of visitors to the village during this period were two people whom Anastasia would always remember fondly. The first was Crown Princess Cecilie of Prussia, the daughter-in-law of Kaiser Wilhelm II. Anastasia had warm feelings toward the late German Emperor and his second wife Hermine and was particularly moved when the Crown Princess began coming to the barrack and almost immediately attested to her authenticity. Well respected among the remaining German nobility, the Crown Princess was tremendously wealthy, and her recognition of the Grand Duchess helped open even more doors. They became good friends, seeing one another frequently, whether at Unterlengenhardt or at the castles and estates Anastasia and Mrs. Heydebrand occasionally visited.

The other important visitor was Lili Dehn, who arrived in 1954. She had been one of the Czarina's closest friends at Czarskoe Selo in the days just prior to the imperial family's exile to Siberia. Mrs. Dehn had settled in South America and, after entreaties by some of Anastasia's relatives, had decided to come to Germany and determine for herself whether Mrs. Anderson was indeed the Grand Duchess. As someone who had known the Romanovs well, Mrs. Dehn had little doubt of her ability to unmask the woman, should she prove a fraud.

Mrs. Dehn brought with her to Unterlengenhardt a copy of a book she had written in 1922 entitled *The Real Tsaritsa*, which contained a black-and-white photograph of Czarina Alexandra. Anastasia had never heard of the book and asked to see it. When she opened the cover and saw the picture of her mother, Anastasia turned to her visitor and said she remembered the dress the Czarina was wearing at the time. It had been made of brown velvet. Mrs. Dehn knew that what Anastasia said was true. She also realized that only those who had been present when the photograph was taken or who had the most intimate familiarity with the Czarina's wardrobe could have made such an accurate identification. As Anastasia would later tell Milukoff, Mrs. Dehn stayed "a bit long"—six days, in fact—but by the time she left, she believed that the woman in this small German village was undeniably the lost Russian princess.

Lili Dehn's visit was but a capstone on the tower of recognition constructed by those who mattered most to Anastasia: old acquaintances, many members of her family, and European nobles. The acceptance she received at this level echoed the support she received at home from the loyal Adele Heydebrand and the small circle of acquaintances in Unterlengenhardt. The "creators" had apparently lost interest in her, and she felt certain that her friend Prince Frederick could deflect any troublesome intrusions. Although money was still a problem, she could feel secure and protected. The Grand Duchess seemed to be on the verge of achieving the kind of existence she had desired for so long.

II.
"There the unhappiness started"

IN DECEMBER 1954, New York anxiously awaited the opening of a new Broadway play, *Anastasia*. The producers had cast Viveca Lindfors, the beautiful Swedish-born star of Hollywood, in the title role. Eugenie Leontovitch, one of the grand dames of the New York stage, was to play the other female lead, the Dowager Czarina Marie.

The play was loosely based on Anastasia's life before her trip to America and even today remains the most famous of the fictionalized accounts of her existence. The story takes place in Berlin. The main character is a young, anonymous Russian woman who has been hospitalized in "Dalsdorf" and has taken the name Anna. After leaving there, she tries to commit suicide by jumping off a bridge, only to be rescued by a Russian prince named "Bounine." He has heard of the lost Romanov Grand Duchess Anastasia and, with his Russian expatriate friends, decides to coach Anna so that she can pose as the Czar's daughter and inherit his estate. Slowly they begin to realize that there is no need to coach the woman, that she is the real Anastasia. A meeting is finally arranged between the woman and her grandmother, Dowager Czarina Marie, the one person who can identify her unquestionably. In the play's most dramatic scene, the two are reunited in a tearful encounter. A few moments before her grandmother is to publicly acknowledge her before a group of Russian nobles and the bankers who have held the Czar's money, Anastasia disappears. The play ends with her grandmother's realization that all Anastasia really wanted was a normal life.

The New York play was an adaptation by Guy Bolton from the work of a French playwright, Marcelle Maurette. There is no indication that the play was ever performed in France before being translated and brought to the London stage, where it was produced by Laurence Olivier. The play was a great success in England, and the New York production achieved even greater acclaim.

Anastasia was not involved in any aspect of the play. In fact, Marcelle Maurette wrote the original version thinking that the woman once known as Anna Tschaikovsky had died. After learning that the Grand Duchess was alive, Maurette paid Anastasia for the use of her story. Some authors report that the payment was voluntary, but Guy Bolton implied that the money was paid only after Anastasia's attorneys threatened to file suit on her behalf prior to a production of the play in Germany.

The letters of Gleb Botkin tell a different story. In November 1953, well over a year before *Anastasia* opened in New York, he wrote to the Grand Duchess regarding the London production and plans that were already underway in the United States to make a movie based on the work:

> One of the biggest motion picture producers in this country, Warner Brothers, have bought that horrible London play and started already to produce it when they remembered me. They started looking for me and finally found me here—in the forest. . . .

One good result has already been achieved. In spite of the money they have put into it and the high hopes they had in connection with it, Warner Brothers will *not* produce the London play [as a movie].

Gleb was very worried about Anastasia's being connected in any way to the Maurette-Bolton play, for it was all fabrication. He felt that if she lent her name or her authorization to the work, whether tacitly or through a legal agreement, her chances for proving her claim and selling her true story would be ruined.

Gleb had already begun negotiating for a different movie, one that would benefit his friend in Germany:

> Now, the rest is as yet quite indefinite and it may happen that Warner Brothers will not be able to do anything at all. . . . Much depends on whether you would be able and willing to come to this country.

> The motion picture would be based . . . as much as possible on what you yourself will dictate. Warner Brothers would give you all the time you want, but on condition that if somebody else would buy the London play which they have now refused, you will authorize a lawyer to bring action against it. The London play is so horrible that you would be absolutely certain to win such an action.

> For dictating the material for the motion picture, Warner Brothers would, of course, make a payment to you. . . . Again, I repeat, that nothing has been decided as yet and perhaps nothing will happen at all. But they are thinking of offering you $250,000—that is a quarter of a million dollars.

> . . . Nobody [else] would get a penny out of this transaction. You alone will be paid.

Gleb obviously felt that, by stopping Warner Brothers from finalizing its purchase of the motion picture rights, he had guaranteed income to Anastasia directly and avoided questions about her identity.

The problem of obtaining income for Anastasia had become a great concern at this point. She had referred to herself as "a milk cow," telling Gleb that her attorneys and those who were overseeing her care in Unterlengenhardt were trying to find any means possible to make money off her. The one exception was Mrs. Heydebrand, whom Anastasia continued to see as her loyal companion.

One month later, although no final offer from Warner Brothers had been received, Gleb still felt that his negotiations would succeed. He wrote to Anastasia at this time, telling her that he had been in touch with her German attorney, Kurt Vermehren, and that "he is sincerely devoted to you and is trying his best." Five months later, in March 1954, however, Gleb learned that the lawyer had been acting on his own and had persuaded Anastasia to take actions contrary to her best interests:

> I have just received a horrible letter from Dr. Vermehren. He writes that he has obtained your consent for the production [of a film] in this country of that outrageous London play which is an atrocious libel on you and all your friends and adherents. I still hope that this is not true, but if it is, then, in my opinion, your case is irretrievably lost.
>
> Dr. Vermehren writes further that you want me to discontinue all attempts at interesting producers and publishers in your true story. . . . I will obey your orders in the matter, but only if I receive them from you directly. I will not take any orders from Dr. Vermehren. . . .
>
> All this baffles me all the more, because you have been so critical of Dr. Vermehren and it was I who so stupidly kept defending him.

No response from Anastasia to Gleb's letter exists, but Anastasia told Gleb later that her attorney had forced her to comply. She said he was "always threatening, always, always and again."

By the time the play opened in New York, nearly ten months later, Vermehren's deal was completed. As *The New York Times* reported in a story hailing the play's premiere: "Previously the acquisition by Warner Brothers of the picture rights was held up. Everything has been straightened out now. The alleged survivor, who resides in Germany, shares in the royalties."

THE success of the play in the United States and the announcement of the movie deal generated tremendous publicity and in March 1955, *Life* magazine prepared to do a story on Anna Anderson. A reporter and crew of photographers came to Unterlengenhardt, apparently unannounced, and went first to the home of the mayor, whose wife contacted Mrs. Heydebrand. Anastasia decided that they could come to the barrack, but only if they paid her. When they agreed to her terms, the Grand Duchess who disdained the press allowed them to enter her home. She recounted the event for Milukoff:

> It started with *Life*. [They] were the first writers at the old barrack. They were hours and hours in the barrack. Hours! . . . They had paid 2,000 marks, they had the right to go in the barrack in every corner. And they went in every corner. . . . They went under the bed, and on the bed, and whatnot everywhere. . . . They were photographing and were busy in all the rooms, in the bathroom. . . . Very nice [people]. But they went like little mice in every corner. . . . and [they] had the right to do that. We permitted them to do . . . they could do what they wanted, and they did.

Despite all the trouble, Anastasia was very pleased and proud of the article that later appeared. But soon she realized that "there the unhappiness started."

Her life in Unterlengenhardt had been quiet. She cared not for the court cases that kept dragging on, and whenever events in the outside world bothered her, Anastasia could always find solace in discussing them with Mrs. Heydebrand, who would patiently explain matters and calm her down. As Anastasia told Milukoff, however, the appearance of the *Life* story changed everything:

> Then started the reporters to come from all over the earth suddenly. And they broke even the doors in, and with one . . . I had a fight. . . . I almost boxed him because Mrs. Heydebrand had gone away . . . and I was alone there, and the doors had to be open because . . . the water was running from the roof and was freezing. When the door was shut we were . . . frozen in. So we had to leave the door open. And so . . . a reporter . . . just came in and . . . I didn't want to permit strangers to enter there. So I had run in [my] nightgown to the door and to prevent that nobody should enter. Already, this beast had his foot in the door and wanted to come in. I told that he had to go out at once. Then he asked if I was Mrs. Heydebrand, I told, 'Yes, I am Mrs. Heydebrand,' and it was terrible. Then he was satisfied that I was Mrs. Heydebrand. . . .

The peaceful existence she had known in Unterlengenhardt up to this time "was at an end. We had no human life anymore at all."

AFTER succeeding on Broadway, the Maurette-Bolton play toured the United States for at least a year. Warner Brothers sold the film rights to Twentieth Century Fox, which released *Anastasia* early in 1956. The story line had changed somewhat: the movie version took place in Paris, not Berlin, and the advertising portrayed it as "the most amazing conspiracy the world has ever known . . . and love as it never happened to a man and woman before!" The film starred Ingrid Bergman as Anastasia, Helen Hayes as the Dowager Czarina Marie, and Yul Brynner as Prince Bounine. Twentieth Century Fox also released a record entitled *Anastasia, Tell Me Who You Are* by the popular American singer Pat Boone that same year. The film was an international success, and Miss Bergman won the Academy Award for Best Actress.

The film's appearance disgruntled some of Anastasia's friends, most especially Gleb, who had already told his friend in Unterlengenhardt that a film based on the Maurette-Bolton play would prove disastrous to her case. Expanding on his earlier criticisms of her attorneys, Gleb accused Leverkuehn and Vermehren of greed in the negotiations with Twentieth Century Fox on her behalf:

> They made an awful mess out of this whole movie business. I had it all stopped beautifully and I was in a wonderful situation to really negotiate. . . . [Warner Brothers] were talking about making a real contract with the lady for very heavy money, but Leverkuehn and Vermehren saw this chance of just getting a little money, and they grabbed at it. And of course, most of the money they took themselves, to which they had no right at all, because they were working on a contingent fee.

Gleb accused Vermehren, in particular, of trying to

> blackmail the American motion picture people . . . [who] thought that they had the exclusive rights on any motion picture like that. But Vermehren had added something in little letters that they overlooked.

And after it was all signed, he came to them and said, 'Well, you don't have exclusive rights. So if you want exclusive rights, pay me more money, or we are going to make another film in Germany.' Well, they were so mad . . . they just threw him out.

Gleb's accusations have never been proven, but Vermehren did proceed with plans for another motion picture to be produced in Germany.

Known in English under the title *Is Anna Anderson Anastasia?*, the German movie appeared in late 1956 and starred the famous German actress Lilli Palmer in the title role. Her performance won a prize at the Berlin Film Festival. This film was not based on the Maurette-Bolton play. It purported to present the true story of Anna Anderson and portrayed real-life figures who had been involved with the controversy surrounding Anastasia after 1922. Besides the Dowager Czarina, the characters included Harriet Rathlef, Clara Peuthert, the Duchess of Leuchtenberg, and Franziska Schanzkowska's sister. False names were given to the characters portraying two American women, a millionairess who founded the Grandanor Corporation and an imperial cousin of Anastasia, but clearly they were meant to represent Miss Jennings and Xenia Leeds. Finally, the character of Gleb Botkin was given the role of male lead.

Although he received reports from Germany that the public had reacted favorably to the film, Gleb took steps to stop its release in America. His letters demonstrate clearly his belief that the German producers had broken their earlier promise to him and Anastasia that the movie would "unequivocally assert . . . the Grand Duchess's identity." Instead, their press materials stated that "they do not assert anything and the so-called Mrs. Anderson may well be the Polish factory hand, Franziska Schanzkowska." Gleb continued to feel that any book or film that stopped short of acknowledging Anastasia's authenticity would only harm her cause, and he found it "incomprehensible" that "such damaging distortions should have been allowed by Vermehren in his capacity of Grand Duchess Anastasia's attorney."

Gleb's concerns about Vermehren and the continuing damage to Anastasia's cause from publicity that failed to conclusively support her case, would be borne out the very next year. In 1957, a German firm published a purported authorized biography, which appeared later in England as *I, Anastasia* and in America as *I Am Anastasia*. Edited by Roland Krug von Nidda, this book was an international best-seller and was translated into at least a dozen languages. Despite its claims to tell her story in her own words, Anastasia was completely unaware of the book until after it was already published.

She would later say that her first knowledge of Roland Nidda's work came when he appeared suddenly one day in Unterlengenhardt with a hundred copies for her to distribute. She had never met the man before and was surprised to learn that he had been engaged in the project at the urging of her German attorneys. Although *I, Anastasia* contained many truths—to which she herself would often point—it was not the memoir she had envisioned herself writing. She remained forever dissatisfied with the work as a whole and felt betrayed that her lawyers had sought to profit by robbing her of the one project in which she would maintain a lifelong interest—the telling of her story in her own words.

ANASTASIA had been cheated of more than that. As a result of the publicity that had begun with the appearance of the play and the two films, she was suddenly international news again. Despite the continued efforts of her group of friends to try to preserve the Grand Duchess's solitude, Unterlengenhardt soon became world famous. Baroness Miltitz described the scene:

> [S]he began to feel the curse of an overdose of publicity. The quiet of her retreat was disturbed. Although the interest of the people was mostly friendly, they began to throng around her. Many cars disregarded the sign forbidding traffic on this section of the road—even big buses came and the passengers alighted in droves to satisfy their curiosity and stare at the grounds. They pressed against the fence, tried to climb over the gate and called the recluse to come out. This popularity became a veritable plague. Even the tourist bureau in a distant town announced Sunday afternoon drives to Unterlengenhardt to see Anastasia. Finally a policeman came up every Sunday, fined all trespassing cars and regulated the traffic. During the turmoil Anastasia sat shivering with fear in her room, full of horror lest the fence might break down and the whole crowd descend upon her.

The Grand Duchess began to retreat more and more into her barrack as her intentional isolation became imposed confinement. The increased attention must have also made her realize that her identity, which had become such an accepted part of her life in Unterlengenhardt, was being questioned anew. Unfortunately, the effort to prove the duplicity of her family suffered a serious setback when she lost an important ally; Grand Duke Andrew, the only immediate relative to have openly acknowledged her, died in 1956, just as the new round of publicity was at its height. The Romanov family immediately seized the hundreds of historical documents and records on which he had based his endorsement. They have not been seen since.

NONETHELESS, Anastasia would always have one comfort in her life. Despite what others might believe of her because of the fictions manufactured during the popularization of her story, she could always count on the support of Gleb, who had been with her when the incognito Anna Anderson was created. As Anastasia would later tell Milukoff, Gleb—the childhood playmate of an imperial grand duchess—always knew "who I am and who I pretend to be."

Her correspondence with Gleb continued apace. By this time, Gleb was firmly committed to his religion, and he began to send Anastasia carefully typed pages on Church of Aphrodite stationery imprinted with the ♀ symbol. He continually expressed concern for her, but he also maintained his habit of ending his letters with descriptions of the forest or occasionally with news of his family. Anastasia was particularly pleased to learn that his daughter, Marina Botkin, had married an American attorney, Richard Schweitzer, in 1956, and had settled in Charlottesville, Virginia. Despite the fact that she had not met them, Anastasia developed a special fondness for the Schweitzers which quickly became mutual. She was godmother to their children, and Marina maintained a strong tie to the Grand Duchess through Gleb. For his part, Richard Schweitzer never hesitated to assist Gleb or Anastasia herself during the course of his successful international legal career.

* * *

THE year 1957 was an important one for Anastasia. Prince Frederick's brother-in-law Prince Sigismund, whom she had known when they were children, made the long trip from his adopted home in Costa Rica to see the woman who claimed to be his childhood friend. Little time passed before he openly acknowledged her.

Sometime during the trip that brought him to the village in Germany, Prince Sigismund went to visit another woman who claimed to be a daughter of Nicholas and Alexandra. Her name was Margda Boodts, and she had lived quietly for years near Lake Como in Italy. Like Anastasia, she had never openly sought any recognition, but Margda Boodts had been able to avoid the sensational press and publicity that plagued Anastasia. Margda had also succeeded in avoiding the hatred of the Romanov family. She claimed to be one of Anastasia's older sisters, Olga, whom Prince Sigismund had loved as a child. She told him that she had tried to contact her "sister" in Berlin. Anastasia was aware of Margda Boodts and her claim, but she had never received any letters from the woman and had always withheld her own judgment about her authenticity. Prince Sigismund, however, was not so circumspect, and after meeting Mrs. Boodts, he readily acknowledged her as Anastasia's sister.

Anastasia's friends in Unterlengenhardt, as well as Prince Frederick and the attorneys preparing her case in Berlin, had been delighted when Prince Sigismund had added his name to those of other important witnesses who had recognized the Grand Duchess. But his endorsement of Margda Boodts upset them greatly. Others had claimed to be this or that member of the imperial family over the years, but all had been dismissed readily, except for the woman who now called herself Mrs. Anderson. Despite the preponderance of evidence in their favor, her supporters had found it difficult enough to try to convince the world that one grand duchess had somehow survived the massacre at Ekaterinburg. Now one of her most recent and unequivocal advocates was saying that he believed two of the grand duchesses had escaped.

Perhaps Anastasia revealed her true belief to Mrs. Heydebrand by stating that Mrs. Boodts "might" be her sister. But in the eyes of Baroness Miltitz, Prince Frederick, and the others, Anastasia's statement and Prince Sigismund's actions meant trouble. Indeed, Lord Louis Mountbatten soon took advantage of the confusion this incident had caused: "So much for the value of [Sigismund's] testimony!" Anastasia's supporters saw no alternative other than to try to control the damage.

EVER since the appearance of the article in *Life* magazine, Anastasia had been withdrawing. The public attention had frightened her and had shown her that the support and acceptance she had found in Unterlengenhardt did not extend beyond its boundaries. She became more self-absorbed and indifferent about how her actions might appear to others.

Mrs. Heydebrand had been able to help allay the renewed bouts of depression and sudden outbursts of anger and disappointment, but she was growing old and less effective as a caretaker. The time had clearly come for others to step in and try to care for Anastasia, but Adele Heydebrand was not so easily replaced. She was the one person who somehow helped Anastasia cope with the turmoil and confusion without trying to shield her by hiding things from her.

Baroness Miltitz and Prince Frederick now took the opportunity to exert an even greater influence on Anastasia's life. Anastasia had never felt entirely comfortable with the Baroness and still became irked when the older woman seemed to be trying to control her. The Baroness began to provide direct advice and fulfill Anastasia's daily needs, as Mrs. Heydebrand had done, but Anastasia resisted strongly. Gleb's letters from this period show that his friend in Germany felt more and more hemmed in by those around her and that the Baroness was a particular problem. Rather than physically rebelling, Anastasia resumed what had always been her greatest defensive mechanism—refusing to speak or to answer questions.

The resulting seclusion came just as the court trials were approaching a crucial stage, and with Anastasia's refusal to cooperate, Prince Frederick took over all aspects of her case. Baroness Miltitz provided for the Grand Duchess's care, but the Prince controlled the more public side of her life. He had held her power of attorney for some time, but he now felt compelled to act as her press agent and financial manager. As might be expected, he was very cautious about allowing reporters to interview Anastasia. Moreover, with the help of Baroness Miltitz, the Prince severely restricted visits to

Unterlengenhardt by anyone other than a few trusted allies. The Prince and the Baroness explained that this last step was necessary, lest Anastasia become even more upset by the intrusions, but they clearly also wanted to keep her from repeating what they viewed as damaging statements—like her utterance about Margda Boodts.

Equal care was given to the handling of the Grand Duchess's meager finances. Vermehren had negotiated royalty payments from the movies, but everyone knew that Anastasia did not know how to manage even these relatively modest amounts. They turned to Baron Ulrich Gienanth, a prominent German industrialist, who agreed to handle her earnings and invest them wisely so that her future could be more secure. At the same time, a will was drawn up for the Grand Duchess. In it, she named Baron Gienanth responsible for collecting and preserving the documents she had gathered in regard to her identity.

ANASTASIA was highly suspicious of the changes occurring in Unterlengenhardt. For the greater part of the past decade, she had lived a relatively quiet life as Anna Anderson. The public had paid little attention to her, and her close circle of acquaintances in the German village had treated her as the Grand Duchess she truly was. But that world was collapsing. Her name—Anastasia—was being tossed about recklessly, and worse, a false image of her now existed in the public mind. She had obtained some money from these ventures, but Gleb's dire prediction had come true: her real identity was no closer to being endorsed or understood than it was before.

Moreover, just at the time that the intrusions and unwanted attention had increased, her own private world had begun to change dramatically. Mrs. Heydebrand's devoted and accepting care was being replaced by what Anastasia began to view as manipulation and control. The more Baroness Miltitz and Prince Frederick tried to insist on her cooperation—for her own good—the more she resisted. She had little regard for the things that seemed to matter so much to them, especially their attempts to establish her identity in the courts, the public, and the press. She now referred to the trials as "this foolery."

III.

"How any jurists could have the effrontery"

IN 1957, the judges reached a decision in the Berlin trial on Anastasia's challenge to the certificate of inheritance awarded to the Romanov survivors in 1933. After ten years of investigation and endless deliberations, the lawyers for the family had presented as a surprise witness an Austrian citizen who claimed to have been a prisoner of war at Ekaterinburg in 1918. He testified that he had been recruited by the Bolsheviks to act as a guard at the Ipatiev House. The witness told the judges that he had been at the house on the night of the massacre and had followed the Bolshevik guards into the woods. He stated that before the bodies were destroyed he saw seven corpses lying on the ground, leaving the court with the clear impression that they had just heard an eyewitness account that the entire imperial family had been assassinated.

This witness was the only one heard by the court, and his story was told with such apparent conviction and lucidity that the judges readily accepted it as true. Believing that Nicholas, Alexandra, and all their children had clearly died in Siberia on that terrible night, the judges ruled against Anastasia's petition to have the certificate of inheritance revoked. For their purposes, the case was at an end.

The judges, however, had refused to allow the rebuttal testimony of Anastasia's lawyers, who were prepared to present evidence and expert opinions that would have proved that the witness was lying. Leverkuehn and Vermehren quickly decided that this omission constituted the basis for an appeal of the court's ruling against their client, and they filed a motion for review by a higher court. Even Gleb, who had already come to suspect the motives of Vermehren in relation to the negotiations for movie rights, wrote from America that "the decision of the Berlin court is so absurd and baseless that one can only wonder how any jurists could have the effrontery of writing it."

The process of appeal had just begun when a judge from the appeals court told Leverkuehn that his review of the case indicated that Anastasia had enough evidence of her identity that she need not bother with trying to have the certificate of inheritance revoked. The judge understood that the real issue was not the money, but rather the need for legal recognition of the Grand Duchess's identity. Leverkuehn and Vermehren took heed of this advice, and the focus of the case now switched from one centered around the money to one concentrated solely on their client's authenticity.

This new strategy was extremely complicated. It required a basic reformulation of the plans that Fallows had carefully laid nearly twenty years previously. He had seen clearly that Anastasia's best chance was to cause the burden of proof to shift from her to her enemies. In other words, rather than have the courts decide that his client was telling the truth—that she was, in fact, Anastasia—he wanted to force her relatives and detractors to defend their stance. Fallows had sought to make the Romanovs: prove that the entire imperial family had died at Ekaterinburg; counter the physical evidence of his client's scars and deformities that matched those of the Grand Duchess exactly; and explain why many of them had first endorsed her only to later recant.

In filing the new suit, however, the German attorneys shifted the burden of proof to Anastasia. Now they would have to prove, first, that the daughter of the last czar had survived and, second, that Anastasia was indeed that survivor. In the end, this new tactic would require that facts long established as truth be argued yet again and would provide countless opportunities for her foes to parade their fictions in front of the public.

A problem more easily solved was how to confine the court case to Germany. They decided to name as a defendant Barbara, Duchess of Mecklenburg, who had inherited some of the money from the Mendelssohn Bank as granddaughter of the Czarina's sister Irene. They accused her of wrongfully denying Anastasia's identity and of spending money that belonged rightfully to their client. In choosing this particular distant relative, they perhaps hoped that the case might be settled before going to the court. Duchess Barbara was the daughter of Prince Sigismund, who had already officially recognized Anastasia, and the niece of Prince Frederick, her most ardent supporter. Prince Frederick appealed to Duchess Barbara to return the money, which would have been tacit recognition of Anastasia's authenticity, but she never responded. Duchess Barbara's stance was bolstered by Prince Louis of Hesse, son of the late Grand Duke who had fought Anastasia until his death in 1937. Prince Louis now voluntarily joined as a defendant. As part of their strategy against Leverkuehn and Vermehren's charges, they filed a countersuit alleging that Anastasia was none other than the Polish factory worker, Franziska Schanzkowska. The trial began in January 1958 at the High Court in Hamburg.

THE press was prepared for a court spectacle that would provide hundreds of pages of intriguing copy. But the chief judge disappointed them—and Anastasia's growing cadre of supporters—by deciding that he and his fellow jurists must first survey the evidence. The judge ordered that more photographs of Anastasia, as a woman and as a child, and samples of her handwriting be presented. He also directed the defendants, who were not present in the court, to make available to the tribunal any and all papers they had in their possession that might relate to the case. Also missing from the courtroom was the plaintiff—Anastasia—and the chief judge let it be known that she must either appear in person before them or explain why not and state where she would be willing to make herself available.

Some of the peculiarities inherent in German court proceedings would play a crucial role in how Anastasia's case would be decided. Judges in Germany are unlike the experienced legal practitioners who sit on American benches. Although German judges, like their counterparts elsewhere, seek to obtain the truth, they do not entertain arguments from the attorneys so much as they rely on the advocates to present evidence and oral arguments that suggest further areas of investigation. There is little or no cross-examination by the attorneys. Normally, only the judges question witnesses, and they have sole discretion as to which witnesses will be heard.

To complicate matters further, the tribunal alone decides whether a witness's testimony should be made part of the official record as a sworn statement. Witnesses are not sworn in before they take the stand and, therefore, those appearing as witnesses are never certain whether they will be asked to affirm their statements officially until after they have been examined by the court. Finally, the length of the trial and the extent of the investigation is solely at the discretion of the judges. When they—not the attorneys—have decided that enough evidence has been presented, the proceedings are brought to an end and a ruling given.

SIX weeks after the chief judge's initial declaration, the case actually commenced. The judges began by interviewing the witnesses who had been named in the documents provided by the lawyers from both sides. One of the first to have his day in court was Pierre Gilliard, who for more than thirty years had worked in conjunction with the Grand Duke of Hesse and others to discredit Anastasia. He briefly recounted his story, which was little more than a summation of the fabrications he had published in his book, *The False Anastasia.* The judges questioned him intensely about all manner of details and learned quickly that the witness could no longer remember crucial points or incidents that supposedly bolstered his charge that Anastasia was a fraud.

Faced with the type of interrogation that the Grand Duchess had been forced to undergo since her first days in Berlin, Gilliard withered. The chief judge reportedly said, "Ordinarily, a witness who knows that he going to be heard finds a way to freshen his memory." Flustered, Gilliard assured the court that whatever his memory now, the book he had written nearly thirty years previously contained the truth. Following this statement, the judges asked to see the original documents on which Gilliard's research had supposedly been founded. But the witness could not produce even the letter from Grand Duchess Olga to his wife. It was this document that had first prompted the Gilliards to visit Anastasia at St. Mary's, where they had initially recognized the patient. Frustrated, the judges told Gilliard to return after a weekend recess, when they would have further questions for him.

His last appearance proved no more beneficial to the Romanov family and their attorneys than had the first. Again, he could not recall where crucial documents could be found, and when the judges asked him to produce the originals of photographs and handwriting samples he had published in his book, he said that he had burned them all. He left disgraced and was injured in a car accident on his way home. Pierre Gilliard never fully recovered, nor was he called to testify again. He died four years later.

During this same session, the judges also heard testimony from Felix Dassel, the young officer who had met Anastasia at the hospital on the grounds of Czarskoe Selo and who had later recognized her at Seeon. Now, some thirty years later, he had become so ill from emphysema that he had great difficulty breathing, and was interviewed by the court in his home. Over the course of two days, Dassel repeatedly stated his conviction that Anastasia was genuine. The judges determined that his testimony was of enough importance to request that he swear to it formally. The old soldier did not hesitate, despite the chief judge's insistence that the witness listen to a long recitation of contradictory testimony already given in court. In the end, he was asked to swear to his *belief* that Anastasia was indeed the daughter of Czar Nicholas II. Dassel reportedly responded, "I did not say 'I believe.' I affirm it! I *affirm* that she is Anastasia. . . ." Despite his weakened physical state, he began to rise from the couch to make his point, but the chief judge became concerned and assured the witness that such a gesture was not necessary. Captain Dassel stared his examiner in the eye and said, "I am going to get up." Standing, supported by his wife, he took a deep and painful breath and announced, "I swear by God to 'have the certitude' that Mrs. Anderson is Anastasia . . . Grand Duchess of Russia." Dassel's testimony was the last significant event in this round of hearings, and the judges and lawyers returned to Hamburg for further investigations.

IN May 1958, the court turned to the false charge raised by the Romanov family in their countersuit—that not only was Anastasia not the Grand Duchess, but that she was, in truth, Franziska Schanzkowska. The prostitute bribed by the agent of the Grand Duke of Hesse, for the fabricated story in the *Nachtausgabe*, was called before the tribunal in Hamburg to recount the story of Franziska Schanzkowska. The judges questioned her thoroughly about the supposed similarities between the missing Polish factory worker and the woman in Unterlengenhardt. Finally, the chief judge asked the woman to produce photographic evidence to support her story. She readily displayed two snapshots. The first showed the witness herself wearing a blue suit that she claimed to have given to Franziska in 1922, when Anastasia had run away from the Kleist's home. The other showed the Grand Duchess at the Berlin Zoo, purportedly wearing the same suit. The chief judge immediately noticed that the first picture had been altered, and the witness explained that she had simply had the face of her male companion erased. However, after further examination of the evidence, the court determined that there were enough questions about the nature of both pictures to order an independent, expert opinion.

Another witness, an old acquaintance of Franziska Schanz-kowska, was called. Given a group of photographs to identify, she recognized each as a picture of her old friend, except the only one that was, indeed, of Franziska.

These witnesses provided the opportunity for Leverkuehn and Vermehren to try to gather countervailing proof of the Schanz-kowska charge, but before they could get very far, the matter was settled in their favor. In October 1958, experts from the Hamburg police department reported the findings of their examination of the photographs produced by the former prostitute in court: not only was the suit worn by the women in the two pictures not the same, but in the photograph of Anastasia, "the buttons and the belt have been drawn in *after the fact.*" Surprisingly, the judges made no comment on this announcement.

BEFORE the Hamburg police report was received, the court had established a commission of inquiry to gather testimony throughout Europe and in America. In Paris they interviewed Felix Youssoupov, who told them that Anastasia was an impostor and that her supporters were all mad. The commission also interviewed Gleb in his home in New Jersey, and he provided an unwavering endorsement of his friend in Unterlengenhardt. One of the commissioners' other destinations was Toronto, where Anastasia's aunt, Grand Duchess Olga, had settled with her husband in 1949. She was in no mood to entertain the commissioners' questions and gave only brief and equivocal answers. After several hours, she declared the interview at an end and left the room.

IV.
"I didn't like this at all"

WHILE THE TRIAL continued, Anastasia remained intent on living an isolated life in Unterlengenhardt. The publicity arising from the play and films had not lessened during the last two years. The curiosity seekers began arriving in tour buses, and she would always hide inside the barrack when the crowds formed. As she felt more confined, she had come to rely to an even greater extent on the companionship of Adele Heydebrand. Even though the nearly eighty-year-old Mrs. Heydebrand was not able to take care of Anastasia as she once had, the two women remained quite close. Anastasia had always insisted that the little group around her speak English, but to help Mrs. Heydebrand practice the Russian language, Anastasia began using it more frequently. The older woman spoke and understood some of the language fairly well, but she had never read or written it to any extent. Anastasia helped her practice the cyrillic alphabet in several exercise books—comparing the strange looking letters and words with their equivalents in English or German.

The two women would eat breakfast in the garden surrounding the barrack, or take walks if the tourists were not peering over the fence. Their time together was filled with such idle pursuits, now that Mrs. Heydebrand was capable of providing little more than conversation and companionship.

Anastasia refused to recognize the need for other arrangements to ensure care for herself. Some of the more burdensome chores had been assumed by the Baroness Miltitz, Miss Mutius, and Miss

Thomasius. They determined that one way to save Mrs. Heydebrand's strength was to keep both her and the Grand Duchess ignorant of what might be upsetting or disruptive news. They knew how distraught Anastasia could become, and they realized that Mrs. Heydebrand would refuse to hide anything from her. They screened the enormous amount of mail that poured in from around the world—addressed variously to the Grand Duchess Anastasia, to Mrs. Anderson, or to Mrs. Tschaikovsky, depending on how much or which parts of her legend the correspondents had chosen to believe.

These women, primarily the Baroness, also kept informed of events involving the courts and filtered the news to Anastasia, trying always to assure her cooperation. She became as removed as possible from the outside world, venturing out of her compound at the small barrack occasionally. Rarely would she react to what she saw or heard with anything other than disgust or fear.

Far from ideal, this situation remained stable until May 12, 1959. The previous night, Anastasia and Mrs. Heydebrand had eaten dinner together, with grapefruit as a treat. Awaking to find that Mrs. Heydebrand was not in the barrack, Anastasia went looking for her and found her body lying on one of the garden paths, where the gentle companion had died of a heart attack. For once, Anastasia did not attribute a friend's death to assassination by Bolsheviks or the British Secret Service, but she found little solace in the fact that natural causes had robbed her of someone so dear.

MRS. Heydebrand's death brought back all the memories of the horrible night in Ekaterinburg more than forty years earlier. Not for the first time, but perhaps more deeply than ever before, Anastasia was forced to consider why she—of all her beloved family—was left to survive. She had emerged into a world that had always treated her as an entity to be studied and debated, not as a human being to be loved and understood.

Her feelings toward God also came into question. She firmly believed in a supreme being, but failed to discern any reason or purpose for having been forced to witness the brutal murder of her family and be brought out of Russia to battle incredible illness and mental distress and survive—only to be spurned and vilified by her aunts and uncles for the most petty and self-serving motives. Still, she had gone on, managing somehow to find people who cared for her and seemed to have her best interests at heart. However, the court trials and the movies had changed all that: she had thought the legal battle would be quick and decisive; and she had been told that the money from the films would secure her well-being. Instead, the attention and intrusion they caused had taken over her life and threatened to destroy what little happiness her seclusion in Unterlengenhardt had provided. Even before Adele Heydebrand's death, Anastasia had begun to feel that the attention and guardianship offered by most of her friends and protectors was little more than a form of oversight and control.

There had been three exceptions. Harriet Rathlef had proven to be a true friend and defender, despite their temporary alienation, but Harriet was long dead. Gleb was a dependable adviser and confidant, but he was far away in America. Adele Heydebrand had been Anastasia's constant friend and had provided her a firm footing in the world, but she was gone, too.

Anastasia's reaction to the death was immediate. She developed a red rash on her arms and face and apparently developed a form of shingles on her chest. She withdrew into herself, succumbing to an overwhelming sense of loss and sadness, and refused to talk to anyone for days. As her own special token of mourning, she said she would never again eat grapefruit; and forever, she would remember that May day as one that "breaks my heart."

THROUGHOUT 1958 and into 1959, the court had continued to gather evidence in Hamburg and in sessions held by the commission in other countries. Finally, in May 1959, the judges determined that they must interview Anastasia. They had announced their intention to do so following the early testimonies of Gilliard and Dassel in March of the previous year, but Anastasia had vehemently declined to meet with the jurists. She had supposedly told Vermehren that she "may receive the president of the tribunal . . . [and] invite him for tea if he is intelligent and a gentleman."

The judges were not so easily dismissed, and just after Adele

Heydebrand's death they traveled to a town near Unterlengenhardt with a Russian language expert to test Anastasia's knowledge of Russian. Moreover, they sought to determine what facts the plaintiff herself could supply to clear up the conflicting evidence that had been presented thus far. The Grand Duchess, however, still refused to see them. The loss of her friend and companion had only strengthened her refusal to be made part of the court proceedings.

Three days of intense lobbying and maneuvering by Baroness Miltitz, Vermehren, and others ensued before a meeting between Anastasia and the judges was finally arranged by Baron Gienanth, who had been summoned by Leverkuehn. When the tribunal arrived at her door on the evening of May 23, 1959, however, she declared that she would agree to meet for ten minutes only and with the chief judge alone—no stenographers, no other jurists, no language expert.

Anastasia refused to shake the judge's hand, explaining that she was afraid of germs. The judge spoke with her in English and asked several questions about her life and her encounters with those who were still making charges against her—Grand Duchess Olga and Gilliard being of greatest note. Her answers were short and not always direct. Her interviewer also attempted to have her speak Russian as a way of proving her detractors wrong. Anastasia said that she knew of the accusations that she could not be the Grand Duchess because she did not choose to speak Russian, but she nevertheless refused to speak it with him now.

When ten minutes had passed, Anastasia remained true to her word, and the meeting was over. The court record of the meeting reads, in part, as follows:

[She] gives the impression of a very self-confident and energetic lady . . . thoroughly clear and mentally competent. She speaks in a regal manner, with a deliberate distance. Sometimes she will look her conversation partner directly in the eye, while burying the lower part of her face in a high collar; sometimes the face turns all the way to the left side and is hidden entirely in the collar of her coat.

It is difficult to get the plaintiff to concentrate on certain questions and events. . . . She turns her gaze away mainly when she hears arguments which speak against her identity with the daughter of the Czar. Repeatedly she says that she cannot understand the arguments of her enemies at all.

In summary, as might have been expected from Anastasia's constant disdain for the court proceedings, the interview was inconclusive. However, before leaving Unterlengenhardt the court managed to acquire one of the exercise books that had been used by the late Mrs. Heydebrand to practice the Russian language. Like another such notebook rescued by Milukoff years later, it contained notations by Anastasia in Russian, demonstrating beyond doubt to the world that she not only knew the language, but was proficient enough to tutor her companion in it. Clearly, her refusal to make this fact known to the judge was but another indication of the imperious disregard she had for the court proceedings and a sign of the extremely private nature of her mourning for Adele Heydebrand.

THE court's intrusion into Anastasia's life had little effect other than to annoy her. More troublesome were the renewed and fierce efforts of Baroness Miltitz to fill the void left by Adele Heydebrand. Gleb's letters from this period show that Anastasia resented the Baroness's actions. Although the Baroness likely felt she could gain some influence over the Grand Duchess by ingratiating herself, Anastasia saw these attempts as a ruse to exert greater and unwanted control. She became particularly angry when she felt that the Baroness was trying to replace Mrs. Heydebrand, for Anastasia knew in her heart that no one could ever do that.

One of the projects in which the Baroness became involved during this time was planning a party at Unterlengenhardt. Sometime prior to Adele Heydebrand's death, a parcel of land had been purchased for Anastasia. The money had come from investments Baron Gienanth had made with some of the royalties paid by the film studios. The land was to be the site of a new home for the Grand Duchess, but before the structure was built, friends decided to arrange a celebration. Anastasia was still in the first months of mourning Mrs. Heydebrand's death and had closed herself off almost totally from personal contacts, but "knowing the sociability of the . . . [the Grand Duchess's] nature," the Baroness said that she was glad to help and "made the arrangements with the greatest pleasure."

The Anthroposophistic Baroness had long felt that Anastasia had a special connection to the land and those who tended it. The villagers, many of them owning small acreages, had always treated the Grand Duchess respectfully. As Anastasia later revealed on the Milukoff tapes, it was primarily for this reason that she agreed to the party: "I consented that this was done for the village people, the farmers. They were kind. . . ." For Anastasia, however, the happy occasion planned by the Baroness—complete with "paper-lanterns . . . hung in the trees, the entrance [to the meadow] . . . marked by torches, and a quartet . . . to play"—was far from a joyous occasion. Her memory was still vivid years later:

> The people were in masses inside [the fence] . . . outside the fence with cars . . . and what was standing outside heard just the same what went on and saw what went on. . . . I was placed under some trees. I didn't like this at all, it was horrible. . . .

She returned to her barrack and her life of solitude. Baroness Miltitz, completely oblivious to Anastasia's feelings, later described a much different scene:

> The invitation had created great enthusiasm. . . . After the concert [by the quartet] everybody rushed up to Anastasia to shake hands and say a few words. She enjoyed herself immensely. . . .

Perhaps buoyed by her impression of this event, the Baroness—along with Prince Frederick—began preparations to build a pre-fabricated, one-story structure on the meadow where the party had been held. They wanted to make certain that the Grand Duchess could live in greater comfort. They made one critical error, although not a surprising one given their attitude toward the ever-reclusive Anastasia: they failed to consult the future occupant of the house about her own wishes.

V.
"She lived in her own world"

THE HEARINGS CONTINUED in Hamburg throughout 1959, but only one other major breakthrough came before the court issued its ruling. The previous year an anthropological study had been conducted at the University of Mainz. The researchers had compared hundreds of photographs of Anastasia as an adult and as a child, as well as pictures of the Romanov family, including the House of Hesse. Such studies had been conducted previously, but the results had always been judged inconclusive. The new report, however, took pains to point out that the earlier work had used only a limited number of photographs, many of them taken by amateurs and then retouched.

The researchers in Mainz addressed particularly the comparisons of the "ear region," based on the pictures that had first been provided by Gilliard to his colleague at Lausanne and on which the first denouncement of Anastasia by anthropologists had been made. After completion of their more careful and scientific analysis, the leader of the project declared that "it is not only possible that we are dealing with an [exact] identity [of the Grand Duchess Anastasia] . . . it is the only acceptable solution." The report was submitted as evidence in Hamburg.

The lawyer for Duchess Barbara and Prince Louis of Hesse refused to accept the new expert opinion, and the entire issue became the subject of another session of the court. Finally, with the agreement of both sides in the case, the judges ordered a new study to be conducted and indicated that it would accept only those findings as the last word on the matter. The judges chose Professor Otto Reche, the founder of the German Anthropological Society and the most respected practitioner in his field at the time. As an adjunct, the court ordered a detailed examination of the many handwriting samples it had gathered and enlisted the services of Dr. Minna Becker, a renowned graphologist who had authenticated the identity of another lost child, Anne Frank, by reviewing her famous diary.

Reche and Becker completed their reports in early 1960, and their conclusions were submitted to the judges soon afterward. Professor Reche had spent more than a year on his investigations and had collected a vast array of photographs of the Grand Duchess as a child, of the imperial family, and of members of the Hesse family. He had even won the cooperation of Anastasia in Unterlengenhardt, and had taken pictures of her posed to reflect exactly the angles and lighting of the childhood pictures. Finally, the professor had analyzed blood tests and—because of the countersuit filed by the defense—compared Anastasia's physical features with those of Franziska Schanzkowska and her family. His conclusions were firm: the woman living at Unterlengenhardt was *not* the Polish factory worker; she was the Grand Duchess Anastasia of Russia.

As heartening as this news was, Minna Becker's report bolstered Anastasia's case even more: "I have never seen this many identical traits in two scripts that did not come from the same hand." She, too, concluded without doubt that "Mrs. Anderson is no one else than Grand Duchess Anastasia."

Following the issuance of the reports, attorneys for both parties prepared to present their final evidence and arguments. The court's term was coming to an end, and Leverkuehn had died shortly after the Reche analysis had been made public. Vermehren organized his final pleadings somewhat hurriedly. He knew that if the court declined to finish its business before the term expired, a new chief judge would have to be appointed and familiarize himself with the evidence and arguments gathered since 1958, when this particular hearing had begun.

To help prevent such a long delay in the proceedings, Vermehren enlisted the aid of Dominique Auclères, a journalist assigned to cover the case by the French publication *Figaro*. In addition to writing reports favorable to Anastasia for the French press, Mrs. Auclères had already been involved in helping the attorneys gather evidence. She had also become friendly with Prince Frederick but, until this point, had remained for all appearances only an observer.

Her newspaper editors were aware of the direct assistance she now provided to Vermehren and approved it.

APART from the release of the reports by the court experts and the death of Leverkuehn, two other events significant for Anastasia occurred in 1960. The first was the death in England of her aunt, Grand Duchess Xenia. Surprisingly, perhaps because she had lived in a certain amount of seclusion under the protection of the British royal family, Xenia's death did not receive a great deal of public attention. Her involvement in the court trials had diminished greatly over the previous two decades, but her death marked the disappearance of one of Anastasia's first and most vehement enemies within the Romanov family.

The other significant event was the death of her remaining aunt, Grand Duchess Olga, whose emigration to Canada and subsequent decline in fortunes provided a poignant story for the international press. Aunt Olga died as a penniless old woman in a flat above Ray's Barber Shop in a poor section of Toronto. Evidence indicates that in the end, she may have felt some remorse over the manner in which she had treated her niece. Several reports of her in old age characterized her as pacing the floor of her tiny home in Canada, wringing her hands, and exclaiming, "What have I done to my niece? What have I done to my niece?" Nevertheless, the media portrayed her as the last Russian grand duchess, and her public funeral drew a great deal of attention. It was noted, for example, that Sir Edward Peacock of the Bank of England had visited her on her deathbed.

ANASTASIA could hardly have avoided realizing that, of all the Romanov relatives she had known from her days at Czarskoe Selo, she alone survived. This realization must have led her to begin rethinking how and why she had come to live as she did, secluded in a small town on the edge of the Black Forest. Now nearing sixty, and purposely walled off from outside contacts, she had nothing other than her thoughts, her memories, her sadness.

No one, not even Gleb, could penetrate Anastasia's self-imposed and reflective silence following the loss of Adele Heydebrand. His letters from this period show almost no communication with her. Rather, she asked one of her friends—Miss Thomasius or Miss Mutius—to write and give her thoughts, thereby putting a new and greater distance between herself and her old friend. The Grand Duchess would sit alone for hours in her barrack. She wanted to see as little as possible of the Baroness, who continued trying to replace Adele Heydebrand. As the year progressed and Anastasia kept avoiding personal contacts, the Baroness became increasingly aware that "she live[d] in her own world and ha[d] not the slightest understanding of the reality of present conditions. . . ."

What Anastasia was trying to comprehend was not so much the present as the past. She had often had her own way of viewing events and people who were involved in her life. Her interpretation was apt not only to be unique, but also to change with the circumstances. The clearest example thus far had been her attitude toward Harriet Rathlef. Anastasia had viewed Harriet as a most trusted friend, then as the betrayer who had written the serialized book, and finally as a friend again. Alone with her thoughts and her many mementos, Anastasia now began to create a whole series of new interpretations of her life.

The enemies who had arisen in the 1920s were dead and no longer posed a threat to her. Moreover, most of these people—certainly, to her mind, the most important of them—had been family. She had sought reconciliation with these relatives as the only, if still inadequate, means of finding some way of overcoming the terrible loss of her parents, brother, and sisters. Although she understood their treachery, she irrationally felt that, because she was at the center of the controversy, she must somehow be the cause for the disharmony of the family. While they lived, her aunts and uncle had intentionally kept her at a distance and she had had no means of overcoming their hatred and pettiness. But now that their deaths had silenced them, Anastasia was free to pursue her own means of reconciliation.

It was an essential act for her, and the fantastical explanations she gave for what she had once called their "treason" show the extent to which she still longed for the reconciliation. The Grand Duke of Hesse, whose devious and selfish motives were by now clear to all, became, for her, a misguided man. Anastasia knew that her uncle had turned against her because of the revelation of his wartime trip to

Russia; she now insisted that his assistants had convinced him at the earliest stages that she was an impostor and then kept from him important evidence to the contrary.

She had been furious when she left her cousin Xenia Leeds because Mrs. Leeds had not fulfilled her promise to arrange a reunion with the Dowager Czarina. She also knew that her cousin had conspired with her aunt, the Grand Duchess Xenia, to gain control of the money in the Bank of England and to keep Anastasia quiet. Now, however, she felt that Xenia Leeds was not at fault; her husband had obviously forced her to behave so deplorably. Anastasia even had occasion to reconstruct the image of Miss Jennings, who had arranged her kidnapping and exile back to Germany. To the Grand Duchess, Miss Jennings was no longer "the ugly old woman," but a glorious society figure who had provided only the greatest comfort and luxury—prior to the now-forgotten confinement at Four Winds, of course.

The process of remaking enemies into friends also required the creation of new wrongdoers. Anastasia always saw life portrayed in the starkness of black and white. If she had friends, she had to have enemies. When mistakes occurred or events turned against her, there was always a cause and, undoubtedly, a person behind that cause. Her understanding of these purposes, actions, and those responsible, might change, but everything was always a matter of right against wrong. Thus, when she began to recast her relatives as saints, she had nowhere to turn to see devils except among those she had formerly considered allies.

The Empress Hermine, who was once one of Anastasia's "greatest friends" and who had provided the Kaiser's tacit recognition of her, was now to become "not quite right in the head. . . . This idiot was crazy, one cannot call her normal." Her suspicions about the actions of her attorneys also mounted. She accused them of stealing her money and ruining her case—an opinion not entirely new but certainly stated with an increased vehemence and intensity. To Baroness Miltitz, no longer viewed as a simple interloper, Anastasia often ascribed the most venal acts—spying, theft, and incredible incompetence in trying to handle her affairs. Her old friend Prince Frederick was subjected to the suspicion that his efforts on her behalf were little more than a way of using her to gain fame and money.

*　　*　　*

AT first, few people were aware of Anastasia's changing state of mind. Miss Thomasius and Miss Mutius were her favored companions whenever she felt the need for company. Both were old women who had always seen her as the Russian Grand Duchess, whose temperament was to be soothed and whose wishes were to be met as best they could. Miss Thomasius and Miss Mutius would sit and listen to her newly constructed tales, not contradicting her with what they—and she—knew to be the truth. Understanding that to counter Anastasia would be futile and would lead only to more upset and turmoil, they could only try to turn the conversation to another point when she began her harangues.

Nevertheless, word of these conversations and her changed attitude could not be kept from those who had taken over responsibility for her care. The Baroness and Prince Frederick both quickly realized that she could not be allowed to talk openly about her thoughts. Otherwise, the press and the attorneys for those fighting her in court would portray her as a raving lunatic whose memories and utterances were not to be trusted. They began trying to find ways of controlling her even more in order to prevent her from endangering her own case and their one cause in life. Gleb was informed, and he agreed that the new development was potentially very damaging, although temporary. Those who could observe her closely felt that the change was probably permanent. At this point, both the Baroness and the Prince attempted to take over virtually every aspect of her life. Anastasia reacted by transferring even more enmity to them, and the more they pushed, the more she resisted. It was a stalemate that would eventually grow intolerable for all concerned.

THE house the Baroness and the Prince had planned for Anastasia was completed by the spring of 1960. The barrack had become almost dangerous to inhabit. The small space had always been crammed with Anastasia's mementos and gifts, but once her caretaker had died, the Grand Duchess had neither the capability nor the desire to keep things in any semblance of order. The lawn was overgrown with weeds, because she would allow no one near enough to tend it; she had neglected the daily maintenance chores, and the dwelling had deteriorated quickly.

The Baroness and Prince Frederick knew that she must be moved, but Anastasia resented the fact that they were trying to interfere in her life; and she was still furious at them for not consulting her about the plans for the house. As a result, she refused to move. She was happy sitting with her most valued possessions—paper bags filled with photographs, documents, and books, as well as paintings of her relatives. She had also begun to take care of stray cats and dogs, turning to them for the undemanding companionship and love that she could find nowhere else. She seemed to be putting her life at risk, living in a fire trap of a hut. But the chaos that was so apparent to outsiders was to her a refuge where—surrounded by the random memories of happier times—she found peace.

In July 1960, Tatiana Botkin visited Unterlengenhardt with the French journalist Dominique Auclères. The Baroness and some of the other women who looked after Anastasia had decided that this would be a good excuse to persuade her to move into the house; surely she would want to greet Tatiana in decent surroundings. But Anastasia refused to budge. Only after much cajoling did they induce her to even go to the new house to have tea with the two women. During this visit, she asked Tatiana to write to Gleb for her, complaining to him that she could not find "an inner connection" with the new house. Her attitude remained the same for many months thereafter, and she continued to do everything she could to thwart the plans for her to move.

Eventually, however, her resistance wore down. Exactly when or why she agreed to make the change is unknown, but evidence suggests that she moved in July 1961. There is a postcard with a picture of the new house on the front signed in a formal—almost ceremonious—manner by Baroness Miltitz, Prince Frederick, and one of Anastasia's local acquaintances. The card had clearly been printed for sale to the tourists who still flocked to Unterlengenhardt. On the bottom of the picture is a printed description of "The Anastasia House in Unterlengenhardt." The crass commercialism of printing postcards of her new residence demonstrates clearly why she was so reluctant to leave the relative anonymity of the barrack. In the new house, she would face the glare of public attention again.

Anastasia's negative feelings about the new dwelling never waned. To say that she hated it would not be an exaggeration. She referred to the house as the "new barrack," hinting in a way at a sense of confinement, although the house was by far more spacious and commodious than the other residence. Still, she would always compare it in the most derisive terms with what she began to fondly remember as the "old barrack."

She soon managed to create much the same environment in the new home as she had in the previous one. She refused visitors and felt intruded upon whenever someone tried to bring any type of order to her life. The cats and dogs multiplied, she never cleaned, and the garden was left to grow untended. Because of the continued interest of the public—which now, thanks to the postcards, did not even need guided tours to find the famous Mrs. Anderson—new fences and an iron gate were constructed around the property. As she had done in the old barrack, Anastasia now remained alone inside the new barrack, finding companionship chiefly in her many pets, who were allowed free reign over the house and property.

VI.

"They do not seem to want the Grand Duchess to really trust anybody"

AS ANASTASIA'S LIFE underwent changes in Unterlengenhardt, Gleb remained concerned about her well-being and wrote to her regularly. His active involvement in Anastasia's case had all but ended. The geographic distance and the increased control over the Grand Duchess exerted by Baroness Miltitz, Prince Frederick, and the attorneys all contributed to his inability to influence events. Nevertheless he continued to do what he could to help her, and she continued to seek his advice and assistance. As part of his efforts, he encouraged those who expressed an interest in helping her. Sometimes he endorsed their willingness to provide Anastasia donations of cash or other gifts that he knew might please her. Others times, he simply recommended ways in which they could let the Grand Duchess know of their support in the effort to win the court case.

Among those who contacted him during this period was Alexis Milukoff, one of the most enigmatic figures to ever become involved in Anastasia's life. Little is known about him—even his age is a mystery—and he has provided few verifiable facts. Milukoff was a Russian emigre who claimed to have served in the horse guard under the Czar. After fleeing Russia, he had settled in California and become an American citizen. At the time he contacted Gleb, he was working for the U.S. Army Corps of Engineers in Germany and undoubtedly became aware of Anastasia's presence in that country while serving there.

Milukoff wrote to Gleb early in 1960 as someone who was unalterably convinced of the Grand Duchess's identity and willing to offer his aid. Over the course of the next three years the two men exchanged numerous letters and visited in America, and Gleb attempted to persuade Anastasia to accept the Russian emigre's support.

The only record of these activities comes from letters written by Gleb, but they provide some revealing insights into the intensity of Milukoff's attempts to become directly involved in Anastasia's affairs. They also demonstrate clearly the level of Gleb's understanding of how her psychology and the attitudes of those surrounding her could hinder those efforts. From the beginning, Milukoff showed himself to be an inveterate researcher and chronicler. Gleb's letters are filled with detailed answers about the genealogies and activities of many of Anastasia's relatives, as well as the lives and personalities of people who opposed her. Milukoff also apparently asked many questions about those who had aided the Grand Duchess in the past, including the Leuchtenberg family, Prince Frederick, and Baroness Miltitz. More than anything else, however, he sought advice about how best to ingratiate himself with the famous woman in Unterlengenhardt. Inexplicably, Gleb seemed almost immediately to have developed a remarkable level of trust and intimacy with Milukoff. Perhaps it was the fact that the Russian emigre was an expert charmer. His first letter to Gleb indicated that he had come to believe so fervently in Anastasia because he had read Gleb's books, the last of which was published in 1937 and had long been out of print. Another reason may be that Milukoff showed an extremely intense interest in helping Anastasia and seemed ready to accept Gleb's opinions and advice without question. It is also possible that Gleb somehow felt that Milukoff would be able to provide a source of reliable and objective information about Anastasia, now that her overseers in Unterlengenhardt had come to view Gleb as a meddler. However Milukoff managed to convince the older man of his sincerity and abilities, from the start of their contact Gleb gave him explicitly frank and insightful advice.

The first problem for the newcomer was how to gain access to Anastasia. Since taking up residence in the new barrack, the Grand Duchess had become more determined than ever to be alone. The enormous iron gates, topped with barbed wire, and the fence around her property were meant to ensure her privacy. And in addition to her growing number of cats, she had four gigantic dogs: Baby, Naughty, Polly, and Tiny. These dogs were there to protect her from tourists and other curiosity seekers, but she also saw them as her first defense against assassination. All these efforts did help ensure her privacy, but they also made her more of a mystery to a public that continued to feed on the most sensational news of her past life and the most decrepit portrayal of her present existence.

Very few people were allowed into her little house or into her thoughts. Gleb was kept informed of the Grand Duchess's views through her letters, as Milukoff must have somehow discovered. In addition, Anastasia still allowed Miss Thomasius and Miss Mutius to visit her and gossip, but Baroness Miltitz was generally not welcome. More and more, Anastasia would accuse the Baroness of spying, and anyone whom Anastasia perceived to be involved with the woman was immediately suspect.

She also had growing suspicions about the money she had been promised from the films. Anastasia had never had any grasp of financial affairs, but she now decided that she could not trust her advisers. She fired Baron Gienanth, her financial manager, even though an independent audit that he insisted be conducted showed that all transactions had been properly authorized and accounted for. Prince Frederick was no longer the favored intimate he had once been. She would speak directly to fewer and fewer of her acquaintances in Unterlengenhardt and complained to Gleb about virtually everyone. She was as wary of strangers as she had always been, and when outsiders dared to approach, she turned them away without comment or explanation.

Gleb wrote to Anastasia to request that she see Milukoff, but she refused. Milukoff was insistent, however, so Gleb counseled him carefully about how to approach Anastasia and sought to reassure Milukoff that Anastasia's refusal was not directed toward him personally, noting that "her reluctance to see people is almost a pathological condition." He painted a very sympathetic and detailed portrait of her character, noting that part of her reluctance to see people could be attributed to ". . . sheer vanity, because she thinks of herself as terribly old and unattractive." Gleb cautioned further that any approach must be made with the utmost care and consideration because of the many ordeals the Grand Duchess had undergone during the court trials.

Gleb suggested that Milukoff would do well to first approach her in a most solicitous manner, perhaps appealing to her vanity. Gleb knew that she had always loved receiving gifts—even if she seldom acknowledged them—and that anyone who provided her with some of her favorite things would be that much closer to a positive reception:

> [T]he best way for you to achieve your purpose is to start sending nice, friendly letters to the Grand Duchess, without for the time being asking her for anything, and, perhaps, also some small presents. I imagine, she would be glad to get coffee. . . . One thing she always wants to have is Yardley's lavender soap. I know, she loves perfume, but, unhappily, do not remember her favorite scents. Besides, she loves only good perfume which is very expensive. But, I am sure, she would like lavender toilet water (once again, Yardley's). She had those Yardley things in her childhood. She eats very little, but she does love citrus fruit of whatever kind. You could make her very happy by supplying her with oranges.

As important as it was to gain Anastasia's confidence, Gleb knew Milukoff would need to avoid whatever barriers Baroness Miltitz and Prince Frederick might pose. In regard to the Baroness, Gleb advised the newcomer that, despite the growing alienation between her and Anastasia, she still assumed the role of go-between, a position that Milukoff would be wise to respect. For example, Gleb explained, answers to Milukoff's letters might be dictated by the Grand Duchess but written by Baroness Miltitz. She in turn would be aware of his intentions and—because of her intimate familiarity with Anastasia's feelings and opinions after many years' experience—would know whether Anastasia showed him any favor. As for the Prince, Gleb provided a succinct interpretation of his character:

> . . . a rather peculiar person, not always easy to talk to, but essentially quite good natured and body and soul devoted to Grand Duchess Anastasia. Like the Grand Duchess, he can be very suspicious and very abrupt, but can also be most friendly and charming. You will see at once that they are cousins. There is even a bit of resemblance between them.

Finally, Gleb encouraged Milukoff not to give up hope and suggested that he "lay a systematic siege" on Unterlengenhardt in an effort to win access to Anastasia. In the meantime, he would at least achieve a better understanding of her condition and the concerns of those around her.

As frank as Gleb was in assessing the situation in the small German village, he was even more open regarding the need to find a solution to Anastasia's dilemma. He encouraged Milukoff to talk to anyone and everyone—especially if he felt he could be of any assistance in coming to an arrangement with the family about the money. Gleb was growing increasingly concerned about the state of Anastasia's well-being, particularly since she was beginning to suffer health problems again.

As early as 1929, Gleb had proposed that Anastasia come to some agreement with her family to divide the money. He had always shared her feeling that the question of her identity—especially acknowledgment by the family—was of prime importance. All of her immediate relatives had died, however, and the issue had grown far beyond the question of Anastasia's authenticity. Gleb was practical enough to know that the best means of assuring her future care was for her to gain control over some of the money that had been left by the Czar. From the perspective of Anastasia's opponents, the inheritance had been at the center of the dispute from the very beginning. By now it was clearly the only reason that Duchess Barbara and Prince Louis were continuing the battle.

Gleb repeated to Milukoff his long-standing belief that "the Grand Duchess is both very clannish and very generous. Were she to be acknowledged by all her relatives and enabled to inherit her fortune, she would, no doubt, take care of them all, as well as become a rallying point for the whole family." Since Milukoff had shown such a great interest in Anastasia and her relatives, Gleb encouraged him to see whether his efforts in obtaining an agreement with the family might succeed where all others had failed.

Milukoff apparently went about the task with a fervent, if misguided, zeal. In July 1961, a little more than a year after his first contact with Gleb, he wrote back to America reporting that he had contacted, of all people, Felix Youssoupov. Apparently Milukoff had learned from Baroness Miltitz on a visit to Unterlengenhardt that she considered Youssoupov to be the spokesman for the Romanov family. Milukoff therefore probably knew little more than the fact that Youssoupov was the late Grand Duchess Xenia's son-in-law. The man obviously knew nothing about Youssoupov's attempt to murder Anastasia at Castle Seeon.

Milukoff had written to tell Gleb of Youssoupov's offer to now acknowledge Anastasia—and perjure his testimony before the Hamburg court just two years previously—in exchange for a share of the money that was supposedly in the Bank of England. Gleb quickly downplayed Youssoupov's purported importance and exposed his true character without mercy:

> [T]he Romanovs are very snobbish and to them, Youssoupov is just a commoner. Further, they know as well as I do how dishonest and dirty a person he is. Even if we were [to] assume that Rasputin was a horrible villain, his murder as engineered and performed by Youssoupov, must still be adjudged as one of the filthiest crimes in history, as well as an act of monumental idiocy.
>
> . . . Youssoupov is a self-confessed murderer, perjurer and traitor. As everyone knows, he is also a homosexual, a drunkard and a hooligan. . . .

[He] testified under oath that Anastasia is an impostor and that all her supporters are either lunatics or crooks. But now he tells you that he is willing to have Anastasia acknowledged, but only if there is money in the Bank of England and if he is assured of a share of it. . . . [H]is willingness to acknowledge her as the real Grand Duchess in return for a large sum of money would . . . prove him to be a scoundrel. . . . [H]e knows perfectly well that Anastasia is what she claims to be and his fight against her is a crime more horrible and cruel by far than even the murder of Rasputin.

Nevertheless, Gleb clearly did not blame Milukoff for this gaffe and continued to encourage him to seek out other members of the Romanov family, particularly those still living in England.

Gleb also advised him to remain persistent in his efforts to see Anastasia, who did finally speak with Milukoff briefly through the window of her house in Unterlengenhardt. But she remained suspicious of him, despite the continued entreaties from America. Gleb felt that the problem lay perhaps not with the Grand Duchess, but with her friends:

[Y]ou may well be the victim, not of the Grand Duchess's suspiciousness, but of the intrigues of . . . Baroness Miltitz, or even of Prince Frederick. Both can appear to be so very friendly to the rest of us, but I am not so sure that they are as friendly, in fact. They certainly do not seem to want the Grand Duchess to really trust anybody but themselves. . . . I too seem to be in disfavor for the time being, for both the Prince and the Baroness have failed to answer several of my letters, in spite of the fact (or possibly for the very reason) that they contained some important and urgent questions.

Despite these obstacles, Milukoff persisted and, over the next three years, visited all manner of people interested in Anastasia's case. In doing so, he won their apparent confidence long before he ever succeeded in gaining entrance into the world the Grand Duchess had created for herself in the new barrack.

THE final court session opened on May 9, 1961. The judges began with a long recounting of all the facts that they considered important. As they proceeded through their summary, it became apparent that they had chosen to ignore key points that favored Anastasia. The tribunal overlooked the fact that the Zahle papers had been suppressed by the Danish royal family, that Pierre Gilliard had mysteriously burned all the documentation he claimed to have once had in his possession, and that the photographs purporting to show that Anastasia was Franziska Schanzkowska had been retouched. Most shocking, however, as the judges completed their summation, was the fact that they obviously had no intention of calling Professor Reche or Minna Becker. Anastasia's supporters could not believe that the judges would decline to hear testimony of their own independent, expert authorities in open court. Vermehren, however, provided a markedly weak closing argument, failing to point out even the most glaring omissions in the judges' summation.

Given the obviously slanted interpretation of the evidence, the final decision handed down on May 15, 1961, should not have been surprising. The court judged Anastasia's claim of authenticity to be totally unfounded. After noting the testimony of those who said they had not recognized her, the judges falsely asserted—despite the numerous witnesses presented by Vermehren and Leverkuehn— that no one had acknowledged her at first sight. The court also dismissed the countersuit filed by the defendants, but explained that it had done so merely on the grounds that the issue was irrelevant, given its first decision. The judges seemed to take pains, however, to say that they did believe the identity of the plaintiff as Franziska Schanzkowska was "eminently likely." They went so far as to apologize to Duchess Barbara and Prince Louis of Hesse, lest they had been embarrassed by the proceedings.

Finally, concerning their own expert witnesses, the judges explained that they had not considered their testimony for two primary reasons. First, they felt that Professor Reche—in determining that Anastasia was indeed the Grand Duchess and not Franziska Schanzkowska—had erred and should have considered whether the plaintiff might be somebody else altogether. Second, in regard to the evidence provided by the graphologist Minna Becker, they simply said that she had not compared enough samples to make an accurate analysis.

This was all the explanation necessary under German law and reflected the absolute autonomy the tribunal assumed. After all, it was solely at their discretion that any of the witnesses had been heard, and they alone had final say as to what evidence presented to the court could be deemed relevant. Still, from the view of any objective observer—particularly when considering their refusal to weigh the testimony of their own expert witnesses—the tribunal's decision was at best bad law and at worst a duplicitous shirking of its duty to determine the truth.

Not surprisingly, the attorneys representing Anastasia decided that they must appeal.

ANASTASIA was not at all ready to proceed with further court action and for weeks refused to speak to anyone about the decision in Hamburg. Only after months of arguments by Prince Frederick and Vermehren did she finally agree that they could take the case forward. Confident of her own identity, she had always looked upon the legal battles with suspicion, which had eventually turned into disregard and even boredom. She had refused to cooperate with the judges and was purposefully becoming more and more withdrawn from the world. Yet her defenders—soon to become known as "Anastasians"—persisted. Although they viewed their efforts as benefiting the Grand Duchess, they were defending their own reputations as much as hers.

Many of Anastasia's supporters, chief among them Prince Frederick, had been actively involved in aiding the attorneys during the most crucial moments of the Hamburg trial. They had gathered evidence, sought witnesses—and most importantly—tried to mollify Anastasia while cajoling her into cooperating. As the first hearing drew to a close, they had been joined in this task by Dominique Auclères, the journalist from *Figaro*.

As had so many of her defenders before them, these people had come to Anastasia's aid with the best of intentions. They felt that if her identity could be accepted in a court of law, she would gain access to the means of guaranteeing her future well-being. For their devotion, they were rewarded with vilification by her enemies, who succeeded in making their interest in the case as much an issue as the Grand Duchess's identity. Now, after all these years of involvement they could not allow the matter to drop.

Anastasia, however, was nearing sixty and did not want the vindication or wealth that these people pursued on her behalf. All she required was the kind of comfort and care Mrs. Heydebrand had shown her. It was the only thing that could substitute for the love the Romanovs had denied her.

Nevertheless, once Vermehren had obtained Anastasia's begrudging agreement, he went ahead with his plans and filed papers with the High Court of Appeals to hear the case. This court acknowledged that the earlier tribunal had erred gravely in not considering the testimony of its own expert witnesses and agreed to consider the matter. Shortly thereafter, in October 1962, Vermehren was killed in an automobile accident. Prince Frederick thought the lawyer's death was "destiny," but Anastasia felt certain that he had been assassinated by agents of her enemies. Whatever the cause, his death would further delay the judicial proceedings.

The power of attorney that Vermehren had held now passed to Prince Frederick. When the court informed him in early 1963 that he must find another attorney within six weeks or face dismissal of the case, he quickly located a qualified lawyer. The new advocate was Carl-August Wollmann, an aggressive legal practitioner who, like Dominique Auclères, had become convinced of Anastasia's authenticity after only a brief familiarity with her story.

Wollmann's desire to help the Grand Duchess increased after the Hamburg tribunal issued its written verdict, and he now set about reviewing the vast amount of material compiled by his predecessors. A year would elapse before he was prepared to present the case to the Court of Appeals. He was readily assisted by Prince Frederick, who in turn enlisted the aid of a friend from England named Ian Lilburn. Dominique Auclères, having earlier won the approval of her editors at *Figaro* to help Vermehren after his partner's death, now became an open and vocal ally of Anastasia's new attorney. These three, and others, would form what amounted to a small band of ever-willing investigators and advisers who would eventually attend nearly every court session and map out strategies or compare notes at a nearby hotel.

 The Romanov children were celebrities, their likenesses reproduced all over the world. This German postcard features Anastasia at center.

Czar Nicholas II

Czarina Alexandra

The symbol of the imperial double eagle indicates illustrations from Anastasia's personal collection, now in the James Blair Lovell Collection

Anastasia, the "Clown," playing on an exercise bar in the palace at Czarskoe Selo. The identity of the photographer is unknown, but it was most likely a family member.

Nicholas, Alexandra, and their hemophiliac son Czarevitch Alexis at one of the rare public occasions when the frail boy was seen walking. He was often carried in the arms of a guard.

Nicholas and Alexis feeding the elephant at the children's private menagerie at Czarskoe Selo. Photograph by Czarina Alexandra.

Anastasia, far right, on the tennis court at Czarskoe Selo. Photograph by Czar Nicholas II, from the photo album compiled by Grand Duchess Marie and presented to Tatiana Botkin.

An "animal picture," painted by Gleb Botkin in 1915. These paintings formed the basis of his childhood games with Anastasia. This is one of only two which have survived from the pre-revolutionary period.

Rasputin. Anastasia believed he was "God's gift to Russia." (*The Bettmann Archive*)

Anastasia, center, with her sister Marie at the hospital they sponsored during the First World War. Felix Dassel stands behind Anastasia. The Czarina often commented during this period that Anastasia was growing quite plump.

Harriet Rathlef, photographed by Anastasia, on the Hotel Tivoli balcony at Lugano, March 1926.

Ernest Ludwig, Grand Duke of
Hesse-Darmstadt, the Czarina's
brother.

Grand Duchess Olga,
youngest sister of the Czar.

Pierre Gilliard

Grand Duchess Xenia,
eldest of the Czar's sisters,
in 1912. She is escorted by
Grand Duke Nicholas, one
of the Czar's uncles.

Anastasia, self-portrait in a mirror at the Hotel Tivoli, Lugano, March 1926.

Anastasia, center, with Tatiana Botkin and Dr. Theodor Eitel at the Stillachhaus, September 1926.

Prince Felix Youssoupov. (*The Bettmann Archive*)

Castle Seeon in Germany where Anastasia lived in 1927. Its Russian architecture influenced her to want to buy the castle years later. Her ashes are buried there.

Gleb Botkin in the 1930s.

Annie Burr Jennings in the 1930s. (*Fairfield Historical Society*)

Anastasia's favorite portrait of herself, taken in 1930 at the Jennings estate by the Bridgeport, Connecticut, society photographer, Haley. She is holding the parrots from the West Indies given to her by Xenia Leeds. In later years she refused to allow the picture to be reproduced for publication, saying, "I am saving it for Jemmy's book. It is my best photograph."

Baroness Monica Miltitz, photograph by Alexis Milukoff. (*Lovell Collection*)

Lord Louis Mountbatten (*The Bettmann Archive*)

Germany, 1954, left to right, Adele Heydebrand, Gertrude Lamerdin, Anastasia, Baroness Gienanth.

The symbol of the imperial double eagle indicates illustrations from Anastasia's personal collection, now in the James Blair Lovell Collection

Ingrid Bergman, right, in the Academy Award-winning 1956 film, *Anastasia*. Helen Hayes played the Dowager Czarina and Yul Brynner portrayed a character who seemed to be based in part on Gleb Botkin. (*Twentieth-Century Fox*)

Viveca Lindfors, left, in the title role of the 1954 Broadway production of *Anastasia*. Eugenie Leontovich, seated, as the Dowager Czarina Marie.

Lilli Palmer in the title role of the 1956 film, *Is Anna Anderson Anastasia?*

Amy Irving as Anastasia in the 1986 television mini-series. (*Telecom Entertainment, Inc.*)

ABOVE: Prince Frederick Ernest of Saxe-Altenburg, seated, with Alexis Milukoff, in the mid-1960s. (*Lovell Collection*)

LEFT: Anastasia in the 1950s. She was aware that she looked nothing like the glamorous actresses who portrayed her.

Anastasia's own copy of the German postcard of the new barrack in Unterlengenhardt, presented to her and signed on the back by Prince Frederick and Baroness Miltitz.

Das Anastasia-Haus in Unterlengenhardt

Anastasia with her dog, Baby. She felt closer to her pets than to most people; they were also a source of protection.

Anastasia with her oil self-portrait. "I look like a monkey," she told Milukoff. (*Lovell Collection*)

Anastasia in the hospital in Germany after her breakdown in 1968. She had just agreed to travel to the United States when Milukoff snapped this picture. (*Lovell Collection*)

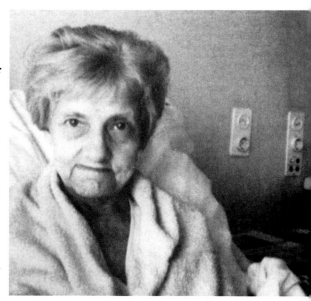

Gleb Botkin's drawing of Anastasia and
Jack, 1969. (*Andrew Hartsook Collection*)

Jack Manahan and Gleb Botkin,
photographed by Milukoff, the day after
Anastasia's arrival in Charlottesville,
Virginia, July 1968. (*Lovell Collection*)

The Manahan
residence at 35
University Circle,
Charlottesville, as
Anastasia first saw it
in 1968. (*Transgas*)

A similar view of the house about ten years later. (*Bill Sublette*)

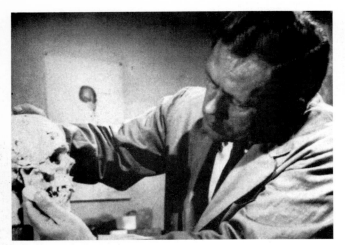

Moritz Furtmayr, the eminent German forensics expert whose PIK ear identification test scientifically established Anastasia's identity in 1977. (*Lovell Collection*)

 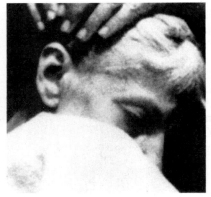

Two of the photographs used by Furtmayr. Left, an enlargement of a childhood picture of Anastasia, clearly showing her right ear. Right, the same ear in 1959, from a series of pictures taken for Professor Otto Reche's anthropological report. (*Furtmayr Collection*)

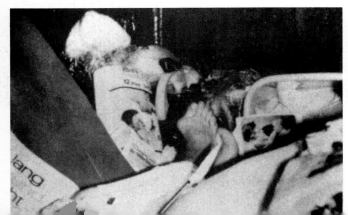

Detail of a photograph depicting Anastasia's bare feet. The *hallux valgus* is clearly evident on the right foot. Taken by Milukoff in the new barrack about 1967. (*Lovell Collection*)

Two views of the living room of the Manahan residence at 35 University Circle after Anastasia married Jack. (*Bill Sublette*)

BELOW, LEFT: Jack and Anastasia in the late 1970s. (*Bill Sublette*)

BELOW, RIGHT: Anastasia's last photograph, taken by Jane Holt, Christmas 1983. Mrs. Holt's daughter, Vicki Branham, standing, and granddaughter, Amy Branham, kneeling. Anastasia had less than two months to live. (*Lovell Collection*)

Suzanna Catharina de Graaff in the garden at Unterlengenhardt, June 24, 1952. Photograph taken by Anastasia, who called her "Princess Alexandra." (*Isaac Don Levine Collection*)

Antoon van Weelden identified this man as his grandfather, Leendert Johannes Hemmes, the psychic "pisswatcher." (*Jaap Bottema Collection*)

The signed photograph of Czarina Alexandra in its original silver frame which Anastasia always kept at her bedside. (*Bill Sublette*)

VII.

"To get the Grand Duchess out of Germany"

ON APRIL 9, 1964, the High Court of Appeals in Hamburg began its hearing. The chief judge of the panel was nearing retirement, and this was the last case he was supposed to hear. He planned to finish the proceedings by the end of the year, and his opening statement restricted possible disruption by the press and barred cameras from the courtroom. He downplayed the previous notoriety by stating that the case was not one of "world-historical significance." Like the earlier tribunal, the judge announced, the Court of Appeals would conduct its own investigation and wanted the evidence limited solely to what was presented in court by the attorneys from both sides. He particularly cautioned Wollmann that Anastasia alone would have to bear the burden of proof, precisely what the American attorney Fallows had originally tried to avoid and what had proved one of the major problems in the previous trial.

Thorough investigations had already been conducted and the judge indicated he preferred to exclude evidence other than that contained in the existing records. But the documents and evidence amassed over the previous thirty years could not be dispensed with in a matter of months. As a result, even though little new information regarding the case came to light, this trial lasted nearly three years.

The first witnesses to testify before the court were the anthropological expert, Professor Otto Reche, and the graphologist, Minna Becker, whose testimony the previous tribunal had refused to hear. Despite a constant barrage of irrelevant assertions from an expert supplied by the attorneys for the Romanov family, Reche was successful in arguing his conclusions that Anastasia was indeed the lost Grand Duchess. In a careful manner, he explained to the tribunal his detailed study of the vast photographic and medical evidence.

Reche concentrated particularly on four points of identification involving measurements of the cheekbones, eyesockets, and forehead, noting that in some cases the features of Anastasia matched those of the young princess to within a fraction of a millimeter. The expert witness provided by the attorneys for Duchess Barbara and Grand Duke Louis challenged Reche specifically on one point. He referred to the pictures of the ears that had first been studied in 1927 and used by the Grand Duke of Hesse as the basis for his denouncement of Anastasia. The court determined to have its own expert make further investigations, and the findings he reported back to the judges clearly supported Reche's arguments for the Grand Duchess's authenticity. The court itself, however, never came to a conclusion on this point.

Minna Becker's oral testimony was equally strong:

> I have never before seen two sets of handwriting bearing all of these concordant signs, which belonged to two different people. . . . I also know what difficulty people can have with writing after they have passed through some tragic or traumatic event. . . . There remain in Mrs. Anderson's handwriting [however] *all* of the traits that were already apparent in the handwriting of the young Anastasia.

To counter this witness, the defense attorney presented his own expert, and the arguments grew so tedious and complicated over the next two days that the court appointed yet another expert to resolve the debate. This last report completely denigrated the defense's expert and tacitly confirmed the conclusion that Becker had reached about Anastasia's authenticity. The judges now ordered a set of pleadings by the attorneys that would help the court determine whether further evidence was needed before they recessed to issue a judgment.

IN February 1965, the court finally returned to hear the arguments of the two counsels as to whether to continue with the accumulation of evidence before a judgment was issued. This session had been delayed because of a prolonged illness by Wollmann, but he was now prepared to argue that further investigations were warranted. One of the demands the Court of Appeals had made early in its proceedings was that Anastasia submit to a physical examination by medical experts. The judges had taken the action with the hope that the doctors would be able to determine when and how she had received the wounds that had left so many scars on her body. Anastasia had agreed, and Wollman made the results known at this session.

Although the medical findings echoed almost precisely some of the conclusions reached by Dr. Rudnev, who had examined Anastasia at St. Mary's Hospital in 1925, the debate among the lawyers and their own experts became so involved that no statement was deemed too absurd to utter. At one point, the Romanovs' lawyer implied that some of the scars could have resulted from suicide attempts. After hours of charges and countercharges, the issues became incredibly confused and the judges recessed without giving any indication of whether they were prepared to reach a decision.

BY 1965, Gleb had become increasingly—almost obsessively—concerned about the future well-being of the Grand Duchess. Prince Frederick assured him that the latest appeal of her case would prove favorable and would, therefore, ensure eventual access to the Czar's fortune. Gleb remained skeptical. He was apparently able to gather only sporadic information about the case from press reports or from the opinions of friends and supporters who wrote to him about the Grand Duchess.

To make matters worse, Gleb and his wife Nadine had been forced to leave their cottage in New Jersey after a forest fire. They had first moved to a small town in Maryland where one of their sons lived, before eventually settling in Charlottesville, Virginia, near their daughter, Marina Botkin Schweitzer, and her husband, Richard. Even though Gleb told both Anastasia and Milukoff of his happiness at finding the Virginia town reminiscent of Czarskoe Selo, the process of moving and resettling had further hindered his ability to monitor the situation in Germany.

Gleb's letters to Milukoff during 1963 and 1964 show a growing irritation with the lack of information provided by Prince Frederick and a mistrust of the assessments offered by Baroness Miltitz:

I have found it impossible to get from . . . [Prince Frederick] answers to the simplest questions. My last letter, he did not deign to answer personally, but turned it over to Baroness Miltitz who responded with the usual incomprehensible gobbledygook.

Being thus deliberately kept in complete ignorance of current developments, I have no means of forming any definite opinion as to how well the good Prince is conducting Grand Duchess Anastasia's case, but am puzzled and worried on several counts, including the Prince's inexplicably high opinion of German courts. So far, those courts have shown themselves as straight as corkscrews.

As Anastasia became increasingly reluctant to cooperate in any way with the court's deliberations, Gleb was certain that the judges would use her aversion as an excuse to issue another negative ruling. If that happened, he informed Milukoff, then the Grand Duchess could face enormous legal fees, as well as a possible countersuit by the defendants. One or both of these events would leave her penniless.

GLEB feared most a successful countersuit. Not only could such an outcome result in the loss of her home, but the final condemnation would also thrust her into an irreversible depression. The reports he received from Milukoff more than confirmed his own strong belief that Anastasia was on the verge of critical mental instability. Since Gleb could not travel to Germany to ascertain what was really happening, he turned to Milukoff as a source of information and help.

Despite repeated rebuffs by Anastasia, Milukoff had followed Gleb's early advice and had remained persistent in his attempts to see the Grand Duchess. Finally, on her birthday—June 18, 1963—the Russian emigre had arrived at her house in Unterlengenhardt complete with presents and photographs that he knew would interest her. From that day, he apparently began to win her confidence, although she preferred him to visit in the company of one of the women who still cared for her.

Because Milukoff now had access to Anastasia and demonstrated an interest in Gleb's advice and opinions on matters affecting the

Grand Duchess, the two men began making plans for shielding her from the effects of an adverse ruling by the Hamburg Court of Appeals. Gleb asked Milukoff to keep him directly informed of all developments—particularly Anastasia's physical and mental states and the latest maneuverings in court—and began to solicit Milukoff's active participation in protecting her.

Anastasia certainly seemed to be in the direst straits she had been in since the end of the Second World War. She had limited her contacts with the outside world to a bare minimum and remained suspicious of everyone. Gleb had long ago begun to feel that the Baroness and the Prince were happy at this development, for it meant that they could control the Grand Duchess completely. Gleb knew her retreat was dangerous, because previous periods of self-imposed seclusion had ended disastrously. Her retreats from the abuses she had suffered from the Kleists, Xenia Leeds, and Miss Jennings had had terrible consequences for her physical and psychological health.

Gleb knew that Anastasia had been ill from time to time since moving into the new barrack, and that her living conditions continued to deteriorate. It was partly Anastasia's own fault, now that she had made her house off-limits to nearly everyone and preferred to fend for herself and her growing menagerie of cats and dogs. Gleb sensed that she was once again attempting to avoid the unpleasantness of the world outside. He knew that, to her mind, withdrawing was the only way to avoid being manipulated by events beyond her control, especially the court trials. At the same time, however, he realized that practical considerations and consequences could not be ignored. The authority of the court in Hamburg could not be discounted. The seeming reluctance of Baroness Miltitz and Prince Frederick to admit to the possibility of an adverse decision, let alone plan for it, made the situation even more critical. Gleb felt completely powerless to help his friend and determined that the time had come for desperate moves.

In January 1965, he wrote to Milukoff with his idea for saving Anastasia:

To me, it seems imperative to get the Grand Duchess out of Germany. . . .

I should like very much to bring . . . [her] to this country, but so far have been unable to find any means of getting an American visa for her. . . .

I have enough money pledged by various friends for the Grand Duchess's journey to this country and her support here. I am still trying to get that visa, but if I fail, shall try to talk those friends into supporting the Grand Duchess in Europe. But she must be taken out of Germany as soon as the court rules against her.

Please . . . give the matter serious thought. Do not discuss it with the Prince, or the Baroness, or anybody in Unterlengenhardt, except possibly the Grand Duchess herself and then only if you can stay alone with her.

Milukoff readily agreed to Gleb's plan, and they began preparations for obtaining a visa for Anastasia to go to America.

The amount of detailed planning they accomplished in the first few weeks was nothing short of amazing. Soon after making his proposal to Milukoff and obtaining a promise of cooperation, Gleb wrote again. He outlined the bureaucratic hurdles they would have to overcome as well as the practical concerns he had already taken into consideration. The first issue was whether the American consul would grant a visa for Anastasia to travel to the United States based only on her German identification papers. The Grand Duchess held no valid passport, and Gleb feared that the Americans would not approve a visa without formal travel documents.

Adding to this difficulty, Anastasia held two sets of German identification papers under two different names. The first were issued to Anastasia Tschaikovsky with the correct birth date, June 18, 1901, and her birthplace properly stated as Peterhof, Russia. The Grand Duchess had traveled to the United States in 1928 under this identity and the American officials were certain to have that information in their records. The second set of papers had been surreptitiously prepared by Miss Jennings and her friends at the German consulate in New York when they sent the Grand Duchess back to Germany for confinement at the Ilten Sanatorium. Those papers gave her name as Anna Anderson, which she still used and by which she had come to be generally known, and listed her birthplace as Berlin.

Gleb cautioned Milukoff that the Americans would know about the first set of identification papers, and reminded him of the unrelenting attempts by her opponents to portray her as an impostor. Given these circumstances, Gleb explained, Anastasia should apply for a visa only under the name Anastasia Tschaikovsky. Otherwise, she might be refused entry into the United States—or later expelled—for providing false information on her visa application. Either event would strengthen the accusations made by her Romanov relatives that she was a liar.

Besides his detailed explanation of this facet of the process, Gleb also informed Milukoff that he had already seen to the problem of caring for Anastasia once she reached America:

> Were the Grand Duchess to come to this country, her support would be guaranteed for life. There may be a brief period of some inconvenience, but before long the Grand Duchess would have at her disposal a lovely apartment on an estate only a few miles from . . . [Charlottesville], in one of the most beautiful places to be found anywhere in the world. It would not be possible to bring any of her dogs or cats into this country, but one puppy of a somewhat similar breed and with a perfect pedigree has already been reserved and there will be no difficulty at all in finding more of them. . . .

> Parenthetically, were it to prove possible to take the Grand Duchess by plane directly from Germany to the United States, she will be properly escorted all the way and properly met here. Money necessary for her transportation has already been deposited in a German bank.

Finally, Gleb let Milukoff know that he had made these proposals directly in a letter to Anastasia and that he expected her to be agreeable to the plan. Gleb cautioned that he did not want to raise her hopes unnecessarily and encouraged Milukoff to continue quietly doing all he could from Germany to speed things along.

Despite all Gleb's precautions and warnings that these plans should remain as secretive as possible, others soon became directly involved. Suddenly, what had seemed like a straightforward plan became extremely complicated. First, Baroness Miltitz and Prince Frederick learned of the strategy, perhaps from Anastasia herself. Sometimes they supported the idea, although Gleb suspected that each wanted merely to come to the United States on a free trip as Anastasia's escort. Most of the time they seemed unwilling to let go of the Grand Duchess. Perhaps they felt that if she were to flee Germany before a final outcome of the court case, the tribunal in Hamburg would misconstrue her departure and find in favor of Duchess Barbara and Prince Louis.

At the same time, far from being enthusiastic about the idea, Anastasia balked. She refused to cooperate in filling out the visa form that had been obtained from the American consul in Germany. Gleb had gone to a great deal of trouble in trying to arrange an easy escape for Anastasia from her troubles in Europe, but he was quickly growing frustrated. Adding to his burden, his wife Nadine had become seriously ill in early 1965 and Gleb was required to expend more and more of his physical and emotional energy for her care. At one point, he seemed completely discouraged at the way events were turning out:

> I have . . . managed to arrange everything that could possibly have been arranged from here. Now, it is the Grand Duchess herself who must act and if she refuses to do so, there is nothing else either I myself, or her other friends in this country could possibly do for her. In such a case, the Grand Duchess will have nobody to rely upon, except Prince Frederick; and that would be about as comfortable and secure a situation as having to sit on a chair with rubber legs.

Gleb's devotion to Anastasia, however, could not be so easily dissuaded, and he continued to work with Milukoff, the Grand Duchess, and his many friends in America to help take her out of Germany.

ONE of those in Charlottesville to whom Gleb had turned, and who had enthusiastically lent his support, was Professor John Eacott Manahan. At first, their relationship had been rather formal, but as Manahan developed an intense and detailed interest in Anastasia and her case, the two men began to talk often. By 1965, Gleb had begun referring to Manahan as Jack and informed Milukoff that Jack had agreed to act as Anastasia's sponsor in the United States. Jack was the one who had promised Gleb that the Grand Duchess could live on his estate outside Charlottesville, and he later sent money to pay for her trip.

Jack Manahan was a wealthy, well-respected member of the community and a personal acquaintance of influential American government figures. As such, he felt no compunction about making repeated inquiries to the U.S. Department of State and the American consul in Germany. He pursued these personal contacts by signing many affidavits and writing numerous letters to American officials attesting to his promise of support for the Grand Duchess once she reached the United States. As his efforts intensified over the course of the next three years, Jack Manahan would become very knowledgeable about her affairs. Apparently, he even visited Anastasia in Unterlengenhardt to assure her of his sincere desire to be of help.

GLEB'S frustration with Anastasia's unwillingness to cooperate in filling out papers and forms reemerged often. He also felt constantly stymied by the apparent interference of Baroness Miltitz and Prince Frederick and, from time to time, would express his disappointment when Jack acted on his own without first informing him. Nevertheless, Gleb never wavered in his desire to see his plan enacted and his attempts to save Anastasia succeed.

All sorts of plans were considered. An early thought was to drive the Grand Duchess across the border to escape the reach of German authorities, if need be. Later, someone suggested that Anastasia apply for political asylum as a means of acquiring permanent residency in the United States. In the end, Gleb realized that no matter what the plan, he would have to rely on the help of others. He was left with only two sources of aid: Jack's able, if sometimes misguided, actions in America; and Milukoff's growing influence with Anastasia in Unterlengenhardt.

VIII.

"Yes, write, write, write"

AFTER HIS first face-to-face encounter with Anastasia in 1963, Milukoff had begun attempting to gain her trust. The task proved difficult at first. Nevertheless, he slowly managed to assume a key role in her life. In large part this was due to his own character, particularly his extreme persistence. Milukoff had written many letters to Gleb and visited him in America as a means of assuring his introduction to the Grand Duchess. Afterward, he had made numerous trips to Unterlengenhardt and all over Europe in an attempt to gather as much information as possible about Anastasia, her history, and the ongoing court trials. All these efforts had provided him with a detailed comprehension of her personality, especially of the people and things she liked and those she would not tolerate. The fact that, as a complete stranger, he had been able to gain the confidence of so many people was an indication of his charm and his almost instinctive ability to ingratiate himself. Getting close to Anastasia was quite a different matter, however, and the success he had in that regard cannot be attributed to his personality alone.

When Milukoff first appeared, Anastasia had already established a world of her own liking. After finally moving to the new barrack, she had constructed both a physical and mental wall around herself. The fence and iron gates topped with barbed wire were but a material extension of the protection she built around her thoughts and emotions. Within the house were hundreds of books, thousands of photographs, and dozens of priceless mementos of her family and her history. They had mostly been gifts from the many friends who supported her and her case. Now they were her only solace, and she would sit for hours alone or with the occasional visitor, reminiscing as she shuffled through what she often called her "precious goods."

But the number of visitors decreased rapidly, as Anastasia refused to see anyone she did not know and most of those she did. Having as much as banned Baroness Miltitz from entering the new barrack, she began to suspect that others were spying for the Baroness. She saw conspiracy everywhere, and even Prince Frederick was not immune from her mistrust, especially as she began to realize that the court trials might go badly and cost her what little security she had achieved. Protection was of the utmost importance to Anastasia now, and her unwavering attempt to maintain a sense of security explains what has often been observed as her strange behavior during this period.

WHEN she retreated into a world of her own creation, there was no question of who she was. This world was a place where she alone could control which questions to ask, which answers to give, and most important, which motives would govern. Her universe evolved from a single constellation—one formed from the feelings and perceptions of a young imperial princess, the person she had never ceased to be.

Anastasia's only chance for a life of happiness had died even before Ekaterinburg, but after the murder of her family and her failed attempts to reconcile with her other relatives, that chance was beyond resurrection. She had no choice but to try to recapture those hopes, and she had nowhere else to turn but to her memories. She was not capable of facing memories that frightened or saddened her, so she began to rearrange otherwise inexplicable events to her own purpose. She continued to reinvent the past, even the most recent past, which was perhaps the hardest to understand. Her earlier reassessments of her aunts, her uncle, Xenia Leeds, and Miss Jennings were but the first indications of her capacity for creating the most absurd exonerations. Her belief that assassins and conspirators pursued her became an obsession. At this time, she also began reviving the secrets of her childhood that only she knew, whether they were closely guarded facts about her family or mere gossip from the imperial court. She must have felt that she had at least achieved some command over her own circumstances simply by establishing a world whose order only she defined, and only she could alter.

Along with the control came undoubtedly a certain sense of freedom and power. She soon felt unencumbered enough to tell Miss Mutius and Miss Thomasius the most fantastic things when they were allowed to visit. The two women reported to Baroness Miltitz and Prince Frederick that Anastasia was spinning imaginary stories. They may have understood that this was Anastasia's way of newly defining what she had once been and what she had become, but they more likely felt that this development signaled her complete mental collapse.

Despite her withdrawal, Anastasia had a certain awareness of what was happening around her. She knew that she looked like a withered old woman, aged far beyond her years by tragedy. She never forgave the "creators" who sought to construct make-believe images of her, especially the "creators" who had profited so much more than she from the films and books and press stories. They were very much responsible for forcing her to retreat from the world. They had brought the tourists and curiosity seekers who had come expecting to find a beautiful princess living in the fairy-tale world that they had seen portrayed. What these outsiders found instead were fences and iron gates that protected a deteriorating house and property that graphically revealed Anastasia's true condition and her rejection of the world outside.

Together, the revolution and her own relatives had denied her the life to which she had been born and raised to expect. Later, the unrelenting publicity and the unfolding of the Anastasia legend on stage and screen had robbed her of even the possibility of living in dignity as the person she had been forced to become. She viewed the efforts of her self-proclaimed protectors and defenders as merely further attempts to manipulate and distort her image. Their concern was that the world would think her a befuddled and mysterious woman, but she saw their efforts as another means of denying her what little solace she could find in what her life had become. She must have felt abandoned to wander between dreams of what should have been and the reality of what was. But the knowledge and constant reminders of her predicament only increased her contempt for it.

Anastasia never retreated so far into her own world that she forgot the controversy that surrounded her. Along with her piles of photographs and treasures, she also kept dozens of boxes filled with documents and objects that she felt proved her authenticity beyond doubt. She rarely showed them to even those few people she now identified as friends, which reflected in large part her disdain at ever having been challenged on the matter. But the fact that she guarded them so closely demonstrated clearly that she understood that others could use the issue of identity against her. The court trials had made this point dramatically.

Gleb, who in spite of his distance perhaps understood her best, was certainly aware of Anastasia's ability to see the consequences of her withdrawal. He did not hesitate to give her his frank opinion of her attorneys, the judges, and the case in general, and although the Grand Duchess did not always abide by his judgments or advice, she seldom failed to seek it. In this role, however, Gleb was unique.

Anastasia often expressed her contempt through an imperious refusal to cooperate and a condescension reflected in sarcasm. These attitudes only served to isolate her even more, as those who sought to help her were often turned away in an unaccountably rude manner. Thus Anastasia was, by design and circumstances, alone. Nearly all those who knew the truth of her past—and who had suffered much of it with her—had either died or been purposely driven away.

THEN appeared Milukoff, a man who said he had served in her father's horse guard. Gleb had solidly endorsed Milukoff. Moreover, during his first real visit, this charming Russian emigre had presented the Grand Duchess with photographs and presents. The gifts provided both a kind of tribute to her stolen grandeur and a means of impressing her with his own remarkable efforts in gathering information about her life. At first, Milukoff was allowed to visit only sporadically, but even these brief stays served two important purposes. He learned to judge her moods more accurately and earned her begrudging acceptance. She began to talk more openly to him and came to rely on him for information. She showed a particular interest in the gossip surrounding the trials and in news about Gleb, whose letters became more infrequent as he had been shunted to the side by Baroness Miltitz and Prince Frederick.

By the fall of 1964, Gleb wrote to Milukoff expressing pleasure that Anastasia was treating him "as the true friend you actually are." Although she continued trying to avoid contact with most outsiders, she had developed a strange affection for the Russian emigre. She would still see him only when one of the Unterlengenhardt women—Miss Thomasius or Miss Mutius—was also present, but he was eventually allowed to visit more frequently. Anastasia felt that he posed no threat and undoubtedly she began to trust in his willingness to help as much as had Gleb, who had little doubt that he could rely on Milukoff to further his plan for taking Anastasia out of Germany. Over the course of many months, she allowed a more significant level of friendship to develop. Finally, she began to reveal her confidences to Milukoff.

GLEB'S concerns about the outcome of the trial seemed completely justified, as the Hamburg Court of Appeals in 1965 announced that the hearing first begun four years earlier would continue. The judges wanted to hear the testimony of new witnesses, but little of consequence came out in the next few months. One witness charged that Anastasia had worked as a spy for the Soviet government after the First World War. He claimed that she had been enlisted with the aid of Grand Duke Andrew, the member of the Romanov family who had conducted his own study in the 1920s and had been highly criticized by his family for acknowledging Anastasia. Wollmann, Anastasia's attorney, was quickly able to prove that the man had been coached by the defense attorney, and his testimony was discredited on the spot.

Of apparently greater importance were the statements provided by another witness, who testified that he had lived near the Ipatiev House and had sheltered the wounded Grand Duchess Anastasia in his home after the assassination. This seemed to be clear proof that the youngest daughter of Czar Nicholas had lived—a crucial point in the entire legal debate—but by the time the lawyers had argued the many points raised, the validity of this testimony, too, was cast in doubt.

* * *

IN September 1965, Wollmann arranged for the chief judge to visit Unterlengenhardt with a Russian language expert to test Anastasia's knowledge of that language. Since this was a formal court proceeding, the defense attorney was also to be present. Wollmann, however, had not informed his client of their arrival beforehand. It was only with the help of his fellow Anastasians—Prince Frederick and Ian Lilburn—that he was able to convince his client after many hours to see the judge. Anastasia remained unaware, however, that her knowledge of Russian was to be tested.

When Anastasia entered the room where the interview was to take place, she was incensed to see the defense attorney present and insisted that he leave. After his departure, she told the judge that he was "a copy of Youssoupov when he was young. . . . You can believe me, everybody fell in love with him."

The test began almost immediately after this. According to those present, including some of the Anastasians, she was questioned by the language expert in Russian for one and a half hours, but she always responded in English. She engaged the judge in casual conversation and seemed to be enjoying herself. As the questions continued, however, she was constantly prodded by others in the room, Prince Frederick among them. Eventually, she grew exhausted and would speak no more. As the meeting ended, Anastasia—still unaware of the real purpose of the session—asked when the questions about her case would begin.

THAT the court seemed strangely uninterested in hearing Anastasia's testimony on her own behalf was but one sign of how the world beyond the new barrack continued to view her. For most people, Anastasia had become a personality, not a person, and they were generally unaware of the woman living in Unterlengenhardt. What fascinated people almost exclusively were the myths and legends that were forever repeated, even though these were little more than hollow fabrications of the young woman she had once been.

In 1965, plans were underway for a new version of the Maurette-Bolton play, this time in the form of a full-scale Broadway musical entitled *Anya*, with a score based on the compositions of Rachmaninov. Constance Towers played the role of Anastasia and Lillian

Gish, the Dowager Czarina. It premiered at the Ziegfeld Theatre on November 29, 1965, and Anastasia—who was still entitled to a portion of the rights of all works based on the earlier play—was probably aware of the size and scope of the production long before it opened. For years she had been trying to escape precisely the kind of distortions that were at the core of the play. The public clamor had never really ended from the earlier stage and film productions, and now it would surely intensify.

Anya was to be just one more effort at profiting from Anastasia's image and her predicament, as she felt her former protectors and defenders had done. By this time, she was convinced that Baroness Miltitz and Prince Frederick merely disguised their real intentions in offers of help. In truth, they sought only to control her so that she could do nothing to interfere with their determination to prove her identity and then have her take possession of the Czar's fortune.

Anastasia had been made acutely aware that she was in danger of financial ruin. She heard this sensible assessment of her situation constantly from Gleb and Milukoff, just as they echoed her suspicions about the Baroness and the Prince. The Grand Duchess was far from an uninterested observer of her own life, and she came to realize what was happening and, more importantly, what might yet unfold.

As these events began to converge, Milukoff was formulating his own plans, which Anastasia would see as an opportunity to fulfill one of her lifelong desires. When he had first become interested in her case and begun his correspondence with Gleb, Milukoff had attempted to write an article supporting the Grand Duchess's authenticity. The effort had proved unsuccessful and the story was never published, partly because Baroness Miltitz had convinced Anastasia that it would harm her image. Nevertheless, he had remained an unstoppable chronicler of Anastasia's life and an unrelenting defender of her authenticity. By 1965, Milukoff had traveled and met with nearly every major representative of the Romanov family, in addition to visiting Russian emigre communities in Europe and America. He had taken up the task of detailing every aspect of the Grand Duchess's life and had read the numerous books and articles both for and against her. He had collected hundreds of photographs and taken even more himself, compiling a personal travelogue of all the places where Anastasia had lived.

Anastasia had come to trust Milukoff, in large part because she felt comfortable with him. He was as much a gossip as she, and with his knowledge and recent updates on the family, they would sit and chat for hours. They would analyze the events of her life, discuss the people who had played important roles in her story, and criticize the "creators" who had prevented her from gaining happiness. She allowed Milukoff a certain degree of familiarity because she found him entertaining.

One of the interests Anastasia shared with her new friend was a love of gadgetry. Milukoff was, after all, an engineer, and he naturally used the most modern tools in exercising his penchant for gathering facts and information. A self-styled historian like Milukoff would have been lost in the 1960s without his portable tape recorder and sixteen-millimeter camera. Anastasia's fascination with photography was by this time widely known, and she was naturally intrigued by the moving pictures that Milukoff was able to show her. More than that, however, she loved the idea of recording her own voice. She was as interested in the manner in which the recording was accomplished as in the importance, or lack of it, of what she said. Her new friend soon convinced her that she should allow him to tape her voice whenever he came to visit as a means of capturing in sound what had always eluded her otherwise—an authentic record of who she was.

The first tapes made in Unterlengenhardt recorded informal conversations ranging over an array of topics. Although either Miss Mutius or Miss Thomasius was always present, the conversation took place almost exclusively between the two principals. Milukoff sought to have Anastasia teach him even more about her life, and she was delighted to have an interested and attentive listener, someone who did not try to stop her from talking about anything. He would provide her with photographs of people and places from her past and ask her to explain or simply to recollect. She was happy to become lost in these memories. In turn, she would also tell stories and reveal some of the secrets she had ordered and structured in her own fashion during the years she spent alone.

Anastasia often taunted Milukoff—"he who knows so much," as she would say—during the recording sessions. Part of her method of mocking him was to tell him what she knew to be the most absurd tales, perhaps as a means of testing their effect, but more likely as a way of investigating just how much Milukoff really knew and how far she could trust him. For example, she might recite as fact the notion that her brother, the Czarevitch, had not been the natural child of their parents or that he had never suffered from hemophilia. Mixed with these wild stories would be her reconstruction of history, formed from the new images she had created of those who had turned against her in the past. She would tell him of what she now saw as the truly pure intentions of the Grand Duchesses Xenia and Olga, and the Grand Duke of Hesse, of Xenia Leeds and Miss Jennings, forgetting the awful consequences. But above all, she would supply him with the facts and dates and names that no one else knew or that few others could now remember.

Milukoff recorded it all and reported back to Gleb what she had said, seeking his help in separating fact from fiction. Gleb was "delighted" that she had begun recording her reminiscences, and he told Milukoff he felt certain that "in the end [you will] assemble material of the greatest value." As he learned the full extent of the taping sessions, however, Gleb expressed alarm that some of the material Anastasia provided was "delirious nonsense." He warned Milukoff to "be very careful with the Grand Duchess's tapes. You can easily imagine what her enemies could do if they get hold of such utter nonsense dictated in her own voice." Yet the taping continued, and as Anastasia grew more comfortable with the process, she became increasingly willing to reveal all she could. The value of these revelations, when separated from the fantasies she would also spin, became as clear as Gleb had predicted.

ON August 14, 1965, Milukoff arrived at the new barrack, where Anastasia was expecting him. As was his practice, he brought out the tape recorder and began asking questions. The tape begins with one of their normal discussions about photographs he brought along with him. As she admires the pictures, he tells her that he would like to take some of the better photos and produce a book about her. He begins to discuss the barest details of what the project might mean, but his remarks are drowned out by her immediate reaction: "You have my permission, you can do that. Yes, write, write, write. Do, do, do, do. Yes, yes. Write it, write it. Do it at once! Yes, yes. Write, write, write!" The enthusiasm that comes through clearly in her words and voice is not surprising. Almost certainly with full knowledge of Anastasia's past attempts to write her autobiography, Milukoff had finally presented her with the one project for which she never lacked a will and desire to see completed—her own story, in her own words.

IX.
"The free development of the personality"

THE TAPES SHOW that both Anastasia and Milukoff intended from the very beginning to record a thorough compendium of her understanding of what had happened, both before and after Ekaterinburg. Such an organized result was never achieved, in part because events and characters as random and surreptitious as those in Anastasia's life were not easily rationalized. Moreover, Anastasia had spent the last several years developing her own explanations for what had happened. Her rationalizations had been completely personal, and she saw no need for them to make sense to anyone other than herself. Her attitude was reinforced when she began speaking into Milukoff's microphone.

Ever the imperious arbiter of her immediate surroundings, Anastasia often insists on the tapes that she, alone, control how her story is told. As the conversations unfold, it is she who determines which topics are discussed, and if Milukoff tries to refine her course, she either refuses to acknowledge him or simply changes the subject altogether. Her choice of important topics and her interpretations of them clearly indicate the thought processes she had developed since living alone.

What the Milukoff tapes offer, then, is not so much a wealth of historical fact but a better understanding of precisely who Anastasia was. As the interviews begin to fill more and more tapes, she becomes almost completely comfortable with Milukoff and shows a willingness to discuss all manner of things. When she opens a story on a new subject, she is invariably intent on telling all she wants to remember about it. At times, the topics are those of clear historical importance to her life. In other instances, they might be nothing more than detailed recitations of gossip and innuendo. In every case, though, Anastasia reveals much about herself.

ONE of their conversations concerns Eugenia Smith, an American woman living outside Chicago who claimed to be the real Anastasia. Other than the Franziska Schanzkowska myth, Mrs. Smith's account was the most publicized of many such frauds, probably because she appeared in 1963 during the court trials. Some of Anastasia's supporters worried that Lord Mountbatten may have aided her as a means of further confusing the situation, but Anastasia was amused by Eugenia Smith's claim and the attention it gained.

Mrs. Smith had approached the New York publishers, Robert Speller & Sons, with a manuscript. The Spellers questioned her but, before agreeing to a book project, they investigated the matter more closely. One of the persons they contacted was Gleb Botkin, who in 1963 reported that "originally Mrs. Smith submitted a manuscript of her memoirs . . . in which she . . . claimed only to have known the Grand Duchess at the time of her stay in Romania." The Spellers told Gleb that only after they informed Mrs. Smith of their suspicion that she herself was Anastasia that "she modestly admitted that she was." They scheduled her to undergo a lie detector test and a psychiatric evaluation, after which they accepted Mrs. Smith as genuine and asked her to rewrite her manuscript. Gleb "told them their lie detector must have had a screw loose somewhere" and cautioned the Spellers not to proceed.

In October 1963, *Life* magazine printed an article containing portions of the Smith book prior to publication, as well as the findings of an investigative reporter who concluded Mrs. Smith was a fraud. The Spellers, however, published her book and continued to try and prove their author's authenticity. As part of their efforts, they agreed to a request by another purported Romanov survivor, Michal Goleniewsky, to meet with Mrs. Smith. Goleniewsky claimed to be the Czarevitch Alexis, but was really a former Polish army officer who had covertly helped the American Central Intelligence Agency during the 1950s before they brought him to the United States. Once he was in America, Goleniewsky revealed his claim and said that he had been "miraculously" cured of his childhood hemophilia. He also stated that his three sisters in Poland were really the Grand Duchesses Olga, Tatiana, and Marie. Mrs. Smith insisted that the meeting between herself and Goleniewsky on December 31, 1963, at the offices of Speller & Sons, be taped. Within a few minutes, the two impostors tearfully embraced and affirmed one another's authenticity. Shortly thereafter, however, they met again privately, only to later publicly denounce each other as a fraud.

Goleniewsky quickly disappeared from view but the CIA provided him further support and protection. Eugenia Smith was again seen only when she posed as a victim in photographic recreations in true-crime magazines. In 1965, Speller & Sons announced their intention to file suit claiming fraud in order to recover payments made to Mrs. Smith, although they have since denied ever doubting her.

Anastasia asks Milukoff a simple question as their conversation ends: "Is it not incredible?"

A particularly favorite, and more serious, subject of hers is the immoral, especially licentiousness, behavior of royalty—past and present, great or minor. Like a Romanov princess, she can and does provide the most detailed history of many branches of European royalty:

> King Konstantine, the finer king from the Danish royal family, they won't have, you know, as they have. There cannot be a finer being as this is. He really looks elegant and beautiful, and has brains. And the people love him tenderly. . . . [The Greek royal family are] English, they all are English. You see, they come over from Denmark. The

footing of this family is Denmark. The footing of this house is the brother of the empress of Russia. That was the first king, from the Danish royal family. . . . His real name was William and he became George the First.

She also gives other intangible evidence of her Romanov past. As might be expected from the descendant of a family that used pogroms effectively for centuries to help maintain its power, her speech is sprinkled with remarks that reveal her to be virulently anti-Semitic. She also blames the Freemasons for every political and economic disaster to ever befall mankind. Surprisingly, given her constant refusal to cooperate in obtaining a visa, Anastasia extols the virtues of the United States. There is a tone of reverent respect for the nation's accomplishments. Unlike Unterlengenhardt, where Anastasia feels that Baroness Miltitz is spying on her and where Prince Frederick and the Anastasians overseeing her court case continue to manipulate her, everything in America is better; everyone there is happy.

In addition to these topics, she also discusses at length her spiritual beliefs. Although she favors any peace movement, her hatred for revolution and love of a strong leader comes through often. Russia and its people are a particularly important theme for her, and she predicts for Milukoff the future of her homeland:

> There sure will be a czar of Russia again. . . . There is no mistake about this. So, as the things are, it doesn't stay forever. Never! A Peter the Great must be born again—that is necessary—who understands to use the axe again and behead what is wrong. That sure is necessary just . . . now.

The tapes also provide a very private portrait of Anastasia, for Milukoff was unabashed about asking the most personal questions. One aspect of her personality to which Gleb had referred in his first letters to Milukoff was her extreme vanity. Anastasia knew that she was not a beautiful woman, that her disfigurements and prematurely grey hair did nothing to enhance her appearance. Milukoff often plays the charming courtier, extolling her beauty, telling her half-jokingly how he would love to know her secrets.

Although Anastasia has already accepted his more familiar attitude, it is still astonishing to hear how freely she admits to her vanity. Even more remarkable from this solitary woman is the detail of her beauty regimen, in which Milukoff is so obviously interested:

ANASTASIA: Some type [of women] understand this business very well—I not. . . . There is a type of woman . . . who understand to keep themselves grandly up, that one doesn't see their age. This business I don't understand . . . and am not interested. . . . [If] I would be interested . . . then I maybe would understand it. I know of course what is to be done, but I don't do it. . . . I am lazy, that is the real reason. I take my baths in ocean salt . . . in the morning. I take always half a package [of] ocean salt in each bath. That's quite a lot. I look like I don't do anything [to myself], but I do. And lemons I take [in the bath]. In the evening, I do other things. . . .

MILUKOFF: What things you do in the evening?

ANASTASIA: Ah! [laughing] You are going too far!

MILUKOFF: [also laughing] You have to tell me. What do you do in the evening?

ANASTASIA: A thousand things, what one does. [nervously giggling] Three-quarter. . . .

MILUKOFF: Douche?

ANASTASIA: Yes, and such things. Just the same, mountains of money is spent . . . twice a week are cosmetical things bought. . . . [Lipstick] is not interesting. . . .

MILUKOFF: Do you want some color for your hair?

ANASTASIA: That is what I want, exactly. . . . My old brown color with a reddish tint, which I use . . . a tiny bit [of]. . . . So like I had it. . . . I feel myself displaced with this damned [grey] hair color. [Beauty shops] are out of the question. That I did many years ago when Mrs. Heydebrand was [alive], but not anymore. But I am buying frightful masses [of cosmetics] just the same.

Have you seen the painting I did [of] myself? I will show you this painting . . . it's a big, colored painting. I have painted it myself in oil colors. . . . [Y]ou can use it for your book . . . but I don't look pleasant. I look like a monkey.

The taping sessions in Unterlengenhardt continued over the course of the next three years. As the conversations progressed, Anastasia freely discussed any sort of topic. She spoke in an almost conspiratorial intimacy with Milukoff, so that in the end he had clearly gathered more of her opinions—whether justifiable or not— than had any of her previous chroniclers.

THE fact that these conversations were taking place soon became known outside the walls surrounding the new barrack. Rumors about the nature of their content spread just as quickly. Miss Mutius or Miss Thomasius were witnesses to every session. Anastasia and Milukoff both talked freely and proudly of their work. From any one or all of these sources, the outsiders who were responsible for and interested in the Grand Duchess's well-being learned some of the wild tales and terrible accusations that were being stored away. The more they realized what potential harm could come to Anastasia's cause if such remarks were made public, the more concerned they became about what was being put on tape.

Gleb had already expressed reservations about certain of Anastasia's stories. He had always encouraged the Russian emigre to go ahead with the work, but in a letter dated 1967, Gleb felt compelled to point out that "her recordings would have to be edited before being published." Baroness Miltitz, Prince Frederick, and the many other Anastasians involved in the court trials were even more concerned. They had always been suspicious of Milukoff, particularly so after they learned that he was in frequent contact with Gleb. To them, Anastasia's friend in America had turned into a long-distance interloper, and they suspected anyone who sought his opinion.

The Baroness must have been aware that the Grand Duchess was relating to Milukoff her increasingly negative and suspicious opinions about the Anastasians, including the Baroness. If so, she had also realized that, far worse than the threat the tapes posed to the successful conclusion of Anastasia's case, was the possibility that they would also cast serious doubt on the efforts the Baroness and others had made on behalf of the Grand Duchess, thereby ruining all their reputations.

As long as Milukoff enjoyed Anastasia's favor, there was little that the Baroness and the other supporters could do to stop the taping. Nor could they eliminate the danger that Milukoff might actually make all the material public. The level of Anastasia's interest in the project never seemed to waiver, and she began instructing Milukoff about whom he should see and whom he should avoid. If he countered her suggestions, or if she suspected that he was talking to people she no longer trusted—especially the Baroness, the Prince, or anyone connected to them—she became irate. She also told him that he should travel and see the places where she had lived. Only then could he understand the events she considered so crucial to her life.

During one of the sessions recorded on the tapes, Anastasia and Milukoff spoke of her stay at the Stillachhaus. As she reminisces, the past becomes the present, and she insists that he go there to visit Dr. Eitel, who is still overseeing the facility in the 1960s. Milukoff agrees to the suggestion and, in turn, proposes that the Grand Duchess record a greeting to Dr. Eitel, which Milukoff will then present to him. In a very formal and respectful manner, she begins:

> I remember with greatest pleasure [the] Stillachhaus, and I don't forgot the moments which were very pleasant to me when I arrived there. . . . You and your wife . . . shall belong always to the kindest remembrances of my life, . . . and the very fine, beautiful Stillachhaus.

As usual, however, Anastasia becomes too involved in the story and continues on with memories of how she was forced to leave the Stillachhaus and went to stay with the Leuchtenbergs at Castle Seeon:

> From Stillachhaus . . . Dr. Eitel brought me by train to Munich, and there [I] was expecting . . . the wife of Zahle. . . . Tatiana [Botkin] came the next day and then we went . . . on the train to Castle Seeon, and then Duke Leuchtenberg fetched me.

It is clear from her tales of Castle Seeon that it had become for Anastasia an ideal. Her selective memory had erased the unpleasantness of being forced to face the relatives of Franziska Schanzkowska. Even the horror of Felix Youssoupov's attempt on her life—spoken of elsewhere on the tapes—she had somehow severed from her happier impressions of Seeon. By 1967, she had formulated a completely unthreatening picture of her days there, and the castle had come to symbolize one of the happiest times in her life—beautiful, secluded, palatial, Russian.

At some point, Anastasia and Milukoff learned that Castle Seeon might be sold. The Grand Duchess began to formulate an idea—just as inexplicable but also just as fixed as many others she had at this time—and she soon stated flatly that she intended to buy Castle Seeon. She wanted it, not to use as a residence for herself, but to turn into a hotel. As absurd as the notion may sound, it was her way of helping to allay the growing concerns about her future well-being that Milukoff and Gleb had repeatedly expressed as part of their effort to get Anastasia to apply for a visa to America. Yet Milukoff agreed wholeheartedly with her scheme to buy the castle and assumed the task of finding someone who could afford to finance the undertaking.

THE Court of Appeals continued its investigations into early 1967, but after the interview with Anastasia two years earlier in Unterlengenhardt, only two developments of any note had occurred. One was the reappearance of the Franziska Schanzkowska story, which this time was mercifully and finally put to rest. The prostitute whose testimony had first been bought by an agent of the Grand Duke of Hesse and who had continued her perjury during the first trial, took the stand and repeated the same story. This time, however, Wollmann succeeded in showing the judges the nature of the woman's deceit, and she left the courtroom completely disgraced.

The other issue that occupied the court's time was the veracity of Anastasia's statement that the Grand Duke of Hesse had traveled to Russia during the First World War. This court would fail to establish the truth of the matter, and the unintentional intervention by the one of the Anastasians did not help the cause. The first witness to testify on this point was a former Russian prince who had been located by Dominique Auclères. He testified that he had been employed at Czarskoe Selo in 1916, when he learned from a highly placed court official that the Grand Duke was visiting. His testimony was apparently convincing and unequivocating. The defense attorney, however, got the witness to admit that he would not have testified, without the urging of the well-known Anastasian journalist. There would be other lengthy debates on the subject of the Grand Duke's trip and more witnesses would be called, but by the end, no more light could be shed on the facts than had been made public for more than forty years.

Finally, on February 28, 1967, the Court of Appeals announced its decision. In nearly three years, the judges had listened to the expert testimony of Otto Reche and Minna Becker, had seen a clear demonstration by Anastasia of her knowledge of Russian, and had recorded the final and total discrediting of the Franziska Schanzkowska myth. Nonetheless, the opinion they issued stated that Anastasia's lawyers had not provided sufficient proof of her identity. Wollmann and the other Anastasians were not left without some hope, however, for the tribunal took pains to say that their decision was not meant to be interpreted as a denial of the claim, but as a signal that it had not been proved to the court's satisfaction. Moreover, the written opinion issued later declared that "the death of Grand Duchess Anastasia at Ekaterinburg cannot be accepted as a conclusively historical fact," in effect completely nullifying the 1933 decision that had originally granted the certificate of inheritance to Anastasia's relatives.

Nevertheless, this was not a clear victory for the Anastasians, and immediately after the judges had given their verdict, Wollmann announced that he would appeal the case to the German Federal Supreme Court.

Wollmann would remain involved with the case for another few weeks, while the Hamburg Court of Appeals prepared its written judgment. He was not a member of the bar of the Supreme Court, however, so Prince Frederick had to find another attorney. The lawyer chosen to argue the case before this tribunal was Baron Curt Stackelberg. Already a well-respected barrister, he would later serve as president of the association of attorneys granted status to practice before the Supreme Court.

In preparing his appeal, Stackelberg saw the need to convince the Court to recognize that the burden of proof rightfully lay with the Duchess Barbara and Prince Louis of Hesse. If he were successful in this strategy, he would undo the fatal error that Leverkuehn and Vermehren had made when they accepted the advice of the Hamburg judge in 1957 and deviated from the strategy first advocated by Fallows. He determined to frame his legal scheme within the context of constitutional arguments, specifically the "fundamental rights of man" that were a key element of the German Federal Constitution:

> The right to identity, as well as the right to a name, is included in the basic rights of human dignity and the free development of the personality. . . . [I]n cases of this sort . . . the procedural rules of civil law . . . must be modified in consideration of those rights. At the least, this leads to an alleviation of the burden of proof. . . . In cases where a fundamental right is at stake, the burden of proof must be reversed: it must be borne by the person *contesting* the claim.

As for the Hamburg court's reading of the evidence, he noted that even if the burden of proof had properly lain with the plaintiff, Anastasia had been put at a clear disadvantage by the judges. He noted that this last court, like its predecessor, had refused to give credence to the anthropological evidence given by Otto Reche and the additional photographic expert it had appointed. It had also ignored the incontrovertible testimony of Minna Becker regarding handwriting samples. Worse, he charged, whereas both tribunals had accepted with little question the testimony of witnesses for the Romanovs, they had required extraordinary corroboration of any statements provided in favor of Anastasia. Stackelberg acknowledged that since the burden of proof had been shifted to his client, the jurists would, of course, have wanted to make doubly sure of the evidence. Even so, the degree to which they questioned every aspect of the witnesses' possible connection to Anastasia went far beyond the need to eliminate reasonable doubt and certainly warranted review of the decision by the Supreme Court. He completed his final brief in May 1968 and submitted it to the court, but more than a year and a half would pass before a judgment was issued.

X.

"I shall not stay anymore alone"

As Anastasia's lawyers awaited the outcome of their appeal, she was again unavoidably occupied with facing the effects of her past on her present. In 1968 she shared the shock of the entire world as events seemed to point toward revolution: students protested that spring in Europe and America, and Dr. Martin Luther King, Jr., and Senator Robert F. Kennedy—both men dedicated to peace—were assassinated. These events heightened her awareness that this same year marked the hundredth anniversary of her father's birth and the fiftieth anniversary of the events at Ekaterinburg. Ever-fearful that she would be murdered by conspirators or spies, she watched as the world seemed to be crumbling. Her paranoia went unchecked.

Anastasia's suspicions about the activities of those whom she had long considered her enemies also increased. She particularly came to resent Prince Frederick's habit of referring to her as "Madame Mutabor," a Latin term meaning "I will be changed." Baroness Miltitz was completely banned from the new barrack by now. She would still occasionally burst into the house unannounced to bring what she considered important news or to demand Anastasia's attention on some matter. But from the conversations on the Milukoff tapes, it is clear that each such incident only made Anastasia more determined to have absolutely nothing to do with her. The Baroness was now part of the group of people who, as far as the Grand Duchess was concerned, were "not quite right in the head."

She began to fear even those nearest her. She refused entrance to the new barrack to Gertrude Lamerdin, one of the women who delivered food to her almost daily. Miss Lamerdin had lived across the road since Anastasia had moved from the old barrack, but the

Grand Duchess had never fully trusted her. At one time, Anastasia declined to see her at all, having somehow reached the conclusion that Miss Lamerdin had been acting as a sleuth for Baroness Miltitz. Now that Anastasia felt that everyone was against her, she refused to allow Miss Lamerdin to cross her doorstep. Anastasia reached the point where she declined to invite visitors inside the new barrack, and if someone did appear—whether expected or not—she held conversations with them through a high, open window situated at the front of the cottage.

The grounds of her house were as forbidding as her hovering presence inside. The gardens went untended and the weeds and grass were never cut, for Anastasia would allow no workmen near. The sixty cats and four dogs had long since overtaken the house. When Milukoff came, he would find them everywhere—even lying in the mess of papers and discarded food that covered the bed in which Queen Victoria had once slept. As their numbers grew, the pets began to roam the neighborhood, despite the high fence that surrounded Anastasia's property.

In the spring of 1968, Prince Frederick traveled to Unterlengenhardt to warn Anastasia that the local officials were planning legal action because of her animals. The cats posed a health hazard to the community, and the farmers had complained. With the approach of warm weather and spring planting, they had begun killing the cats they found digging in their fields. As had become her practice, Anastasia turned a deaf ear to the Prince—whom she made stand on a ladder outside the window to give his report—and chose to ignore the problem completely.

She had also disregarded her health. Although her companions made certain that food was delivered, she seldom ate it. By now a strict vegetarian, she would partake sparingly of the food that had been especially prepared for her. She would tell others that she simply preferred something else, but she confessed to Milukoff that she feared poison. Yet she spent little of her own money on food for herself, using it instead to pay the local butcher for delivery of the best cuts of meat for her cats and dogs. The reports that Gleb received from Milukoff were alarming, and he began to share the fears of her other friends that the Grand Duchess might be in precarious health.

* * *

MAY 18 marked the centennial of the Czar's birth, and the local citizenry planned a celebration in honor of Anastasia's father. It might seem odd that, in a town where she was regarded as a curious nuisance, the citizenry would go to such trouble. The Grand Duchess was Unterlengenhardt's most famous resident, however, and interest in her father and mother was at its peak. About six months earlier, Robert K. Massie's book, *Nicholas and Alexandra*, had appeared. A biography of her parents and a popular history of the last years of the Romanov dynasty, the book personalized the story of the imperial couple and their family. The book was written in a manner clearly meant to appeal to a wide audience and had been a spectacular international success. Since its publication Anastasia had been bombarded with questions about her parents, and the tour buses had returned.

The new wave of public attention, together with the sensationalism of the recent decision by the Hamburg Court of Appeals, brought many encounters like one Milukoff had taped earlier:

MUTIUS: When we go away, come and bring us to the gate. When [we] go away now. Can't you bring us to the gate?
ANASTASIA: What shall I?
MILUKOFF: To make the walk together us with to the gate. . . . You don't like to walk in your garden? Just to walk for exercise.
MUTIUS: It would be so good for you.
ANASTASIA: Really, you go too far! You forgot that it is Saturday [and] what [on] that day happens. Nothing happens to you, but to me. When they are sitting there in the apple trees, yes, you don't mind . . . but I get it. When there some swine sits in the apple tree and photographs. He doesn't photograph you, but he will photograph me.

Afraid even to walk outside, she was supposed to face a party to commemorate the birth of her murdered father.

On that warm and sunny May afternoon, Anastasia's neighbors and friends gathered in the front garden of the new barrack, many of them holding bouquets of flowers for her. She would not invite them in, nor would she even come out to see them. Finally, Milukoff coaxed her to the front window. This scene, so indicative of Anastasia's idiosyncratic behavior at the time, is captured in an awkward, amateurish home movie Milukoff made that day. It shows a sickly Anastasia surveying the crowd from the isolation of a window overlooking the yard, as the people below sing in memory of her dead father. Their smiling faces are in stark contrast to the melancholy stare that never leaves her face.

Finally, the film ends with scenes of the visitors as they leave the grounds of the new barrack. Their faces now seem solemn, perhaps reflecting disappointment over Anastasia's reaction to their celebration. A once-joyful occasion has suddenly turned sour, even black, and the participants murmur to one another as they leave, perhaps speculating at the Grand Duchess's self-imposed isolation, her failing health, and the possibility that she might actually be dying.

In the closing days of May 1968, Anastasia bolted the door to her house from the inside and refused to acknowledge the presence of any visitors. After four days, a woman living nearby who knew that there was no food in the new barrack, took it upon herself to order that the door be broken down. Thinking that the Grand Duchess might be dead, the concerned friend rushed into the house and found Anastasia lying on the sofa that she used as a bed. Semiconscious and delirious, she repeatedly murmured "Mamma! Mamma! Where is Mamma? Mamma, I'm dying."

The woman quickly spread the word to the others who regularly attended to Anastasia, and they all—including Baroness Miltitz—gathered at the new barrack. Someone called a doctor, who in turn ordered an ambulance to take the patient to the district hospital in a nearby town. Before the attendants lifted her onto a stretcher, the doctor administered a morphine injection—at the request of the Baroness—which seemed to bring the Grand Duchess to consciousness. Looking about wildly, yet seeming to grasp what was happening, she became frenzied and screamed, "I will not go to the hospital! You will not take me to a hospital! I forbid it!" Then she fainted, and her tiny limp body was lifted carefully into the ambulance.

WHEN Anastasia awoke at the hospital, she immediately demanded to see Milukoff. He arrived—with his tape recorder—and began to explain to her how she had come to be at the institution. When he told her that Baroness Miltitz had ordered that she be sedated, her anger was uncontrollable. Anastasia had confessed to the Baroness—as she had to many others—her fear that morphine would rob her of conscious control over her life, just as it had left her dazed and weakened at the Mommsen Nursing Home forty-odd years before. That the Baroness would now use this method of trying to quiet Anastasia was unforgivable. Milukoff suggested that perhaps Anastasia should speak to the Baroness personally, and she responds on tape:

ANASTASIA: I don't see her, I have told you!
MILUKOFF: Yeah, just one moment. . . .
ANASTASIA: I don't see her, have you understood?
MILUKOFF: Yes, understood.
ANASTASIA: I have told here to the physician lady that this woman
 doesn't come here in, and she has here not to come. This I tell you!
MILUKOFF: Okay . . . well. . . .
ANASTASIA: She will be thrown out!

Soon Anastasia calmed down and, as the days passed, she began to enjoy the constant care and attention she received from the staff of the hospital. She accepted the doctors' explanation that she had suffered a nervous breakdown and that she might leave the hospital but not to return to a life by herself.

Milukoff came frequently to visit her and clearly saw the opportunity to take advantage of the circumstances. He began finally to put into action the plans to take the Grand Duchess to America. She had continued to resist obtaining the visa, despite continued pleas from both Milukoff and Gleb to act quickly. Gleb's letters following the court decision earlier in 1968 were filled with exhortations to all concerned to make certain the papers were completed properly and submitted as quickly as possible. Conversations about the visa and her need to leave the hospital are numerous on the tapes that Milukoff recorded in Anastasia's hospital room, so it is clear when and how she began to cooperate:

ANASTASIA: Sit down. That is not pleasant. Absolute not. It's a
 mess. But I shall not stay any more alone. . . .
MILUKOFF: Certainly not.

ANASTASIA: . . . that I get in such a dirty mess.

MILUKOFF: Yeah, I think it is good idea for you to have visa, you go or not, to have visa, you see? You don't have to go to America if you don't want, but at least you'll have visa. . . . So I'd like to get the visa for you and next time I will come and say, "This is visa for you," and passport I give back, so you have everything. But you don't have to go if you don't want to.

Once her interest is engaged during the taping of their conversations that day, Milukoff is able to explain to her some of the detailed problems involved in obtaining a visa. He tells her that he has managed to obtain a passport issued under the name of Anna Anderson, with a false birth date and birth place. It is much like the one Gleb had often railed against in his letters. Anastasia explains to him that Baroness Miltitz and Prince Frederick used this document to take her on a trip to Paris the year before. She had not wanted to go, but they had insisted and had made all the arrangements. She explains further:

ANASTASIA: This was the greatest mistake I did, that I had myself talked into go to Paris.

MILUKOFF: You didn't like to go to Paris?

ANASTASIA: Not at all.

MILUKOFF: . . . but, of course, at least you have seen this Eiffel Tower, and you have seen Notre Dame Cathedral. You have seen all those nice places.

ANASTASIA: Yes, but . . . I have been . . . in Paris and I was there misused only.

MILUKOFF: Yeah, that's right.

ANASTASIA: I have been only misused.

Still, Milukoff's primary concern is with the passport, and how it had been issued to enable Anastasia to cross the German frontier successfully. He suggests that they speak with Baroness Miltitz, but Anastasia bristles:

ANASTASIA: I have nothing to tell and don't tell not a word to the Baroness Miltitz.

MILUKOFF: Maybe we should never get this passport then. You see . . . because this passport, I don't know. According to Botkin . . . this is not good passport, because it is written "Berlin."

Botkin says "Berlin" not right, you see? And so, they have to change
and put it right, to put . . . that it is *"Peterhof"* and "18 June." It says
"official business" because otherwise with this we shouldn't go to
America. Because in Munich [at the American consulate] it is written everything correct. You know, that you are Anastasia, that your
father Nicholas, mama Alexandra, that you were born at *Peterhof*,
18 June. And here it is written "Berlin, June. . . ."

ANASTASIA: That has done the Baroness Miltitz, is her work.

MILUKOFF: Yeah, and now they have to correct this, they have to go
to. . . .

ANASTASIA: I don't see the Baroness Miltitz, for life and death
not. . . .

MILUKOFF: Well, then I tell them that I. . . .

ANASTASIA: The Baroness Miltitz, I don't see.

MILUKOFF: Okay.

ANASTASIA: You can do what on earth you want. Never! I never do
that.

MILUKOFF: All right, okay.

ANASTASIA: Under no any condition will I see this woman.

Milukoff remains more concerned with the issue at hand, and he
proposes next that they try to contact Prince Frederick for an explanation of the passport:

MILUKOFF: How about Prince Frederick? You see him?

ANASTASIA: Neither. Never.

MILUKOFF: You don't like Prince Frederick?

ANASTASIA: No!

MILUKOFF: But . . . [for] thirty years you like him very much!

ANASTASIA: I didn't never like him. You forgot that I hardly saw
him. Hardly, that is the truth.

Despite Milukoff's best efforts to discuss the problem of the visa,
Anastasia is now intent on finishing the topic she has begun. She
feels used—"misused" in her words—by the Baroness, the Prince,
and their friends, the Anastasians. She accuses them of being concerned only with their court trials, forcing her to give interviews and
making her a public spectacle, from which they made money that
rightly belongs to her. Milukoff stops her:

MILUKOFF: But you like to talk to reporters?

ANASTASIA: I had to. I was always forced. I have done that, and look, for what? You see it yourself, what have I done that? For what? Only tell me this: for what? I have seen television people and who knows what. And for what?

MILUKOFF: Well, because . . . they are interested in your story, huh? What you have to tell them. Right?

ANASTASIA: I have been palavering and I have been, I don't know, they would do just what they pleased, all the time. And that was nonsense.

MILUKOFF: And who brought these reporters? Baroness Miltitz?

ANASTASIA: The Prince!

MILUKOFF: The Prince.

ANASTASIA: Always the Prince, yes. And this is the thanking I get. . . .

Milukoff is quite aware that Anastasia is referring to much more than being placed in a hospital. They have often discussed the fact that her assets could be seized at any time by the courts, if they ever finally decided against her. A few months ago, Milukoff and Anastasia also talked about a plan proposed by the Prince—who still held her power-of-attorney and managed her finances—to hide her few remaining assets. She was not at all pleased to learn that Prince Frederick planned to sell her house and property, take the money under his own control, and provide her with care in a nursing home. She now tells Milukoff that "[if] . . . Mrs. Madsack would have been alive, this would not have been done with me. They wouldn't dare it! Oh no, only because she is dead, the Baroness Miltitz and the Prince dare to do this, what they do."

The conversation that day was as far-ranging as it was detailed and revealing. For example, there is evidence for the first time that Milukoff had come to imagine himself as much more than Anastasia's biographer and friend. It has always seemed odd that this Russian emigre would devote more than seven years of his life to the Grand Duchess—incurring great expense—merely as a selfless gesture of fidelity. But in an exchange following one of Anastasia's offhand comments about sickness and health, we hear precisely what Milukoff's plan had become:

ANASTASIA: The Prince is ill too.
MILUKOFF: What sickness he has?
ANASTASIA: He maybe has the same illness.
MILUKOFF: Like [Duchess] Barbara, cancer.
ANASTASIA: Yes.
MILUKOFF: Well, then he will not live long.
ANASTASIA: No, the Prince is not long alive.
MILUKOFF: Good, uh-huh.

From this point, he begins to almost naturally assume the role of chief adviser and discusses financial affairs with her. The topic turns to the subject of buying Castle Seeon and the efforts he has undertaken to find a sponsor for Anastasia's dream of turning the property into a hotel. Gleb had kept him and Anastasia well-informed of Jack Manahan's unrelenting interest in helping her go to the United States. Jack himself had sent numerous letters and deposited money in a German checking account to pay for their travel expenses. Most important, he clearly had a good deal of money, for he had repeatedly assured everyone—including the American consul—that once Anastasia reached Charlottesville, he would provide for her indefinitely. To Milukoff's mind, then, Jack would serve two purposes. His offer of help would assure that Anastasia had somewhere to go when she left the hospital, and his money might be available to finance the scheme for buying Castle Seeon:

MILUKOFF: [W]e might as well make a trip and see America. Don't you see, after that, you talk to Manahan, you talk to Botkin, and say you'd like to come back and . . . open hotel with . . . [me]. . . . But first we have to have lots of money.
ANASTASIA: And that we must in America get somehow together.
MILUKOFF: America will help, because especially if you get interested in this Mr. Manahan, he has lots of money. You say, "Mr. Manahan, why don't you make together, like partners." And you and Manahan. . . .

Anastasia still does not seem to quite understand, or her thoughts are occupied with other matters, particularly whether she will be

expected to travel alone and what she will do once she is in the
United States:

> ANASTASIA: Don't you want, don't you want to spend your vacation
> in America?
> MILUKOFF: Maybe I will stay a few days, sure. I will take you there
> and then maybe go to California, and maybe come again, and travel
> to Charlottesville and stay there.

The Grand Duchess is growing suddenly comfortable with the
idea of seeing the United States. Although she appreciated the offer
of hospitality that has been extended by Jack Manahan, she had told
Milukoff and Gleb both that she did not want him to spend all his
money on her. She now expresses concern about how she and
Milukoff will be able to afford their stay once they reach America.
Still not thinking of Jack as a source of income for the hotel project,
she also implies that they might find a way to earn funds in America
that will allow them to return and buy Castle Seeon:

> ANASTASIA: Maybe . . . we go to the lecturing and such things that I
> show myself that one gets money together.
> MILUKOFF: No, we don't need money if we are friends with Man-
> ahan. You don't need money, he will help you.
> ANASTASIA: I want to buy the hotel.
> MILUKOFF: Well, you'll be like a partner, you see? Manahan give . . .
> his dollars and from this many money you can do it. Sure, but
> important that you should be interested in Manahan, you know,
> because he is an important man and he has—
> ANASTASIA: Then come and help me.
> MILUKOFF: Sure, I will come, certainly I will come with you.
> ANASTASIA: A hotel must be bought.
> MILUKOFF: I know.
> ANASTASIA: Then one has a footing, because the physician told me
> still something more.
> MILUKOFF: What?
> ANASTASIA: It is not very pleasant, that I might . . . get older . . .
> longer than still twenty years.
> MILUKOFF: Uh-huh, that's all right.
> ANASTASIA: Is that not unpleasant?
> MILUKOFF: Twenty years you have to live?

ANASTASIA: I shall be still longer living than twenty years.

MILUKOFF: Well, this is nice.

ANASTASIA: Is it not horrid?

MILUKOFF: Why? You like to live longer, huh?

ANASTASIA: No, not at all.

MILUKOFF: Why? But why do you want hotel?

ANASTASIA: I would like to have this hotel.

MILUKOFF: Sure. You'd like to have this hotel? So you'd like to live longer, huh? You'd like to live longer because you'd like to have hotel. Of course, everything would be much better when you are in America. Then you talk to . . . Botkin, you talk to Manahan and tell him your idea and he says his idea. . . .

ANASTASIA: All right, then I consent. I go.

Just that quickly, her years of resistance disappear, and the idea is fixed. She will travel to America, where she can see Gleb. Milukoff will be along to help, and together they will convince Jack Manahan to finance the project for a hotel at Castle Seeon. Before their conversation ends, she and Milukoff—like happy tourists—begin planning the second journey of Grand Duchess Anastasia to America:

MILUKOFF: As soon as we shall get visa then we shall simply take an airplane, a jet, and start moving, at once.

ANASTASIA: At once.

MILUKOFF: And I think it takes about, I don't know . . .

ANASTASIA: How many hours?

MILUKOFF: About eight hours or something.

ANASTASIA: Eight hours? That's a bit much.

MILUKOFF: Too much? No, but it is, here like in the room now, it is a big—

ANASTASIA: Are you with me then?

MILUKOFF: Certainly, I will be next to you all the time.

ANASTASIA: All right.

MILUKOFF: Sure. We should come first to Washington, D.C.

ANASTASIA: D.C.

MILUKOFF: Washington. In Washington.

ANASTASIA: All right.

MILUKOFF: From Washington we shall go to—

ANASTASIA: I like to see Washington. I have never seen Washington.

MILUKOFF: Well, then, we shall make a trip. See White House and Congress building, and—
ANASTASIA: Yes, I pay to the president a visit.
MILUKOFF: Sure, if you—
ANASTASIA: And that I would like to do.
MILUKOFF: Good, yeah, and then, and talk to . . . Johnson?
ANASTASIA: Yes, I will . . . speak with him.
MILUKOFF: What would you like to speak with him?
ANASTASIA: I . . . ask him, "How do you do, Mr. President?" And he surely will tell, "Thank you."
MILUKOFF: And what else?
ANASTASIA: And then, "Goodbye."

ONCE Milukoff had obtained Anastasia's acquiescence, he moved quickly to finalize plans for the trip to America. His enthusiasm was, however, not matched by Gleb's. For some time now, he had been growing frustrated with both Milukoff and Jack Manahan. The Russian emigre now seemed an unreliable assistant, someone who was likely to take his own course of action without regard to Gleb's advice or what he considered to be Anastasia's best interests. The taping sessions and the possibility that they would be published in a book worried him constantly. His letters to Milukoff also showed a great suspicion about the latter's motives in helping the Grand Duchess. The doubts were particularly evident when the subject of money and Jack's ability and desire to pay became important topics of discussion.

As for Jack Manahan, Gleb appreciated his generosity but had begun to feel that he might prove as unreliable as Milukoff. The American had taken to writing to Anastasia directly, without consulting Gleb, and his efforts on her behalf in Charlottesville were beginning to cause problems. In a letter from 1967, Gleb had outlined for Milukoff his precise concerns about Jack Manahan:

I am . . . increasingly worried by the question of how . . . [Anastasia], if she comes here, will get along with Jack Manahan. He has always been a bit of an eccentric . . . but of late he has become very irritating, as well as insolent. I am afraid, the fortune he has inherited has gone to his head. . . . Among other things, he permits himself to write . . .

that I fully agree with everything he does and says, which is totally untrue. . . . I told him in no uncertain terms that I am very much annoyed and that he has no right whatever to make any statements in my name.

The plan that Gleb had initiated was out of his control. He was very much against having the Grand Duchess travel in the company of a man whom he now considered to be a fortune hunter. He was equally unhappy about seeing her placed under the care of a person who had become an uncontrollable nuisance.

But Gleb had no choice. His wife Nadine had recently died, and he was growing older. His lifelong mission had been the well-being of the Grand Duchess, and he realized "that anything would be better than for . . . [Anastasia] to remain homeless and penniless . . . and . . . completely at the mercy of her enemies." Finally, he agreed to the plan to have Milukoff travel with her by plane to Washington and dutifully helped in finalizing the arrangements. But he would continue to do all he could to assure that Anastasia was not subjected to any further exploitation and that she be allowed to live out her life in comfort and security.

BOOK FIVE

———

"The Czarina of Charlottesville"

My policy has differed from the others, has always been to try to have Anastasia meet and know as many people as possible so that there will be many, many memories—particularly with young people—long after she has gone. So that the strength of her case will be buttressed by an enormous number of friends who have had personal, eye witness of her.

Now, I am not a publicity seeker myself . . . but I believe that the truth has to be shouted from the housetops.

—JOHN EACOTT MANAHAN

I.

"What her future would be"

"DO YOU KNOW where John Manahan is today?" the southern dowager asked as she reached with her delicate, manicured hands to pour tea from a silver pot. The question caught Mildred Ewell off guard. She realized she didn't know where Jack was. As she accepted a teacup with her white-gloved hand she said, "No, I don't. Where is Jack?"

"He has gone to the airport in Washington to meet the *Grand Duchess Anastasia*," her hostess said in an offended tone.

Years later, Mildred Ewell would laugh about this conversation. The genteel southern community of Charlottesville, Virginia, was scandalized that John Eacott Manahan, the bachelor scion of a prominent University of Virginia faculty family, would invite an unmarried woman to stay in his home.

Mildred recalled a much different Jack from the one who now seemed to be the subject of everyone's gossip in this small community of Virginia aristocracy. She had first met Jack in 1938, when he was a student at the University of Virginia. She was attending a Sigma Phi Epsilon fraternity party with her future husband, also a student at the University, whom Jack was sponsoring for membership in the exclusive brotherhood. From that point on, they would remain friends.

Jack was the only child of the dean of the University's School of Education. His father had made millions investing in Virginia real estate and Jack had been raised in a wealthy household. Although pampered and protected, he lived a regimented lifestyle dictated by his father, who wanted to make the most of his young son's obvious genius. Jack was a brilliant student who had graduated from the

University and gone on to earn a Ph.D. in history from Harvard, but he could not live up to his father's exacting standards.

Jack had served as an officer in the Navy during the Second World War and later traveled widely, living for long periods in Europe and teaching at small, exclusive colleges in the South. Mildred and her husband, Dr. Nathaniel McGregor Ewell, Jr., had remained in Charlottesville and raised five children. But the friendship they had established in those early years, combined with the interests they shared with Jack, had helped maintain and strengthen their ties despite the distances that sometimes separated them.

When Jack had returned to Charlottesville about ten years ago, he had grown even closer to both of the Ewells. He was still the brilliant and inquiring scholar and had used his substantial inherited wealth to establish an unequaled library of historical and genealogical material, which became his passion. Indeed, Mildred knew that his love of learning and search for knowledge meant more to Jack than almost anything else, a characteristic that added to his image as somewhat of an eccentric. His love of learning might be one reason that he had never dated frequently, but now he was rumored to be bringing a Russian grand duchess to live at his country estate in Scottsville, a hamlet just outside Charlottesville.

CRADLED in the foothills of the lush Blue Ridge Mountains, Charlottesville has always been an enclave of academe. The town was founded in 1762 and named for Princess Charlotte, the bride of King George III of England. Thomas Jefferson planned and founded the University of Virginia, and built his home, Monticello, overlooking the town. Despite the democratic principles of its most famous resident and the intellectual life that thrives there, Charlottesville cleaves to English pretensions and is a bastion of Old South culture and affectation. The beautiful tree-lined avenues and mock-Georgian buildings contrast sharply with spray-painted graffiti extolling the virtues of the music of Jimmy Buffet, the antics of college fraternity life.

Charlottesville today remains much like the quaint little city that Anastasia saw for the first time on July 13, 1968, as Jack drove into town on Highway 29. Even before they arrived, the cloistered circle of university society was passing the word in hushed tones that she was coming to town.

REMEMBERING how the mob had surrounded Anastasia when she arrived in New York harbor in 1928, and how the crush of onlookers and the popping flashbulbs had unnerved her, Gleb feared that something similar would occur if Milukoff escorted her around Washington. To preempt Milukoff's plans, Gleb enlisted the help of Jack, who agreed to drive to Washington and meet the plane. Always the southern gentleman, Jack was concerned about appearances, so he took Mrs. Alicia Flynn along to act as Anastasia's chaperon. Mrs. Flynn had been his mother's friend and contemporary, and he hoped that her presence would help deflect some of the gossip he knew was inevitable.

"Her mind was certainly cloudy at the time she got off the plane at Dulles as to what her future would be," Jack later remembered. "And she was a rather pathetic individual at that time."

Anastasia had nothing to declare to the customs officials, so the little group was able to pass quickly and unnoticed through the terminal to Jack's car. The two-hour drive to Charlottesville was one of the few times Milukoff did not have his tape recorder running, so there is no record of what was said.

They stopped at the Boxwood House in Culpepper, Virginia, for dinner before proceeding to Fairview Farms, Jack's country estate near Scottsville, where Anastasia would spend the night in the company of Mrs. Flynn. Jack planned to lodge her at the farm for the duration of her visit to avoid any hint of impropriety. Milukoff was to stay in town with Jack at the house at 35 University Circle.

II.

"Now I am safe"

ALL OF THE PARTICIPANTS are now dead—with the exception of Milukoff, who lives in Spain and whose recollections are best reactivated with periodic cash payments—so we have no eyewitness account of the reunion between Anastasia and Gleb. Perhaps it took place the next morning, when Jack fetched his guest from the farm and brought her into Charlottesville for breakfast with himself and Milukoff.

University Circle was a Charlottesville showplace, a collection of stately Virginia residences modeled along the lines of the Thomas Jefferson architecture common in the older, finer neighborhoods. The houses were carefully placed amid immaculately tended lawns and gardens. The Manahan home seemed modest when viewed from the front, but it possessed the understated elegance that characterized this exclusive section of the town.

Jack and his two guests approached the painted brick house along a stone path through the ample front lawn. At the end, a small courtyard was separated from the rest of the yard by ivy-covered walls framing a simple arched doorway.

Jack opened the French doors, and they crossed the threshold into a foyer with a sparkling black-and-white tiled floor. Archways led to either wing of the residence. The home was carefully tended and arranged. Since Jack's parents died, his butler James had cared for the place. "It was so clean you could eat off the floors," as Mildred Ewell described it.

Entering the living room, Anastasia noted the tastefully muted decor. On either side of the doorway, painted wooden shelves were recessed into the walls and filled with porcelain pieces collected by Jack's mother. Capping each set of shelves was a hand-carved escalloped arch in the Georgian manner, with a wooden keystone reaching to the crown molding that framed the ceiling. Wainscotting added to the intimacy of this apparently formal setting. Morning light streamed through the balcony doors to illuminate a free-standing stained-glass window—removed from Exeter Cathedral in England before the Blitz—depicting the coat of arms of Edward the Confessor. Damask swag curtains draped the doors and complemented the sumptuous period pieces in this meticulously appointed room.

MILUKOFF taped the three of them talking that morning in the living room before Gleb arrived. Taking pictures, Milukoff moves around Anastasia and Jack, suggesting they pose this way and that. Finally Anastasia snaps, "That's enough."

Intent upon making a good impression on her host and potential benefactor, Anastasia has planned a surprise for Jack. As they talk, she takes a small package from her pocketbook and lays it on a table beside Jack's chair, indicating that he should open it.

"Mmmm . . . I don't know what this is going to be," Jack says, surprised.

"Nor do I," Milukoff adds. He had carefully coached Anastasia about how to deal with Jack; and now, at the beginning of their first full day together, she is pulling a surprise out of her purse. "I don't know nothing," he disclaims.

"I waited till the last minute," Anastasia states proudly. "He," she says, indicating Milukoff, "doesn't know this."

Anxious to distance himself from any deviation of their plan, Milukoff nervously repeats, "I don't know nothing."

"Go on. Open it," Anastasia prompts, as Jack begins to tear the paper.

"Say!" Jack exclaims. "That is *something* now! Just a moment. That looks to be—"

Inside the paper is what Anastasia describes as "a very important handkerchief," with the initials of Czar Nicholas II mounted by a crown.

"I should not have that!" her host says. "Nothing that good for me, please. I am overpowered, overpowered."

"Yes, of course," she assents, "I saved it." Then she pulls another package from her purse and opens it herself, displaying its contents. There are nine pieces of silver cutlery lying in her outstretched hands, each emblazoned with a royal coat of arms at the top of the stem.

Milukoff is clearly as surprised as Jack and, unable to identify the coat of arms, asks, "Which family is it, Anastasia?"

Before she can answer, Jack interjects, "Reuss."

Anastasia explains that they were given to her by "the cousin of the Empress Hermine. And Miss Thomasius brought it to me in the hospital. . . . I didn't tell a word. I wanted to have it secret and so I had to put it secretly in my bag. . . . And I brought it over that it was saved. It comes from the Reuss family. And this I brought secretly over and nobody know anything. Did I not do this right? I packed it in this bag. I couldn't save it otherwise. So I brought it here over. . . ."

"This is overpowering," Jack says, obviously awed. "I am over-whelmed. I am completely overwhelmed."

Anastasia next says that she wants Jack, Gleb, and Milukoff to divide the pieces amongst themselves. "I love to have all of them," Milukoff says. But she insists that the cutlery be evenly divided between the three men.

"Now I know why you wanted the car locked when we went into the Boxwood House," Jack laughs. "I'm going to hide this now. At this moment, it's going into the candlebox." He walks across the room and puts eight pieces of the Reuss silverware in a wooden box used to store candles. Anastasia keeps one of the forks, turning it over in her hands.

"You see, I—all is taken from me. All," she begins, but Jack interrupts her, "Yes, I know. I know."

"You don't know yet everything," she replies, her voice lowering to almost a whisper. "Botkin knows more. But therefore I kept it quiet. I didn't speak a word. She brought it to me, Miss Tho-masius . . . because she was the nurse of the Princess. And this she wanted that should be my birthday present, and I have brought it for Botkin and you."

Later, Jack would tell people that her decision to travel to Char-lottesville "meant abandoning every bit of her worldly property, and with the idea of perhaps building a new and happy life—and perhaps not." Sitting in the living room, looking at the only meaningful possession that Anastasia had been able to carry with her and that she now wanted to bestow on her few remaining friends, Jack must have been deeply moved.

As the tape continues, Anastasia hears a familiar sound. "A cat is calling!" she exclaims.

Jack, knowing her devotion to animals, especially her near-obsession with cats, had presented one to her that morning. Hearing the cry, she grows very excited and begins looking around for it, "It is here somewhere about. Yes, yes, yes." Thinking she hears the cat on the lower level of the house, she insists that they all go to find it.

The downstairs housed a renowned library of more than 30,000 historical and genealogical volumes. These books, many of which were rare limited editions, bound in leather with gilt edges and splendid, hand-painted illuminations and illustrations, filled the room. They testified to Jack's expertise in and obsession with tracing family lineages, particularly those of prominent Americans and their Old World antecedents. He was a Life Member of The Sovereign Colonial Society, Americans of Royal Descent, and had become extremely well-versed in the genealogy of European aristocratic families.

In addition to the books, Jack had an unmatched collection of paintings and artifacts relating to these families. As Milukoff continues to record and Anastasia searches for the cat in the library, Jack begins to expound on his collection of materials, pointing out from time to time some of the more unusual and unique items in his collection. He has Sir Walter Scott's tea service, suits of medieval armor, and the Western Hemisphere's only portrait painted from life of King Philip II of Spain.

In the midst of this discourse, Jack pulls down a volume in German from one of the shelves and begins to leaf through it. He turns to Anastasia, who is still holding the silver fork in her hand, and says, "This is your family from Reuss. Heinrich von Reuss."

"Heinrich Reuss," she says emphatically. "Heinrich Reuss. And the Empress Hermine. Yes, they are the richest of Europe. They were intensely rich. They had possessions and mines, coal mines, and what-not in Silesia. And they were very important . . . and this," she continues, indicating the fork, "comes from their own silver mines, Mr. Manahan."

He examines the fork carefully, "This is a fork that shows a lion, a griffin, and two storks." Switching to German, he expounds on the Reuss family history and the meaning of their heraldic symbols.

Heretofore, Anastasia has had little idea of the breadth of Jack's genealogical knowledge, and she is clearly amazed as he effortlessly reels off names, titles, dates, and places associated with the Reuss family. He recites for several minutes, and when he finishes, Anastasia turns to Milukoff and says, almost breathlessly, "You see, he knows *everything*. It's wonderful."

Milukoff seems very pleased to see that Anastasia likes Jack. Obviously, he knows the hotel scheme will have a better chance if she can feel comfortable with their host. "Very good. Are you happy that you are here, Anastasia?" he asks.

Her voice is as excited as a child's. "Very happy, very happy."

"You hesitated to come," Milukoff reminds her, "and now everything is all right?"

"Yes," she says decisively.

Jack pays them little attention. He is beginning to wind up with enthusiasm about the Reuss family, repeating a litany of facts from his vast storehouse of historical reference.

Milukoff perhaps sees at this point that Anastasia and Jack are beginning to warm to one another and that their plans are working well. In a moment of excitement, he turns to her and says, "Can I kiss your hand because you are so good?"

But Anastasia, enthralled by the range of Jack's knowledge, dismisses him with a gruff, "No."

Turning back to Jack, she goes on, "The Princess Reuss was my kind friend, and the Emperor."

Seeing that she is still holding the Reuss fork, Jack looks at it and says, "The division is not going to take place now. The division will take place when we have Botkin and Alex and myself and you together."

Outside, a dog barks and Anastasia becomes concerned for her cat. Jack reassures her that it is only the neighbor's dog, who has grown up with cats and will not harm her new pet.

"I know someone who likes dogs very much," Milukoff says, undoubtedly pointing to Anastasia. "I know one person and could put finger on that person. Likes dogs very, very much."

"Oh, dogs," Anastasia responds fondly, "I had wonderful dogs . . . a shepherd dog and lion-heart." The subject of her dogs brings a melancholy tone to her voice. She knows that Miss Lamerdin and the citizens of Unterlengenhardt had her dogs destroyed while she was in the hospital in June. She sighs and must look so tired that Jack asks if she would like to sit down.

THE Milukoff tape breaks off at this point, but we know from later reports that the three participants went into an adjoining room. She took a seat in an easy chair and her little body seemed to collapse inward. The journey had been long and fraught with misgivings, but now she seemed genuinely relaxed and accepting of her surroundings. She felt at ease with this man who had an intimate and encyclopedic knowledge of her family and their equals, and who talked about them much as she did. Perhaps he could understand her situation as well as anyone. As the great-granddaughter of Queen Victoria, she had been groomed for marriage into the British royal family which had eventually betrayed the Romanovs. After her reemergence in Berlin, she remained deeply interested in and drawn to her English relatives but had also grown to deeply fear and mistrust their motives and actions. Indeed, as time passed Anastasia learned that she and Jack were in almost complete accord in many of their opinions about her supporters and detractors, but particularly the English ones, whom he characterized as "rascals."

In addition to their immediate affinity, the careful and splendid manner in which he lived reassured her that Jack Manahan could provide whatever money she and Milukoff needed for their hotel scheme. Things could not have turned out any better.

She opened her pocketbook and rummaged through it. Jack and Milukoff were surprised when she pulled from it a short, highly sharpened dagger and laid it on the table next to the chair. "Now I am safe. Now I do not need this."

Neither Jack nor Milukoff spoke. Instead, they exchanged glances. Anastasia, always anticipating assassination, had carried a dagger with her for protection. Somehow, it had escaped detection by the airport security personnel in Germany and Washington.

The dagger rested for months on the table where she laid it, mute testimony to the fear and anxiety that had overshadowed Anastasia throughout the half century since Ekaterinburg.

MILUKOFF did not begin taping again until after Gleb Botkin had arrived and joined them at the breakfast table. Aware that Anastasia was a strict vegetarian, Jack had ordered the butler James to prepare a suitable breakfast. Having had no acquaintance with vegetarianism, James understood the request to mean that no meat could be served.

The tape depicts the scene as they begin to eat. Passing a compote of jam to Anastasia, Jack says, "We can put this on bread. We can have cheese with bread. We can have celery. And then we can have watermelon, and we have ice cream. And then the raisins are to be passed around as bonbons along with the mints. It's a very strange meal."

Surveying James's attempt at a vegetarian breakfast, Gleb chuckles. Anastasia eats sparingly, apparently too excited by the long trip and by finally being in Gleb's company again.

The conversation at table continues with Gleb reminiscing about Anastasia's case, particularly about the lawyers who have represented her over the years. Anastasia listens intently, seldom taking her eyes off him. Jack and Milukoff can see that she worships Gleb, for she asks dreamily, "Is he not sweet?"

Gleb remained silent amid this praise. Gazing across the table, he saw his childhood friend, now an old woman, thin and tired. Their long history together could not obscure the fact that the years had more than taken their toll on the Grand Duchess.

Fifty years had passed since she waved to him from the window of the Governor's house in Tobolsk. She had been a teenager then, young and innocent. Forty years had elapsed since he saw her in the hallway at Castle Seeon. They had enjoyed the carefree days of their childhood only to experience long years of heartbreak and separation as adults. Now, just two days before the fiftieth anniversary of their fathers' deaths, they were together once again in the little Virginia town that reminded him so much of Czarskoe Selo.

Gleb, like Anastasia, must have been weary. With Nadine dead and Jack acting so strange, Gleb must have almost wished that his friend hadn't come. He also thought Milukoff untrustworthy. For years he had tried to arrange another, more successful visit to America for Anastasia and now, sitting at Jack's breakfast table, he had doubts.

APART from her interest in the hotel scheme with Milukoff, Anastasia had her own agenda of subjects she wished to discuss with Jack and Gleb, as the conversations taped that day indicate. One was her strong desire for an accurate motion picture about her life. Many writers have mistakenly assumed that Anastasia had seen Ingrid Bergman's Academy Award-winning portrayal of her, but Milukoff's tapes reveal she had not.

Jack still knew relatively little about the details of what he called "the case," so the Russians began to try to give him a short course in the history of Anastasia.

As Milukoff's tape recorder runs, Jack exclaims, "There's so much to talk about. There's so many things. There are so many facets to the case. . . ."

"This movie with Ingrid Bergman," Anastasia says, "I never see. . . . Nothing."

Speaking to the group, Jack tells them, "She wants to see the movie. Here's the way we can see it. We will watch the television columns in the paper until the program is going to come on. . . . Then we can see the whole thing right here in the house."

The possibility excites Anastasia, who says, "Yes. I must see it. All together, yes?" She has only seen clips of the film and is adamant about viewing it in its entirety.

"I didn't see it either," Gleb interjects, "because it made me too angry."

"It is possible to see it, it is," the Grand Duchess enthusiastically chimes, "I must see it."

Jack makes a reassuring murmur and she repeats, "*I must see it.*"

Milukoff brings up the fact that the movie "isn't true. It isn't correct." A conversation ensues about the film's accuracy. Anastasia has heard much about it and has been led to believe that "it is a nice piece of work."

Gleb notes that he read the screenplay, "I read it, but I didn't see it. . . . They said it's just a lot of nonsense. It ended with a happy marriage with some mysterious prince. They selected such an actress, this big, huge, Swedish horse."

"How do you think about a new movie, about a quite new movie?" Anastasia asks. "A new movie could be arranged."

Gleb agrees, "That would be nice."

"Would be nice," their host says, "to have a true movie, wouldn't it?"

"Just now, the big question is whether there is any interest," Gleb muses. "I doubt it, just now."

"For the *new* movie?" Anastasia asks.

"For the new movie," Gleb repeats, "find the right time, the right place. . . ." He tells a story about a friend of his from Virginia who became "a big movie man," and wonders if he might be someone to approach.

"Will you inquire about it?" Anastasia asks anxiously. "I think this would be very good when a new movie would be produced."

"It would be," Gleb agrees, "if it were based on fact. And we always, always, made the demand, and Vermehren spoiled everything."

The tapes continue beyond this point, recording everyday, trivial conversations among the four friends. Finally, Gleb expresses regret that he has a great deal of work to do, and Jack agrees to drive him back to his house while Anastasia and Milukoff remain at the Circle.

III.
"Just part of the illness"

UP TO THIS POINT, Anastasia and Milukoff had every reason to believe that their trip was proving to be a success. The plan to involve Jack as the primary investor in the hotel scheme seemed to be working. Throughout, he remained politely attentive to Anastasia.

He responded positively to her gift of the Reuss silver cutlery and the Romanov handkerchief, which had appealed to his fascination with genealogy and heraldry.

But now, just at the point when Milukoff was beginning to feel comfortable enough to leave Anastasia alone in Charlottesville so that he might continue his trip to California, disaster struck. It came in the form of a simple letter from Gertrude Lamerdin, Anastasia's neighbor in Unterlengenhardt.

Jack had planned to take his two guests to the farm in Scottsville that day, where he thought the three of them might have lunch before driving Milukoff to the airport. As they were leaving the house at University Circle, the postman arrived with the mail—which Jack quickly thrust into one of his coat pockets on the way to the car, as was his habit.

After lunch, as they sat around the dining table, Jack searched through his pockets, pulled out the mail, and began leafing through the envelopes. When he noticed the postmark of Unterlengenhardt on one letter, he opened it and began reading aloud, translating Gertrude's German to English as he went along. Milukoff switched on his tape recorder.

" 'I am writing openly just exactly how the situation lies, since she can bring up the greatest aberrations with such ridiculous ideas and . . . misunderstandings about her friends for whom she has everything to thank. I am a psychologist and I know . . . this is what she said in the hospital and she probably says it also to you, dear, most honored, Mr. Manahan, and she will tell this to Gleb Botkin. Mr. Botkin knows her also from this side.' "

It seems that Gertrude's intention was to warn Jack of Anastasia's erratic behavior and to bring him up to date on the events immediately preceding Anastasia's departure from Germany.

The tape records Anastasia whispering something inaudible to Milukoff. Jack stops her to explain, "She's trying to say that you were beside yourself, you were out of your mind. She's trying to say that."

Anastasia and Milukoff have been lively conversationalists so far this day, but now they sit in shocked silence.

Jack continues translating Gertrude's description of the situation that resulted in Anastasia's pets being destroyed. " 'The people demanded that the whole house and garden, which was in an undescribable condition, should be cleansed and disinfected. There was hardly enough money for the cats' nourishment and they could have brought a plague into the whole neighborhood. . . .' "

As Jack pauses, silently translating the next paragraph, Anastasia erupts, "That's all a lie! Only some milk and some bones, that was all, that was their food."

By now, Milukoff must be furious at Gertrude. Part of the reason he was eager to get Anastasia out of Germany was to separate her from the interference of her neighbors in Unterlengenhardt. Now, Gertrude Lamerdin's harping voice has followed them across the ocean.

If Jack takes the letter seriously, it could compromise their carefully made plans. Milukoff is so intent on figuring out how to counter this unexpected interruption that he forgets and leaves his tape recorder on.

Just then, the conversation takes another turn. Jack, still translating, reads aloud, " 'The cats had to be killed. The last dog, Baby. . . .' "

At the name Baby, he bursts out laughing at the irony; he has seen photographs of Anastasia's dogs, which were absolutely massive. Trying to control his laughter, he reads on, " 'We wanted to bring Baby to a neighbor's, but he howled all night long and would not eat any more after she left. So that. . . .' "

Again, he laughs but tries to collect himself. " 'So that unfortunately they were compelled. . . .' "

He begins laughing again.

"Please excuse me for laughing," he says to Anastasia.

"Yes," she replies, ". . . read on."

" 'They shot Baby, they shot Baby.' "

Anastasia, seeing an opportunity to rebut Gertrude, says, "Yes. That Lamerdin attended. Yes. It was her work."

But Jack pays no attention. He is caught in a paroxysm of laughter, knowing that he should control himself, but unable to do so. "It's very, very tragic they shot him," he giggles.

"Yes," Anastasia replies curtly, unable to understand why Jack is suddenly displaying a lack of manners and sensitivity.

Milukoff remains silent, hoping that Anastasia will hold her own against Gertrude's epistolary onslaught because, if the letter achieves its intended effect, his plans might be ruined.

But as Jack continues to read, one can hear in his voice that he begins to see the reality of conditions in Unterlengenhardt.

" 'Her motherly friend, Baroness Miltitz, who had a morphine injection given to her in order to bring her to the hospital in order to put the animals to death and preserve the written and other valuable things belonging to Anastasia.' "

"Wonderful are they preserved," Anastasia says cryptically, "when they are divided and taken away."

The letter continues with the subject of the slaughter of Anastasia's pets. " 'For Anastasia, whose whole life history has been of animals, this was naturally a terrible blow and whether she later, indeed, again a dog or one or two cats should have. . . .' "

The tape catches Anastasia again whispering something under her breath.

Jack does not seem to hear this time and continues to read, " 'And because of these dogs and the cats, she decided that she would no longer go into her house but she would go to America.' "

He bursts into laughter, "Well, that's all right."

Anastasia and Milukoff are silent, as Jack reads on, " 'And she, those whom she had everything to be indebted for, to be thank for, for years, she had lived not only on the money but also on the relatives of the Prince, the Prince. . . .' "

"It's a lie, Mr. Manahan," Anastasia says, anger rising in her voice.

Jack pays her no mind, " '. . . The friends of Baroness Miltitz. . . .' "

"It's all a lie. . . . The Red Cross helped me."

Jack still does not pay much attention to what Anastasia says and keeps reading, " 'And the help of her dear friends, to the Prince, who for forty years. . . .' "

"The Prince now," Anastasia is trying to contain herself but is quickly losing her temper, "was in South America with *my* money. . . . Three thousands marks which I have. . . ."

The recitation of the letter goes on and on, listing all of Anastasia's faults and foibles. Occasionally, she interjects a sarcastic "yeah" and mumbles about people "misusing my money."

But as Jack nears the end of the letter, the purpose of Gertrude's rambling prose becomes more evident. Referring to the Prince, who for years took upon himself the task of managing her affairs, she writes sympathetically, " 'This dearest and selfless friend who for her sacrifices all, who always took away unpleasantness from her knowing that . . . [it] was—just part of the illness.' "

Gertrude's thinly veiled warning would forever be lost on Jack.

MILUKOFF left the next day for California to visit his children. He fully anticipated that by the time he returned, Anastasia would have been able to charm Jack.

Anastasia remained at Fairview Farms, where she received frequent visits from Gleb and daily visits from Jack. Gleb's attitude toward her began to change. He had long suspected that Milukoff was using Anastasia and that angered him, because he had seen many people use her over the years. As Gleb spent more time with her in Charlottesville, however, he began to see that Anastasia was now a willing participant in Milukoff's plans. He also sensed her mental imbalance and felt increasingly suspicious of her.

Gleb quickly realized that Anastasia had no intention of returning to Germany, despite the fact that she had been granted a visa for only six months. In one of her earliest private conversations with her old friend, she informed him that he looked ill and that she had decided to stay in America, to take driving lessons, and to care for him. At the same time, she was becoming more attached to Jack, and was comfortable around him, although she continued to address him formally as Mr. Manahan.

Milukoff returned from California expecting to find his plans complete. By this time, Anastasia should have been able to persuade Jack to provide the money for the purchase and conversion of Castle Seeon into the hotel she had longed to own. Instead, Anastasia informed Milukoff that he was to return to Unterlengenhardt by himself. Even before coming to the United States, she had prepared a document stipulating that he was to have access to her house there, and she now instructed him to pack up her belongings and ship them to Charlottesville. Milukoff, who undoubtedly realized not only that their plans for the hotel had fallen through, but that he could no longer count on proceeding with the book collaboration, made no more tape recordings of Anastasia. Nevertheless, he would remain in touch with her for another few years.

Milukoff did perform one last, notable service for Anastasia. Upon returning to Unterlengenhardt to carry out his assignment, he encountered Prince Frederick and Ian Lilburn at Anastasia's home, cleaning out the mess she had left behind. While discarding the mounds of trash and refuse, they had also apparently carted away some of her most important documents, letters, books, and the countless photographs she had amassed. Milukoff reported back to Anastasia that he had retrieved what he could and sent her what he had been able to save—except for some choice mementos that Anastasia allowed him to keep for himself.

IV.

"The Rasputins were always trouble"

SHORTLY AFTER Anastasia's arrival in mid-July, she and Jack heard from Maria Rasputin, the daughter of Father Gregory and one of the Grand Duchess's childhood friends. Maria was living in California, and Anastasia had not heard from her in more than fifty years. She had traveled the world as an animal-tamer with Ringling Brothers Circus and lived as a White Russian emigre who had once had connections at the imperial court. As such, she moved in wealthy social circles in and around Los Angeles, where many White Russian immigrants lived.

Maria wanted to visit, and Anastasia agreed to the meeting, which was quickly set for August 10. The local press had been contacted, and reporter Rey Barry was assigned to cover the visit. Jack also invited Gleb and other close friends to be present when the two women met.

Maria arrived at Fairview Farms, Jack's country home, accompanied by Patricia Barham. Ms. Barham was a wealthy Los Angeles socialite and former newspaper columnist who was already collaborating with Maria in writing a biography of Rasputin. When Anastasia entered the room, she looked at Maria and said simply, "Mara."

Anastasia had called her visitor by the pet name the imperial family had given her, a name known only among their most intimate friends. Maria, however, did not recognize the Grand Duchess, whose appearance had changed significantly after a half-century of physical neglect. Maria insisted that they go alone into an adjoining room so that she could examine Anastasia's body for the distinguishing marks Maria remembered her childhood playmate having.

They were alone together briefly, and when they reentered the room Maria declared that her recognition of Anastasia had been "almost instant."

Rey Barry's article on the meeting, which appeared a few days later in the Charlottesville *Daily Progress*, quoted Maria as saying, "She reminded me of things I had forgotten. There was one time when I was dressed up like a Red Cross nurse, the kind who accompanied wounded soldiers on the trains. I'd entirely forgotten the incident, until being reminded." The story of the meeting proved so interesting that *Time* magazine reported it.

Jack's friend Wilbur Crews also confirmed later that Maria was indisputably convinced that Anastasia was real. He also reported having accompanied Jack and Maria Rasputin to a downtown bank, now The Jefferson National Bank, where the daughter of the Mad Monk dictated and signed—at Jack's insistence—a notarized statement in which she confirmed her recognition of the lost daughter of Nicholas and Alexandra. Jack later forwarded the document to Anastasia's lawyers in Germany.

The one person who remained unimpressed with Maria's visit was Gleb. He had never trusted her family and wrote a scathing report of the encounter between the two women:

I met Maria at Manahan's house and found her to be just what one would expect—a very homely Siberian peasant with the small eyes of a sly pig and saccharin manners of very doubtful sincerity. As she proceeded to expand on her ardent love for and devotion to Anastasia,

I asked her where she had been all these years. My question embarrassed her visibly and she mumbled something to the effect that she had been very busy and had not heard about Anastasia until recently, which was, of course, a lie. I cannot help but suspect that Maria's acknowledgment of Anastasia was just a publicity stunt to advertise [her] book [about Rasputin]. . . .

Maria and Patricia Barham returned to California. On August 22 of that year, Ms. Barham wrote an article for the *Los Angeles Herald Examiner*, reporting that "Maria is sure that this is her long lost friend and everything I have seen, read, and studied, convinces me of the same." Sometime shortly thereafter, she and Maria began to formulate plans for a gala tea to be held at Ms. Barham's spacious home in Los Angeles, reportedly to benefit a local charity. According to the invitations, however, the event was to be in honor of the Grand Duchess Anastasia. Undoubtedly, those invited included representatives of the White Russian community.

One week before the scheduled date of the tea, Maria and Patricia Barham returned to Charlottesville to inform the guest of honor of their plans. Completely unaware of the preparations that had been made on the West Coast, Anastasia seemed intrigued. Although neither Gleb nor Jack would be invited to go along, she and Jack agreed that she would attend the event. On the eve of their scheduled departure, however, she suddenly changed her mind and refused to accompany Maria and Ms. Barham to California.

Her refusal destroyed the two women's well-laid plans, which must have been personally devastating to Maria. Nevertheless, a few hours after this second meeting, she would again reaffirm her conviction that Anastasia was telling the truth.

Charlottesville reporter Rey Barry recounted his second conversation with Maria at a local restaurant, The Gaslight:

Over hamburgers and too much to drink, Maria told me why she was convinced Anna Anderson was really Anastasia. She said that during their meetings, she would start to recount some childhood experience no one but she and Anastasia had shared, and Anna would finish the story. After a time, Anna also began to recall distant events they shared, games they played, that Maria could corroborate. It didn't happen once or twice, it happened in a score of specific instances.

Very matter-of-factly, Maria told me, it was certain beyond question that Anna Anderson was the real Anastasia. . . .

According to Barry, Maria also did a poor job of disguising her disappointment at seeing a social coup escape her grasp.

The Los Angeles press had given her plenty of publicity when she arrived there . . . and then, as the press will do, had moved on.

Perhaps that's one reason Maria asked Anna to come out to her home in California for an extended visit. It was clear—a better word is transparent—that Maria felt she could recapture the caviar circuit if hosts could count on Anna coming along with her for at least as long as the novelty lasted.

(Rey Barry's assessment was echoed by noted American entrepreneur and collector of Romanov memorabilia Malcolm Forbes, who in 1990 wrote that "Maria was never able to regain privileged status, either for her father's memory or for herself.")

The very next day, Maria and Ms. Barham recanted the statements they had made in front of many witnesses. Speaking to a reporter at Washington's Dulles Airport, Maria now said, "I've been bluffed by her." She also claimed to have reexamined Anastasia's body at this second meeting and said that the identifying marks had inexplicably disappeared. Patricia Barham called Anastasia "the cleverest fraud we've ever seen."

Rey Barry's assessment: "It got good press in L.A. and they probably dined out on it quite a lot. I knew Pat. She was a Hollywood product, tough and calculating."

Jack's assessment: "The Rasputins were always trouble."

FOR Gleb, this incident confirmed his belief that something was seriously wrong with Anastasia. He was also unwell, and his worsening health only exacerbated his frustration where Anastasia's future was concerned. In a letter to Milukoff in Germany, dated November 19, he said:

Things here are in a pretty bad mess. Among other things, those horrible women from California, the Misses Barham and Rasputin, turned out to be precisely the kind of dirty creatures I had been warning everyone from the start that they are. All they wanted from our poor A.N. [Anastasia Nicolaievna] is that she permit herself to be exploited to create publicity for their book on Rasputin and some kind of dubious charities . . . and the two California bitches instantly turned from friends and admirers into A.N.'s bitterest enemies, declared her an impostor and began to write horrible articles and give out equally horrible interviews.

To make it worse, Jack thought of nothing better to do than to keep bringing all those articles and interviews to A.N. Now A.N. decided that it is Jack himself who is writing or paying for those articles, and she telephones me several times a day, saying that she cannot stay in Jack's place any longer. . . . I'm doing my best to calm her, but have no idea how all will end.

In this same letter, however, Gleb noted that even though Anastasia and Jack occasionally battled, "at least he is very kind to A.N. and permits her to do anything she pleases." Perhaps this is one reason Jack continued to enjoy an amiable relationship with Gleb during these early months.

V.
"A marriage of protection"

THE PROBLEMS facing the group in Charlottesville were serious. Anastasia insisted that she would not return to Europe, so something had to be done about her visa status in the United States. She had come to America with a six-month visa, which meant she had to return to Germany no later than January 13, 1969. By November, Gleb was thoroughly convinced that Anastasia would be much better off remaining in America. She and Jack seemed to be getting along very well. Jack certainly had the financial means that would be required to care for her, but he also displayed genuine interest and affection for Anastasia. Moreover, it was clear that Anastasia could not return to Unterlengenhardt, especially after the greatest portion of her possessions had been cleared out by Prince Frederick and Ian Lilburn and the rest shipped off by Milukoff.

Over the course of the next few weeks, both Jack and Gleb made efforts to resolve the visa problem. At one point, Jack even drove Anastasia to Washington, D.C., to appeal to officials of the West German embassy. He had decided that they should speak personally to officials at the embassy and not simply rely on the written requests previously sent to American and West German immigration authorities. They drove up to the capital on a Saturday. Not surprisingly, few people were at work on the weekend, and they achieved no success from this trip. The event demonstrated Jack's innate kindness and concern but also his naivete in regard to planning practical solutions to everyday problems.

As time grew short and no resolution of Anastasia's legal status was forthcoming, all three realized that drastic measures would have to be taken in order to keep her in America. Gleb knew that the best means of achieving the goal would be to have Anastasia marry an American citizen. Realistically, there were only two possible candidates, himself and Jack.

Without doubt, she would have accepted a proposal from Gleb, who had become a U.S. citizen decades earlier. He was her childhood friend and a man who had stood by her and protected her since those first terrible years in Germany. She also felt particularly close to his children, especially his daughter, Marina Botkin Schweitzer, who lived with her husband in Alabama at the time. Although Anastasia had never seen the young woman, she was godmother to Marina's children, and they corresponded regularly over the years. Gleb was certainly aware of Anastasia's fondness for himself and his family, but he knew that what she wanted most was "a man to fight her battles for her, that she could trust." Gleb's health was deteriorating markedly, and his wife Nadine had been dead only a short time. Moreover, he lacked the financial resources required for Anastasia's care. A marriage between these two old friends would alleviate the immediate problem but would not resolve Anastasia's long-term predicament.

In a conversation late that November, Gleb again discussed the situation in detail with Jack. Both recognized that her only solution was marriage to an American, and Gleb confessed frankly, "Jack, I can't marry her." With no hesitation, Jack said, "Okay, then I'll do it."

It does seem odd that Jack, who had spent very little time with Anastasia prior to her arrival in Charlottesville the previous July, would so readily agree to marry her, but he was well known as an overly generous, kind-hearted soul. Despite his eccentricities and obsessions, he was the first to help those in trouble, even if he did not know them intimately. He had, for example, helped save a local book dealer's fledgling business by going in once a month and purposely buying enough books to cover the store's rent.

In addition to being generous, however, Jack was a brilliant historian and genealogist, and his interest in the royal families of Europe was inexhaustible. His theory of history was that:

> everything that ever has happened is happening and the whole thing is like a river and the bank. If we could just get in a time machine and go back, upstream or downstream or whatever it is, we could see the things on the bank that are the events that are happening. . . . They are happenings that never end. . . . All these things perhaps have not been lost.

Given this view, a dedicated scholar of European royal genealogy might readily see a marriage to the last daughter of the Czar as his opportunity to journey down the river of time and regain events that he believed were never really lost. By marrying Anastasia, Jack himself would become a Romanov of sorts. He and Botkin explained their proposed solution to Anastasia, and she accepted what she would later term "a marriage of protection."

Jack and Anastasia were wed on December 23, 1968, at the Charlottesville City Hall in a simple civil ceremony by City Sergeant Raymond C. Pace. Gleb acted as best man. On the marriage certificate, Anastasia listed her name as Anna Anderson, née Romanov. She noted her father's name as Nicholas Romanov and gave her mother's maiden name as Alexandra Hessen-Darmstadt. In the space provided for describing her education, she said "taught by governess." She listed her address as Fairview Farms.

Following the ceremony, Jack asked Gleb what he thought the Czar would have felt about his marrying Anastasia. Gleb knew that Jack was keenly aware that he would have been a mere untitled commoner in the eyes of the Romanovs, who had groomed their daughters to marry into the most powerful European royal houses. Yet Gleb also knew that Anastasia had been forced to lead a life full of dashed hopes and continuous manipulations at the hands of others. She was sometimes irrational, and dealing with her could wear down anyone's patience. Caring for her now would be a trying task. Knowing how saddened Nicholas would have been if he had lived to see what had happened to Anastasia during her life, and knowing the love and protection the Czar had showered on his children, Gleb gave a simple response to Jack's question: "I think he would be grateful."

ANASTASIA and Jack returned to live at the house on University Circle, where his butler James—although growing old and less capable—managed the house and took care of their needs. The Manahans seemed a curious but compatible couple. Jack was eighteen years younger than his new wife, and the difference in their ages was always apparent, but he evidently was completely dedicated to her, never questioned her authenticity, and acted as a shield between her and the world outside. She seemed quite happy with Jack. Gleb also appeared pleased with the match, more for Anastasia's sake than for Jack's. He wrote to Milukoff in Germany within two weeks of the marriage, noting that "A.N. and Jack seem to be very well satisfied with their married status and are having a very busy social life. Everybody here treats A.N. as the Grand Duchess she actually is; and it is an infinite relief for me to know that A.N. is now completely safe and may well be expected to end her days in peace and security."

Even before their marriage, Jack had fully endorsed Anastasia's claim, and he now took pains to make certain that everyone else recognized her authenticity. As a prominent and wealthy citizen, he was very much a part of the Charlottesville social scene. He was also a participating member of numerous genealogical and historical associations, where his expertise was well respected. Jack continued to attend all types of events, and Anastasia—always fearful of being left alone—accompanied him everywhere. On each occasion, whether in Charlottesville or elsewhere, Jack would do his best to advance his wife's cause.

The couple traveled up and down the East Coast and through the South to attend meetings of regional or local historical societies to which Jack belonged. Invariably the arrival of the purported Grand Duchess would interest the local press. While Jack explained her story in detail and ardently put forth her case to the reporters and photographers, Anastasia would sit quietly to the side, saying little. He loved giving interviews, whereas his wife projected regal indifference.

Even during this period, however, those who knew Jack and Anastasia began to understand that the new Mrs. Manahan was far from the placid bystander portrayed in the press. The Grand Duchess had always been temperamental, but her desire to be rid of curiosity seekers and self-appointed overseers seemed to have turned into a fixation on living her life with little regard for the consequences of her actions—or for the feelings of others. Certainly the deterioration of the houses in Unterlengenhardt and the plans she had made with Milukoff to play on Jack's sympathy in order to buy Castle Seeon reflected these characteristics. Moreover, observers in Charlottesville noted that she soon became more assertive in her dealings with her husband, and that her self-absorption sometimes exhibited itself as cruelty where he was concerned. Even in the first few months of the marriage, Anastasia would vociferously challenge and berate Jack over the least little thing, especially if she felt her privacy and security were threatened. Nonetheless, the eruptions always subsided. Eventually, perhaps after days of Anastasia's pouting, the matter would be resolved, generally with Jack ignoring whatever objections she had raised and proceeding with what he considered the best course of action.

ALTHOUGH Gleb at first endorsed the marriage, the continuing arguments between the two Manahans put a strain on his relationship with Jack. He despised the strategies Anastasia's husband devised to call attention to her case by repeated public appearances. Gleb and Jack would argue for hours about these matters. For forty years, Gleb had been the one person to whom the Grand Duchess deferred for advice and guidance. Now, however, Anastasia seemed to ignore his opinions, and he felt strongly that the current course of action would lead only to more disappointment and ridicule.

Jack's obvious eccentricities came to grate on Gleb's nerves, and he began criticizing Jack personally. A particular annoyance was Jack's love of collecting mechanical toys. One night at University Circle, as the three of them sat around arguing, Anastasia began screaming in her high-pitched voice. Suddenly, around the corner walked a five-foot-tall mechanical penguin, one of Jack's acquisitions, which moved when activated by a whistle. Its mechanism had been triggered by Anastasia's voice. The penguin was a toy that Gleb found especially annoying. He had always had a sense of humor—perhaps necessarily so, given the trying times he had shared with his childhood playmate—but rather than viewing this interruption as a comic coincidence, he grew very angry. He told his daughter, Marina Schweitzer, that the penguin incident was the last straw. From Gleb's perspective, the couple's life had descended into ridiculousness, and he wanted nothing further to do with their foolish plans. "From now on, I am keeping completely out of it," he declared. Nevertheless, the three remained in touch. Anastasia continued to value and trust his advice, and Jack gave no indication of anger toward her old friend.

By December 1969, Gleb was seriously ill. On Christmas Day, Jack planned to deliver their presents, despite a heavy snowstorm. Anastasia urged him not to go to Gleb's. She was concerned not about the weather, but about Gleb's health. She told Jack, "Gleb is dying," but Jack went ahead and made the trip to Gleb's house on Stonefield Lane.

Within two days, Gleb was dead, and Anastasia was devastated. He had encouraged her to come to America to be near him and had helped arrange for Jack to take over the financial responsibilities for her care. He had remained a confidante, her best friend. Now, just eighteen months after she had abandoned Unterlengenhardt, Gleb was dead, and she had only Jack to shield her from the intrusive world outside. *The New York Times* quoted her as saying, "Everything is changed entirely with his death."

WITHIN a few weeks, Anastasia's prediction seemed to be coming true. On February 17, 1970, fifty years to the day that she had fallen into the Landwehr Canal in Berlin, the German Supreme Court declined her appeal without expressing an opinion as to her identity. The Court specifically allowed the case to remain open and rendered no judgment of its own. This was the end of Anastasia's thirty-seven-year odyssey through the German judicial system. Her proponents could offer no new evidence to support her case, and she was intent on remaining in America to live out her life removed from the ordeals she had undergone in Europe. Attempts to pursue the matter would probably be futile, from a legal perspective, and unhealthy for Anastasia.

ALTHOUGH Jack agreed that Anastasia's legal case was, in effect, finished, he began to display increasing interest in championing her cause elsewhere. He pursued many strategies with zeal, but not all of them can be viewed as rational. Jack was a remarkable scholar with an incredible mind for obscure details, but his interpretations of facts and events were often skewed where Anastasia was concerned.

His Christmas gift to her that year illustrated his quirky reasoning. After tracing her lineage, he drew up a genealogical chart listing 1,023 of her ancestors. In his view, the chart demonstrated to her his belief in her claim, while helping him understand her psychology. Jack was not surprised, for example, to learn that so many of her ancestors were German. He felt that her German heritage made seeking refuge in Berlin in 1920 only natural. The observation might have some validity, but his other major deduction from the evidence on the chart can only be termed bizarre. It says as much about Jack's psychology as he believed it told about Anastasia's:

> Now comes the surprise. The stars in the outer ring [of the chart], and there are 88 of them, if they are all on there . . . each is a separate line

of descent from Ferdinand and Isabella of Spain. So that I was perfectly aware within a week after we were married that I was married to what I have always wanted to marry, which was a Spanish personality. She is, to me, in every way a Spanish person. She hates Spain, she hates everything connected with Spain, she is Protestant and Orthodox by background, has nothing to do with Catholicism whatsoever, but when you get to know her, you realize that this inbred thing back to Ferdinand and Isabella is pretty important to her background.

Regardless of whether anyone accepted Jack's interpretation of Anastasia's "Spanish personality," or his willingness to assign personality traits to national characters, he clearly believed in it. And his conviction is perhaps as good as any other explanation regarding why he remained wholly and unalterably devoted to his wife, even when she subjected him to her imperious, sometimes contemptuous, anger.

VI.
"Grand Duke-in-Waiting"

JACK AND ANASTASIA were both furious that her possessions in Unterlengenhardt were gone. She had collected thousands of invaluable artifacts relating to the Romanovs and felt that Prince Frederick and Ian Lilburn had absconded with the lion's share. Jack would later say "that of her 600 books, we have received fewer than 150, so that the proportion of her things that we have, I would say, is roughly one out of four, one in four." Perhaps because he knew so much had been irretrievably lost to them, he was especially determined to continue gathering these types of materials for his wife, who loved being surrounded by remembrances of her family and her royal heritage. Indeed, it is not unfair to say that the search for such materials preoccupied both of them. They would travel far and wide to pursue even the most spurious leads and ridiculous stories about possibly valuable artifacts.

In 1972, a woman in Tampa, Florida, contacted the Manahans and wanted to sell a portrait of the Czar. She originally asked $30,000 for the painting, but Jack explained that the price was too high. Even when the seller offered to lower the price to $15,000, the multimillionaire from Charlottesville refused, explaining curiously that the cost was still prohibitive. He remained intrigued, however, and drove Anastasia all the way to Tampa just to view the painting. During a conversation there, the woman tried once again to interest the couple in buying the piece. According to Jack, the woman reported that

> Mrs. Merriweather Post [had] accepted [the offer of sale], and said she would pay her immediately $25,000 for it . . . and the lady doesn't want Mrs. Post to have it. . . . She said, 'You know, Mrs. Merriweather Post wanted this painting for $25,000. We were ready to crate it up and send it to her. On the night we were going to do it I dreamed that the Czar came in and there were tears weeping down his face. I said to my husband, we can never let Mrs. Post have this painting.'

Despite this inspired story, both Jack and Anastasia remained unimpressed, and they never bought this particular portrait. But they continued purchasing Romanov-related materials to the end. Even at this early date, they had amassed enough material to enable Jack to persuade the University of Virginia to grant him permission to mount an exhibition in the main lobby of the Alderman Library. Contained within four enormous showcases was a disorganized display of eclectic mementos designed to establish Anna Anderson undeniably as the Romanov Grand Duchess Anastasia.

Jack remained forever preoccupied with winning recognition for Anastasia, and like the search for artifacts, his efforts to publicize her case were not always as tasteful as his exhibition in Charlottesville. Indeed, they sometimes bordered on the ridiculous. In 1978, for example, they received an invitation to the premiere of a ballet about Rasputin produced by the Fort Worth (Texas) Ballet Association. The organizers of the event were very interested in having the supposed last Grand Duchess of Russia attend the gala, and they spared no expense to assure that Anastasia and Jack would come. According to *Saturday Review*, the couple flew to Fort Worth by private plane as guests of the Tandy Corporation. Their sponsors supplied the finest accommodations and lavish entertainment. The two were escorted everywhere, and Anastasia received the key to the city. She stopped short of wearing a tiara, as Jack had wanted.

In truth, their participation in the gala opening was little more than a well-orchestrated effort to publicize the performance. A ballet about Rasputin would hardly have warranted any special notice without some kind of added feature. What better way to achieve such notoriety than to invite the woman who claimed to be the daughter of the last Russian czar, a woman who had known the Mad Monk? But Jack did not ever seem to realize that both he and Anastasia were being used in such an obvious way. Instead, he considered the occasion one of their greatest triumphs, characterizing their treatment—and especially the proclamation awarding Anastasia the key to the city—as official recognition of her authenticity by the State of Texas.

WITHIN a year after Jack married Anastasia, the butler James passed away. He had maintained the Manahan residence in excellent condition for many years and had seen to the needs of both his employer and his employer's new wife. He was a trusted and loyal caretaker, and Jack knew that he would be difficult to replace.

He turned out to be impossible to replace. With her life-long fear of strangers and her terror of being assassinated by poisoning, Anastasia did not like having servants prepare her food or take care of her personal needs.

Jack was generally willing to accede to Anastasia's requests, particularly when he felt they were not unreasonable and when placating his wife would avoid scenes and tantrums. He was still relatively young and had lived without servants before. He likely felt that he could care for her and keep up the house at the same time, needing additional help only when major work was required.

At the beginning, the arrangement seemed to work well. Because the couple traveled frequently in the first months and often attended receptions and dinners when they were in Charlottesville, they spent relatively little time at the house on University Circle. Basic housekeeping was enough to maintain the home in livable condition, although their standards for cleanliness were far below the ones James had set in his day.

Gradually, however, both their living habits and their failure to perform routine maintenance began to take their toll. Anastasia had always loved animals, and Jack seemed unable to deny her anything when she was attracted to a new pet. He knew about what had happened at Unterlengenhardt, and eventually the same pattern began to occur in Charlottesville. Over time they acquired more than twenty dogs and between forty and sixty cats, all of whom lived at either the house or the farm. The mess these animals created never bothered Anastasia, who felt she had no right to inhibit nature in any way. Jack made apologies for the disorder at first, but he eventually gave up worrying about it and focused on his desire to make his wife happy. The number of animals, along with the problems they caused, continued to increase.

Jack also had other concerns and interests that occupied his time. With unrelenting zeal, Jack continued trying to compensate Anastasia for the many items lost to Prince Frederick and Ian Lilburn. He gathered thousands of books, documents, paintings, and artifacts—enough to fill a small museum, let alone the house on University Circle—and he constantly brought his wife toys and other objects for her amusement. None of these items was ever discarded, even if it broke. Priceless antiques were piled together with broken dolls, and the cats and dogs roamed freely throughout the house.

Routine cleaning became impossible, and even necessary upkeep on the property all but stopped. Anastasia was suspicious of any workman who came to the property, and word around town was that the Manahan house was not a welcome place. Repairmen began declining requests to come out to the home, knowing that they were likely to be observed from behind a curtain by a suspicious old lady and, if they ever got inside the door, to encounter a revolting stench and piles of discarded trash.

In a sense, the worsening condition of the house only added to the public attention that Jack kept pursuing as a means of promoting his wife's cause. He continued to give frequent interviews, often from their home. Several local press photographers made excellent supplemental income by taking pictures of the Manahans for European—chiefly German—publications, many of them tabloids. Jack was always willing to accommodate any request by the press and take advantage of an opportunity to tell Anastasia's story, and photos of their deteriorating living condition made for excellent copy.

THE Charlottesville community began to view Jack and Anastasia more and more suspiciously. It was one thing, in this staid and elite southern enclave, to tolerate a certain degree of eccentricity, but it was quite another to associate with people who brought so much distasteful notoriety to the town. The social circles in which Jack had traveled as a prominent young bachelor now ostracized the Manahans. The isolation merely strengthened Jack and Anastasia's desire, especially hers, to avoid contact with others and to live as they wanted.

Naturally, their growing seclusion only exacerbated the problem. They took little care of their appearance, dressing shabbily and ignoring their personal hygiene. They acted in public as they did alone, often making remarks that were incomprehensible to others or raging at each other in front of complete strangers. Gossip in the community drove them further into isolation and closer together.

From time to time, the neighbors would file suit against the Manahans, trying to get them to clean up their property. Jack would appear before the magistrate, usually accompanied by his attorney, and develop elaborate arguments for his defense. Many of the disputes centered around the outside appearance of the house, particularly the lawn, which grew waist-high and threatened to infect the neighboring yards with weeds. During one hearing, Jack took pains to explain that he could not cut the yard because his wife—who hated the British—would not allow a manicured, English-like setting outside her window. Needless to say, the judge was not sympathetic. The charges became more serious over the years, and Jack was jailed in an effort to get him to adhere to the court's orders.

Jack began to espouse some of the same paranoia for which Anastasia had long been noted. He started seeing enemies everywhere, and believed he and Anastasia were both under surveillance by the

CIA, the KGB, and especially the British Secret Service—she because of her Romanov heritage, he because he was her foremost champion. Using his genealogical training, he drew up elaborate, color-coded charts to analyze various aspects of Anastasia's life, particularly who had acted as her friend and who as her enemy.

Even though they had less and less contact with the citizens of Charlottesville, Jack and Anastasia corresponded with distant relatives and minor nobility in Europe who had befriended Anastasia over the years. And the visits from reporters did not abate. As Jack grew older and less in touch with the everyday world around him, however, his statements to these supporters and to the press became more outrageous. He referred to the Grand Duchess as "the refugee of all refugees" and argued that the only appropriate forum for a hearing of her identity claim was the World Court. The idea for establishing the Court had originated with Czar Nicholas, and Jack somehow felt that, because of this fact, the tribunal would be inclined to favor his wife, even though he knew that only sovereign states could bring cases before the Court. He also began attacking public figures, naming the American industrialist Armand Hammer as a threat to U.S. national security, because of the close ties he maintained to Soviet leaders back to Lenin. Such statements and the repeated reports of Anastasia's odd lifestyle began to alienate her supporters overseas and in America, so that only a small cadre of ardent loyalists remained.

Jack and Anastasia still seemed relatively unaffected by the criticism swirling around them, except for two notable instances involving important segments of the Charlottesville community. Although Jack had never taught at the University of Virginia, his father had been a respected member the faculty, and Jack continued to be included as part of the school's academic and social community, after his father's death. This status did not change upon his marriage, but as the Manahans' behavior—both privately and publicly—became increasingly bizarre, the University establishment shied away from them.

A similar situation developed at the exclusive Farmington Country Club. The Club was the pinnacle of social distinction in Charlottesville, where pillars of the community often gathered for entertainment and dining. Jack's parents had been members, and he had joined as a young man. Although Jack and Anastasia began attending events at the Club less frequently, they never failed to make an impression on the other members: they would come to dinner dressed inappropriately and invariably exchange loud words in the genteel, conservative surroundings. Almost always, Anastasia would take her uneaten food from the plate and wrap it in foil for the dogs waiting outside in the car. The Manahans' appearances at Farmington became so disturbing that the governing board let Jack know that they would prefer that he not renew his membership.

Far from understanding why they had been spurned by these two important circles of Charlottesville society, Jack lashed out at them. He accused the University community of being biased against his wife's claim and repeatedly told their few remaining friends that they had been "thrown out" of Farmington Country Club because Anastasia "spoke German in the dining room."

By the late 1970s, most people viewed the Grand Duchess and her husband—who characterized himself as "a duchyless, but not duchessless, Grand Duke-in-Waiting"—as an eccentric, even crazy, old couple. As Jack and Anastasia, accompanied by some of their pets, drove around town in one of their dilapidated vehicles, whispers and shaking heads followed them.

ONLY the press continued its pursuit of the Manahans. Now older, Anastasia was one of the few remaining witnesses to a bygone era, whose very mention elicited countless stories. Her notoriety, combined with her bizarre lifestyle, served as a magnet to news organizations around the world. Every new and unusual event in the Manahans' lives seemed to be fodder for pages of press coverage.

In 1974, Jack had the telephone removed from 35 University Circle because he was tired of paying the charges for Anastasia's frequent trans-Atlantic calls. The press found itself cut off from instantaneous contact with the Manahans, but the various parties agreed that a local reporter, Bill Sublette of the *Daily Progress*, would act as liaison between the couple and the press corps outside Charlottesville. Any reporter wanting an interview with Anastasia would first call Sublette. He, in turn, wrote detailed notes to Jack, outlining proposed interviews, and left them in the mailbox.

If Jack agreed to the interview, he would go to a public phone booth or to his friend Mildred Ewell's home and call Sublette, who then confirmed the arrangements.

They usually conducted interviews at University Circle, until its condition worsened to the point that even Jack was embarrassed for anyone to see it. For a short time he arranged events at the Farmington Country Club, until he and Anastasia were unwelcome there. Dr. and Mrs. Ewell finally agreed to host the interviews at their home on Rugby Road.

Anastasia had always been reluctant to speak to the press, seeing no need to explain her case to inquiring reporters, but now she was absolutely cantankerous. Reporters from other cities often asked Bill Sublette to accompany them on interviews. Many came ill-prepared, expecting to find a sensation-seeking old woman experienced at telling her story. After all, so much had been written about her over the decades, much of it repetitious. What they found, instead, was a reluctant and petulant subject who sat glaring, while her husband espoused theories about his wife and her family or told endless anecdotes which did not seem to relate at all to the story.

Strangely, according to Bill Sublette, the effect of Anastasia's sphinx-like behavior was to persuade the reporters that she was telling the truth. Most felt that, had she been an impostor, she would have taken advantage of opportunities to put forth her case. As the daughter of the last Russian czar, however, she would naturally demonstrate regal disdain for their incessant questioning.

At other times she became animated about something unrelated to the interview. She evinced this attitude especially when visitors evoked happy memories. Anastasia had maintained a lifelong fondness for the family of Hugh D. Auchincloss, whom she first met during her brief stay on Long Island in the 1920s. She and Jack were excited when they discovered that an interviewer would be arriving in Charlottesville accompanied by Hugh's son, James Lee Auchincloss. Once the interview commenced, she ignored the reporter and turned her attention toward Auchincloss's son and their mutual enjoyment of photography.

After Bill Sublette left the *Daily Progress*, the Ewells became primary contacts for the media. Mildred Ewell, one of Jack's oldest friends in town, received an initial inquiry, consulted briefly with him on the matter, and then completed all the arrangements. Despite this attempt to organize more formally, the desired effect was lost. Jack remained eager to see his wife's story published, but most press accounts in the last few years concentrated on sensationalism. Serious attempts to investigate the facts and myths surrounding the Grand Duchess Anastasia were sorely lacking.

VII.
"Watch out for the booby traps"

I HAD LONG BEEN INTERESTED in Anastasia's story and continued to read accounts of her, as well as books on Romanov history, for many years before becoming a writer. A chance to write a feature article had led to my first meeting with Jack and Anastasia. Although no story resulted from this contact, I remained in touch with them after our first meeting in 1972.

In the autumn of 1976, BBC reporter Anthony Summers and his editor, Tom Mangold, published *The File on the Tsar*, accompanied by a television documentary of the same name. The book presented new evidence overturning the accepted account of the last days of the imperial family, documenting that the family had been separated at Ekaterinburg and the women sent by train to the city of Perm. The book reported that the Czar and his son were shot in a military-style execution—probably the following day. The story had circulated in the 1920s but was discounted after the White government issued the results of Nicholas Sokolov's investigation into the assassination of the imperial family. Summers and Mangold, however, had discovered documents that supported the theory that Anastasia and the other Romanov women had spent their final days in Perm, not Ekaterinburg. No one challenged their conclusions.

The book also contained an entire chapter on Anastasia, including a chronology of her life, and an account of the evidence presented by both sides during her various court cases. Summers and Mangold virtually handed Anastasia Manahan her identity on a silver platter. Riveted by this highly readable, documented account, I tried to reach Manahan, but by then he had had the phone removed.

IN December 1976, a well-known writer who was interested in collaborating with Anastasia on a book asked me to go to Charlottesville and offer her a million dollars for her story. I had mentioned my interest in her life casually to him and never imagined our conversation would lead to such an offer, or that he would ask me to be his research assistant on the project.

I spent the week before Christmas in New York searching for the books I would need to begin the preliminary research. I planned to visit the Manahans in Charlottesville on Christmas and sent ahead a wire to that effect, knowing that the lack of response meant that they agreed to see me.

In preparation for the trip I again telephoned my former English professor from the College of William and Mary, J. Lewis Walker, III, who was then teaching in Rocky Mount, North Carolina. He told me that Jack's "relationship to reality [was] distorted," and that he had "not much contact with reality, but [had] his own reality, which [was] kind of fun." Walker had once lived in the Manahans' apartments and his living room window had looked into their rear living room, providing an intimate view into their lives. He recounted a number of random details: Anastasia would drape her underwear, which "looked like chain metal armor," over the balcony to dry; thirty cats lived in and around the Manahan house, and the smell was so offensive that the tenants refused to go inside to pay their rents; Manahan let people in dire financial straits live in the apartments for free, even though Anastasia thought immorality ran rampant in the apartments; when she spoke to Jack her voice was so loud it sounded like one side of a violent argument.

Mr. Walker also gave me descriptions of the Manahan vehicles, so I could determine whether they were home when I arrived. He warned that I would find the exterior of the house much changed, the grounds overgrown and impenetrable. "Watch out for the booby traps," he laughed. I thought the comment strange. But our entire conversation about these famous recluses had been odd, and I dismissed this last point as unimportant.

I also discussed Anastasia with people who had already researched her story. On the afternoon of December 22, I arranged to meet first with Robert Speller, of Robert Speller & Sons publishers, in his New York office. Speller had published the autobiography of a fake "Anastasia," Mrs. Eugenia Smith, in 1963. In 1971, he had issued the first English translation of the famous Sokolov Report.

Speller's offices were located on the fifth floor of a shabby building at 10 East 23rd Street, reached by a creaking freight elevator. While he virtually admitted that Mrs. Smith was not Anastasia, Speller would not concede that Mrs. Manahan was genuine. But he had a curious respect for her and suggested several questions for me to pose to her. When I asked why he should care about her answers if he thought her a fraud, he replied, "She's so damned knowledgeable."

That evening I spoke with Guy Richards, author of *The Hunt for the Czar*, who had his own list of questions for me to pose. He had thought her a fake, but the Summers-Mangold book made a deep impression on him. "If any of them were Anastasia, it is Mrs. Manahan. There's no doubt now," he said. Along with the questions, he offered to arrange for me to meet Tony Summers, but time was running short, so I could not see the British author before going to Charlottesville.

I went home on Christmas Eve to see my family, then flew to Charlottesville on Christmas Day and checked into the Downtowner Motor Inn, the hotel closest to the Manahans' house. Later that day, Dr. Glenn Stoner, the grandson of a family friend and a scientist at the University of Virginia, drove me past the house. The house looked just as my friend Mr. Walker had described it. A low chicken-wire fence surrounded the property. Boxes of huge canvas bags filled with mail lay in the street; the mailman reportedly refused to navigate around the side of the house to the kitchen door, which was now the only visible entrance. Anastasia had ordered the front door boarded over, the windows barricaded, and junk piled in the yard to further dissuade anyone from approaching the house. The path to the side door was littered with big rocks, tree stumps and knives protruding at odd angles. Shotgun barrels had reportedly been sighted sticking out of a window or two, on occasion.

After our drive, I had dinner with the Stoners, who told me troubling stories about the Manahans. They said, for example, that Anastasia had begun cremating her dead cats in the living room fireplace, causing the neighbors to file several complaints with local health authorities.

Dr. Stoner took me back to University Circle at about 9 P.M. A light was on, and the cars Mr. Walker had described to me were parked in the driveway, indicating the Manahans were home. Having heard about the dangerous path, Dr. Stoner insisted on waiting in his car with the headlights shining until I had safely reached the side door and knocked on it. I waved to Dr. Stoner, and he drove away as Jack answered my knock with a jolly Christmas greeting and invited me in.

The smell inside was overwhelming, and I feared for a moment that I might start retching. Cats were everywhere, and the house was in much worse disarray than before. The carpet was now covered with pieces of cardboard, which the Manahans laid over the messes made by the cats. Walking was tricky, but Jack steered me into the living room. A huge tree stump stood in the middle of the room "to remind Anastasia of her years in the Black Forest," he explained.

It was much the scene described by Alan Haas, one of the few journalists allowed inside the Manahan house during the late 1970s:

> Inside, the house is a total shambles. The main room, where we are received, is dark and forbidding. The furniture is falling apart. Most of the shades are drawn. On shelves around the room are literally thousands of items of memorabilia, old photographs, icons, religious statues, porcelain and china figurines, faded news clippings and letters. Almost everything is in a disarray. Genealogical charts and ancient portraits of the Romanovs predominate. On the floor, in various places, and on plates in corners, cat food, appearing days old, is decaying.
>
> Although it is [winter], the only heat comes from a single log, smoldering fitfully in the grate. In a jumbled heap in the middle of the

room is a pile of twigs, branches, and small logs to feed the blaze. Everything is covered with the dust of ages. In truth, it is not unlike the room in Dickens' *Great Expectations* where Miss Haversham brooded for a lifetime, awaiting her never-to-appear bridegroom. "My wife likes to live in total confusion," comments John Manahan.

Anastasia sat huddled in front of a roaring fireplace, not, thankfully, conducting a cremation. The house was very cold, and Jack explained that the furnace had broken and he refused to pay the money necessary to fix it, "so we do without."

I had brought Christmas presents for them, books for Jack and a jade brooch for Anastasia. She smiled and refused her package, "No, Jemmy, not for me." Manahan urged her to open it, and after unwrapping it she exclaimed, "Ach, but it is too nice. Very expensive, it looks. I cannot wear such a thing."

She liked to call me "Jemmy," saying it was a "good name."

"That was the name of your dog in Russia, wasn't it? I've seen photographs of you holding him."

"No, he was Tatiana's. I just liked to hold him. And I shall call you for him."

The three of us talked for about an hour, Anastasia reminiscing about Christmases past, including those in Russia, before she got sleepy and retired. Jack led me downstairs to a room where he said it would be warmer. Only then did I reveal the true purpose of my visit. We sat up until 5 A.M. talking.

"She won't do it," he answered emphatically. "She hates New York, distrusts publishers and all journalists, and the money has no interest to her."

But he conceded his desire that she tell her story to someone. She had never told even him how she had escaped Russia or what had happened to the rest of her family.

Then he startled me with the confession that caring for Anastasia was wearing him down, physically and emotionally. He offered a detailed accounting of his finances, which seemed more than adequate for their needs and certainly included enough to repair the furnace. He said he was tired, and afraid of what might happen to her if his health failed—or worse. He had tried to coax her into applying for American citizenship, which would guarantee her right to remain in this country if he should die before she did.

"What am I to do?" he asked. "I need help, but who can I trust?" He added that Anastasia seemed unwilling and unable to live with anyone else.

As dawn approached, I realized that I had been awake for twenty-four hours and wanted to get some sleep. Our conversation ended, and Jack offered three options regarding the approach to Anastasia: he would ask her; I could ask her; or it could go unmentioned.

"Be aware that this idea may make her very angry with you, and you could lose her friendship, Jimmy," he warned. I said I would ask her myself, if he agreed not to mention it to her before I had raised the subject on my own. He assented.

Jack drove me back to the hotel, and as I got out of the car he said he hoped that Anastasia would be able to get some sleep. "She's been walking the floors all night for weeks."

VIII.
"I am here; I am real"

THE NEXT DAY we got into one of Jack's ancient automobiles and drove around sightseeing, starting out for Monticello, as I had suggested the night before. I sat in the back, surrounded by books, papers, and empty soda cans. Anastasia sat in front with Jack and didn't say a word to me. She seemed furious, and I felt certain Jack had told her of my mission.

Almost as if reading my mind, Jack said to pay no attention to Anastasia because she was very angry with him. At that, she launched into an abusive tirade in German. Jack laughed and continued talking to me as if Anastasia had said nothing.

We first stopped at the Virginia Visitors' Center. As we parked, Anastasia announced she did not wish to go inside. Unable to persuade her, Jack said, "Well, in that case, stay in the car. Be that way, Anastasia. We're going in." Anastasia seemed content to sit alone in the car, drinking a can of warm soda and reading an Agatha Christie novel as Jack and I toured the center.

When we arrived at Monticello, it was closed. I was hungry and offered to take them to dinner. Anastasia agreed that she would eat, but Jack insisted that this be their treat, not mine. A long discussion followed about where we would go for dinner. Finally, Anastasia announced, "I want to go to Farmington." Jack replied that none of us were dressed for Farmington. Indeed, we had dressed hurriedly for a casual tourist expedition. Jack looked like a sloppy preppie, Anastasia like a bag lady, and I still needed a good night's sleep.

But Anastasia insisted upon Farmington. Jack suggested that because it was the day after Christmas, the club might not be open.

She said, "They would open it for me!"

"Now Anastasia, even if it is open, the downstairs. . . ." He turned toward me and, without lowering his voice in the least, said, "Watch this. I'll use psychology on her.

"Anastasia, if Farmington is open, then probably only the lower dining room is open tonight. Remember the fat waitress that you don't like? Maybe she's working tonight, angry that she has to work the day after Christmas. And she might try to poison your food."

"We don't go to Farmington," she firmly replied.

Knowing that Anastasia did not eat meat, I suggested the dining room of my hotel, which specialized in seafood. The night before, Jack had seemed unusually pleased that I had chosen to stay at that particular hotel. He said it was Anastasia's favorite, and that she wanted him to buy it for her.

Jack wanted to go to a nearby cafeteria instead. "Ugh!" was Anastasia's reaction. But we had been driving around town for more than an hour debating where to eat, and in ravenous desperation I begged them to go back to the hotel.

Jack still wouldn't agree, but suddenly Anastasia looked at him hard and said, "We go to the hotel." So we went.

JACK got out of the car first and announced his intention of using the lavatory. I got out of the back seat on Anastasia's side of the car. As I opened her door, I realized that this was the first time I had ever been alone with her.

Stepping out of the car, Anastasia looked up at me and said, "I am tired of journalists, always pestering me for my story. For fifty years it has been so. And now you. . . ."

So Jack *had* told her of our conversation the night before. My heart sank. He had promised not to. I was supposed to ask her. But I knew what she was telling me, and her answer was no.

She reached back into the car and put the Agatha Christie paperback into her purse. As we started toward the restaurant, I had an idea.

"Anastasia, you really like Agatha Christie, don't you?"

"Oh, yes," she answered enthusiastically, almost cooing.

"How many have you read?"

"I don't know. All of them, I'm sure. Many times again I have read the same ones."

"You read the same ones over again?"

"Well, of course! There are so many that one after a while forgets, you know?"

I said I understood that many Agatha Christie fans read her work over and over again.

"It is so," she said. "Miss Christie has created so many mysteries that one forgets after a few years and can read them again."

"So she is like you," I said in what I hoped sounded like an offhand and casual tone.

We were walking across the parking lot and she stopped. "What? What do you mean by saying such things?"

"She is like you."

"What! Miss Christie, she is a creator. It is all . . . how do you say. . . ."

"Fiction."

"Yes, but *I* am not so! You are looking at me. I am here; I am real. I am standing here. I am not . . . how do you say it?"

"Fiction."

"Yes." She enunciated slowly, "Fiction."

This was the opening I had been searching for. "Anastasia, you are a fiction, a mystery, to many people. . . ."

She cut in sharply. "Too many people have bothered me. Always they are asking that I prove again and again who I am. It's rubbish. And he [Jack] said I should show myself to people, to young people, so that they will remember me when I am dead. I am not long alive. Soon I shall die. I want to die."

A bitter winter wind cut across the parking lot as we stood facing each other. It almost knocked her down, and I leaned forward and put my arm around her frail body to steady her. She relaxed against my chest.

I inclined my head downward and said softly, "And when you die the mystery will go with you. The mystery of Anastasia will never be solved, will it? Do you want to be remembered as a mystery, or as who you really are?"

"I do not know of what you speak." Her body stiffened, and she seemed about to pull away.

"Anastasia, if you don't tell the whole truth to somebody someday, you will always remain a mystery. Like a fiction by Miss Christie. People will remember Ingrid Bergman, not you."

She pulled herself up straight. "That Swedish cow! That film was the work of creators. You know it had nothing to do with me. This you already know!"

"Yes, ma'am, I know that. Your friends know that. But to the rest of the world you are a fiction, a mystery that, unlike Miss Christie's mysteries, may never be solved."

She said nothing in response, but as we walked into the building she held my arm tight. She was trembling violently, but I could not tell whether it was from the emotion or the cold.

JACK stood in the lobby, looking surprised as we came through the door. "Anastasia never lets anyone touch her," he said. I had given it no thought at the time. Putting my arm around an old, feeble woman had seemed such a natural thing to do. But now I quickly removed my arm. Anastasia patted me and said, "Ach, Jack, it is Jemmy. I like him, you know."

We sat in a booth on the left side of the dining room. The waitress brought menus and asked if we would like coffee. Jack and I declined, but Anastasia's eyes lit up. "I want coffee."

Immediately, Jack said, "No, Anastasia, no, no, no, no, no. You can't have coffee. You know how it affects you."

She repeated, "I want coffee!"

And he said, "No, Anastasia!" He was strict about her diet.

Again she declared, "I want coffee!"

And again he answered "No, no, no, no, no, no coffee. Now Anastasia, you know you'll be up all night and all day tomorrow, if you drink just one cup of coffee now."

Anastasia looked across the table at me with the pleading eyes of a child. She knew that I was the host for this evening, and her silent appeal was touching. Jack was shaking his head at me, but I said to the waitress, "Whatever the Grand Duchess wants, she may have."

The waitress brought a cup and poured the coffee. Anastasia emptied the sugar bowl into the cup and stirred.

Then the strangest thing happened. The hand that she usually kept over her mouth, to cover her missing teeth, suddenly dropped into her lap, and she began speaking in nearly perfect English, her accent gone. She said, "You want to write this?"

I had not expected this offer, but as she had made it clear that she would not work with anyone else, I replied, "Yes, I do."

"All right."

I was shocked. Jack looked stunned. I said, "But a few minutes ago you said—"

"I like you, Jemmy," she interrupted. "I have always like you. I tell Jack I like you."

I told her that I did not know what to say or where to begin. She said, "This is where we begin. I will not work with your friends in New York. No publishers from New York." She grimaced each time she said New York.

"I will tell all only to you."

"But Anastasia, why me?"

"Go look in a mirror."

I went to the lavatory and looked in the mirror. When I returned to the table, the Manahans were arguing. Anastasia was furious and screaming at Jack in German.

"So, what do you see?" she asked.

"Myself."

"When I look into your eyes, I see the Czar. You look more like the Czar than anyone I have ever seen."

"But Anastasia, the Czar's eyes were blue, like yours. Mine are brown."

"But this," she said, pointing to the circles surrounding my eyes. "This is beautiful, just like the Czar. And when I see into your eyes, I see the soul of the Czar. You I can trust. With you, Jemmy, all is well, and I am safe."

Then she added, "I believe in reincarnation—"

"Oh, Anastasia, you don't mean—"

"Who is to know?" She shrugged.

Her cup was empty, and she looked at it and then at me, as if asking whether she could have another. She was charming in those moments, as if she were trying to weave a little web of intimacy between us.

She continued, "You will write the story. No one else. No one has ever written about the Czar and Mama properly. Or myself. Or Father Gregory. Everyone says I am crazy. You will come back to Charlottesville. . . . No, you stay here and I will tell you everything."

Jack murmured something in another language, and she shouted a response. He said something else, and she screamed at him again. He seemed unfazed by her reactions, but their exchange lasted several minutes until Jack demurred in English, "All right, Anastasia, all right."

I said to Anastasia, "I must go to London next month on business. I cannot stay here now. And in London, perhaps I shall see Summers or Mangold."

This seemed to upset her deeply. She frowned and studied her coffee cup intently.

I explained to her that my business necessitated a visit to London, and that I might not be able to return to Charlottesville for a long time. I told her that I had to find a publisher before I could offer her money for a book.

"You may involve yourself with publishers, but I shall not. I will tell only you everything."

I asked if she would write or sign an endorsement of the book. She had to confer with Jack on the meaning of the word "endorsement."

"No," she answered, shaking her head.

I asked her why not.

"I will write nothing. I will tell you everything, and you write it as you wish. That is all."

I told her that the venture would be purposeless, if she later failed to acknowledge her own participation. But she seemed confused by my repeated use of the word "endorsement." Finally, I asked if she would authorize me as her biographer. She immediately understood the word "authorize."

"Yes. Authorize. You are the chosen one. I authorize you to write for me. I will tell everyone you are the chosen, the authorized one."

Jack gasped, and she shot him a mean look.

I said, "Anastasia, I cannot financially afford to do this on my own," explaining that a publisher would want something substantive before agreeing to pay any money. I told her that she must give me something to work with, something to entice a publisher's interest.

"What do you mean?"

I said I would need facts, facts that had never been published anywhere.

She seemed to understand this and replied, "Yes. There was no massacre."

I reminded her that she had said the same thing to Tony Summers and "Good Morning, America."

She considered this for a moment and added, "The Czar never abdicated." The Czar went to Berlin in 1913 to attend a royal wedding, she said, and stayed in a hotel. Assassins tried to kill him with a bomb made in Switzerland, but they were foiled somehow and the bomb was thrown down a laundry chute. After the attack, the Czar secretly ordered the construction of another duplicate of his sumptuous blue trains. Identical doubles of each member of the immediate imperial family were recruited to stand in for them at public events where the possibility of assassination existed. She said that the real family later escaped Russia on the duplicate train and that the doubles were killed at Ekaterinburg.

Jack had never heard the story, and he got so excited that he grabbed a menu from the hands of a passing waitress and began furiously taking notes on its blank rear pages. Occasionally, he interjected questions in German.

While Anastasia talked, a young child behind her began to climb over the top of the booth and pull Anastasia's hair, then attempted to sit on top of Anastasia's head. Anastasia screamed and flailed at the child, but the scene continued without a word from the apparently oblivious parents, until a waitress intervened on Anastasia's behalf. All the time she was fighting off the child, Anastasia continued telling the story in English and answering Jack in German.

If the story itself was unconvincing, the circumstances of its telling made it seem ludicrous.

I asked Anastasia whether she minded if I took notes, but she said, "Today Jack will write."

Although Jack was thrilled by the revelation of the doubles and even offered to serve her more coffee, I was certain the story was untrue and could not be corroborated. I decided to ask her to tell me something unpublished but verifiable.

She thought for a moment, then said, "Ahhh, I know a thing no one else knows. . . ."

"Not 'no one,' Anastasia," I said. I had to have information that could be verified.

"Only the Duke of Leuchtenberg and his wife know this."

She said that in the late 1920s, while she was staying at Castle Seeon as the guest of the Leuchtenbergs, a woman of noble rank was sent to care for her following a bone operation on her left arm.

Every afternoon, the woman fixed tea and small almond cookies for her, but Anastasia grew weaker rather than stronger. Finally, convinced that something unrelated to her operation was wrong, she declined the tea and cookies. The woman became distraught, and later committed suicide after admitting to the Leuchtenbergs that she had been slowly poisoning Anastasia on the instructions of Prince Felix Youssoupov, the organizer of Rasputin's assassination.

I listened, while Jack took notes. Anastasia seemed pleased with herself, but I was deeply disappointed. The doubles story simply couldn't be true, at least not completely. Too much documentary evidence existed about the family's captivity at Ekaterinburg and Tobolsk for the story to have any credence. Even her tale about the attempted poisoning—although intriguing—probably could not be verified. If this was the kind of story she would tell, there would be no book.

As we ate, Anastasia seemed to sense my disappointment. She spoke of Rasputin always as Father Gregory, in reverential tones, her eyes shining. The years had not dimmed her admiration for him and she called him "a saint." I did not refer to the doubles story again, but asked for further elaboration of the poisoning story, to which she added a few more impressions of the event. But she said nothing of consequence and looked almost moonily into my eyes, like a young girl playing the coquette. Then she brought up the doubles story again in passing.

I decided to be more forceful in dealing with this elusive woman and said, "Anastasia!" in a tone of mild reproof. Lowering her head like a rebuked child, she got my point.

Her adamant insistence about the doubles story finally had become too much for me. If she would hand me a line like that with a straight face, she might say anything. Yet I felt instinctively that she was the genuine Grand Duchess. But how to get the truth out of her, if she had any that she would or could still reveal. Frustrated, I told myself then and there to forget the whole thing and go home, admitting defeat.

IX.
"The death of kings"

JACK, whom she now often called "Hans," remarked that Anastasia loved movies. Earlier that day I had noticed that the newly released Dino De Laurentiis film, *King Kong*, was playing at the Barracks Road Theatre. They agreed that a movie would be fun, so we finished our meal and went to the theater, putting the mystery of Anastasia behind us.

The place was almost empty that night. After Jeff Bridges captured Kong, Anastasia said something to Jack, got out of her seat, and left the auditorium. Jack leaned over to me and whispered that she abhorred violence of any kind, especially to animals, and preferred to wait in the lobby until the movie was over.

After a while, I got up to go to the lavatory. Anastasia was sitting alone on a bench in the lobby staring ahead, frozen like a statue. I asked her whether she wanted anything, and she accepted a Coke without ice. I returned to the theater.

I could no longer concentrate on the film, but Jack was engrossed in it and seemed especially taken with "Dwan," the character played by Jessica Lange. I slipped out of my seat and wandered into the lobby. As I approached Anastasia, she looked up as if she had been expecting me and gestured toward the seat beside her. Neither of us said anything for a while. Then I asked, "Don't you like this movie?"

"No. The death of kings is bad. They will kill this King?"

"Yes."

"Is bad."

"Yes."

"Everyone wants to kill kings."

"The girl loves him."

"She is a bad actress."

"She tries to save him in the end, I think."

"Was the same for us."

I asked what she meant. She began to talk, still looking straight ahead. She said that, "at the end," obviously meaning Ekaterinburg, the Red guards told her family that plots were being hatched to rescue them. They also heard rumors of German and British rescue teams gathering near the city.

"In the end was hell," she said. "Sometimes I wish I die then, so I would not now remember."

I told her that she didn't have to remember this for me, but she seemed oddly reflective and said she wanted to say certain things "so the world would know."

The Bolshevik guards had forced every indignity imaginable upon the family, tying them to chairs and repeatedly raping all of them, except the Czarevich. While one member of the family was being violated, the others were forced to watch. The Reds formed a line outside the door, each awaiting his turn. If the family members closed or covered their eyes or tried to look away, they were held by the guards and forced to watch. While the Czarina was being abused, the guards taunted her with comparisons of their size to that of Rasputin. The Czar was often taken by two men at once.

That the Ipatiev House guards might have sexually violated members of the Romanov family had long been a subject of whispered speculation. But as far as I knew, no one had ever dared ask Anastasia about it. Nor had she voluntarily broached the matter—except perhaps to Mrs. Rathlef, who was long dead. I didn't know how to respond when she raised it. Rather than displaying the demeanor of an Edwardian-era child, as she often did, she now appeared a very contemporary person, worldly and unafraid.

"In this book you will write, you must tell all. *All.* All what *they* have done to us. All what I have seen."

I nodded, "I'll try."

"You must tell how they have hurt us. Tell that they. . . ." She fell silent. I did not know what to say and certainly did not want to risk interrupting her train of thought, so I remained quiet.

"This would not have been so if King George had saved us. But the English—*the English*—they have on their hands our blood. They left us there to be so hurt . . ." her voice trailed off.

"I—"

"Not interrupting! They hurt us, they made us not anymore *ladies.* First Mama."

She began describing a horrific scene. When the guard approached, the Czarina reached down to her breast and pulled from it the cross made from the relic of Noah's Ark. Anastasia repeated the gesture she remembered, as if warding off a strange demon. She recalled screaming at the stunned guard, "That is a relic of the True Ark." He only laughed and began the rape of his sovereign.

"Then Olga. And I. I fight with them, but they hold me. *Many* hold me. The pain was not the worst. It was the *words*, those *terrible* words. And my Father's face! And he can nothing do to help me. They hold him there and force to watch. My own *Father!*"

"Anastasia—"

"Let me tell this! The Bolsheviks have done these things to me and to the family of their Czar. And what they have done to us, they have done in other ways to all their own people."

"Do you mean 'rape'?"

"The *entire* country—"

I started to speak but she interrupted again. "Listen only! This they have done to *millions*, 'X' number of people. They have taken Russia and *used* it."

Her metaphor was graphically clear.

"And some day . . . when I am dead, the Russian people will have enough of this. They are strong. And good, *very, very good*. But *I* must first be dead. This *will* happen!"

I was cautious about speaking, but felt somehow that I must reassure her. I put my hand on hers.

"You spoke with Jack about this movie—" she said.

"*King Kong?*"

"No. The *other* movie about which you spoke with Jack."

Jack had asked me about *The Exorcist* earlier in the day, but Anastasia had seemed not to be listening.

"You mean *The Exorcist*? The movie about demons?"

"Yes."

"What about it?"

"These things I have seen."

"You saw *The Exorcist*?" I couldn't believe it.

"No, Jemmy. Such movies I should *never* see. But such *things I have seen. They are real*. The Bolsheviks were *devils*! They were devils *inside*, not normal. *Not at all!* No movie can show what I have seen men do. No movie can tell what they did to us."

She had been staring straight ahead as she spoke. But suddenly she raised her right hand and seemed to point at the air in front of her. It was as if she were warding off an image that only she could see. Her hand made a fluttering gesture and fell limply back into her lap.

"It is many years ago. *Many years ago*. But I shall never forget. They used *us all. All* except my brother. The Czar gave himself *again* to save his son. For many days after, he was not walking. This is why I think God left me. If there was a God, then—*you* tell me—why should I live? Why? With such memories. *Why?*"

I was speechless and embarrassed for her. I felt hot, confined, uncomfortable. I opened my mouth to speak, and she shook her head.

"Say nothing now. Wait. Wait until I am dead. Then tell the world what they have done. Tell English people what their king has done to a little child. Tell the Russian people what their 'revolution' did. To a *child*. To a *girl* child. And to *all* Russian people. *All* of the children. They are slaves!

"Even I have become a slave to what they did. I have no home, no family. I am a slave to only memories. But when I die, all will be at an end. When my suffering is finished Russia will soon be without the devils.

"The world must know what Bolsheviks are," she added flatly.

Speaking rapidly, Anastasia said that one night the Czarina and the girls were taken from the Czar and his son and put onto a train. They never saw the men again. The train took the women to Perm, where they were imprisoned for at least two months. They were first kept together, then separated, later reunited for a while, and finally separated again.

Anastasia escaped three times, and was recaptured each time. Back in captivity, she was beaten and raped. Once she was shot. After the third failed escape, she was taken to a room where a woman, apparently of the lower nobility, was asked to identify her. The woman told the Reds that she was not Anastasia, so they let her go. In the street, she met a peasant named Alexander Tschaikovsky, who helped her run away.

I risked interrupting her again, but I had to know whether she was telling the truth this time and, if so, why she had concocted the doubles story just hours before.

She said that I had mentioned my trip to England and plans to meet Summers or Mangold, and she hoped the doubles story would confuse them. She said she did not want to give anyone from England the satisfaction of having the last word on the Romanovs.

"All English are scoundrels. Never trust the English. But now you know, Jemmy. The last word shall be yours."

Anastasia continued to look straight ahead, but obviously her memories were as clear and detailed as the action on the movie screen. Her poise had an innate regality.

She described her flight across Russia with Tschaikovsky. The sounds of King Kong's rampage through New York City, filtering into the lobby where we sat, added a strange resonance to her tales of apocalyptic civil war. She seemed to be watching the scenes of those bygone years, looking back through the decades to the bleakest months of her life. Although her eyes filled with tears, her voice, in broken but perfectly pronounced English, was strong.

"I left Mama," she repeated several times. "That I am ashamed. Makes my heart heavy. I left Mama. . . ."

She said that Bucharest was "cold, dark in the day," when she and Tschaikovsky arrived there. "Many people moaning. Many die."

Her words were chilling. Obviously moved, she nevertheless controlled her emotions. As the story came pouring out, I was overcome with frustration. This was a journalist's nightmare—to finally discover the truth and be unprepared. My tape recorder and notebooks were at the hotel. I had come all the way across the country loaded with equipment only to have this happen in a movie theater. I concentrated hard on every word, every inflection, hoping I could get it all down later.

I tried to keep calm and not get caught up too much in the drama of what I heard. Quietly I asked where she had lived in Bucharest. She said that Tschaikovsky had taken her to the German embassy, where they refused to believe she was Anastasia until she removed her handmade silk undergarment monogrammed with the Romanov crest.

I asked why she had tried to kill herself by jumping off the bridge in Berlin. She said she had been pushed.

After that, she said, everything had become "a mess." She had no idea what had happened to the Czar or her brother, but perhaps one of her sisters, Olga, was still living near Lake Como. She wasn't sure.

"Wait for me to die when you tell," she said, turning and taking my hands in hers. "Let me die. Is better." She looked deeply into my eyes as if gazing down into my soul. I held her hands and promised.

A few minutes of uncomfortable silence passed before I asked another question. Did she ever wonder what had happened to her son?

"No," came the sharp reply.

I said I thought she liked Tschaikovsky.

"He was good man. Loyal to his Czar. But not father."

Who was the father?

"A Bolshevik devil."

Did she ever really marry Tschaikovsky?

"No, it was a story."

Was his name really Tschaikovsky?

"Yes."

I continued asking questions and she continued answering them, some at length, some with just a word or two. I could have gone on all night. She seemed comfortable, too, but I wondered when the movie would end; it seemed to be going on forever.

I put my arm around her and she laid her head on my shoulder. "Anastasia, why didn't you tell all this to people years earlier?" I asked. The answer was the one I had heard before that same day.

"You, I trust," she answered. "You are the chosen one. When I look into your eyes I see the soul of the Czar. You are good. I told Hans to bring you back for this. You are my heir. To you alone I leave these truths. How you tell the world is for you to decide, but you will do so in my name, I know."

This was too much for me. After a few minutes of silence, I stood up and again she put her hands in mine. "History, truth, is yours now, Jemmy. This is all I have to give, and to you I give it. I trust you."

I slipped away and rejoined Jack in the theater in time to hear Jessica Lange's final scream. As Jack and the members of the audience rose and made their way to the exits, I could only sit there. This had all been so unreal. I felt numb. Finally, I arose and walked up the aisle, feeling as if my every movement were in slow motion.

Jack was waiting at the exit door. He had loved the movie and was chattering about it, but I couldn't concentrate on him or what he was saying. As we walked across the lobby where Anastasia still sat, I lagged behind, looking at the faces of the other moviegoers. Most were teenagers on dates, holding hands, laughing, talking. I stood in the center of the lobby for a few seconds, trying to preserve the moment in my memory. Everything seemed so commonplace, yet what I had experienced that evening had been extraordinary.

I thought of the decades of litigation, the thousands of newspaper and magazine articles, the years of scholarly research by historians probing the mystery of Anastasia. And it had ended like this. In a movie theater. At *King Kong*. The incongruity, the irrationality of it was so strange that I smiled. And Anastasia, taking Jack's hand as she rose from the bench, looked over at me and smiled back.

Typically, she wanted a photograph of the occasion. When Jack asked where, she pointed to the *King Kong* movie poster outside the theater. Just before he snapped the shutter Anastasia murmured, "Remember the death of kings, Jemmy."

THE next day, December 27, I slept late and then wandered around Charlottesville thinking about what Anastasia had said. She had offered me the opportunity of a lifetime, yet I felt inadequate to the task and especially uncomfortable with the restrictions she had imposed about recording her on tape or taking notes. I tried not to think too much about her fixation with reincarnation and how it applied to me. In order to write a book with her, I would have to move to Charlottesville and find part-time employment. I would need income, but also adequate time to spend interviewing her. Without the financial backing of a publisher, this could be a long and costly project, and I knew my age and credentials would be viewed skeptically. As I continued walking, I felt blessed by circumstances and cursed by my youth and inexperience.

Late in the afternoon I visited the Manahans and we sat outside, wrapped in coats and blankets, on the back lawn.

"This weather reminds me of home," Anastasia said. Jack commented that I might encounter colder weather in England when I traveled there the next month.

"You should see the queen while you are there," Anastasia said, smiling at me mischievously. "She is the last sovereign of England, but one." Jack nodded approvingly.

"What do you mean?" I asked.

"This I know from Father Gregory. It was he who told that when a Battenberg becomes king of England, all is at the end."

"Are you saying that Rasputin said that a Battenberg would become king of England?"

"Yes. Absolute. And when that happens—when a Battenberg

ascends the throne of England, he will be their last king. So when Prince Charles of England becomes king, he is—England is—will see the end of monarchy."

"Rasputin said this?"

"Yes."

"To whom?" I asked.

"To the Empress. We always don't like the Battenbergs and Mama was worried about them. They come from nothing and marry for money and titles only. Lord Louis Mountbatten is my greatest enemy. It is he who has caused such a mess."

Jack began another of his long dissertations, this time about the evils of Lord Mountbatten. He bemoaned all the money and time Mountbatten had spent trying to discredit his cousin Anastasia. His motive was to disqualify her from her inheritance so that he, as a collateral descendant of the Czar, would inherit whatever was left of the Czar's estate in England.

"True. All true. He and Youssoupov are the same," Anastasia added.

There was little similarity I could see between Lord Louis Mountbatten and Prince Felix Youssoupov, and I said so.

Looking at Jack in dismay, Anastasia said, "Could it be he does not know?" Jack responded that I was young and perhaps a bit unworldly "about these things."

"Lord Louis Mountbatten and Youssoupov are—both of them—hermaphrodites," Anastasia said blithely.

Her vocabulary was normally so simple and repetitive, to hear her say such a word was a shock. I couldn't believe what I had heard. "Hermaphrodites?" I said slowly. "Are you sure?"

"But of course. *Everyone* knows," she said, in an unconcerned, matter-of-fact tone.

Jack began to giggle and said, "Anastasia, I don't think that's quite what you mean."

"Yes. That is exactly what I mean. Each are," she slowed her enunciation and repeated, "hermaphrodites. Part man, but inside, a woman."

I knew that Youssoupov had admitted in his autobiography that he was a transvestite and had been rumored to be a homosexual. The more likely choice, I asked her if she meant "homosexual," but she looked perplexed and said she had never heard that word. Jack couldn't contain his laughter any longer and said, "That's exactly what she means."

AT noon the next day, Jack and Anastasia arrived at the hotel, and we went to a cafeteria for lunch. Afterward, we drove to a bookstore at the same shopping center where the movie theater was located.

In the bookstore, Anastasia gazed longingly at the paperback Agatha Christie novels. I bought her a dozen of them. Anastasia loved presents, and it was the least I could do after what she had offered me. As I turned from paying for her books, they stood together, smiling broadly. "Anastasia insisted I buy these books for you. God only knows why," Jack said, handing me two paperbacks, the novel *King Kong* and a book about the filming of the movie.

Anastasia winked as she placed a colorful book mark in one of the books and said, "Jemmy knows why."

At her insistence we visited the pet store next-door, where she became enthralled by a bird feeder, so I bought it for her. As Jack and I both stood at the cash register, Anastasia slipped out the door.

When Jack realized she was gone, he was frantic. He went to look in the bookstore, and I searched the parking lot. As I passed the theater, there she stood in front of the King Kong poster. When I approached, she said that someday there would be a marker here, for it was here that the truth had finally been told. She said that last night she had finally slept well.

"Because you know. Now someone knows."

At the airport, Anastasia stayed in the car. "She hates to say goodbye," Jack explained. In the terminal, he became very somber. I still had not mentioned my conversations with Anastasia in the theater lobby. I wondered whether she had told him.

He said that Anastasia had become very fond of me, so much that he wondered if she was tired of him and wanted "a new, younger knight to be her champion." He still thought he might predecease her and mused aloud if she would marry me when that happened. I assured him I could not marry someone my grandmother's age.

"She will need protection if I die," he said sadly.

I promised him that I would care for her if she needed me, but I knew he would be fine. I told him I could tell she loved him for what he had done for her.

"Please take good care of her should something happen," he said, almost begging, as tears came into his eyes. There was a pause.

I said I didn't know when I would be back, and he answered, "You have the most important information now. She has entrusted it to you. Cherish and honor it. You know she thinks you are her father, in some way, and she would never lie to the Czar."

I was astonished by that remark. But before I could react, he removed a handkerchief covered with heraldic crests from his breast pocket and put it in my jacket pocket. "Wear this in memory of me, sir," he said.

My eyes began to well, too. We hugged, and I boarded the plane. As it taxied down the runway, I could see Jack waving and wiping his eyes.

X .

"You merely have to prove that she believed it"

EVEN AFTER these dramatic events, I hesitated. Every Anastasia biography had been an exercise in special pleading, apologias by her friends. I had no wish to be considered one of what the French call Anastasia *cultistes*. If I wrote about her, I decided, it would be a dispassionate report based on whatever the facts indicated.

But I knew I didn't have enough material for a book. She had refused to allow me to take notes in her presence or to record our conversations because it distracted her. So I had no way of proving what she had told me.

She said she viewed our projected collaboration as something akin to the French Empress Eugénie's conversations with Maurice Paléologue in his book, *The Tragic Empress*. Paléologue had spoken with Eugénie once a year over a period of nineteen years. I was unwilling to commit to such a casual—and long—project. And I could not compare myself with Paléologue, who was the French ambassador to the Court of Nicholas II, and later a member of the *Académie Française*. His undisputed reputation as a diarist and historian made his transcriptions of his conversations with the Empress acceptable. We lived in different times, I reasoned. Modern journalism dictated that I prove her every statement, if possible. But I could not do that without tape recordings or documentation.

In January 1977, I traveled to England, where my old family friend, author Robin Maugham (Viscount Maugham of Hartfield), gave me some advice: "You don't have to prove that *what* she said was true. You merely have to prove that she *said* it, and she *believed* it."

THE following month came news that Moritz Furtmayr, one of Germany's leading forensic scientists, had developed improved techniques for a new identification test called PIK. Furtmayr, a forty-seven-year-old renowned criminologist in the German law-enforcement community, had earlier studied in Washington, D.C., and Chicago, and had once served as a detective in Hesse. He used the PIK test to scientifically compare the anatomical points of the ear in cases where fingerprints and dental records were not available. In order to prove someone's identity, twelve identical anatomical points had to match exactly. Comparing photographs of the right ear of the historical Anastasia to that of Anna Anderson, Furtmayr found *seventeen* identical anatomical points.

The wire services flashed the news around the world: science had conclusively proven that she was Anastasia. The Furtmayr tests so impressed the German Supreme Court that it took the unprecedented step of offering to reopen the Anastasia case. This, combined with the weight of the previously submitted anthropological, graphological, and forensic evidence, substantiated her claim beyond any reasonable doubt. Believing she had finally achieved her lifelong quest for recognition, Anastasia refused to enter into any further legal actions. After decades of notoriety, the lost princess was now an old woman seeking solace in anonymity.

Strangely, although the Furtmayr tests were recognized in international courts of law as a form of positive identification, they seemed to make little impression on the public. Perhaps the legend of Anastasia was so entrenched in people's minds that they had trouble accepting scientific resolution of a modern fairy tale. But Anastasia did not mind. Indeed, the lack of public interest was a blessing for her.

The confirmation of Anastasia's identity was certainly difficult for Lord Louis Mountbatten to accept. British writer Michael Thornton showed him a copy of the Furtmayr report and later recounted the meeting:

> I can still see him sitting opposite me. . . . As he read it, his face was a picture of doubt and confusion. 'But this isn't possible,' he said. 'No impostor could be as lucky as that.' Behind the words, I could see his thought: 'Is it possible that I could have been mistaken all these years?'

THAT same year brought another resolution of sorts for Anastasia. Ever since Milukoff had reported finding Prince Frederick and Ian Lilburn clearing out her possessions in Unterlengenhardt, she had resented the two men. She had missed few opportunities to present her view of the incident, based on Milukoff's reports, and the Prince was certainly aware of —and disconcerted by—his old friend's dissatisfaction.

Several of their mutual friends had lobbied Jack over the years, encouraging him to persuade Anastasia to reconcile with the Prince. They felt that, whatever indiscretion the Prince might have committed, his proven devotion to the Grand Duchess should not be so easily overlooked because of one of Anastasia's frequent, temperamental outbursts.

These pleas eventually moved Jack enough that he agreed to arrange for the Prince and his companion Ian Lilburn to visit in Charlottesville. He spared no expense to assure that the visit would occur, patiently accepting the many costly changes in itinerary demanded by the two men. Finally, all was arranged, and they arrived—with little prior notice to Anastasia—on November 19, 1977.

Published reports of the reunion indicated that the reconciliation was complete. Jack wrote to Richard and Marina Schweitzer later, however, reporting tensions in the visit. The Prince and Ian Lilburn remained with them for more than three weeks, and the four of them frequently reminisced and shared stories about European royalty. Over dinner one night at the Boxwood House, where Jack had first entertained his future wife upon her arrival in America, the Prince revealed that his companion, Ian Lilburn, was the illegitimate grandson of King Christian IX of Denmark. This made him a distant cousin of both Anastasia and Prince Philip of England.

Normally this tenuous royal connection would have impressed the Grand Duchess and her husband, but Anastasia and Jack remained suspicious of their guests. Jack explained their reasons:

> Anastasia and I learned so very much. . . . Many, many, many of the things Anastasia has told me were completely verified (in some cases by unwitting admissions) by Prince Frederick, who at age 72 is quite a 'charmeur' and one of the most informed men I have ever met. . . . That they were fascinated by our zoo-library is borne out by their desire to return and 'clean it up,' by which Anastasia understands 'clean us out' of all Anastasia memorabilia to join the rest [that] Anastasia says are in Lilburn's London house.

Regardless of whatever doubts remained in Anastasia's mind, the four parted as friends. They continued to correspond, and the Prince never abandoned his interest in her.

ANASTASIA maintained a vehement hatred of the English, particularly the royal family. She reserved particular scorn for Lord Louis Mountbatten, her first cousin, uncle to Prince Philip, and one of the hated Battenbergs. To her mind, he had victimized her by using his money and power to disgrace her publicly and to ruin her chances for legal recognition.

One evening in 1979, Anastasia and Jack were invited for dinner at the Ewells. Before eating, they sat watching television. As Anastasia sipped her favorite Danish cherry wine, the evening news began with an overview of the day's events. The lead story reported the assassination of Lord Louis Mountbatten on his converted fishing boat off the west coast of Ireland. He had been the victim of Irish Republican Army terrorists.

Anastasia leaned forward slowly in her chair, staring at the television set. *"Mein Gott!"* she said, reverting to the German that both she and Mountbatten would understand. A look of horror came across her face, as she carefully viewed the news footage that filled the screen while the reporter provided the grisly details.

She remained gravely shaken throughout the evening. Over dinner, she condemned the assassination as "an evil thing." Her greatest enemy was dead, but he had suffered the worst kind of death for a royal—to be brutally cut down at the hands of revolutionaries.

ANASTASIA'S life continued to take bizarre twists and turns. In November 1981, the Russian Orthodox Church Outside Russia decided to recognize the martyrdom of the Czar and his family by canonizing them as saints. Unlike the Roman Catholic Church, which demands evidence of miracles before elevation to sainthood, the Russian Orthodox religion accepts death for the cause of Russian Orthodoxy as qualification for canonization.

In a ceremony held at the Cathedral of Our Lady of the Sign in New York, a large crowd of the faithful had gathered to hear the church's prelate, Bishop Gregory, conduct the rites. He said that because the Czar and his family had given their lives in defense of Russian Orthodoxy, he was now empowered to declare them "Holy Royal Martyrs." Special icons depicting Jesus welcoming the Romanovs to heaven were produced, and a special hymn composed, for the occasion.

Anastasia was aware of the planned service, although whether she was invited or what feelings she had about this odd development remains unknown. She did not attend and was only later given a copy of the icon produced for the event. She made no comment about her own premature canonization, but did cherish the religious object for its depiction of her beloved parents and siblings as martyred saints.

While the faithful considered her a martyred Grand Duchess ascended to heaven, Anastasia remained secluded with Jack in Charlottesville, isolated as much as possible from the real world.

XI.

"You'll never take me alive"

BY 1983, the house at University Circle had deteriorated markedly. The years without upkeep, Jack and Anastasia's penchant for
collecting everything and discarding nothing, and the ridiculous
number of pets that Jack felt he could not deny the Grand Duchess
all took their toll. To the outside observer, they must have seemed to
be living in a garbage bin with four walls and a roof.

The neighbors had continued complaining about the state of the
property over the years. There had been many lawsuits, and Jack—
ever the stickler for details—repeatedly appeared in court to defend
himself and Anastasia and their lifestyle. But he clearly was incapable of maintaining the home, and the neighbors began expressing
fear for the couple's welfare.

When the furnace at 35 University Circle had stopped working in
the mid-1970s, Anastasia insisted that heating systems harbored
germs and disease, so the doors and windows were left open day and
night, even in very cold weather. Visitors from the city's social
services department worried that at the age of eighty-two, the frail
Anastasia might suffer from exposure, even though she and Jack
moved to one of his nearby apartments on University Circle during
the winter.

Buttressed by complaints from neighbors, the Charlottesville Social Services Department finally petitioned for a guardian for both
Anastasia and Jack. The Circuit Court determined that Anastasia
needed a temporary guardian and, in August 1983, appointed local
attorney William C. Preston to act in that capacity. The question of
permanent guardianship and her husband's own competency to care
for himself were put off until hearings could be held in October.

As a result of the proceedings that autumn, the court determined that although Jack was "eccentric," he was capable of caring for himself. The court decided that Jack could not provide adequately for his wife's welfare, however, and Mr. Preston was appointed her permanent legal guardian. Anastasia attended these deliberations, sitting quietly in a wheelchair.

At first, Jack and Anastasia continued to live together in the apartment on University Circle, but Preston and Jack clashed from the very start. According to the attorney, Jack refused to cooperate. As Anastasia's health declined, additional help was clearly needed to care for her, but Preston reported that Jack would not allow a practical nurse into their residence to care for his wife. Finally, in late November, acting in his capacity as legal guardian, Preston had Anastasia committed to Blue Ridge Hospital, where she was placed in the psychiatric ward for observation and examination.

Jack was allowed to visit her there every day, but Anastasia was extremely upset about being taken from her home and separated from the man who had acted as her buffer against strangers. Once again institutionalized and subjected to what must have seemed like endless questions and proddings, Anastasia begged Jack to take her back to the apartment where they had been living.

As early as September, Jack had expressed his opinion that the appointment of Preston as temporary guardian was but the first step in an attempt to separate him from Anastasia. He must have also had some idea that, under the conditions of Anastasia's commitment to the hospital, the doctors had full control over the types of tests and procedures they could use on their patient. Knowing of his wife's concerns about assassination and poisoning, and understanding her paranoia, Jack agreed to her request to be reunited with him.

One day during a visit, according to Jack, Anastasia asked him to take her from the hospital. She was so demanding that he could not quiet her. Finally, he decided to pick her up and take her away. As he proceeded down the hall with her, the hospital personnel—aware that Jack had no status as legal guardian—approached and insisted that he return her to the room. Once back in her bed, Anastasia became very upset and continued to call for "Hans" long after her husband had been escorted from the building.

Visiting privileges were unaffected, and Jack knew that Anastasia was scheduled to be moved from the Blue Ridge facility in a few days. Having found no evidence of mental illness, the doctors had decided to transfer her to the nearby University of Virginia Medical Center by ambulance.

The evening before the planned transfer, Jack devised a plan for taking Anastasia during the move, using one of their twenty-three dogs as a decoy. When the ambulance attendants brought Anastasia out of the hospital, Jack and the dog would be waiting. Jack would divert the attendants' attention by asking them to have a look at the pet, who was pregnant. Jack would then grab Anastasia and drive off with her.

He arrived at the hospital parking lot on the morning of November 29, 1983, with enough money and supplies to last about six days. A single attendant wheeled Anastasia out into the parking lot and left her alone briefly. Seizing his opportunity, Jack picked her up out of the wheelchair and carried her to his waiting station wagon. Meanwhile, the dog had jumped from the car, but Jack did not take the time to look for it. He and Anastasia drove off to the cheers of some of the elderly patients watching from the windows of their rooms.

WILLIAM Preston swore out a warrant for Jack's arrest on felony abduction charges the next day, and an immediate search began. Police officials in thirteen states were alerted by bulletins of the kidnapping, and numerous press stories—published internationally—contained pleas for their return.

Jack and Anastasia first tried to enlist aid from friends. When that proved unsuccessful, they checked into a motel in a nearby central Virginia town, where they registered under their correct names. The next day, other friends located a rural farmhouse near Sweet Briar College in Amherst County where the couple could stay. They remained at the farm for two nights, during which time Jack read to his invalid wife from *The Escape of Charles II After the Battle of Worcester.* The story of her English ancestors had always interested her, and to Jack it aptly paralleled their own predicament. By day, they would drive around the countryside, and during these amblings, as Jack called them, Anastasia seemed thrilled to be on such an adventure.

The station wagon, which was in bad repair, finally broke down in front of the house. Jack had to make frequent trips on foot to a local shopping center to obtain parts.

After three days, their appearances in the small community near the farmhouse began to rouse suspicion. On December 2, Jack went into town to get help fixing a flat tire. He left Anastasia sitting in the car in front of the house. Acting on reports made by a restaurant owner who had noted Jack's frequent trips into town, two sheriff's deputies observed Anastasia bundled in blankets and hunched down in the front seat of the station wagon. They approached the vehicle and asked her name.

"Jones," came the reply from the incapacitated daughter of the last Russian czar.

The officers explained that they knew she was Mrs. Manahan and that they had been searching for her and her husband. They asked where he was, to which Anastasia replied defiantly, "You'll never take me alive!"

The police waited with her by the car for about fifteen minutes when they saw Jack walking back up the lane toward the house. His first remark was, "Well, I see we've been caught." He complimented the officers on their efficiency and cooperated with them fully. The couple was taken back to the Amherst County sheriff's office, where they spent an hour waiting for the law enforcement officials from Charlottesville to arrive. During that time, Jack reportedly regaled the sheriff with stories of Anastasia's life and showed him snapshots and books about her.

Anastasia was taken to the emergency room at the Blue Ridge Hospital and greeted by a crowd of reporters, photographers, and the usual curiosity seekers. Pictures taken that day show her wearing a Russian babushka and frowning in disgust. When the sheriff's officers tried to remove her from the car, she began screaming. Jack calmed her and lifted her into a wheelchair before attendants took her into the facility for examination.

Jack was taken to the Juvenile and Domestic Relations Court, where a judge ordered him to post a $1,000 bond, pending trial on the charges, and limited his visitation rights to Anastasia. The police fingerprinted and photographed him, then allowed him to return to his apartment on University Circle.

Doctors determined that Anastasia was unharmed. William Preston ordered her transferred, after a few days, to an adult-care facility run by Jane Holt in Charlottesville. The charges against Jack were dropped within a month, and all restrictions on his visits to his wife were lifted.

ANASTASIA was miserable in the new facility, which was located in Mrs. Holt's home and served only three patients at a time. Like most others in Charlottesville, Mrs. Holt had followed the press reports about Dr. and Mrs. Manahan over the years, and her interest had heightened during the sensational coverage of the kidnapping. After the police brought the couple back to Charlottesville and Mrs. Holt learned Preston wanted to place Anastasia under supervised care, Mrs. Holt knew just the place for her: "So when I saw it in the paper, I wanted to have somebody famous like that. I said, 'Well, maybe they'll bring her to me.' Preston, he knew my lawyer real good. He was a friend of my lawyer. . . . But it was such a hush-hush deal. I wasn't allowed to let anybody come to visit her," with the exception of Jack and his attorney, James Hingeley.

Anastasia required a great deal of care. From the moment she arrived at Mrs. Holt's, she screamed repeatedly, "Hans! Hans!" Crippled from arthritis, incontinent and requiring diapers, the patient was livid about her treatment and fearful of being poisoned. She allowed no one to touch her. Mrs. Holt reported that during her stay, Anastasia slept fitfully—at most an hour each night. She wanted Jack with her at all times and continued to scream "Hans!" constantly.

Jack decorated Anastasia's room with pictures of the Romanovs, including a small signed photograph of the Czarina in a silver frame and a czarist-era flag. On his daily visits, he brought sealed bags of snacks and candy from the local store. Anastasia would not eat any food prepared by Mrs. Holt other than Lipton's Cup-a-Soup mixes and boiled eggs, the latter only if they were peeled in her presence. The pre-packaged snack foods Jack provided were the only other sustenance Anastasia would agree to take.

She remained with Mrs. Holt roughly two months. During that time, her only visitors were Jack and, rarely, Mr. Hingeley. Mildred Ewell recalls visiting Anastasia once, after which guardian William

Preston told her never to return. Mrs. Holt has no recollection of any visits by Mr. Preston himself, or by any employees of the social services department, which had previously expressed so much concern over the patient's welfare.

As Anastasia's condition worsened, she wanted Jack to stay with her constantly. He continued to come every day at about the same hour, and they talked for long periods. Jack often asked Mrs. Holt to come and listen to these conversations, and she became intrigued, developing such an interest in Anastasia's story that she went to the local library and checked out several books about her patient and the Romanovs: "I wanted to know all the things about her."

Mr. Preston had forbidden Mrs. Holt to discuss Anastasia's whereabouts or her care with anyone, but she found it impossible to completely avoid talking about the subject.

> All my friends would call me. They knew she was there, but I told them they couldn't come. My daughter would come [and] my family, of course. . . . They'd ask me, 'Do you believe it?' . . . And I didn't . . . but then I got to thinking, the way he talked to her about 'Nicolai,' and this and that. . . . Then she would answer him back in . . . English. . . . And this went on day after day until you saw, well, they couldn't be making up all the stuff. So then they made a believer out of me.

One afternoon, Mrs. Holt was present when Jack asked Anastasia about her father, the Czar. "Gone, gone," was the mournful reply. Listening to conversations like these, Mrs. Holt naturally developed a curiosity about Charlottesville's most famous resident, but like so many others, she became more interested in the legend than in the person of Anastasia and began scrutinizing her in an effort to fathom her mystery.

On January 28, Jack arrived earlier than usual. He talked with Anastasia for a while then, according to Mrs. Holt, walked out the door saying, "I'm going to be back at 4:30." Anastasia became very upset and suffered a stroke.

> [She was] just hollering 'Hans!' and kicking the cover. . . . Then, right there in front of my eyes . . . [as if] automatically, her . . . lip went way up, eyes drooped up. . . . It was funny to just sit there and watch her. I'd taken care of a lot of stroke patients but . . . I've never seen it. She

kept her eyes open. Stayed conscious all the time. I put ice on her head. . . . I kept that ice all over and she kind of relaxed. Her mouth went down a little bit, but not all the way. . . . She was staring there, with her eyes open. . . .

Remembering that Jack had just left, Mrs. Holt ran to the front door, but his car was gone. "[S]he was having this and I didn't know where he was." Mrs. Holt went to the telephone and called the rescue squad. "They were only five minutes away."

As she waited for the ambulance, Mrs. Holt said, "I was thinking she'd died . . . but I could feel her pulse, that she was living. . . ."

XII.
"It's all over"

WITH SIRENS blaring, the rescue squad ambulance rushed Anastasia, near death, to the emergency entrance of Martha Jefferson Hospital. The doctors stabilized her, and Mildred Ewell visited the next day without suspecting that her friend's life was in danger. The news was quietly dispatched from Charlottesville to friends around the world that Anastasia had suffered a stroke.

Days passed with little medical progress. Jack never gave up hope. His friend from Richmond, Robert Crouch, drove over to Charlottesville to be with him, and together they kept a vigil at Anastasia's bedside. Crouch remembered how uncomfortable she seemed, and when the doctors diagnosed pneumonia, he noticed an increasing restlessness in her body.

She was very tiny now, her weight having dropped below sixty pounds, but she continued to fight. Crouch recalled her thrashing in the huge hospital bed, which seemed to engulf her shrivelled frame, and incessantly calling out, "Hans! Hans!"

Slowly, over the period of a week, the virus consumed her. Mrs. Ewell visited again on the last Saturday and thought Anastasia could die at any moment. Noticing how quiet Anastasia had become, Mrs. Ewell hoped the end would arrive peacefully.

The next morning, Sunday, February 12, the shadows grew longer. Her Anthroposophist friends might have said that the "spirit group" of the czars was surrounding her.

Crouch overslept that morning and awoke with a start; "I knew something was terribly wrong and that I should get to the hospital as fast as I could." But meanwhile, Jack sat alone in a chair beside her bed. He was unwilling to leave her while she was conscious. Certain that she was the victim of a conspiracy of doctors and nurses, he refused to admit that nature might have a hand in her destruction.

We do not know much about their last moments together, because Jack later told conflicting stories, but she was unconscious and un-aware of the pain of the pneumonia.

Jack left the room at about 11:30 A.M., perhaps to use the lavatory. During the few minutes he was gone, his wife—the lifelong symbol of the archaic divine right of kings—expired in the hospital named for Thomas Jefferson's wife. The mystery of Anastasia was finished. The last of the imperial Romanovs was dead. She died as she had lived since those terrible last days in Russia—alone.

One can only hope that her spirit at last knew the peace that had so long eluded it.

When Jack returned to the room, Anastasia was gone. A few minutes later, Robert Crouch arrived at the hospital and saw Jack coming out the door to the parking lot, holding a box of Valentine candy Crouch had given Anastasia and a twenty-five-pound dog-food bag in which Jack had placed Anastasia's belongings. The men met in the middle of the street.

"It's all over. Anastasia died a few minutes ago," Jack said in a broken voice, tears streaming down his cheeks. Crouch sat down in the middle of the street, and Jack knelt beside him, sobbing. Neither spoke. After a moment, Crouch said, "I think we'd better get out of the street."

Later the two friends drove to Fairview Farms. "He wanted to be with their dogs," Crouch said. "It was really quite pitiful. At that moment, he seemed to feel that those dogs were his last link to Anastasia—like they were their children.

"He was in shock, I think. I didn't know what to do for him except to stay with him—to share his grief."

XIII.
"A publicity carnival"

CONTRARY TO JACK'S LATER STORIES, which were repeated in the European press, Anastasia died of natural causes, the result of the pneumonia. According to her attending physician, James D. Aller, "Mrs. Mahanan [*sic*] had straightforward medical problems leading to her death, which is why a standard death certificate was signed listing things as they were. There was no suspicion of foul play, therefore a medical examiner's form was not used."

No autopsy was performed, and later that afternoon Jack called the Teague Funeral Home and asked them to handle the arrangements. Mr. Teague sent a hearse to Martha Jefferson Hospital, and the attendants collected Anastasia's body and transported it to the nearest crematorium, the Kyger-Trobough Funeral Home on South Main Street in Harrisonburg.

To the crematorium's employees, the corpse was probably just another old lady, shriveled by age, whose time on this earth had run out. Now, sixty-five years after the Grand Duchess's life was destroyed in Ekaterinburg, her earthly remains were consigned—as she had wished—to the crematory flames she had believed would ensure her soul's reincarnation.

Reports of Anastasia's memorial service at the University of Virginia Chapel, Tuesday, February 14, vary widely. Not only do estimates of the crowd run from two-hundred-fifty to numbers that spilled over on to the lawn outside the church, but descriptions of the service itself have little in common. The only point on which most witnesses agree is that Jack's words and behavior that day were exceedingly bizarre.

Richard and Marina Botkin Schweitzer drove down from their home near Washington and entered the chapel with Mildred Ewell. Jack insisted that all three were family and should occupy the first pew. Prior to the service, Jack had placed a brass candelabrum decorated with the Russian imperial double eagle and a pair of playing cards on the altar. At the rear of the chapel, by the entrance, he had also arranged an assortment of Romanov memorabilia and stacks of old newspaper clippings about Anastasia, including an article from a supermarket tabloid that proclaimed Anastasia would soon be placed on the restored Russian throne.

Officiating was the Reverend Ramsey Richardson, who had been close to Jack and Anastasia. According to the printed program, the religious service was to be combined with personal remarks—in the form of a "Historical Comment"—by Jack. The rambling, disjointed diatribe lasted for thirty minutes, twice the length of the religious service. "I don't think that anyone there could have told you what he said," Mildred Ewell would comment later. The *Richmond News Leader* described Jack's remarks as "a densely detailed body of historical footnotes and personal anecdotes."

Jack began by explaining that he had been uncertain as to what type of religious service to hold in his wife's memory. He noted that the Russian Orthodox Church Outside Russia had canonized the Czar and his family and asked, "How can you have a funeral service for a saint who's already dead?" As he continued, he harangued the audience with sentimental, highly personalized reminiscences, which sometimes focused on Anastasia's confusion in her last days. He often gestured toward the candelabrum and playing cards on the altar, making obscure references to them and his wife's life. At one point, Jack pointed to the cards and referred to Anastasia—as he had so often—as the "White Queen." Many of his listeners were used to this unexplained metaphor, but this time they were aghast when Jack went on to characterize Queen Elizabeth II of England as the "Black Queen," and referred to her as an international drug dealer. He also repeated dubious accounts related to Anastasia's authenticity, including the story of the Czar escaping from Russia using doubles, which Anastasia had admitted concocting.

Perhaps the most remarkable part of the ceremony came when Jack asked a woman to stand and read a poem in honor of Anastasia. She was the daughter of one of Jack's elderly tenants, but although few knew who she was, her poetry made quite an impression: " 'A' is for Anastasia, eating apples in the kitchen," she began, and went on to spell out the dead woman's name in rhythmic nonsense sentences.

"It was embarrassing. Marina and I hung our heads, not knowing whether to laugh or cry," Mrs. Ewell said. Indeed, it was an ignoble way to eulogize Anastasia. "He degraded her," Mrs. Schweitzer said. "I can never forget that."

At the end of the service, as the mourners left the chapel, the organist began playing *God Save the Czar.* Richard Schweitzer, pleased to hear such a tribute, which had not been noted on the program, stopped to thank the musician. The crowd gathered outside the chapel, and Jack spoke to his friends and a large assembly of reporters. He told them he was "bitter" because "Anastasia died from lack of hope."

Marina Schweitzer left the chapel by the front door, but turned to the side of the building to avoid the crush of people and Jack's performance. "I just couldn't take any more, so I actually hid behind a bush," she said. "Jack turned Anastasia's last rites into a publicity carnival." The international press gave considerable coverage to Anastasia's demise. Several headlines proclaimed, " 'The Czarina of Charlottesville' is dead."

JACK took Anastasia's ashes back to the apartment and began protracted efforts to honor her wish to have the urn interred at the cemetery at Castle Seeon. Weeks became months, as Prince Frederick and others negotiated with the numerous parties involved. Although the town of Seebruck-Seeon now administered the cemetery, it had been ceded to the municipality by the Leuchtenberg family in 1969, under certain conditions. A dispute now arose over the legalities of the agreement. According to newspaper reports, Duchess Katharina von Leuchtenberg objected to Anastasia's burial for several reasons. The Duchess, who lived in Montreal, believed the agreement stipulated that no one outside the family was to be buried on the grounds. Furthermore, she argued, the Russian Orthodox Church, under whose authority the grounds were consecrated, did not sanction cremation. Only after Prince Frederick hired a local attorney to review the agreement and present his arguments to the town's mayor did the council conclude it had the authority to allow additional burials in the cemetery and approve the plans for interment.

The ceremony took place on what would have been Anastasia's eighty-third birthday, June 18, 1984. In attendance were Jack and Prince Frederick and other members of minor nobility, in addition to a large contingent of the European press corps. After a short ceremony officiated by a former minister of the town, Jack gave several interviews, emotionally defending Anastasia's claim to her identity. But for most of the world, the story was over. Jack was left alone to fly back to America and take up residence in his squalid apartment.

XIV.
"I'm the son-in-law of Czar Nicholas II"

OVER THE COURSE of the previous few years, Jack's renowned eccentricity had begun to edge toward mental imbalance. After losing Anastasia, he began concocting theories regarding her death. At times he blamed the adult-care provider, Jane Holt, and Anastasia's court-appointed guardian, William Preston, of entering into a conspiracy of maltreatment and neglect. He hypothesized that Anastasia's "totally unnecessary demise [was] brought on by an unfeeling agent of cruel guardian and misinformed JUDEX," and stated that it "was high time that I plead murder by Preston's agent, Jane Holt," whom he claimed had beaten Anastasia. For her part, Mrs. Holt completely denied such charges and remembered how grateful her patient's husband had been for her efforts to alleviate the stroke.

On other occasions, Jack claimed that Anastasia had been murdered by a conspiracy of doctors and nurses employed at Martha Jefferson Hospital because he believed these people feared the consequences of restoring the Romanovs to the Russian throne.

Strange as these conjectures may appear, they were widely reported in the European press and accorded some acceptance among scholars. For example, British biographer Michael Thornton—one of Anastasia's most vocal supporters in England—gave an interview in which he expressed his belief in the very real possibility that she had been murdered in her hospital bed.

For the most part, however, Jack's statements and claims were dismissed as the ramblings of a lonely and pitiable old man.

JACK increasingly lived in a world of his own, the cause to which he had devoted so many years now apparently lost and of little interest to anyone else. His physical appearance mirrored the mental strain from which he was clearly suffering. A disheveled figure with worn clothing and dirty fingernails, he wandered the streets of Charlottesville and became more and more the subject of unkind and condescending gossip.

Althea Hurt, however, did not participate in the gossip. The daughter of a wealthy local physician who had become a major land developer, she had not been close to either Jack or Anastasia before Anastasia's death. But she had attended Anastasia's memorial service and—as Jack later related the story to several friends—had approached him afterward. He thought that she was going to offer her condolences, as so many of those in attendance had done. Instead, he reported, she said she wanted to "become his partner," a phrase that he interpreted as a marriage proposal. He was intrigued enough by this offer to invite her to come and speak with him later.

Now that Jack had become so isolated and lonely, Althea became an important part of his life. As it developed, her interest in being Jack's "partner" chiefly related to his property interests. He allowed her to become involved in his financial affairs, and she began to monitor everything, including Jack's contact with lifelong friends.

Jack eventually decided that despite the forty years that separated them, he wanted to marry her. He offered to sign over or sell to her most of his property, and her attorneys drew up papers for the sale of several parcels, the terms of which have since been questioned.

In June 1986, Jack told several of his friends that Althea had finally agreed to his marriage proposal. He began making arrangements for a ceremony to be performed on the south portico of Monticello on the Fourth of July of that year. On the appointed date, Jack waited on the porch with a magistrate who had agreed to marry them.

As part of the day's events, Jack had planned a special surprise for his bride and the world at large. He had earlier commissioned the printing of certificates and postcards proclaiming the former Althea Hurt to be Czarina Althea-Pravda I of Russia. In Jack's mind, as "Widower of Anastasia Buried at Seeon" he had the authority to anoint the next ruler of Russia, and he felt the announcement would lead to the downfall of the communist government there. So sure was he of this outcome that he had sent copies of the official proclamation to various world leaders, including Mikhail Gorbachev, Emperor Hirohito of Japan, Queen Elizabeth II of England, and King Juan Carlos of Spain. He hoped that they would all recognize the legitimacy of Althea-Pravda's rule. None responded to the proclamation.

Althea spent the holiday in New York.

Undeterred by the absence of his bride at the Fourth of July ceremony, Jack persisted in courting the apparently agreeable Althea, and never failed to think of her as Althea-Pravda I. She seemed undismayed by this curious conduct and continued to visit him, discussing her interest in his property. As they spent more time together, others began to make comparisons between the young Virginia real estate heiress and Anastasia, often disparagingly. When she became aware of such talk, Althea did not hesitate to dismiss the late Mrs. Manahan in a jealous and belittling manner.

Althea had by now convinced Jack to sell her the house at 35 University Circle, and she quickly took possession of the property. Her first act was to have the contents of the upper floor of the house—much of the irreplaceable collection of Romanov artifacts Anastasia had bequeathed to her godchildren—removed to the Charlottesville city dump. When Jack learned what was happening, he became distraught at the thought of all those precious objects being destroyed. He called several friends to help save what little they could, but most of it was lost. Althea denied all knowledge of the articles and proceeded to restore the upper story of the house to its former elegance. Jack's vast library was apparently left untouched, as were some other materials from their fabulous collection. These included: Czarina Alexandra's wedding portrait with the imperial crown carved into the top panel of the frame molding; an oil portrait of the Dowager Czarina Marie painted from life when she was the Princess Dagmar of Denmark; a full-length portrait of Czar Nicholas II; a five-hundred-year-old Russian icon; one of the Czar's monogrammed handkerchiefs; a signed photograph of the Czarina in a solid silver frame; the only oil self-portrait of Anastasia; an album bound in red morocco leather containing childhood photographs of the Czar's family; pastel pictures painted by Anastasia's sisters before the Russian revolution; an illuminated and embossed invitation to the Czar's coronation; a hand-lettered menu from the wedding banquet of the Czar and Czarina; and many uncatalogued pieces by Fabergé.

Despite such disagreements, Jack remained fully dependent on Althea and continued to see her as the rightfully anointed heir to the Russian throne. Even his once brilliant genealogical expertise became distorted and befuddled, as he devised a hereditary chart for Althea-Pravda, listing her as "The Center of the Universe," around whom revolved Napoleon Bonaparte, Czar Nicholas II, Thomas Jefferson, the Vatican, and the fictional Conan the Barbarian.

For her part, Althea remained solicitous of Jack and gained greater control of his affairs. He would later tell several of his close friends that Althea had confiscated the contents of his safety-deposit box—containing both Anastasia's and his executed wills—and forced him to sign a new document, drawn up by her own attorneys, designating her as sole heir to all his property, except for a small parcel of land in rural Virginia.

DURING the last two years of his life, Jack's health declined precipitously. He had developed diabetes before Anastasia's death, and it worsened. He suffered a series of strokes, was repeatedly hospitalized, and underwent brain surgery. Finally, his condition deteriorated to the extent that the city's social services division had him admitted to Heritage Hall nursing home. Although Althea let it be known that she visited him there every day over the course of the next year, some of the nurses at Heritage Hall flatly denied this.

Jack had many visitors at Heritage Hall, old friends, cousins from Indiana, and former neighbors. All of them reported being shocked at his physical appearance, for his body had degenerated quickly. His mind also became more confused, and he could reason clearly only on rare good days. At other times, he could not even remember lifelong neighbors and friends.

In early autumn 1989, two visitors entered his room and found him fully dressed, seated in a chair next to his bed, crying like a baby. Althea sat on the bed.

"I'm dying," he whimpered through streams of tears. "I'm dying and *she*," he said, feebly gesturing toward Althea on the bed, "won't let me be buried as I wish."

"Now, Jack," she responded, trying to soothe him, "we've already been through this."

"I'm dying, and I want an Episcopal service with Ramsey Richardson presiding, just like I had for my dear wife."

Althea bristled, "Jack, I really think—"

He cut her off immediately, and became so adamant in his protests that Althea excused herself and left.

Jack continued talking.

"I want my wishes *known*. Please *help* me!! Althea has taken everything I have, but *please* don't let her take away my dignity in death. I don't want Bill Smith [the minister of the Westminster Presbyterian Church in Charlottesville] to bury me. . . . *Please!*"

The diabetes had made him nearly blind, and when his visitors did not answer, he stared wildly around the room, searching for them. "Are you there? Don't leave me with just *her*. Oh God, forgive me! She desecrated my Anastasia by throwing her things away, and I couldn't stop her. I tried, but I was too weak. She took over my parents' home. She has taken *everything* from me. And now she won't let me die and be buried and go wherever God sends me . . . as an Episcopalian."

He calmed down somewhat, but was still distressed.

"I'm the son-in-law of Czar Nicholas II, a Romanov by marriage," he said, "and I've been used by a woman named Hurt. Is there any greater irony? Anastasia was used by so many people, and I protected her with everything I had. But when she was gone, there was no one to protect me. Don't let Bill Smith bury me. *Please!*"

Over the next six months, Jack grew incoherent, and his physical condition deteriorated markedly. He became completely blind, lost control of all bodily functions, and on March 22, 1990, died alone in his room.

Some of Jack's friends had lost touch with him as Althea assumed a more prominent role in his life and carefully controlled access to him. Now they and his many remaining relatives began to inquire about arrangements for his funeral and burial. Not unnaturally, they called on Althea, who seemed at first oddly dismayed that others would presume that she would oversee such an onerous task. "Why are they calling me," she asked, "I was only *one* of his friends." In short order, however, she had completely taken over control of all arrangements.

Jack was buried in the University Cemetery in Charlottesville after a brief graveside service where the only attendees were the few people Althea allowed to come. Following the interment, the Reverend Bill Smith conducted a memorial service at the Westminster Presbyterian Church. No eulogy was given—indeed, Jack's name was mentioned only once. Begrudgingly, Althea did allow this ceremony to be open to the public. Both she and Reverend Smith pointedly refused to explain why Jack's wishes for his final tribute were ignored.

Later that evening she hosted a reception at Jack's former home at 35 University Circle for a limited number of his friends and relatives. As one of Jack's cousins later reported, "It made me sick to be in that house she stole from my family."

Outside the family, many of the citizens in Charlottesville were outraged at what they felt had been Althea's machinations to gain control of the vast Manahan estate. And Althea could not help but sense the disfavor of the community. Early one Saturday morning she awoke to find a sign in her front yard. In handmade letters, it read "STOLEN PROPERTY." According to the anonymous friend of Jack and Anastasia who placed it there, the sign was not a mere fraternity prank. It was a calculated effort to send a message to Althea and all of University Circle—that someone knew what she had done, and that someone would not forget.

Controversy still rages over the nature of Althea's relationship with Jack, as well as how many of Anastasia's possessions remain in the house. Althea has told conflicting stories about the Anastasia material, at one point stating that if she did find any documents relating to Anastasia still in the home, she "would burn the Aspern Papers." One can only hope that she will not.

AFTER Anastasia's death, and despite Jack's hopeless attempts to continue the fight for her recognition, the public paid little attention to her story. The one major exception was a 1986 American television mini-series, *Anastasia: The Mystery of Anna*, based on an unauthorized biography published shortly before she died. The author of the book actively participated in publicizing what was a disappointing production. Like other efforts before it, the film invited the viewer to believe that the mystery surrounding Anastasia had been effectively resolved in the 1930s. The movie contained imaginary scenes in which Anastasia's nursemaid Shura failed to recognize her former charge and Gleb repudiated his old friend and left her alone and abandoned on the streets of New York nearly sixty years before. In addition to altering established facts, the screenwriters attempted to sensationalize her story by portraying her nude in bed with a character remarkably similar to Prince Frederick. In the end, the viewer was left with only one possible conclusion: the title character was not the Grand Duchess Anastasia, but an impostor who had been unmasked decades before and whose life thereafter was without meaning or importance. Travesty that it was, the real tragedy of the production was that it lent credence—through the powerful medium of television—to a myth that, like the movie itself, had always been based on deception, innuendo, and the wildest fiction. Even after death, it seemed, Anastasia could not escape the "creators."

LONG before the appearance of the television movie, I had determined that Anastasia's true story must be told. The movie only strengthened that resolve. Fortunately, three years before Jack died I had learned that Alexis Milukoff possessed what was reported to be a large cache of documents and memorabilia relating to Anastasia. He had already contacted a Paris auction house, intending to sell the material in various lots. I did not hesitate to investigate the matter further, for I was concerned that, like Anastasia's effects in Charlottesville, these items might be forever lost if they were sold as curiosities rather than treated properly as a historical archive. I contacted Milukoff through Brien Horan, an Anastasian who was in touch with him.

Horan provided me with only the briefest description of the materials, for which Milukoff was asking $100,000, sight unseen. During two years of negotiations, eventually directly with Milukoff, I finally obtained permission to view the collection—for fifteen minutes only. Even after this cursory examination, I had seen enough: the three crates contained the largest single collection of Anastasia- and Romanov-related artifacts still in private hands, including material dating back to the time of the czarist court. I gladly handed over two cashier's checks in the amount demanded.

BOOK SIX

"This Is Such a Great Mystery"

Even if all parts of a problem seem to fit together like the pieces of a jigsaw puzzle, one has to remember that the probable need not necessarily be the truth and the truth not always probable.

—SIGMUND FREUD

I.
"Entirely a Romanov"

IF JACK MANAHAN WAS sometimes too eager to believe Anastasia, he was nonetheless a skilled historian with a unique talent for genealogical research. Genealogy was Jack's passion, and he enjoyed nothing more than to regale his listeners for hours with long litanies of familial interconnections. As skilled as these presentations were, however, I had often felt that something important was being left unsaid. Certainly genealogy can provide insight into history, particularly where dynastic studies are concerned. Anastasia's story is a case in point.

But to concentrate solely on genealogy, or even to give it the prime importance that Jack did, risks ignoring the influence of equally important factors. Where actions occur, when events happen, and how other circumstances play a role—these are all questions that any responsible biographer must first consider and then answer. His conclusions can then be logically formulated, based on a full range of facts. Without providing answers in a manner that is clearly explained and easily verified, the biographer cannot expect to be taken seriously.

Anastasia repeatedly tried to mislead people. After so many years of enduring doubters and "creators," she had developed a particular talent for telling the most outrageous lies in a very convincing manner. Many were no more sensational than the events of her real life, but she knew that one good story—true or not—could so overwhelm her interrogator that she might be left in peace for a while. From almost the beginning of my research into her story, I knew that it would be pure folly to believe everything she said. To get to the truth, I had to ask and seek answers to those important questions.

By the time I purchased the Milukoff collection, I felt myself quite skilled in discerning fact from myth in regard to Anastasia and her life. I had read dozens of books and countless documents. I had personally interviewed Anastasia and was, therefore, better able to judge her believability. It had become clear to me that she was the daughter of the last Russian czar, but I was still uncertain how to present this truth most effectively.

The information contained in the Milukoff tapes and the Botkin letters helped solve my dilemma. They provided the first real insight into her thoughts and feelings at a time when she had been intensely interested in doing everything possible to tell her version of her story. It was clear from both sources that she understood what had happened to her, even though she forever remained confused about why it had happened. Gleb's chronicles of her insights and Anastasia's recitation of facts to Milukoff are invaluable. They provide convincing proof of both her authenticity and her authoritative knowledge of events and dates.

Perhaps the most fascinating aspect of her conversations with Milukoff was the fact that she told so many stories. Time after time, she would recite what seemed the most preposterous assertions of fact. Just as she had done with Jack in telling the doubles story, she clearly told Milukoff some tales that were pure fiction. She reverted to this device often, when she had tired of her interrogator and his many interruptions.

Yet as I had learned from my own encounters with Anastasia, by listening closely one could discern which of the stories were true. She used the same tone and urgency that I remembered from many of my conversations with her. Ever the skeptical investigator, I had at first returned to the source material to check some of the seemingly preposterous memories she had shared with me. I had learned long ago not to be surprised by what I found. If independent researchers and accepted authorities did not confirm Anastasia's recollection, neither could they conclusively contradict it. Moreover, I knew that in some instances her memory of events had been at first dismissed, only to be proved precisely correct years later.

The very first tape I heard had contained one such story told in the familiar tones. It did not relate directly to her own fate, and at the time I ignored its potential importance. I was concentrating on gathering all the information I could in order to provide a clear explanation of Anastasia's own story. Until that goal was achieved, I refused to be diverted.

I returned to this tape sometime later, however, and listened to the story again. I paid closer attention to her manner of speaking and her initial reluctance to reveal the secret to Milukoff. It was apparent that she fully believed in the truth of this story, and I knew that, because of its nature, I would have to investigate it thoroughly.

As was the case with so much of Anastasia's life, it began with a simple statement of fact:

ANASTASIA: I was born at three o'clock in the morning.
MILUKOFF: Certainly. And you have been the youngest daughter of the Czar—
ANASTASIA: The youngest daughter?
MILUKOFF: Youngest.
ANASTASIA: Nnnnnnn . . . that is a question—
MILUKOFF: Uh-oh! You mean—
ANASTASIA: I was not the last child. There are questions. I was *not at all* the last child.
MILUKOFF: No. You have been the last *daughter*.
ANASTASIA: That is a big question.
MILUKOFF: Oh! I didn't know that. You think after you there was another daughter? And she was living? No, she was not living. Or was she living? Anastasia, that was very interesting because I knew that after that was Alexis, 1904. Oh, you think that between you and Alexis there was another child?

There was a very long pause. Neither of them spoke. I stared at the revolving tape as if it were a living thing. Another daughter? A *sixth* child of Nicholas and Alexandra? Maybe I had not heard correctly. Just as I moved to rewind the tape, the conversation continued:

MILUKOFF: How come? It was *many* years ago. *Sixty* years ago!
ANASTASIA: [cautiously] This is a *very dangerous thing*. Is it not so?

The voice of an elderly woman in the background says, "Yes." I picked up the tape box and pulled out Milukoff's notes. Annemarie Mutius was present at this taping.

ANASTASIA: And it is better that I don't touch it. It is better put under the table. In any case, it is not to be published in this way. That doesn't go! Because there was a *terrible* mess—

What in the world was she talking about? Milukoff is confused too.

MILUKOFF: But who was . . . ? Uh . . . Kschessinska?
ANASTASIA: *No!* Oh no, no, no, no, no! These things put out of your head! There is something quite different. This is a *very important thing*. And a very *dangerous* thing.

Mathilde Kschessinska, one of imperial Russia's prima ballerinas, was the Czar's mistress before his marriage. But according to Anastasia, this birth did not involve her. But if not, who was it about?

ANASTASIA: [her voice calm and confidential] This is a very mysterious story which happened in nineteen-hundred-three. In nineteen-hundred-three there was a French physician and from this French physician, Philippe, there came such terrible things about, and who knows what this man may have done. He can have done crookery, maybe he has stolen this child, it can be. Who knows what maybe he have done for money, one doesn't know. This can have happened. That he has done there something horrible. It can be that one had the Empress drugged and that one had stolen the child because it was again a girl, and one wanted for life or death a boy. That can be . . . that can be, but I cannot swear it. But so it looks . . . so it looks, you know?

In the background, Miss Mutius concurs with a murmur. Whatever this story was, she knew about it, too.

Milukoff is uncharacteristically silent now. I wondered whether he had been as stunned when he heard this in 1965 as I was twenty-four years later. He, who had hardly allowed me to get a word in during our numerous telephone conversations, was now saying nothing. If this conversation really meant what it seemed, this was yet another mystery. But Anastasia and Miss Mutius begin warming to the topic.

ANASTASIA: So [there] are . . . reasons, which is Alexandra, you know?

MUTIUS: Yes, yes.

ANASTASIA: You know we have the proofs. Here [in Unterlengen-hardt] the ladies know there are proofs. This lady is living in Doorn.

MUTIUS: In Doorn.

ANASTASIA: She is living. And looks very beautiful. Looked beautiful when she was here, yes?

MUTIUS: Beautiful face, yes.

ANASTASIA: Beautiful. And entirely . . . hair color, everything, our family hair color. And [a] thousand things [of] our family . . . thousand things. And she knows this herself: what she is and what she was born, and what she was told by her official father and official mother who had taken her in.

MILUKOFF: [meekly] Who had taken her in?

Anastasia, who began this conversation reluctantly, seems to forget that this subject should be "put under the table."

ANASTASIA: Other people had taken her in. She was brought up by other people. It is not so?

Miss Mutius again murmurs agreement.

ANASTASIA: And she has other proofs, enormous masses of Russian money and other Russian precious goods. She has married in the Netherlands. Had a daughter. They have become Catholics now.

Miss Mutius reminded Anastasia that this woman—whoever she was—and her several children lived near Castle Doorn. Milukoff must have thought, at that point, that he understood what was going on because he interrupts.

MILUKOFF: But I have heard this story Irina told, Irina Youssoupov, that it was the *oldest* daughter, Alexandra, and she died young. I have seen her [Irina] maybe a year ago and she told that there was one more daughter but she had [been] born, I think, very first and she died.

ANASTASIA: [surprised] What?

MILUKOFF: Irina, Irina Youssoupov.

ANASTASIA: [disdainfully] Yes.

MILUKOFF: She told that it was one daughter, but she died when she was a child. And also in this book of Convoy, also they have writing that Alexandra was born, and Convoy was invited for the funeral. You will read it in that book, you know?

ANASTASIA: I have not yet time to read. It lies before me. But I have not yet time to look even in.

MILUKOFF: So you see, in that book of Convoy, they have all sort of things.

ANASTASIA: What now? Please, tell me once again, what do you mean? What is told? Who was born? By whom?

MILUKOFF: By Alexandra and Nicholas II. It was another daughter but she died [when] a child.

ANASTASIA: [loudly] *That's a lie!*

MILUKOFF: Well, you see . . .

ANASTASIA: [shouting] *A dirty lie!* When these swines have told you something [it] *is a lie!*

MILUKOFF: No, I mean in the book. It was also in Convoy.

ANASTASIA: But they have told you a lie!

MILUKOFF: [sheepishly] Uh-huh.

ANASTASIA: [screaming] *We had the proof here. The lady* [was] *sitting here.* And the proof is *alive* in the Netherlands. *Living! She was here.*

Miss Mutius murmurs again.

MILUKOFF: And she was your sister?

There was another long pause. I had not taken my eyes off the tape, and I waited—as Milukoff must have waited—for the crucial answer, but the silence continued. Apparently Anastasia nodded, because Milukoff meekly says, "Of course, then."

Any mention of the Youssoupovs always inspired Anastasia's strongest ire, I knew, but now she was angrier, more upset, than I had ever heard. Something about this conversation must have touched a deep inner chord in her psyche and unleashed a tirade.

ANASTASIA: They have drugged her out! They had made sure . . . drugged the Empress and . . . because she was a daughter, too. There had been a terrible story at the time. The Empress got deadly ill, you know. They [had] done terrible things with her. This is fact!

Milukoff was probably startled by Anastasia's vehemence, because he allowed the conversation to diminish into small talk for a while. I turned off the tape and wondered about what I had heard. The notes Milukoff made to accompany the tape indicated that the mysterious, unknown daughter was named "Alexandra de Graf" and beside her name was written "Dr. Philippe."

Who were these people? What did this mean? The story must continue somewhere on the other tapes because Anastasia had referred to the woman only as "Alexandra" but Milukoff had filled in her last name in his notes. I sorted through all twenty-six of the reel-to-reel tape boxes, reading the notes accompanying each. There were references to Alexandra de Graf on other tapes and I played them, trying to piece information together. Here is what unfolded:

MILUKOFF: This story about Alexandra, you have heard in Russia or already when you have been out?

ANASTASIA: This story was *wild* in Russia.

MILUKOFF: You had heard already there?

ANASTASIA: Yes, that was from home that I know. . . . In Russia was spoken that there was a child. There was a child. It was constantly spoken about that there *was* a child, *had to be a child*.

MILUKOFF: You—sisters—talked between yourselves?

ANASTASIA: Yes. There *was* a child. What was done with this child was a mystery. One never was sure at home what happened, one wasn't sure. Because narcotics were used. One started at that time to use the first narcotics when a child was born. That was the start, Queen Victoria of England was the first [to be given] such narcotics, you know, by her many child-bearings. That was the wrongest thing on earth! One cannot take poison when a child is born. The child must go insane, or blind, or who knows what, when one uses such poisons. And here, by this birth, was poison used. A narcotical poison to bring the sleep about. Therefore, the Empress could nothing know what was round her happening. It was impossible because she was lying in deepest sleep under these narcotical drugs which [were being used on her] for the first time. He [Dr. Philippe] had told that it would be a *boy*, and that was the reason he let the girl disappear. And the girl was given to some people who were in Russia, and just happened to be Dutch people. And so it happened that this child came [to be] in the hands of Dutch people because so

391

many Dutch people were living in Russia. In Moscow, Dutch people were living in masses. It was again a girl, so he let this girl disappear.

It [this disappearance] has to do with the wedding of the oldest sister of the Lord Mountbatten, Alice [the Czarina's niece], to Prince Andrew of Greece, nineteen-hundred-three and there has been some strange mess. Some strange mess was there, you know, which has never been cleared up. That is a fact!

[lowering her voice] I am always afraid that Miss Lamerdin could be on the ladder, listening. Yes, this is my greatest fear that this woman could suddenly be on the ladder and listening. But it's not possible.

The most important witness[es] were the sisters of the Empress. The older sister, who is dead, [and] Princess Alice, her daughter. That she, as young as she was, just the same would know something. But you see, these are the points which are so important. She, Princess Alice, can soon be dead, you know. She is more than eighty years old, and it can be that she is soon at the end. Her last photograph which I saw was not very pleasant-looking. Still, besides this Princess Alexandra, could somebody know most, would be she [Princess Alice]. Because this taken father, this adopted father [who would also know, is] dead. They are all dead, there is nobody alive. If there is still somebody alive that could be she [Princess Alice] or still somebody from the ladies' maids in England. Ladies' maids, they know most secrets. They know most of these secrets. There were still a number of maids alive, quite a number. I don't know how many still today are alive, but twenty years ago was quite a number still alive.

Then, adopting a coy, conspiratorial tone, Anastasia encourages Milukoff to visit and question the reclusive octogenarian Princess Alice at her residence, the Mary and Martha Convent in Greece. She carefully instructs him in the proven method of getting Prince Philip's mother drunk:

ANASTASIA: That could be only under a great cover, though, and you must not come as my friend. You have to come as my deadliest enemy.
[turning to Miss Mutius] And then he would get what he wants,

when he comes as my mad, deadliest enemy. Then he gets to know what he wants to know. He cannot come as my friend; that doesn't go. Then he comes and he tells he is . . . yes, he has heard about that crazy woman who calls herself Anastasia, that he's sure she is insane and she's crazy, but he has heard such and such story that there is still so and so and so and so.

This part of the conversation clearly demonstrated Anastasia's understanding of the Mountbatten family's attitude toward her and showed that she thought it was humorous. Her remarks evince not the slightest concern that some people characterized her as crazy:

ANASTASIA: Maybe in this way you could get the cream out of the cream out in this direction. That could be the place where you could get what you want to know. Could you manage to find the possibility to visit the Princess Alice of Battenberg, who is now a very, very old woman, and maybe a bit la-la in the head, too. [W]hat would maybe be of greatest importance—Princess Alice of Greece, the Princess Battenberg. I think that would be of greatest importance that you had not to tell your intentions. You have to come as an American, you know? You have not to tell that you are a Russian. You have to be very clever, and you must not tell that you know Anastasia at all, it is the best thing. Come as an American visiting her monastery . . . and maybe you make a little money present or something to her monastery.

MILUKOFF: Bring a bottle of vodka?

ANASTASIA: [laughing] That is the best thing, yes. And please, so in this way if you could manage to get her there, if you could drug her with vodka or whiskey and some sweet cake, what this lady always likes. If you could manage this, if you could drug her a bit, and then take care [unintelligible]. . . . That would be very important for this case when you should step-by-step could do this.

MILUKOFF: Could it help you?

ANASTASIA: Maybe *more* than you think. Maybe *more* than you think, for many reasons. Yes, for many reasons.

Milukoff steers the conversation back to Alexandra de Graf, "When she came here?"

ANASTASIA: Many years ago. Sixteen or seventeen years ago.

MILUKOFF: 1950?

ANASTASIA: Yes, it was. You see, she was here when we were in the old barrack, and she got first at Mrs. Heydebrand, and so . . . I did see her. Miss Mutius and Mrs. Heydebrand are two sisters . . . their mother was a Dutch lady. They come from a big house [of] tea importers. She [Alexandra] came from the Netherlands to here. I have forgotten [by] whom she was sent, from the Netherlands to me.

MILUKOFF: She is rich?

ANASTASIA: Yes, she has precious goods from Russia. She has masses of rubles, Russian rubles.

MILUKOFF: Gold?

ANASTASIA: She has *everything* . . . she has thousand things. She was living near the castle of the Queen of the Netherlands and of the castle of the German Emperor, not far from Doorn. And she had brought things here which were from Russia. She had brought a tea service from Russia, that I should see it. She had at the same time brought a big bunch of rubles, I don't know how many hundreds of thousands. She had other goods. Everything she had was *unbelievable, jewelry and all*. She had brought all type[s] of strange jewelry from Russia. . . .

This girl [was] beautiful. So now she is grown. You have not seen her. You should see her. You should visit her. She has the most beautiful large head and beautiful Russian hair, so like it came from Denmark. She's *beautiful*! You would fall in love with her.

And so it happened that this is such a great mystery, and stays a mystery, but she looks entirely a Romanov. *Entirely! Entirely!*

I did not know what to make of this. If Alexandra de Graf were alive, she would now be, according to Anastasia, the last surviving child of Nicholas and Alexandra. Would her own children throw the line of Romanov succession into dispute? And what of the Czar's fortune, some of which may never have been disbursed? Would Mrs. de Graf and her children be heirs?

IT was not difficult to confirm the identity of the "Dr. Philippe," whose name was prominent in the story. Philippe Vachot was the psychic doctor who practiced "astral medicine" in a vain attempt to make the Czarina pregnant with a male child. He served the Romanovs from 1901 to 1905, and so would have been present in 1903, the year Anastasia believed the fifth daughter had been born. Vachot ·boasted of the ability to both predict and control the gender of a fetus. His "treatments" of the Czarina are well documented. He dispensed "prescriptions" that included hallucinogenic herbal concoctions and advised the Czarina to "bathe" in moonlight during astrologically propitious nights. She followed his instructions fanatically, and would accept no criticism of him from family members or courtiers. She was undeniably desperate to deliver a male heir to the Romanov dynasty.

In most of the standard historical works, and in several volumes of minor importance, I found vague references to a "false pregnancy" or "miscarriage" by the Czarina sometime in 1902 or 1903—the sources did not agree on the date; no historian seemed to know exactly what happened to that pregnancy. I found this murky area strange in an otherwise copiously documented life.

Several biographies and histories of the period contained descriptions of the marriage of Princess Alice to Prince Andrew of Greece on October 7, 1903, in Darmstadt, but none of them shed any light on the story of the fifth daughter.

"Alexandra de Graf" rang a vague bell somewhere in the recesses of my memory. I had heard her name, or read it. But where? I spent the next several days combing my Romanov files, without success. She was not indexed in any book or mentioned in the thousands of letters and documents I had collected. Nor could I find a reference to a Mr. Convoy or a book by him.

I called Milukoff at his home in Spain, but he could not remember her. "It was more than twenty years ago when I made those tapes. I am now in my eighties and do not remember so well. I am still in good health, my girlfriend says so, but my memory is not as strong as other parts, ha-ha-ha." He suggested that his memory *might* return if I paid him to fly to Washington to review the material. But I knew money always motivated Milukoff, and decided I would have to try to find more about Mrs. de Graf without his help.

Then, late one evening, I took from a shelf *Anastasia's Money & the Czar's Wealth*, a mimeographed booklet Jack Manahan wrote and distributed to his and Anastasia's friends in 1974. The text was printed from pages typed on a manual typewriter with keys so dirty that most of the vowels were indistinguishable. In addition to the barely readable text, the contents were so disjointed that most recipients of this strange "Christmas card like no other," as Jack called it, had been unable to comprehend it.

I leafed through the pages, trying to decipher sentences here and there, when my eyes fell upon this passage:

> [A] plausible sister springing up in Doorn, Holland, educated by Queen Juliana's governess, whose five million *paper* rubles were given to her in 1912 at age 9 by her father the Czar, thus removing her from rival claims against the dowries of 5,000,000 each for the four other sisters!

> In fact, Alexandra de Graaf-Hemmes visited Anastasia's new home in Unterlengenhardt in the Black Forest, where her claim to be the younger daughter of the Czarina and Czar, born during the so-called "false pregnancy" of 1903, met with a friendly reception from Anastasia herself, from Gleb Botkin in America, and from myself as I was reading her 18 page letter to us the day she died, November 25, 1968. Posing no threat to Anastasia's money claims, since she had already received her share in 1912 equal to the other children, her claim seems almost as worthy of careful examination by the 'relations' as Anastasia's, though it has nothing like the half century seniority her claim has.

Here is where I had encountered Alexandra de Graf, but discredited her as another of Jack's innumerable fantasies. The name, spelled "de Graaf," stared back at me from the page where it had lain forgotten for fifteen years. And November 25, 1968—she was dead. Obviously I needed to talk to Jack and glean from his memory whatever other information might be stored there.

IN the five years since Anastasia's death, Jack's health had eventually deteriorated to the point where he no longer recognized close friends. He required constant nursing care at the Heritage Hall facility. If I went to Charlottesville, he might not recognize me, much less remember anything about Mrs. de Graaf, but he was an old friend and I owed him the respect of a visit.

When I entered his room at Heritage Hall, Althea Hurt was with him. He was seated in a lounge chair, slumped to the left, suffering from a loss of equilibrium. His eyes stared upward, unfocused.

Althea said, "Jack, you have company. Do you know who it is?"

"Speak to me," he said, trying to raise his right hand and point in my direction.

"Hello, Jack."

"You are James Blair Lovell, born in Missouri, formerly a resident of Georgia, now living in the District of Columbia."

This, thankfully, was one of the days Jack could remember people. His memory, legendary among genealogists, was at least partially intact and functional. But it was tragic to see this once vital, brilliant mind imprisoned in a dying body.

"Speak to me. Let us talk. It has been too long since your last visit. I understand you bought Milukoff's collection. I hope you didn't let him overcharge you. Was it worth it? Speak to me of history! Ask me something. My mind is clear."

"Yes, Jack, I bought it, and it was worth it. Do you remember Alexandra de Graaf?"

"Yes. She died November 25, 1968. Her maiden name was Suzanna Catharina Hemmes and—"

Suddenly, he burst into sobs. His body slumped further to the left as his chest heaved violently. Althea tried to right him in the chair and dabbed his cheeks with a tissue.

"I can't remember, I can't remember anymore," he moaned. "What was her name?"

What was who's name? As his sobs waned, he choked, "What was the name of the Czar's mother? You, Jimmy, will know this."

"She was the Princess Dagmar of Denmark, who took the name Marie."

He exhaled a long painful sigh, "Yeeeeess."

"He's been asking me that question for two weeks," said Althea. She said he had been obsessed with the desire to recall the name of the Dowager Czarina, and was often reduced to tears by his inability to remember.

I could not understand why, with access to his library of more than thirty thousand volumes, Althea could not have eased Jack's suffering by looking up one of the simplest Romanov facts, available in any elementary reference work.

When I returned the next day, Jack was alone. We had another conversation about Mrs. de Graaf in which he confirmed, to the best of his knowledge, the spelling of her name. He said her maiden name was Hemmes and, in the tradition of some European women, she hyphenated it after her husband's name, thus de Graaf-Hemmes.

It was a painful visit, and my last one with him.

I wondered what, if anything, I should do with this information. Obviously, from her adamant tone of voice on the tapes, the story of Mrs. de Graaf was of great importance to Anastasia.

But was it logical, much less realistic, to even entertain the idea that Nicholas and Alexandra had begotten an unknown child and then allowed it to be whisked away—or stolen—and raised by foreign commoners in a distant land? Theirs had been one of history's most famous romances. The Russian empire fell, in part, because of their blind devotion. Their lives are among the most thoroughly recorded in all history. It was almost inconceivable—fantastic—to think that there might be such a bizarre undisclosed chapter in their tragic existence.

A brief review of the information I had collected so far revealed that I knew relatively little. Anastasia believed that the Czarina had been pregnant again between her own birth in 1901 and that of her brother in 1904. She said that "Princess Alexandra" had been born in 1903, and the birth was somehow connected to the marriage of Lord Mountbatten's sister, Alice, to Prince Andrew of Greece, the parents of Prince Philip of England, husband of the present queen.

Anastasia also had raised the possibility that "Princess Alexandra" had been "stolen" from her crib, and seemed to point an accusing finger at Vachot.

According to the information on the tapes and in Jack's booklet, the woman who claimed to be "Princess Alexandra" was Suzanna Catharina de Graaf-Hemmes, who had been raised in the Netherlands by adoptive parents. She lived much of her adult life in, or near, the town of Doorn, which was also the location of Kaiser Wilhelm II's home in exile after the First World War.

Anastasia reported seeing "masses and masses" of paper Russian rubles in Mrs. de Graaf's possession, and Jack wrote that she had five million paper rubles. Anastasia also remembered seeing an impressive array of Russian jewelry, brought by Mrs. de Graaf on her first visit to Unterlengenhardt.

The tapes also indicated that Mrs. de Graaf had had children, and that she had converted to Roman Catholicism.

And she had died November 25, 1968.

This was precious little information upon which to base any further research, and I hesitated to proceed. But on other tapes Milukoff recorded during Anastasia's first days in Charlottesville, she made a point of trying to impress Jack with the importance of Mrs. de Graaf. This story was something Anastasia fervently believed and was committed to. I decided that, as her biographer, I had a duty to investigate it as thoroughly as possible.

I mentioned it in a circumspect manner, vaguely hinting, to a few Romanov scholars. Some of them did not know what I was talking about. A couple of others said they had heard parts of the story, but thought it apocryphal. Someone pointed out that Peter Kurth, the author of a previous biography of Anastasia, had written of "a Dutch housewife who claimed to be the *fifth* daughter of the Czar, kidnapped from Tsarskoe Selo in babyhood." He dismissed the Dutch lady as one of the crazy people who often tried to meet Anastasia.

The source of Kurth's comment was an article in the October 3, 1968, edition of *Figaro*, written by another Anastasian, Dominique Auclères, who had extensively covered the Anna Anderson court trials in Germany. I pulled the article from the files of the Library of Congress and had it translated from the French by three different translators, so as not to miss any nuance. Kurth maintained that the piece had made Mrs. de Graaf "the laughingstock of Europe," but the article was hardly a thorough investigation of her claim.

Admittedly based on reports "just released" by other "press agencies," the story is written in a very personal tone:

> God knows that the existence of this "Alexandra" is known to me. She presented herself about eight years ago at Unterlengenhardt, and was able to be received by Mrs. Anderson. She, according to American correspondents, where she to this day visits, would have recognized

her sister. The truth is that she was at the time shocked by the souvenirs of Russia which the Dutch woman brought to her, and also surprised by the resemblance that she discovered between the visitor and the imperial family.

This tallied exactly with everything Anastasia had said to Milukoff, except the date of Mrs. de Graaf's visit; Anastasia placed it in 1950, Mrs. Auclères "about eight years ago," or 1960.

Mrs. Auclères recounted the story of Philippe Vachot's treatments of the Czarina and the subsequent "nervous" pregnancy, saying both were established historical facts. She then said that Mr. de Graaf "wants to know nothing of the fantastic affirmations of his wife," adding in parentheses, "This is my own personal information." The last remark was not in keeping with Dominique Auclères's reputation for probing, straightforward journalism. In fact, the whole article read as if it had been written in great haste, not at all in the style of the elegant, readable prose for which she was so well respected.

The article made three additional points: Anastasia, born in 1901, would have been too young in 1903 to remember the birth of a sibling; "The lady de Graaf had a civil state ruling, according to which she would have been born in Rotterdam, May 6, 1905"; and "a few years ago" Mrs. Auclères interviewed a Mr. Encausse, whose father had been "a close friend and collaborator" of Vachot, and that Mr. Encausse—his first name is not given—knew nothing about the birth of a fifth daughter.

Mrs. Auclères ended her article with the remark that "the story of Alexandra" was one of those "that one values or not." While raising legitimate questions about Anastasia's cognizance at age two, the "civil state ruling" (whatever that was), and Mrs. de Graaf's birth date, Mrs. Auclères's brief perusal of the Dutch woman's claim fell far short of making her "the laughingstock of Europe."

I also knew that Mrs. Heydebrand, the gatekeeper of Anastasia's little circle and mentioned in the Auclères article, was very tough on people who wanted to bother Anastasia; she never allowed strangers in. But Mrs. Heydebrand had admitted Mrs. de Graaf, which said something for Mrs. de Graaf's credibility at the time.

To be on the safe side and ensure that I was losing nothing from the French, I asked the translators whether they interpreted Mrs.

Auclères's article as making a "laughingstock" of Mrs. de Graaf in any way. Each one said no. I wondered whether it was significant that Mrs. Auclères's article was published only shortly before Mrs. de Graaf's death.

I decided to consult the person who considered himself one of the world's greatest Anastasia experts, Ian Lilburn in London. He worked for the Royal College of Arms, claimed to have drafted the Anna Anderson chapter in *The File on the Tsar*, and was perhaps the most knowledgeable person on the Anna Anderson court cases. I reached him by telephone and said, "Mr. Lilburn, I'd like to ask you what you know about the Alexandra de Graaf story."

He said the story was not true—"I know that they [Anastasia and Mrs. de Graaf] *never met.*" So I asked him to listen to the tape. When it ended, I picked up the receiver. There was silence. At first I thought he might have hung up, but I could hear the transatlantic connection.

"Mr. Lilburn?"

More silence.

"Mr. Lilburn?"

Finally he answered in a cracked voice, "Yes?"

"Could you hear it?"

"Yes."

"What is your response?"

"I never knew."

This proved to me the story had not been properly investigated. Not at all.

THE idea of traveling to the Netherlands to investigate this story was beginning to take root in my thoughts, but I knew very little about the country in general or the history of the Doorn area in particular. A telephone call to the cultural affairs office of the Dutch Embassy in Washington revealed that they had never heard of Doorn, but they recommended I call the Netherlands Board of Tourism in New York City. When I called New York, the young woman who answered the phone said she, too, had never heard of Doorn and could offer no further assistance. Again I called the embassy. Angry that a potential tourist's questions had been casually brushed aside, the official instructed me to call the director of the Board of Tourism after he spoke with her. The second time I called New York, I was connected with the director who said that she would cooperate fully with my research. I asked for maps and information about Doorn. She volunteered to send photocopies of the pages of the local telephone directory listing de Graafs.

A thick package containing the materials arrived a few days later, and I learned that Doorn was an eleven-hundred-year-old village, the major attraction of which was a museum created from Doorn House, the former residence in exile of Kaiser Wilhelm II. I thought that if I went to the Netherlands, the first place I would visit would be Doorn House.

Anastasia had repeatedly made the point to Milukoff that Mrs. de Graaf lived near Castle Doorn, as if it had some significance to the story. Since the Kaiser was a first cousin of the Czarina, I wondered whether there was a connection between the proximity of Mrs. de Graaf's residence to that of the Kaiser's.

This question led me to briefly investigate the Kaiser's life in exile. I checked every English-language biography of him and found that, although he had lived twenty-two years in Doorn, most books devoted less than a single chapter to what amounted to a full third of his life. Still, I was able to gather some interesting facts that related to Anastasia's story.

Almost immediately after the Kaiser took up residence in Doorn, his wife died. Little more than a year later, he married again, this time to the widowed Princess Schoenaich-Garolath, who had been born Princess Hermine of Reuss.

Hermine, a short, plain, dumpy woman, was almost universally disliked and had openly schemed to marry the Kaiser against the wishes of his children. She was a fervent monarchist who believed that when the Hohenzollerns were restored to the German throne, she would be Empress. Although the Kaiser had abdicated his throne and was now referred to in the American and British press as the "former-Kaiser," Hermine always styled herself as Kaiserin and Empress. For example, she wrote her private correspondence in heavy purple pencil, an affectation borrowed from Queen Victoria. She was also known to scribble notes to her intimate friends on postcards which had been privately printed with a picture of herself and the Kaiser on the front.

Scholars have always maintained that Anastasia enjoyed a particularly close friendship with Hermine, and that Hermine was one of her most ardent supporters. Milukoff's tapes contain numerous references by Anastasia to her friendship with Hermine. When I asked various Anastasia experts what documentation proved the women's friendship, the answer was always, "but everyone knows." It soon became clear that none of these experts had ever seen any proof; rather, they were merely repeating what they had heard.

My numerous attempts to find documentation of some type of connection between Anastasia and Hermine—or, at the very least, to confirm that Anastasia considered the relationship special—were continually frustrated. Then, while going through Milukoff's albums one day, I found a picture postcard of the Kaiser and Hermine tucked behind an unrelated photograph. I thought it odd that they should be together in such a manner, the photograph obscuring the postcard from ready view. But I was only slightly curious about why this memento of Hermine was not displayed more prominently in the album or had not been found, separated, and placed elsewhere among the items Anastasia had entrusted to Milukoff.

The card is signed by Hermine and addressed to "Dear Lies" (pronounced "lease"), most likely the Reuss family governess, Annaliese Thomasius, who later lived near Anastasia at Unterlengenhardt and was one of the few people she trusted. On the front of the card Hermine has signed her name in the trademark purple pencil over the picture of herself and the Kaiser. The contents of the note to "Lies" are almost entirely illegible, because the script—written in the same purple pencil—has faded over time.

There is no indication of how a personal note from the self-styled Kaiserin to her former nanny came into Anastasia's possession. Certainly she was always receiving gifts of money or mementos from her supporters, and perhaps someone who knew of her special affection for Hermine gave Anastasia this postcard. Perhaps Annaliese herself had given it to Anastasia. It is highly unlikely that she would have purchased it from a collector. No matter the circumstances that led to its presence in Milukoff's photo album, its mere existence there is factual proof that at the very least Anastasia felt a connection to Hermine. She certainly was an avid collector but was not in the habit of keeping such personal souvenirs of just anyone.

Another indication of a possible, more intimate connection between the two women appears in the tape recording Milukoff made on Anastasia's first full day in Charlottesville in 1968, when Anastasia carefully takes out pieces of silverware engraved with the crest of Hermine's ancestors, the Reuss family. Ceremoniously, she explains what they are and presents them as gifts to the three people closest to her at that time—Jack Manahan, Gleb Botkin, and Alexis Milukoff. The silverware had been brought to her in the hospital by Miss Thomasius, and it is clear from Anastasia's remarks that the pieces are among her most highly prized goods, a gift from a cousin of her friend the Empress Hermine.

As interesting as this documentation relating to the Kaiser's last years and Anastasia's story was, I had not forgotten the subject that had originally led me to research Doorn. The mystery of the Dutch woman would continue to be foremost in my mind.

MRS. de Graaf—Suzanna Catharina, Alexandra, or whatever her real name was—presented a conundrum. If she honestly believed herself to be a natural child of Nicholas and Alexandra, how had she arrived at that conclusion? She could have learned of Vachot and the 1903 pregnancy from a careful study of Romanov biographies and tailored her story to fit. Was she a scheming charlatan who preyed upon the lonely Anastasia?

What had convinced Anastasia that Mrs. de Graaf was genuine? Had her loneliness and despair after an entire adulthood without any immediate family clouded her judgment and led her to accept Mrs. de Graaf out of sheer wish fulfillment?

I reviewed the various bits and pieces I had managed to glean from the conversations and research I had pursued over the course of the previous weeks.

Ian Lilburn said he "knew" that Anastasia and Mrs. de Graaf had never met. That statement was contradicted by Peter Kurth, partially based on the *Figaro* article by Dominique Auclères. According to these two sources, the two women had met.

Anastasia herself confirmed that she had been visited by Mrs. de Graaf as early as 1950. She was convinced of the Dutch woman's authenticity and forcefully maintained that she had been born "Princess Alexandra" in 1903, at the time of the Czarina's so-called "false" or "hysterical" pregnancy.

Dominique Auclères wrote that Mrs. de Graaf "had a civil state ruling, according to which she was born in Rotterdam, May 6, 1905." Moreover, both Milukoff and Auclères had challenged the very idea that Anastasia could have any knowledge of such a birth. Each cited the fact that she was only two years old when the events of Mrs. de Graaf's alleged birth in Russia would have taken place. Milukoff had said, "It was *many* years ago. *Sixty* years ago!"

But Anastasia had been adamant: "This story was *wild* in Russia. Yes, that was from home that I know. . . . In Russia was spoken that there was a child. There was a child. It was constantly spoken about that there *was* a child. . . . This is fact!" She had said that the Czar's daughters had heard the story and discussed it among themselves.

Gleb Botkin's daughter, Marina Botkin Schweitzer, told me that Gleb had cast doubt on Mrs. de Graaf, saying her claim was not provable.

But Jack Manahan had written that Mrs. de Graaf's story had "met with a friendly reception" from "Gleb Botkin in America."

Something was definitely not right. I felt I was being stymied by misrepresentations and contradictions. It seemed that none of the so-called experts wanted to see an investigation of Mrs. de Graaf's claim. Why? Anastasia herself had accepted Mrs. de Graaf. Why could they not at least condone research based on that lead alone, when so much else she purported had proved true? What had happened to the zeal that had fueled their own probings of the Eugenia Smith and Michal Goleniewski cases, which had even less basis for investigation? What was there in this story that they considered too sensitive to reveal?

The more I turned these questions over in my mind, the more I wanted answers. I decided to apply the same logic to the question of Mrs. de Graaf's identity that I had originally applied to the question of Anastasia's identity after meeting her in 1972. That was to try to uncover every fact, every situational nuance, no matter how contradictory or illogical, to arrive at a set of facts that would either prove or disprove the theory. I had no opinion about Mrs. de Graaf, but resolved to investigate her as completely as my resources allowed.

It was then, against the advice of everyone except my agent, that I decided to go to the Netherlands. The self-styled experts said this was a field plowed many times—but I had proven that their furrows were shallow. They said that they had determined the whole Alexandra de Graaf business was a hoax, and that Mrs. Auclères had unmasked Mrs. de Graaf as the "laughingstock of Europe." They warned that I would taint my reputation by going to the Netherlands.

So I went.

II.

Doorn

AMSTERDAM IN EARLY AUTUMN was crisp and invigorating. The American Hotel, an imposing art-nouveau structure bounded by a canal on the famous *Leidseplein*, is a meeting place for artists and writers, and I had reservations there. I checked in Friday, September 29, 1989, and planned to see Amsterdam that weekend, then travel to Doorn on Monday.

At the concierge desk I inquired about transportation to Doorn. "Where is that?" was the puzzled reply. I asked other people, but no one had heard of it. Finally, in one of the many coffee shops for which Amsterdam is well known, I made the acquaintance of Hans Builtjes, a young English-speaking Dutchman who knew of Doorn. He volunteered to show me around Amsterdam, and as we strolled the narrow streets of the ancient city I took Hans into my confidence and told him about my research and the purpose of this trip. He offered to act as translator when I called the de Graafs in the telephone listings provided by the Netherlands Board of Tourism.

The next day Hans came to the hotel and we called every listing in all variant spellings, but to no avail. No one remembered Suzanna Catharina—or Alexandra—de Graaf.

Late Sunday morning, October 1, I awoke to raindrops splashing on the balcony outside the sitting room of my suite. Angry storm clouds blackened the Amsterdam skyline. This was not a day for sightseeing, I thought, as the room service waiter delivered breakfast. Harry Mulisch, the distinguished Dutch writer, had sent me an inscribed copy of his novel, *The Assault*, so I decided to stay inside reading. But after a while, not even Mulisch's brilliant prose could overcome my urge to get out of the hotel, even though it had begun pouring rain. I decided on the spur of the moment to go to Doorn a day early.

I took a taxi to the Amsterdam Central Station and asked a ticket saleswoman about trains to Doorn. "Doorn?" the lady asked, "Where is that?" After consulting several colleagues and making a few telephone calls, she determined that it was not possible to travel to Doorn by train. Instead, I needed to buy a ticket to Driebergen-Zeist, and from there take a bus to Doorn. That seemed simple enough, until I got onto the platform and asked a conductor which train went to Driebergen-Zeist. "Where is that?" he asked quizzically. I began to wonder if I were meant go to Doorn at all, but I finally located my train and with relief took a window seat.

As the train clacked through the flat Dutch countryside, I looked for windmills, but there were none. For miles there was little more than flat pastureland populated by a few cattle, an uninspiring landscape, so, there being no one else in my coach to talk to, I thought it would be good to review my reasons for making the trip. It occurred to me that this sort of reflection is more like a novelist's device than the biographer's penchant for investigating every possible fact. I realized with a sudden, sobering thought that if I found what I was seeking in Doorn, I could not avoid becoming a character in my own book.

At the Driebergen-Zeist station I had no trouble finding the bus to Doorn. It is about a twenty-minute ride, with many stops in between; but the countryside is pleasant, with beautiful villas and large country houses. An elderly Dutch woman in the next seat was eager to practice her English and carried on an animated conversation, encouraging me to see Doorn House. She said I should get off the bus at the first stop, located around the corner from the Kaiser's former residence.

As the bus drove away, I noticed that I was standing in the middle of a five-way intersection and had failed to ask my seat mate which corner to turn. At that moment a middle-aged woman passed on the sidewalk; I stopped her and asked directions to Doorn House. "What is that?" she replied. If this had been France, I would have ascribed it to typical rudeness, but I was then—and remain now—perplexed by the Dutch people's apparent lack of knowledge of their own country.

So, having nothing better to rely on than instinct—and wanting to get out of the rain quickly—I made a right turn, walked one block, and saw a sign pointing toward the parking area of Doorn House. I entered the grounds through a wide Dutch gatehouse where an elderly man was selling admission tickets. He spoke English well and encouraged me to ask questions about the area. He was friendly, knowledgeable, and seemed to be delighted, like the lady on the bus, to practice his English, so I decided to ask if he knew of Suzanna Catharina de Graaf. "I do not speak English. I do not understand," he said, waving me away dismissively. "Hurry to the house, or you will miss the last tour of the day."

Doorn House sits opposite the gatehouse, at the far end of a long park. Just inside the grounds is the chapel, at that time converted to a gift shop. Because it was right in my path, I went in and met Mrs. M. M. Martin, who operated it as a concession. When I asked if she knew of Mrs. de Graaf, she said no. The studied expression on her face, as if she were genuinely straining to recognize the name, was immediately convincing.

As I left the shop and walked across the park toward the house, brilliant sunshine burst from the cloud cover. The immaculate lawn suddenly looked like a sea of diamonds, the rain-soaked grass reflecting the sun's radiance. I hoped this was a portent of better luck.

I walked through the park, across a tiny bridge spanning a moat, and up the steps to the front door of the Kaiser's house, where I rang the bell. A guide opened the door and said, in English, that I had missed the beginning of the final tour of the day, but that if I wanted to view the house I could either catch up with the tour or walk through unguided. I decided to join the tour.

The doorman ushered me into the Marshal's Room, where the Kaiser's gold and silver was displayed in tall polished glass cases. A guide, speaking Dutch, pointed to objects, lecturing. Not understanding, I disengaged from the group and began wandering through the house alone. No one tried to stop me. I noticed that there were no alarm systems; the Kaiser's fabulous collections lay completely in the open, unprotected. In one of the main rooms on the ground floor, a guide appeared and directed me to continue making right turns through the connecting rooms, which would take me full circle to the main hall again. As I strolled, unchaperoned, through the empty rooms of the exiled German Emperor's house, I felt thrown back into the 1920s and 1930s, when this estate had been alive with the domineering presence of Wilhelm.

Each room was furnished exactly as it had been when Doorn House was a residence. The dining room table was set for luncheon, with only the guests missing. I wondered whether Alexandra de Graaf had ever sat at table with the Kaiser, or if Anastasia had visited here.

The magnificently appointed dining room featured a life-size Alfred Schwarz portrait of the Kaiser in military uniform. Pausing before the picture, I gazed into the face of the posturing figure, mustache waxed and upturned, jaw gravely set, eyes staring down at me. Alone in the room, our gazes locked. I thought of my grandfather from Missouri who had suffered the trench warfare that needlessly took millions of lives, and of statues in a hundred American towns, like the one of a charging Doughboy in Bolivar, Missouri, commemorating the thousands of soldiers who had fought to defeat this man. And of my grandfather's pride in military service, tempered by a hatred of war, passions engendered by the actions of the man this house memorialized.

That egomaniac, whose physical deformities and psychological insecurities had plunged the planet into its first world war, might have held the key to the answer I sought. Was it coincidence that brought Alexandra de Graaf—who, if she were a Romanov, would also be a cousin of Wilhelm II—to Doorn? In the Kaiser's time, the name of this tiny town was known worldwide. The international press had maintained a constant vigil outside the Kaiser's walls, blocking the entrance from the street in front of the gatehouse I had so effortlessly passed through. This house, once a hotbed of imperialist intrigue and Nazi sympathy, was now nearly forgotten and certainly isolated.

If there were answers to the questions I had traveled so far to ask, they would not be coaxed from the ghosts of this ancient dwelling. I would have to find them on my own.

My ambling, still unfettered by company, brought me to a closed door. My hand, resting lightly on the cold antique lever, pressed down. The door opened, and I stepped into a room full of elderly people who were gathered around a tall German-speaking guide. As the door hinge creaked, every head turned, including the guide's. He never paused in his remarks, but the elderly Germans angrily glared as if I had noisily interrupted a solemn occasion. Contrite, I stepped over the threshold, closed the door, and stood quietly in the corner until the guide finished his lecture and the group shuffled away.

I was in the Kaiser's Smoking Room, surrounded by displays of snuff boxes once belonging to Frederick the Great. I walked over to one of the display cases of rich dark-toned wood, admiring the magnificence of the boxes, when the German-speaking guide approached. I apologized for interrupting his talk. Nodding imperceptibly, he asked whether I had questions about the house. Somewhat distracted, I inquired about the ethnic composition of the tourists who visited the house, and he quoted some figures. He remarked sadly that the number of Germans who remembered the Kaiser's Reich was quickly dwindling; only the older ones knew or cared enough to visit.

Although he appeared too young to remember Mrs. de Graaf, I asked whether he had ever heard of her. He replied, "No," pointing out that he was not from Doorn and could not be expected to know. The sound of his negative reply hung heavy in the room, as tangible as my discouragement. I was beginning to think that my day was a complete failure and decided to leave.

As I reentered the main hallway, I saw the guide who had been lecturing in the Marshal's Room, a pale fleshy man in his late fifties or early sixties. I approached him asking, "Do you speak English?"

"A little."

"I'm visiting from America, and looking for the family of Suzanna Catharina de Graaf. Have you ever heard of her?"

As I spoke her name, the recognition in his eyes was instantaneous. "Yes, I remember her. She's dead now. She died in 1964, I think."

"No, she died in 1968, on November 25th. What do you remember of her?"

"My father was the milkman, so I grew up here and went with him on his rounds. I remember delivering milk to Mrs. de Graaf. When your father is the milkman, you know everyone and where they live."

"Do you remember much about her?"

"Very little." He started to step back, edging away from me.

"Where are her children?"

"I have to go now," he said nervously. "There is another tour I have to take through the house."

"No, there isn't. The last tour just finished. I was too late for it."

"Well, I . . . I . . . I have to go." He could not seem to form a complete sentence, nor look me directly in the eye. Coughing nervously, he murmured, "We're closing anyway."

"I realize you're closing, but give me five minutes of your time after you close. Just five minutes."

"No, no, no. I can't. I have to go see my wife in the hospital. You wouldn't deprive a man of seeing his wife in the hospital, would you?"

How to respond to a question like that? I left disheartened: the trip, the day seemed to be ending as a futile gesture.

I had turned to leave by the front door when I noticed the doorman standing there. He was the only person I had not questioned, so I asked him whether he knew the family of Mrs. de Graaf. Yes, he said, one of her sons was a local electrician for whom he had done some part-time work. I took a notebook and pen from my pocket and asked him the son's name. Almost before I could finish the sentence, the milkman's son reappeared and urgently called the doorman away. As I began to protest, the milkman's son gruffly informed me that the house was now closed and I must leave immediately.

Something strange was going on, but its significance was confounding. What was the reason the milkman's son did not want to talk about Mrs. de Graaf, or allow anyone else to discuss her with me?

The nearby municipal building was closed because it was Sunday. The only other place I could think to check before returning to Amsterdam was the police station. The police officers were cordial but knew nothing of Suzanna Catharina de Graaf. I had traveled halfway across the globe to find only a milkman's son and a part-time electrician, illusive discoveries at best. As I made my way back to the bus stop, the rain started again. I slumped down in the bus shelter in a mood as dark as the skies, thinking, *What have I done? I've spent a great deal of money to come to the Netherlands, to this town, to find nothing.* I did not know what to do next.

A moment later I heard footsteps approaching the bus shelter and glanced up to see that they belonged to the tall guide who had given the tour to the elderly Germans—the one fellow who, although non-informative, was at least talkative. Entering the bus shelter and seeing me, he nodded. We introduced ourselves. His name was Ronald Trüm. I complimented him on his English, and he said, "Oh, well, no, it's not that good at all."

Not particularly interested in a dialogue regarding his language abilities, I asked, "Are you sure you've never heard of Mrs. de Graaf?"

"I'm positive. I do not live in Doorn; I live in Utrecht. I have never heard that name," he replied.

When the bus arrived, we embarked. Ronald chose a seat next to mine, and I was glad to have someone to talk to. He seemed knowledgeable about monarchial history, especially the Kaiser. I asked him about the house, questioning the care of its contents and commenting on the lack of security. He asked what I was doing in Doorn. I hedged, "Well, I'm researching a book on the Romanovs."

He scoffed, "Here? Whatever for?" I did not answer, asking instead if he knew anything about the Romanovs, particularly at the end of the Russian empire. He made a few appreciative remarks about the reign of the last czar and—to my surprise—brought up and jokingly discredited the story of Anastasia.

Ronald was well educated; he quoted dates and facts effortlessly, revealing an intimate familiarity with European history. I began to think that if I continued to encounter as much difficulty as I had so far in finding the descendants of Mrs. de Graaf, I would need help. So as we talked, I told him a little more about what I was doing. The matter seemed to pique his interest. He suggested that I take the bus with him into Utrecht, where we could go to his apartment for a longer discussion.

Ronald's home was a veritable museum to monarchy, lavishly furnished with life-size paintings and busts of former Dutch and German royalty. On the budget of a graduate student, he had amassed an impressive collection of monarchial art. In the course of our conversation, I told him the details of my book, and he seemed very interested. He was especially intrigued by my encounter with the son of the milkman. I said I felt guilty for having kept him from visiting his sick wife in the hospital. Ronald hooted, "Going to see his wife in the hospital? His wife *works* in a hospital. He fetches her after we close the house."

In Doorn I had suspected that something was wrong, having been put off first by the ticket salesman in the gatehouse and later by the milkman's son. Now I knew for sure. "I feel like I'm being stonewalled, Ronald. I really believe those men, especially the milkman's son, knew more than they were telling."

"Well, I can find out easily enough," Ronald said.

He picked up the phone and called the milkman's son, laughing several times during the conversation. When he hung up he said, "He told me everything."

"What is 'everything'?"

"He told me the names of Mrs. de Graaf's children, their addresses, occupations, who they married. Everything."

"Why wouldn't he tell me?"

"He said he was not going to tell journalists anything. There have been enough pursuing these questions in the past. He is not going to cooperate with anyone. 'Let the family have its privacy.'"

Tell journalists what?

Before I could ask, Ronald said that the name of Mrs. de Graaf's eldest son was Antoon van Weelden, whose surname was that of her first husband. No wonder I was unable to find him by calling the telephone listings for de Graaf. He was the electrician in Doorn. "The milkman's son doesn't want to tell journalists what, Ronald?"

"I think it is that Mrs. de Graaf was a—how do you say it in English?—myth, no . . . ethereal, uh . . . mystic."

"You mean she was a psychic?"

"Yes."

"Ronald, are you telling me that man on the telephone told you Alexandra de Graaf was a *psychic*?"

He laughed heartily. "Yes, that is what he said. She performed— I'm sorry I don't know how it is said in English—with her hands."

"You mean to say she was a faith healer? That she psychically healed people by the laying on of hands?"

He burst out laughing, almost guffawing, nodding his head. "Ridiculous, is it not?"

This was curious information, especially in light of the evasions I had come across earlier in the day. Was Mrs. de Graaf such a figure of local scorn that people refused to discuss her more than twenty years after her death, I wondered aloud.

Ronald sobered. "No, in fact he said many people in the Doorn/ Driebergen-Zeist communities believe they are healthy and alive today because of the powers of Mrs. de Graaf. People are reluctant to discuss her with strangers because they respect her memory and do not wish it to be misrepresented. Mr. van Weelden is—I know this phrase in English—a pillar of the community. The milkman's son said he has heard that Mrs. de Graaf claimed to be Anastasia's daughter, or something. He wasn't sure."

This was bizarre. I had no preconceived ideas about what I might find, but I never expected this. How to proceed? Did I want to pursue these leads? Or should I chalk up Alexandra de Graaf as a crank and catch the earliest flight home?

Well, I thought, *I'm here, and I have spent a lot of money to get here, so I might as well see this through to whatever end may come.* It occurred to me that as a graduate student working on his own time, Ronald might be available to assist me. He certainly had a rapport with his colleagues at Doorn House, so perhaps he could learn more. I asked whether he was interested in doing some research, and we agreed to meet in Amsterdam the next day to discuss it.

I felt fortunate to have met Ronald, especially when he mentioned that he worked in Doorn only every other Sunday. If I had not decided to go there that particular dreary Sunday, we would not have met.

It was nearly midnight when we arrived at the Utrecht station so that I could catch the last train to Amsterdam. As we stood on the platform, our conversation dwindled to small talk and I asked him questions about Doorn House. He was proud of his association with the imperial residence and recited a condensed version of the lecture tour I had missed.

As Ronald held forth on the subject of the Kaiser's residence, I remembered a question about the house, something I did not understand about its designation. Anastasia always referred to it as Castle Doorn, but everyone else called it Doorn House. Which was it, a castle or a house?

"It is a house," Ronald emphatically replied. "But it was a castle."

"How can you downgrade a castle to a house?" I asked.

"Yes. I understand your confusion," he smiled. "It was originally built in the fourteenth century as a small fortified castle for the purpose of safely storing the possessions of the Church. Then it was rather medieval, and remained so until the eighteenth century when it was rebuilt by a private owner, who converted it to a country estate. It was a castle, but is now a house."

The train to Amsterdam pulled into the station, and Ronald continued his litany of facts, figures, and dates. His voice lowered to a whisper when he confided that no inventory existed of the house's contents, and rumor had it that, since the house had become a museum, some of the smaller pieces had disappeared.

I asked what the contents of the house were worth.

"One cannot know," Ronald shook his head, "because there has never been a thorough inventory. We do know that the gold and silver in the Marshal's Room is worth eighty million Dutch guilders. That's roughly forty million American dollars."

ENTERING the eastern outskirts of Amsterdam, my train slowed as it passed a modern, concrete and steel maximum-security prison. A human warehouse without windows, an awesome reminder of how the Dutch—otherwise such an open and tolerant people— would go to extreme lengths to ensure the safety and privacy of their fellow citizens. As the prison disappeared from view I was haunted by a lingering question. If just one room in Doorn House was worth forty million dollars, how could its guardians be so unconcerned with the protection of the material treasures and yet go to great efforts to shield the memory of the dead Mrs. de Graaf?

Later, lying in my hotel bed, I reviewed the events of this peculiar day. Mrs. de Graaf was a psychic, a faith healer who laid hands on ailing Dutch people and restored their health. I turned on the television, with the sound off, and flicked the channel to MTV. Elton John was performing in a video I had never seen, so I raised the volume. The legend in the lower-left corner said it was "Healing Hands" from his *Sleeping with the Past* album.

As I drifted off, a line from the song lingered in my mind—*There's a light where the darkness ends.*

THE next morning Ronald came to the hotel and we discussed my research. I showed him some of my Anastasia materials and played an excerpt of Tape Five, where Anastasia tells Milukoff about "Princess Alexandra." He remained unconvinced of the validity of Anastasia's identity, but his interest in the project was nonetheless aroused. He asked detailed questions, and I was impressed by the energetic skepticism and intellectual enthusiasm that indicated a probing mind. I did not want a research assistant who was a blind-eyed true believer. Instead, I needed someone reluctant to accept things on face value. Yet because my time in the Netherlands was limited, I needed a quick method of educating Ronald on the finer points of the Anastasia case so that he could understand the background of my work.

After lunch, we walked around the city discussing possible strategies that would assure a meeting with Mrs. de Graaf's children. In a bookshop I bought a copy of the Dutch edition of Summers and Mangold's *The File on the Tsar* and asked Ronald to read the "Anna Anderson" chapter, which was the most succinct, accurate recounting of Anastasia's story I knew. It would give him the basic facts necessary to confirm for him the historical value of Anastasia. Eyeing the book suspiciously, he said he doubted anything could alter his opinion that Anna Anderson was a fake. I asked him to call me when he had read it.

That evening he called. He had finished the chapter and was now more inclined to accept Anna Anderson as Anastasia. I listened carefully to his words and his tone; *The File on the Tsar* had persuaded him that there was more probity to Anastasia than he had believed possible.

We agreed to meet in Doorn the next day.

III.

"She was my mother"

MY BUS ARRIVED before Ronald's, so I took a table at a sidewalk cafe near the bus stop and waited. The cafe was a gathering place for teenagers, and I watched the young couples coming and going. Their fashionable, casual clothing and haircuts were in sharp contrast to the Kaiser's house around the corner, full of musty memories of an era long passed. I wondered if any of these young people could be Mrs. de Graaf's grandchildren. Laughing, holding hands, eating snacks, and talking animatedly, they were light-years removed from the world of psychics and Romanov princesses—the events I was trying to unravel.

At this moment, somewhere nearby, Mrs. de Graaf's oldest son was going about his business, unaware that his life was soon to be interrupted—and perhaps forever changed. What kind of man would he be? Would he agree to talk? How much did he know about his mother's claim? With luck, I would soon find out.

"James?" Ronald was seated across the table. I had not even seen him approach, much less sit down. "I have good news."

He had spent the preceding evening calling his colleagues at Doorn House, asking questions about Mrs. de Graaf. Everyone I had approached, except Mrs. Martin in the gift shop, had known Mrs. de Graaf. They each told Ronald essentially the same thing, that Mrs. de Graaf was a revered healer with powerful psychic gifts. She had worn long, flowing robes and carried herself regally. They all knew she claimed to have some connection to the Romanovs; some of them thought she was Anastasia's *daughter*. To them, the eccentric aspect of her nature was not her psychic predilection, but rather her belief in a Romanov connection.

We walked across the street to the Doorn town hall where we acquired certified copies of Mrs. de Graaf's death certificate at the Department of Civil Registration. Ronald wanted to have another conversation with the milkman's son, Cor den Toon, so I waited in a restaurant while he went off to Doorn House.

Cor den Toon had gone to lunch, but at the gatehouse Ronald encountered a local man, Jan Knier, and a Mr. Barneveld, whom he did not know. He asked them whether they remembered Mrs. de Graaf.

"At first," Ronald told me later, "Mr. Knier proved not to be very communicative, but as it became clear that Mr. Barneveld intended to begin an animated conversation about Mrs. de Graaf, Mr. Knier often confirmed or enlarged upon the stories of the more cooperative Mr. Barneveld. From their conversation, it became clear that Mrs. de Graaf had been a familiar figure in Doorn and that many people thought she posed as a Russian princess. The mayor and former director of Doorn House, the late Baron van Nagell, had known of her—so Mr. Knier said—and had seen Russian jewelry in her possession.

"This 'Russian story' proved so widespread that one of the former guides at Doorn House once asked Mrs. de Graaf's son, 'Please tell me, is it true what people say about your mother, that she is a Russian princess?'

"Mr. Knier and Mr. van Barneveld told me that Mrs. de Graaf had practiced as a kind of paranormally gifted healer, and that she had married twice, and her son, born of the first marriage, had an electricity shop. Mr. de Graaf, her second husband, had worked as a therapeutist in the Military Physical Rehabilitation Centre in Doorn."

We already knew most of this, but it was interesting to hear it confirmed and to learn that Mrs. de Graaf had been a respected—if highly unusual—member of the community. It was now time to try to establish contact with her eldest son, Antoon van Weelden. His shop was located on a main thoroughfare and we proceeded in that direction.

Mr. van Weelden had been described as an "electrician," so I expected an electrical contractor's office or repair shop, but the place we entered was an appliance store, full of microwaves, washing machines, dishwashers, and curling irons. A bell rang inside the shop as we opened the door.

A tall handsome woman and a somewhat shorter man stood together behind the counter assisting a customer. Since we did not know whether they spoke English, Ronald and I had already agreed that he would initiate the conversation in Dutch. I had also requested that he not use Mrs. de Graaf's name if there was anyone else in the shop because people in Doorn seemed so sensitive about her.

I lingered by the microwaves while Ronald and the man, who I knew must be Mr. van Weelden, talked in Dutch. I could not see Mr. van Weelden because Ronald stood between us, blocking my view. I felt frustrated—after all this time I was finally in the same room with a child of Alexandra de Graaf, yet I could not understand or observe him. They appeared to agree on something because Ronald said, "Ja, ja," turned toward me, and signaled in the direction of the door.

Outside, he explained that he had told them we had something important to discuss, so Mr. van Weelden asked us to return at 1:45 P.M. when he *might* have time to talk—if there were no customers. Ronald said the lady behind the counter was introduced as Mrs. van Weelden.

We had about an hour to wait and my anticipation was acute. I had not even got a good look at Mr. van Weelden. I told Ronald that when we returned to the store, I wanted to speak to Mr. van Weelden first, in English, and that if he did not understand what I was saying, Ronald could provide a simultaneous translation.

THERE were no customers in the shop when we returned precisely at the appointed time. I approached the counter where Mr. and Mrs. van Weelden stood. He was bending over, taking a hair curling iron out of its box.

"Mr. van Weelden, my name is James Lovell, and I've come all the way from the United States to talk to you about your mother."

Silence descended upon the shop. His wife was standing behind him, and when I spoke, an expression of terror crossed her face, as if I had threatened to kill them. She opened her mouth, but no sound came out.

Mr. van Weelden straightened up and regarded me gravely. As our gazes met, I realized I had seen the unique blue color of his eyes only once before. It was unmistakably "Anastasia Blue," the color popular in the United States in the late 1920s.

"You mean Mrs. de Graaf," he said in perfectly pronounced English.

"Yes, Mrs. de Graaf," I replied.

"What do you want?" He was brusque.

"I am writing a book about Anastasia—at her specific request—and I have brought from America certain materials pertaining to your mother which I think we need to talk about."

After our earlier visit, Ronald had said that Mr. van Weelden had told him he was very busy and might not have any time to talk with us, and that under no circumstances would he be able to leave the shop.

I was therefore surprised when he now turned to his wife and asked her to take over the store. He motioned for us to step behind the counter and through a doorway that connected the appliance store to their residence. We walked a few steps down a hall and made a left turn into a spacious living room equipped with a variety of high-tech electronic gadgets. Mr. van Weelden asked us to be seated.

As I sat down in an easy chair and arranged my briefcase in my lap, I studied Antoon van Weelden carefully. He was speaking Dutch to his wife, who had ignored his request and followed us from the shop. He seemed to be reassuring her of something. She shot me a pained, puzzled glance, looked back at her husband, took a step toward him, stopped, lowered her head and mumbled softly. I wondered whether she feared leaving him alone with us.

Ronald and I had planned how to achieve an initial meeting but not what we would do or say. Perhaps sensing that I wanted to observe Mr. van Weelden, Ronald engaged him in conversation. *So this was the oldest son of Suzanna Catharina de Graaf—"Princess*

Alexandra." Mr. van Weelden was sitting in an easy chair opposite me, a large coffee table between us, his head inclined toward Ronald, listening intently. He was immaculately dressed—slacks, white shirt, and tie. A full head of silver hair crowned a handsome, finely chiseled face. I had expected a rough tradesman, clad perhaps in dirty overalls. Antoon van Weelden, proprietor of a tiny appliance store in a remote rural village, dressed and comported himself in a manner that belied my presuppositions.

He crossed his legs, shifted in the chair, nodded silently. His movements, hand gestures, posture were those of a worldly, sophisticated gentleman. He was refined, but without affectation, unselfconsciously debonair.

The thought that he looked familiar crossed my mind, yet I dismissed it as foolish. He was certainly strikingly handsome, but the idea that he reminded me of someone evaporated as he turned in my direction and asked what I wanted to talk about.

I explained again who I was and said that in the course of researching a biography of Anastasia—one that she had asked me to write—I had come across the story of his mother. "Anastasia believed your mother was her sister. Do you know that?"

"Yes," he said softly, almost whispering, as he pointed to a small shelf mounted on a far wall. "Please, look." There sat a small color photograph of Anastasia with her favorite dog—Baby—taken outside the new barrack in Unterlengenhardt. I recognized it as one of Anastasia's favorite pictures. I had a copy of it in my own collection. He said that Anastasia had acknowledged him as her nephew and had sent presents—signed "Aunt Anastasia"—at Christmas and on other occasions. He admitted that he knew the cards had actually been signed by Mrs. Heydebrand.

As I recounted to him the research that had led me to his door, he leaned forward slightly, quiet, absorbing it all, studying me. When I finished, he asked Ronald to clarify a few points in Dutch. His English was good and he spoke it well, but at times he preferred to have Ronald translate for him. He said that journalists, usually Germans, had been coming to him throughout the twenty years since his mother's death, asking what he knew of her claim to be a Russian princess. He had asked all of them to leave. "Always I say, 'No comment.'" In a couple of instances, he had slammed the door in their faces. Never had he invited a journalist into his home. Not until today.

Mrs. van Weelden reappeared several times during the conversation and, although they were both ill at ease, she offered us coffee and tea. Whenever the bell on the shop door rang, she went out to take care of business.

Both of them were curious about what I knew; how far my research had gone; what I thought of Mrs. de Graaf; and what I intended to do with the information. But the shop bell rang more and more frequently, and it was apparent that this was not the time for a long discussion. They invited us to return after dinner, and we accepted.

"Well, James, what do you think?" Ronald asked, as we walked toward a restaurant. Dusk was beginning to settle over Doorn, bringing with it a renewed sense of excitement.

WE went back after dinner, and I spent the entire evening explaining how I had discovered the story of Mrs. de Graaf. I played the tape for them and said, "Okay, I've told you what I know. Tell me what *you* know."

Mr. van Weelden said he had been born in 1929 in a duplex mansion in Rotterdam, the only child of Mrs. de Graaf's marriage to Antoon van Weelden, for whom he was named. Mrs. de Graaf divorced Mr. van Weelden, Sr., on Christmas Eve, 1932. Her second marriage, to Jan Barend de Graaf, came in November of the following year. From this marriage Mr. van Weelden gained a half-brother and a set of twin half-sisters, one of whom died in 1955 at age ten. He also said that Mr. de Graaf was younger than Mrs. de Graaf; he was born on March 13, 1907, and died July 26, 1981, having outlived his wife by thirteen years.

Mr. van Weelden seemed well able to follow my remarks, yet hesitant to answer in English. He explained that he and his wife had lived in South Africa in the early 1950s, and that his mother had accompanied them there, so their comprehension of English was good.

The van Weeldens warmed to the idea of my book and, surprisingly, agreed to cooperate fully. To have made such inroads so

quickly after a faltering start was exhilarating, but I realized the need
to proceed slowly and to be very specific.

I wanted to be kindly in my approach toward the van Weeldens;
their previous experience with tough German journalists was something I knew I had to overcome. But Ronald had no such com-
punctions and took a different tack. He started out the skeptic but,
having read the chapter in *The File on the Tsar*, was closer to believing that Anastasia was genuine—although not at all ready to believe that the de Graaf story could be true. Abruptly, he turned to
Mr. van Weelden and asked, "Well, do you think your mother was
just crazy?"

I could not believe what I had heard. Mrs. van Weelden was sitting
on the sofa beside Ronald and stiffened.

Mr. van Weelden calmly turned toward him and said, "She was
my mother." That one simple response spoke volumes.

I could tell by the expression on his face, as well as the words he
used, that he was torn by the thought of finally discussing his
mother with strangers. This was a well-dressed, successful businessman, a pillar of his community, active in the church and in civic
affairs. And yet all his life he had lived under the cloud of being the
son of a woman who claimed to be the unknown child of the last czar
and czarina of Russia. Moreover, she had been a psychic faith healer
and local eccentric, albeit a well-loved and respected one. As we
talked, I could sense from the pained expression on his face the
anguish of someone who had long wondered who his ancestors really
were. Were his grandparents really Nicholas and Alexandra? Or
simply poor Dutch peasants?

As I concentrated on these notions, Ronald asked, "Who was your
maternal grandfather, the man who raised your mother?" Mr. van
Weelden said he knew little of Leendert Johannes Hemmes except
that he was a *piskijker*, or in English, a "piss-watcher."

"A *what*?" I said, leaning forward, sure that somehow I had misun-
derstood something in Ronald's translation of Mr. van Weelden's
remarks.

"A piss-watcher," Ronald replied very matter-of-factly. "Do you
not have them in America?"

I looked at all three of them but no one was smiling. A piss-
watcher? Ronald explained that in the late-nineteenth and early-

twentieth centuries, some people who claimed to have psychic powers also claimed that by using those powers to analyze the urine of a sick person, they could diagnose ailments.

It was difficult to hear this and keep a straight face. Then I thought, if a psychic "doctor" like Vachot were trying to find a home for a baby he needed to hide, what more logical candidate than another psychic doctor? It did not strain credulity at all to grasp that connection. Circumstantial though the link was, I was interested and asked Mr. van Weelden to tell us everything he could remember about his grandfather.

All he knew was that his great-grandfather, Leendert Johannes Hemmes, Sr., a sailor, had died at sea, leaving a wife and child in poverty. His son, Leendert, Jr., the future piss-watcher, was then four years old. He went to work at a very young age to support himself and his mother. Mr. van Weelden knew little more about the man he called his grandfather except that, a few years after the First World War, he had built a duplex mansion for himself in Rotterdam.

Ronald was now genuinely excited, and I left most of the questioning to him. He was intrigued by the notion that Mr. Hemmes had risen from destitute young man to wealthy piss-watcher without any apparent means. Obviously there were missing pieces to this puzzle.

I decided to make Mr. van Weelden an offer that I hoped he would not refuse: if he would cooperate with my research, I would guarantee him that, at my expense, Ronald and I and whoever else we needed to hire would undertake the most complete genealogical search of any family ever conducted in the Netherlands, one that would result in the most definitive answers possible about the history of the Hemmes family. He agreed.

Mr. van Weelden did not know whether his mother had been told that she was a Romanov before or after the death of Mr. Hemmes on January 21, 1949. He also could not recollect when it was that she related to him the story about being taken as a young child to Paris and Vienna by Mr. Hemmes. He did recall her saying that both trips were long and arduous, and that she remembered being taken into a room where a man seemed to be waiting, his sole purpose to see her for a few minutes. He also said she had believed that there was apparently no other reason for the trips, for after these brief meetings she and Mr. Hemmes immediately returned home to Rotterdam.

I then turned to the subject of his sister, whom Anastasia said she had met. His brow furrowed, he glanced at his wife nervously, and said he was sure Anastasia must have been mistaken; neither of his sisters could have met her because he was positive his mother herself did not meet Anastasia until about 1959.

This did not tally with Anastasia's tape-recorded recollections in which she was certain about having met Mrs. de Graaf and one of her daughters about 1950. Although many historians consider much that Anastasia had to say as speculative, they agree that her memory for dates was precise. I knew from my own research that her placement of dates could sometimes be off by a few months—a year at most—but never a decade. Yet Mr. van Weelden, even though his memory of some events in his mother's life was sketchy, seemed confident about this. I decided to leave this part of the conversation for later.

Ronald asked about the Russian jewelry that the late Baron van Nagell had reported seeing in Mrs. de Graaf's possession. Mr. van Weelden said that his half-sister, Jeanette, had a ring, a necklace, a gold-embroidered cloth, and a set of earthenware pottery which had belonged to his mother and were believed to be from the Russian imperial family.

I asked to see a photograph of Mrs. de Graaf, and Mr. van Weelden took a framed picture from a cupboard. It was a full-length portrait of a tall woman wearing a hat and standing next to a man. I examined it closely, but had no particular feeling that she looked like a Romanov.

Mrs. van Weelden was interested in reading Ronald's copy of the Dutch edition of *The File on the Tsar*, which he had with him and lent to her.

Almost as an afterthought I explained to Mr. van Weelden the different spellings of de Graaf I had encountered. He laughed and said that both were wrong. The correct spelling was "de Graaff."

I asked them about the cause of Mrs. de Graaff's death, and whether it was unexpected. She died of a heart attack, they said, and yes, it was very sudden.

Mr. van Weelden said that his mother was buried in the *Oude*

Algemene Begraafplaats (Old General Cemetery) in Doorn, and I asked his permission to visit her grave. The cemetery is open to the public, but I thought it only respectful to make the request. He drew a small map showing how to find the gravesite.

He then mentioned, almost as an embarrassed aside, that he and he wife had met Margda Boodts, the woman at Lake Como who claimed to be Olga, the Czar's eldest daughter.

Mrs. Boodts' claim has never been fully investigated; she remains a shadowy figure among Romanov pretenders because she shunned publicity and—unlike Anastasia—never allowed others to press her claim. Very little is known of her except that Prince Sigismund of Prussia was convinced of her authenticity and tried to raise funds for her financial support. I asked Mr. van Weelden when he had met her, where, and under what circumstances.

He glanced over at his wife and shrugged, "Well, it was a long time ago." He seemed very reluctant to discuss it, but I pressed him. Did he know whether Mrs. Boodts and Mrs. de Graaff had met?

He said that they had, and that Mrs. Boodts had accepted Mrs. de Graaff as her sister. I imagined what a meeting between these two women would have been like—two Romanov claimants seeing one another for the first time, wary, each trying to be convincing. Probably not unlike the scene in Guy Richards' book, *The Hunt for the Czar*, when Eugenia Smith, the false Anastasia, meets Michal Goleniewski, the false Czarevitch. Their hesitant, tearful meeting is a black comedy, the ludicrousness of which is underscored by the fact that, just one week following their "reunion," they denounced one another as impostors.

But Mr. van Weelden went on to say that "Olga" of Lake Como had accepted Mrs. de Graaff because she remembered the story of the fifth daughter from her girlhood in Russia; the Romanov sisters had discussed it among themselves. Anastasia, I recalled, had said much the same thing.

Mr. and Mrs. van Weelden had traveled to Lake Como, he implied, at the suggestion of his mother in order to satisfy their curiosity. Mrs. Boodts had welcomed them as her nephew and niece-in-law.

What did he think, I wanted to know.

He shrugged his shoulders again, this time dismissively, and said,

"How could I know whether she was genuine?" I looked at his wife for her reaction; it was the same. Indeed, neither of them were old enough or sufficiently aware of Romanov history to have been able to form a hard and fast—not to say an expert—opinion on the woman's claim.

As they continued talking, however, there was no mistaking their feelings about Anna Anderson. To them, she was the Grand Duchess Anastasia.

Having apparently made more headway in one day than all the other journalists in the preceding twenty years, I decided not to press the van Weeldens too hard. I had most of the information I had come for, and I asked them if they would see me again. We agreed to meet the following evening. As we left, Mr. van Weelden chuckled and told Ronald in Dutch that when we had first come into his store he thought we must be insurance salesmen.

On the bus back to the Driebergen-Zeist station, Ronald said that he was sure this meeting must have exceeded my boldest expectations, and I admitted that it had. At the same time I felt strongly that the only reason I had succeeded where everyone else had failed was because—in the van Weeldens' eyes, as well as in my own—I represented Anastasia.

I asked Ronald to initiate a search for the house in Rotterdam built by Mr. Hemmes; if it no longer existed, I hoped he could find municipal records pertaining to it.

THE next day, Wednesday, October 4, I again met Ronald at the Doorn bus stop. I had asked him to see to some kind of floral arrangement, one that I could lay on Mrs. de Graaff's grave. He approached with his arms full of flowers. Before leaving Utrecht that morning he had purchased a large bouquet for Mrs. van Weelden, and had asked a florist to make a suitable bouquet of violets, greenery, and purple-and-black ribbons for Mrs. de Graaff's grave.

We had no difficulty locating the de Graaff gravesite, plot number 12 at the Doorn cemetery. The marker was simple, and as I placed the flowers next to it, I said a silent prayer for this woman—whoever she was—that she might rest peacefully, because I felt that her children certainly were not at peace.

Ronald withdrew for a moment as I gazed down at the grave. I could not help wondering whether the moldering body in the soil beneath my feet was that of a crazy woman or the youngest daughter of the last Russian czar. Ronald did not seem to realize that the violets he had chosen were the Czarina's favorite flower. If Mrs. de Graaff really were "Princess Alexandra," they were an appropriate choice; if she were crazy or a fraud, it did not matter.

The visit to the grave seemed to confirm at least one thing. Mrs. Auclères wrote in *Figaro* that Mrs. de Graaff's birth date was May 5, 1905; the grave marker bore the same date. Yet Mrs. de Graaff claimed to have been born in 1903. Who, I wondered, had established the 1905 date? And how?

WE arrived at the van Weeldens at about 4 P.M. and were warmly received. One of the first things I asked Mr. van Weelden was about the discrepancy in his mother's birth date. Was she born in 1903 or 1905? He was not sure, but her birth had been registered by a midwife in Rotterdam in 1905.

Birth certificates were not issued back then. Instead, it was customary for the midwife to go to the city hall and report that she had delivered a child. It was a fairly casual process. Many births went unreported or were registered whenever the midwife found time to go to the city hall, filling in the particulars from memory. Still, even such lax recordkeeping techniques could not be made to account for a lapse of more than two years' time.

I also asked what he knew of Anastasia's recollection of the "masses and masses" of Russian paper rubles brought by Mrs. de Graaff to Unterlengenhardt. "One minute," he said, leaving the room.

He returned with a large stack of czarist-era paper rubles, bound by a thick rubber band, and laid them on the table before me. They could hardly be called "masses," I thought. The stack was three or four inches thick.

Milukoff had said, "Well, they're worthless now. You could make wallpaper out of them."

"Well, there aren't many here," I said. "I mean, not 'masses and masses.'"

Mr. van Weelden replied, "There are three children, we divided them when my mother died. We divided her things, and each of us took some of the rubles."

I had never seen a ruble, especially of the czarist-era, and wondered if Nicholas II's picture was on them, so I pulled off the rubber band and leafed through them. They were crisp, clean, and large, almost twice the size of an American dollar bill. Nicholas's likeness was not on them. Then I noticed something odd. The serial numbers were in sequential order.

How could Alexandra de Graaff, psychic faith healer, have acquired crisp new rubles with sequential serial numbers? She might have been able to buy "masses" of old rubles from numismatics dealers, because for years they were virtually worthless. But surely new ones with the serial numbers in order were not so easily obtained or traded.

I pointed this out to Mr. van Weelden and said, "What do you think? Do you have any knowledge of this?"

He shook his head. I could tell the question had troubled him for years, and that it troubled his wife, too. It must also disturb his children, I thought.

On the table next to me was a framed color photograph of a little boy, obviously their grandson. As I looked at it Mr. van Weelden followed my gaze.

"This troubles you, doesn't it?" I asked.

He did not answer.

"Is this your grandson?"

"Yes."

"This mystery has hung over you all of your life, hasn't it?"

"No. No, not all my life," he said. "I'm soon to be sixty, but I have known about it since the 1950s."

"A long time."

"Yes."

"Do you want resolution? Don't you want to know all that can be known?"

He did not verbally respond. He just looked terribly moved, and nodded his head.

"This is your grandson?" I asked again.

"Yes."

"So this cloud of uncertainty about your heritage has hung over you and your children. And now over this grandchild. Do you want him to grow up facing the same unanswered questions? Do you want your grandson to be your age and still be asking the questions we sit here and discuss?"

"No. I want to know the truth. I honestly don't know what the truth is, and I want to know it."

"Other people may come to you. . . ."

"They already have," he said. "For twenty years they've come, and I have not spoken with anyone but you."

"Will you promise to work with me and Ronald—who will remain here in the Netherlands—exclusively and confidentially, until we can come to some determination about your mother's story?"

He said, "Yes."

And I believed him.

He looked almost relieved when we left a little later, agreeing to return again.

MY last visit to the van Weeldens during this trip took place Tuesday, October 10. Ronald and I arrived at about 7:45 P.M., entering, as always, through the shop and the corridor leading into the living room. I went ahead, carrying my camera and tape recording equipment, but stopped midway across the room. On the couch, rising to greet me, was a beautiful woman about my age—a stranger, I knew, but I felt I had seen her somewhere before. My first thought was, what is one of their neighbors doing here? They knew we were coming. This is supposed to be private.

When Mr. van Weelden said, "This is my sister, Jeanette," I regarded her with disbelief—she looked not a little, not vaguely, but *exactly* like the Czarina Alexandra.

She wore a pair of stylish designer jeans, a blouse, and high-heeled shoes. And she was very nervous. Her English was not polished, which probably made her even more nervous. At first, the only thing I could say was, "You look just like the Czarina."

"Yes, I know," she said. "I look more like a Romanov than those people who live in Paris," referring to the family of the present pretender to the Romanov throne. I asked whether I could take their pictures. Mr. van Weelden was himself a photographer, and his work adorned the walls of his home. Jeanette was afraid to have her picture taken for publication, but I said I simply wanted a memento of the visit, so she and her brother consented.

I began our conversation by returning to the topic of the daughter Anastasia said she had met.

"Jeanette," I asked, "so you have met Anastasia?"

"No, never."

"So your sister who died had to have been the one to meet Anastasia?"

And they answered, "No. It is impossible that our mother could have gone to Germany before 1959. We know this."

"Well, just how much do you people know about your mother's involvement with Anastasia?"

"Everything," they answered.

They said Anastasia sent them presents on their birthdays. When Mr. van Weelden got married, Anastasia sent a wedding present with a little card signed, "Aunt Anastasia." But they were sure they had never received any communication from her prior to 1959. I accepted that and thought that it might demonstrate that Anastasia could be fallible about dates, after all.

We had a pleasant evening. I promised to continue our genealogical investigations and to remain in contact with them. Mr. van Weelden gave Ronald the address of the Hemmes house in Rotterdam. It is still standing and is a landmark because of its architectural style. Mr. van Weelden and Jeanette decided to drive us to the Driebergen-Zeist station where we would say goodbye.

Jeanette was as uncomfortable when English was spoken as I was when Dutch was spoken. There is little compatibility between the languages and I understood how she felt, so as we climbed out of the car I stood back as Ronald spoke with them in Dutch on my behalf.

I watched them talking in a tongue incomprehensible to me, heads nodding, smiling, and suddenly I felt somewhat detached from them. Jeanette, illuminated by the lights of her brother's car, was beautiful, almost ethereal. Mr. van Weelden, courtly and distinguished, was shaking Ronald's hand. *Who are they*, I wondered. *They do not even know themselves*. What a terrible thing it must be not to know where you come from, to question your past, your genes, and wonder if your mother was mad, a fraud—or an imperial princess.

Whatever Mrs. de Graaff had been, she had endowed her children with a legacy of uncertainty and mystery. Standing by the Driebergen-Zeist station, I promised myself—and Anastasia—to do whatever it took to help bring these people out from the darkness of their heritage, to help them find the peace of mind they had never known.

IV.

Missing Pieces

ON THE PLANE returning to Washington, I looked out of the window at the deep ocean below and thought of Baroness Monica Miltitz and the other Anthroposophists who had surrounded Anastasia. They had believed that the continent of Atlantis had sunk beneath these waves; I wondered whether the psychic Mrs. de Graaff shared the belief.

Alexandra de Graaff. I might have learned more about her than any other journalist, but it was still not enough. To my mind, she was like a half-finished jigsaw puzzle, the missing pieces as elusive as the lost continent. Yet she had been a living human being—a fact— just a few years ago. I regretted the necessity of returning to the States, for surely, I felt, I would learn nothing more about her there. Still, I planned to travel back to the Netherlands within a few months in order to fulfill my promise to the van Weeldens.

ONCE back home, I wanted to resume my research on Anastasia, in addition to discovering whatever I could about Mrs. de Graaff. Isaac

Don Levine had been important to Anastasia, and even though he had been dead for several years, I wanted to talk to his widow Ruth, who lived in Washington. I thought her memories of her husband's thorough investigations of the Anastasia case might be enlightening and informative. I called her in November, not long after returning from the Netherlands, and she agreed to see me sometime later.

On December 5, I called again and asked whether I could visit her sometime that month, but she said that her schedule was full until the first week of January 1990. When I explained that I was planning to return to the Netherlands the second week of January, however, she became suddenly more interested.

She seemed to falter somewhat and then said, "Why are you going to the Netherlands? Is this about—Could it possibly be about the fifth daughter?"

"Oh, you mean Alexandra de Graaff? Yes, it is. I went there a couple of months ago, found her children in Doorn, and have their complete cooperation. I'm going back next month."

"You know about this?"

"Yes, ma'am, I do," I said.

"Can you come on Friday?" she asked.

"Well, you don't have the time to talk—"

"Can you come this Friday?"

That Friday brought the biggest snowstorm of the winter. Washington, D.C., was immobilized. The appointment was at 1 P.M., so I started through the storm an hour and a half early. I rang her bell at exactly 1 P.M. She answered the door saying, "I can't believe you're on time in this weather." We went inside.

"Tell me what you know," she said.

"More important, Mrs. Levine, tell me what *you* know."

She had on her dining room table a photograph of Alexandra de Graaff seated alone in a garden. A note on the back, in the handwriting of Baroness Miltitz, read "Alexandra taken by A. N. [Anastasia Nicolaievna] 24th of June 1952." There was another picture of Mrs. de Graaff with several of Anastasia's old lady friends at Unterlengenhardt. On the back was an undated note to Gleb Botkin written and signed by Baroness Miltitz. The note said that Anastasia had been examined the previous evening by Professor

Reche, the anthropologist who testified before the German court in 1960. Reche had been preparing his testimony for a year prior to his court appearance, so it was easy to deduce that the Baroness's note was written in 1959 or so.

Mrs. Levine also had a photocopy of a Russian newspaper, published in St. Petersburg in 1903, announcing that the Czarina had recently suffered a miscarriage.

She explained that her husband had considered writing a book about Anastasia, even though he had never published any of his conclusions. Part of the research he had conducted, however, led to an investigation of the story of Mrs. de Graaff. Mrs. Levine had traveled with him to Doorn in order to interview the Dutch woman. Her only memory of the meeting was one of visiting "a tall woman." She concluded by saying that her husband had decided that the matter was too dubious to pursue.

ABOUT a week later I was looking through the Milukoff albums again, and as I turned a page too quickly, two postcards of Wiesbaden slipped out from behind a large photograph, somewhere they should not have been. I recalled that once before, when discovering the postcard signed by Hermine, I had come across a unique and previously unknown document that had also been placed inexplicably behind one of the pictures in the album. I remembered my confusion at that time; there was no logical reason for its being there—especially when I knew Milukoff to be an otherwise thorough organizer and cataloger of Anastasia's property. Now, I wondered whether these two instances of misplaced—perhaps hidden—records had something more in common. Were the two postcards in front of me simply haphazardly put behind a picture and later forgotten? Or had someone not wanted them found, perhaps because they might speak about events and circumstances that had previously been the subject of mere rumor or speculation? The latter possibility continued to plague me as I read the text of the postcards now before me.

The message side of each card was filled with the unmistakable spidery handwriting of Prince Frederick, addressing "Madame Mutabor," his pet name for Anastasia:

Dear Madame Mutabor! Paris 5. VII 67
As you know, you asked me to visit Alexandra to clarify different
points. So I did.

At first I followed for some days an invitation from Alexis to accompany him in his short holidays. We were in the Palatinat and Wiesbaden visited Mrs. Dassel, and had been with her and Madame Olala
with Baron Gienanths, who had been awfully nice.

After 2 days Paris I had been for myself in Doorn—I mean without
Alexis—and before that in Delfzijl with Dr. Bottema. I could explain
Alexandra different mistakes by her then she was very kind. "This so
called *DAUGHTER*" The lady in question is *kind, straightforward* and
intelligent.

You will love her.

Her blue eyes are similar with yours.

She is modest, natural and (without wanting) impressive! In some
weeks Alexandra will come and introduce you to each other, so that
you are able to judge yourself the best thing to do.

From the story-line the Prince was following and the lack of a
closing phrase and signature, I knew that a third or concluding card
was missing. Nevertheless, the abbreviated version in front of me
did reveal that the Prince had just returned from a meeting in Doorn
with Mrs. de Graaff. The cards were dated 1967. He asked Anastasia to agree to meet her. Interestingly, Mrs. de Graaff must not
have confided to the Prince the fact that she already knew Anastasia.
I wondered about the passage where the Prince says that Mrs.
de Graaff was not very knowledgeable about Romanov history, that
she made mistakes. Had she done so deliberately to avoid appearing
to be too well-schooled on the subject?

The dated photograph in the Levine collection of Mrs. de Graaff
is conclusive proof that she was in Germany as early as 1952—
something she had obviously not told her children. The postcards
show that some 15 years after the two women had first met, Anastasia still had not confided her friendship with Mrs. de Graaff to
Prince Frederick. Clearly, neither had told the people most knowl-

edgeable about her life that they had already been in contact. Maybe that would explain why the postcards were secreted away in the album. A question to be considered again later.

GREG Rittenhouse of Los Angeles, California, was the only person to have seen some of the Milukoff collection before I bought it. He purchased a few books from Milukoff, and inside one of these was a letter written by Mrs. de Graaff to Anastasia in 1959. Milukoff had packed Anastasia's belongings in Unterlengenhardt and shipped them to Charlottesville, and at her request, he kept for himself those articles she no longer wanted. The book Rittenhouse bought was one such item.

When he became aware of my research, Rittenhouse gave the de Graaff letter to me.

It reads:

Doorn 2 June 1959

My Dear Anastasia Nikolayevna

How are you? I hope it is alright. I am very very happy that you have Miss Lamerden [sic]. You see my Darling that the Lord make good everything for you. I go today to Amsterdam for the flag of the family Romanov, he is ready 11 June. I give you him if a birthday present of me. When you have birthday my dear Anastasia you have back the flag of the family Romanov and also a cup of the tea set of the family Romanov that you have seen it when I was with you. My dear Anastasia I will give you everything that brings sunshine on your life. Have you receipt my postcard? You have 5 June birthday of Russia. I go to the church for you and pray to the Lord and ask Him make please that Miss Lamerden stay with my dear Anastasia and 18 June have you the present. Good bye my Darling a kiss for you God save and help you. Many greeting for your beautiful dogs and cats and many greeting for Miss Lamerden. You tell her please that I am happy she is with you my dear. When I come to Unterlengenhardt, I bring a beautiful present for these.

I love you
Alexandra

Judged only by the subject matter, the document would appear to be unimportant. There is nothing immediately compelling in this page-and-a-half of English-language script, except that it clearly reads best as part of an ongoing correspondence. Certainly it is not the kind of letter someone like Mrs. de Graaff would have sent to someone like Anastasia after having known one another for only a short time. It is written in a friendly tone and demonstrates a level of intimacy and knowledge of Anastasia's circumstances that would indicate they had known one another for a period longer than commonly believed.

I was also struck by a passage in the de Graaff letter indicating that Miss Lamerdin not only knew of Mrs. de Graaff, but had met her sometime earlier than June 1959. My mind went back to Anastasia's first discussion with Milukoff about Mrs. de Graaff. She had lowered her voice at one point in the conversation and said, "I am always afraid Miss Lamerdin could be on the ladder, listening. Yes, this is my greatest fear, that this woman could suddenly be on the ladder, and listening."

Why would Anastasia not want Miss Lamerdin to overhear a recollection of facts she already knew? We know that Anastasia lost faith in Miss Lamerdin in the mid-1960s and began to believe she was spying on her for Baroness Miltitz, from whom Anastasia was already estranged. The only probable conclusion is that Anastasia was afraid Miss Lamerdin would tell Baroness Miltitz that she, Anastasia, had confided the de Graaff story to Milukoff and that he had recorded it.

IN my garage, I had stacked the crates and box which held the Milukoff collection when I purchased it. They already had been emptied of what I knew were the important materials. All that remained were miscellaneous items, such as Anastasia's Lady Sunbeam electric razor. One afternoon, while searching for something else in the garage, I accidentally knocked over one of the Milukoff crates. As it hit the concrete floor, some papers flew out—ones I had never seen before.

I examined the crate more closely and realized that it had a false bottom in which Milukoff had stashed the papers now lying on my garage floor. My mind raced back to my discoveries of Hermine's postcard and the correspondence from Prince Frederick regarding

Mrs. de Graaff. In the first instance, it was perhaps reasonable to accept that the postcard from the self-styled Kaiserin had been mistakenly or hurriedly stuck behind a photograph in the album with the intention of finding another, more suitable place for it later. When I found the two postcards from Prince Frederick stashed away in a similar manner, however, my willingness to accept coincidence began to erode and was replaced by a growing suspicion that someone had tried to deliberately conceal important evidence. Whatever belief in happenstance I still retained was immediately erased by discovery of the false-bottomed crate. For some reason, Milukoff or Anastasia—or both—had not wanted certain information revealed. However, luckily for me, they did not—or for some reason could not—go so far as to destroy the evidence itself.

I concentrated again on the mess on the floor. As I picked up the papers and began to leaf through them, I noticed they were photocopies of Gleb Botkin's correspondence. The words "Alexandra de Graaff" jumped from one of the pages in my hand.

It was a letter on "Church of Aphrodite" stationery, dated August 24, 1965, written by Botkin to Milukoff. This is what I read:

> The story about a supposed youngest daughter of the Sovereigns is a very odd and dubious one. Some years ago, a Dutch woman by the name of Alexandra de Graaf, appeared in Unterlengenhardt and told Grand Duchess Anastasia the story she has now told you. Dr. Leverkuehn made some investigations, but found that the whole thing was too complicated, too doubtful and, on top of everything else, seemed to be connected with various shady characters involved in criminal activities. Isaac Don Levine visited Mme de Graaf and came to the conclusion that the whole thing was a hoax.

I knew that Botkin was correct about the visit by Mr. Levine. However, I was surprised to read his report that Leverkuehn had investigated the story of Mrs. de Graaff. More questionable was the suggestion that she was ever involved with criminal elements.

The letter continued:

> Personally, I am not entirely convinced of it and, judging by her photographs, Alexandra de Graaf bears a considerable resemblance to the Grand Duchess Tatiana. *I do think that it would be very interesting to*

get that weird affair thoroughly investigated, but have no idea how it could be done. Unhappily, I do not have and never did have Mme de Graaf's address and am no longer in touch with Mr. Levine. A person who does have the address is Baroness von Miltitz. [emphasis added]

I carefully looked through the remaining papers and discovered another letter written less than a year later, May 3, 1966, perhaps after Milukoff visited Mrs. de Graaff in Doorn. Botkin again addressed the issue of her claim: "I do think that she herself is convinced of it [her identity as a Romanov child]. Also, so far, her behavior has been quite correct."

Obviously, Botkin did think there might be something credible to Mrs. de Graaff's story, contrary to the impression I had received from his daughter. I knew by the time he wrote these letters that Baroness Miltitz had sent him the two photographs Mrs. Levine had showed me. Apparently, Botkin had given them to Levine, hoping to encourage him to investigate further. I was also intrigued to read that Botkin, solely on the basis of two photographs, remarked on the resemblance between Mrs. de Graaff and the Grand Duchess Tatiana. Only a few months before, Jeanette, Mrs. de Graaff's daughter, had told me people often said she looked like Tatiana.

V.

"She has the Romanov Eyes"

WHILE I WAS accumulating material in the States, Ronald was busy conducting the exhaustive genealogical research I had promised the van Weeldens. My work proved easier than his. He dug through the files of the Land Registry Office in Rotterdam, the Central Bureau for Genealogy in The Hague, the Archives of the Municipality of Rotterdam, the Archive of the Town Hall of Rotterdam, records in the municipal building at Doorn, the *Bibliotheek der Rijksuniversiteit Utrecht*, the *Rijksarchief Utrecht*, and myriad other sources to reconstruct the lives of the Hemmes'. Everything the van Weeldens had told us about Mr. Hemmes, Jr., was true; he was a "piss-watcher," or an analytical chemist, as he had preferred to call it.

Ronald's research in the various Dutch archives bore other fruit. He consulted the nineteenth-century ledger books of the city of Rotterdam and sent me photocopies of the pertinent pages, together with English translations and summaries.

I had asked him to conduct a complete genealogical search of the Hemmes family, tracing back two generations in order to learn as much as he could about Mr. Hemmes, the "piss-watcher." He sent photocopies of several folios, large ledger pages full of entries in a flowing script written with quill pens.

From the *1837 A Folio 166, Kaart 12, Number 683*, an entry on March 28, 1837, said that on that day Johannes Hemmes, a forty-one year old patternmaker living at Weelengang 1 250 in Rotterdam, appeared before the registrar of births declaring that the day before, March 27, his wife, Cornelia du Chatinier, gave birth to a son, Leendert Johannes, at 5 P.M. Witnesses of the registration were Joannes Brugman, a thirty-eight-year-old cabinetmaker, living at Oppert L 152, and Mattheus van Houten, thirty-three, also a cabinet-maker, residing at Goudseweg N 184. Both were residents of Rotterdam.

This was the birth registration of the father of the "piss-watcher."

From the *1868 B Folio 76, Kaart 13, Number 340*, an entry on May 13, 1868 registered the marriage of Leendert Johannes Hemmes, now age thirty-one, to Adriana de Lezenne Coulander, twenty-five. Mr. Hemmes listed his profession as "fireman on a steamship." His wife was the daughter of Cornelis de Lezenne Coulander, a house-painter, and Kuijntje IJzerdraad, of Rotterdam.

Five years later, the couple had a son, Leendert Johannes Hemmes, Junior, and his birth was registered in *F Folio 81, Kaart 74, Number 4280*, on October 23, 1874. It says that at 4 A.M. on the morning of October 23, the baby was born at the home of his parents "in the Warmoesserstraat," delivered by a midwife, Dina Cornelia Drost, "living in the Breedstraat," who registered the birth herself later that day. The registration was witnessed by two city clerks.

These entries show that the Hemmes family was prompt in setting down in the official records the major events of their lives. From the registration of the marriage of Leendert Hemmes, Sr., to Adriana Coulander, we see where the name Adriana entered the family. Later that name would be passed on to Mrs. de Graaff's younger sister. Ronald located no Suzanna or Catharina in the records of the Hemmes and Coulander families.

Four years after the birth of his son, Leendert Hemmes, Sr., "fireman on a steamship," lost his life at sea, just as his grandson, Mr. van Weelden, had said. Here is the registration of death in its entirety.

1878 E Folio 42 Kaart 52, no. 4423 31 December 1878

(DEATH OF LEENDERT JOHANNES HEMMES)

Certified copy of an entry of death from the municipality VLAARDINGEN.

On the 2nd November 1878 has been recovered from the Northsea (on 52° 20 min. north latitude and 2° 25 min. east longitude), the body of LEENDERT JOHANNES HEMMES, born in Rotterdam, 41 years old, engineer, living in Rotterdam, husband of Adriana de Lezenne Coulander (without profession), living in Rotterdam, son of Johannes Hemmes and Johanna Cornelia du Chatinier (both deceased).

The registrar of deaths of the municipality Vlaardingen declares that the above mentioned summary is in accordance with the register of deaths of the municipality Vlaardingen, drawn up and signed on the 26th November 1878. Registered in the register of death of the municipality Rotterdam on the 31st December 1878.

We were unable to access shipping line records to discover the name of the ship on which Mr. Hemmes served at the time of his death. Nor could we determine the exact date the ship was lost. His body was found floating in the North Sea, off the coast of England, not far from the current auto ferry route between Felixstowe and Hoek van Holland.

It was this tragic demise that left the thirty-five year old Adriana Hemmes a widow with a four-year-old son, Leendert, Jr. Mrs. Hemmes had always been listed as "without profession," and she was, according to her grandson, Mr. van Weelden, left destitute.

She went to work. We do not know what she did, but her son was put to work as soon as he was able.

RONALD visited Rotterdam several times, and drove out to Mr. Hemmes' duplex mansion at Straatweg 5/7 in the Hillegersberg section of the city. According to records in the Land Registry Office, Mr. Hemmes sold the property in the early 1930s for reasons that have never been clear. The house has been well maintained, however, and is still known as the "Villa Suzanna-Adriana," named for the two Hemmes daughters.

The question of Mrs. de Graaff's birthdate was another subject of Ronald's research. According to the Archives of the Municipality of Rotterdam, where records more than twenty years old are stored, Mrs. de Graaff's birth was registered on May 5, 1905, by a midwife, Grietje Weezenarr, who listed herself as "aged 34." Miss Weezenarr testified that the girl was born "in a house at the Oostvarkensweg," and that the father was "without profession." Dutch privacy laws prevent the release of the original twentieth-century birth registration records, and only certified typewritten transcripts can be obtained. This "ridiculous embargo," as Ronald termed it, will not be lifted until the beginning of the next century. In the *Figaro* article, Mrs. Auclères had referred to a "civil state ruling" regarding Mrs. de Graaff's birthdate. Despite our best efforts, we could find neither any record of such a proceeding nor anyone who was familiar with this type of proceeding. It is possible that when she applied for a passport, the midwife registration was not considered sufficient proof of birth and a civil authentification of the birthdate may have been required.

Although an original copy of her birth registration was unavailable, Ronald did manage to acquire a copy of Mrs. de Graaff's record during his visit to the Central Bureau for Genealogy in the Hague. It provides a detailed and interesting record of her trip to South Africa with her son and daughter-in-law, documenting that she left the Netherlands on August 27, 1952, and returned February 2, 1954.

Another line of research uncovered Mrs. de Graaff's younger sister, Adriana, living as a complete recluse in Mijdrecht, in the same house where Mr. Hemmes had died. She never accepted her sister's claim and the controversy surrounding Mrs. de Graaff was a source of alienation between them. I saw no point in pursuing this line of investigation.

MRS. van Weelden gave Ronald a copy of an interview with Mrs. de Graaff which had appeared in the largest circulation Dutch newspaper, *The Telegraph*, October 2, 1968—only seven weeks before she died. Unlike the small piece published in *Figaro* the next day, this article covered an entire page of *The Telegraph* and was accompanied by photographs. It was her first public statement claiming to be "Princess Alexandra" and created a sensation when it appeared, because it also contained statements by Anastasia confirming her belief that Mrs. de Graaff was, indeed, her sister. Ronald photocopied the article and began translating it into English.

Although we were stockpiling documentation on both sides of the Atlantic, Mrs. de Graaff herself remained an elusive figure in my mind. Apart from the few photographs I had seen and her letter to Anastasia, I could not think of her in sharp focus until I received Ronald's translation of the *Telegraph* article.

The article, titled "She Has the Romanov Eyes," began with a quote:

I am the child who is not in a single history book, because three months after her birth she was 'banished'. . . . Russia demanded an heir to the throne. . . . There were already four girls. . . . The reason for my repudiation: I was a girl and not a boy. There were already four girls. Russia demanded an heir to the throne. I was born on 1 September 1903, my only brother Czarevitch Alexei, on 30 July 1904.

This was "Princess Alexandra" speaking for herself. Unearthed from the files of a Dutch newspaper after twenty years, Mrs. de Graaff was telling her story as she wished it to be known. This interview was the first time she had spoken publicly about her claim. It had created a rash of publicity, until she died shortly after its appearance, taking the truth—whatever it was—with her. European journalists had clamored to do follow-up stories, but Mr. van Weelden, speaking for his family as the oldest child, had refused comment.

The author of the article noted, "This new Romanov mystery has been known by a relatively small circle of insiders for a long time. This group, consisting of mostly noble persons who have done their utmost for decades to prove the authenticity of Anastasia, was confronted with it ten years ago. At that time Mrs. de Graaff visited Anastasia for the first time in her life in Unterlengenhardt, Germany."

It was apparent that Anastasia and Mrs. de Graaff had agreed to say that they had first met about 1958 or 1959. We can only speculate why, but the reason may have had something to do with Anastasia's almost obsessive preoccupation with security and assassination.

The article continues with the information that *The Telegraph* had sent special correspondent Jan Rups to Charlottesville to interview Anastasia specifically about Mrs. de Graaff's claim, and quoted her: "I do accept Mrs. Suzanna Catharina de Graaff-Hemmes as my sister Grand Duchess Alexandra. She is the fifth daughter of the Czar and Czarina, but the world didn't know of her existence." Anastasia also admitted that she was struck by Mrs. de Graaff's close resemblance to her mother and sisters.

The Telegraph also interviewed Jaap Bottema from Delfzijl, whom the article described as a "Romanov specialist and historian." Bottema said that Mrs. de Graaff's eyes were characteristic of the Czarina's family and, "as an academic," he considered the story of Mrs. de Graaff "very well possible." He seemed to further accept her story because of the rubles. Bottema stated that Kurt Vermehren, one of Anastasia's attorneys, had seen Mrs. de Graaff's rubles and had identified them as "real Court rubles." He went on to explain that in Russia, "there were two sorts of rubles. The Court rubles were used only by the diplomatic service abroad and by members of the imperial family." Over the course of the next year I spoke with numismatics experts in the United States and Europe and was unable to verify the existence of "Court rubles."

Finally, Bottema is quoted as saying that he knew that Anastasia had accepted Mrs. de Graaff as " 'one of our family.' " From Prince Frederick's two-page note to Anastasia written in 1967 after his visit to Doorn, we know that he consulted with Jaap Bottema during the same trip, apparently to solicit his opinion on the case. The Prince may have told Bottema then that Anastasia recognized Mrs. de Graaff as her sister.

Now came a statement from Mrs. de Graaff I found riveting: "In 1937 my foster father falteringly told me the true story. After much hesitation, I finally got all my Romanov possessions: the five million rubles, a cloth belonging to the crown jewels, which Anastasia immediately recognized, much china and many trinkets. He told me that he had always received hush money to hide the truth from me as long as possible."

Her explanation of the "false" pregnancy was that the Czarina knew she had delivered a healthy baby to full-term and then had allowed the child to be taken away by Vachot. We can only assume that is what Mr. Hemmes told her. We know, of course, that Anastasia did not subscribe to this theory and believed that Vachot had "stolen the child."

Completely in line with her psychic beliefs, Mrs. de Graaff was also quoted as saying she had believed for years that "Providence" had reunited her with her sister.

A few months later my research uncovered two additional articles from Germany. One was an article about Mrs. de Graaff's story, entitled "I Am Anastasia's Sister," published in *The New Review*, October 27, 1968. The other was her obituary, which appeared in the November 27, 1968, issue of *The Stuttgarter*.

The New Review article was of most immediate interest to me. Here was another published report—in yet another language—about her claim to be the lost daughter of the Czar. It was the third of three that had appeared in as many weeks.

I obtained a copy of both articles. I was disappointed when I finally read *The New Review* story. In many ways, it simply restated the information contained in *The Telegraph* piece.

The Stuttgarter obituary provided no additional information. Published two days after her death in Doorn, it gave a short, straightforward report of her death, included a brief recounting of her claim, and linked her with Anna Anderson and Margda Boodts. The report began, however, by describing her death as "surprising."

VI.

"And stays a mystery"

I ASKED Baron Ulrich Gienanth, who had handled Anastasia's financial affairs in the 1950s, what he knew about Mrs. de Graaff's claim. He was careful to point out that his own knowledge of the de Graaff case was limited to what Baroness Miltitz had told him. She had assured him that she was the only person who knew the story. Based on my own knowledge, as well as the documentation I had amassed, I was certain Baroness Miltitz had patently lied to Baron Gienanth. The list of people aware of the de Graaff story was almost a *Who's Who* of Anastasia's later life: Gertrude Lamerdin, Gleb Botkin, Alexis Milukoff, Isaac Don and Ruth Levine, Paul Lever-kuehn, Annemarie Mutius, Adele Heydebrand, Prince Frederick, Dominique Auclères, Jack Manahan, Ian Lilburn, and Annaliese Thomasius, among others. Her existence and her claim to be the Czar's youngest daughter were known to many people. It is evident from Prince Frederick's postcards to Anastasia, however, that Anastasia carefully concealed what she knew to be the whole story and limited what information she did reveal on a need-to-know basis. Evidently no one was privy to the entire de Graaff saga, yet from my research, I had learned that everyone apparently thought that someone else had thoroughly investigated the matter.

The story—or people's perceptions of it—was replete with contradictions and inconsistencies. I compiled a chronology of what the various participants asserted had happened, and when.

> 1950 *Anastasia and Mrs. Heydebrand meet Mrs. de Graaff and her daughter in Unterlengenhardt.* Anastasia reported the meeting to Milukoff in 1965—noting that "here [in Unterlengenhardt]

446

the ladies know" the story. Miss Mutius, Mrs. Heydebrand's sister, remembered the visit, as well.

1952 June 24—*Mrs. de Graaff visits Unterlengenhardt.* A photograph of Mrs. de Graaff in the Levine collection was labeled, in the handwriting of Baroness Miltitz, as having been taken by Anastasia on this date.

August 27—*Mrs. de Graaff departs for South Africa.* She was accompanied by Mr. and Mrs. van Weelden, who were emigrating to live and work there.

1954 *Mrs. de Graaff and the van Weeldens return to the Netherlands, February 2, and take up residence in Doorn.*

1958–9 *Baroness Miltitz says this is the time period when first contact between Anastasia and Mrs. de Graaff occurs.* The Baroness told Baron Gienanth that only she knew the story of Mrs. de Graaff.

1959 June 2—*Mrs. de Graaff writes an English-language letter to Anastasia dated June 2, 1959.* The letter's contents indicated that a relationship between the two women had been established some time ago.

June 5—*Photograph from the Levine collection showing Mrs. de Graaff with a group of people in Unterlengenhardt—including Baroness Miltitz—is sent to Gleb Botkin by the Baroness.* A note on the back of the photograph, written by the Baroness, was dated June 5 but omitted the year. The contents of the note, however, showed that it was written in 1959.

Mrs. de Graaff's children fix this year as the earliest possible time when their mother could have made contact with Anastasia. Jeanette, one of the de Graaff twins born in 1944, said she did not go to Unterlengenhardt. The other twin, Adriana, known as "Addy," died April 16, 1955, at age 10.

1965 August 15—*Anastasia first discusses Mrs. de Graaff with Milukoff.* He recorded the conversation and wrote to Gleb Botkin, asking for his opinion of the de Graaff story.

August 24—*Botkin answers Milukoff's letter:* "I do think that it would be very interesting to get that weird affair thoroughly investigated. . . ."

1966 *Milukoff visits Mrs. de Graaff and tells Anastasia that she cannot speak English or German.*

1967 *Prince Frederick visits Mrs. de Graaff and writes to Anastasia suggesting she meet her.* Mrs. de Graaff gave the Prince no indication that she already knew Anastasia.

1968 July 14—*Anastasia and Milukoff travel to Charlottesville, Virginia, to visit Gleb Botkin and Jack Manahan.* Subsequently, Anastasia told her friends in Europe that she would remain in the United States indefinitely.

October 2—*First published report of Mrs. de Graaff's claim to be the Czar's fifth daughter appears.* The interview with *The Telegraph* indicated that Mrs. de Graaff first visited Unterlengenhardt "ten years ago."

October 3—Figaro *publishes second article reporting Mrs. de Graaff's claim.* Dominique Auclères wrote that Mrs. de Graaff "presented herself about eight years ago."

October 27—The New Review *article, "I Am Anastasia's Sister," is published.*

November 25—Mrs. de Graaff dies suddenly in Doorn. Anastasia and Jack Manahan received an eighteen-page letter from her and learned by telegram of her death on this date.

November 27—*Obituary in* The Stuttgarter *characterizes Mrs. de Graaff's death as "surprising."*

MY promise to the children of Alexandra de Graaff was twofold: to conduct an all-out investigation of their ancestors and to arrive at a positive conclusion about their mother's story, one way or another. Ronald Trüm and I delivered on the first part of my promise by searching archives, libraries, and private collections on two continents. The materials we discovered did not, however, provide sufficient information to arrive at a definitive answer regarding Mrs. de Graaff's claim. Three important potential sources that might help resolve this issue have been closed to us: the Royal Dutch Archives; the Royal Danish Archives; and the Soviet State Archives in the Kremlin. Ironically, the source that may become available earliest is the Soviet archive, maintained all these years by the successors to the Bolsheviks.

From what I have discovered in archival materials, from documents heretofore unknown, and through anecdotes, two mysteries pertaining to Mrs. de Graaff stand out. The first is whether there ever was a fifth daughter of the Czar. The second is the nature and length of the relationship between Anastasia and the Dutch faith healer.

Let us look first at the story of the fifth daughter. In 1901, the Czar and Czarina visited Paris and were introduced to Philippe Vachot, the psychic doctor from Lyon who promised that he could predict and determine the gender of an unborn child. At that time, the Czarina was again pregnant and the imperial couple desperately needed to produce a male heir. Vachot was engaged to return to Russia as part of the court and began prescribing treatments for Alexandra. On the 5th of June that year, another daughter, Anastasia, was born. Vachot's explanation for his failed promise was that he had been consulted too late in the pregnancy.

In 1903, newspapers in St. Petersburg and across Western Europe published stories announcing that the Czarina was pregnant yet again. On September 1, she "suffered a pain," collapsed and was incommunicado for a long period. Medical doctors, when finally allowed to examine her, reported that she had not been pregnant, and the story circulated that she had only experienced a "false" or "hysterical" pregnancy. Irina Youssoupov and Convoy (whom we have never been able to identify) both reported that they had heard of a daughter named Alexandra who had "died a child." On July 30, 1904, the Czarina, still under Vachot's care, delivered to the Romanov dynasty a male heir, Alexis. Not long thereafter Vachot, rich in praise and money, left Russia.

Anastasia told Milukoff she believed that "Dr. Philippe" had delivered a healthy female child. She could not believe that her parents would willingly give up a child of whatever sex. She thought Vachot had drugged the Czarina so that "she could not know what was round her happening," and spirited the child away in order to preserve his standing at court. Anastasia also remembered talking with her sisters about the possibility of their mother's having given birth to another daughter who disappeared.

On the other hand, Mrs. de Graaff claimed that Vachot had removed her from Russia because her parents "banished" her, realizing the birth of another daughter would be a political embarrassment and would destabilize the throne. She claimed to have received her dowry money, five million paper rubles, in 1912.

Mrs. de Graaff further said that she had been taken as a child on visits to meet a mysterious man in Paris and Vienna, apparently solely for the purpose of being viewed. The implication is that the man was a representative of the Czar, sent to confirm her well-being. Mrs. de Graaff also claimed to have met the Czar and his oldest daughter, Olga, in Vienna before the First World War, but I have found no record of any such trip made by the Czar. All the while, she said, she was being tutored in one of the Dutch royal palaces.

It is known that Leendert Hemmes, Jr., the man Anastasia called Mrs. de Graaff's "adopted father," was an impoverished psychic "piss-watcher" who suddenly and inexplicably managed to build himself an expensive duplex mansion in Rotterdam in 1919. According to Mrs. de Graaff, her adoptive father had been overseeing her dowry money and had been paid hush money to conceal her identity. These funds might well have been used to build a grand house for Mr. Hemmes and his alleged daughter following the fall of the Russian empire in 1917 and the Czar's death in 1918. We do know that Mr. Hemmes was an inept businessman who eventually lost his properties and died almost as destitute as he had been after his father drowned at sea. The paper rubles now belonging to Mrs. de Graaff's children provide an intriguing postscript to this part of her story.

Clearly, based on such sporadic evidence and lacking access to pertinent archival material, a researcher cannot corroborate the story of a fifth child, let alone determine whether such a child was stolen from or shamefully banished by its imperial parents. From Anastasia's history, we know research into this period can be at best a mixture of accepted fact and practiced deduction. There remain some compelling circumstances that make Mrs. de Graaff's claim most intriguing. The vagaries surrounding the reports of the Czarina's false pregnancy of 1903 and the appearance later of a woman of approximately the right age with a resemblance to the Russian imperial family, and in possession of some remarkable artifacts, are in themselves enough to raise interest in the story. When coupled with the tales told by Mrs. de Graaff about her childhood, these unsolved riddles at the very least point to the fascinating possibility that the Dutch woman was telling the truth. Certainly we know that she wholeheartedly believed her story and, without doubt, Anastasia accepted its authenticity, to the point of protectively concealing the full details about her relationship with Mrs. de Graaff.

Let us now turn to the issues of how long the two women had known one another and why they were so secretive about their friendship. According to Anastasia, in her 1965 tape-recorded conversations with Alexis Milukoff, Alexandra de Graaff arrived at Unterlengenhardt in 1950 and spoke to Adele Heydebrand, seeking an audience with Anastasia. Anastasia remembered that she was accompanied by a young daughter and claimed to be the child of the "false" or "hysterical" pregnancy. As proof, the Dutch woman brought with her "masses and masses" of czarist-era rubles and "other precious goods that were from Russia." Mrs. Heydebrand's sister, Annemarie Mutius, remembered the meeting as well.

On June 24, 1952, Anastasia, in keeping with her lifelong hobby of photographing friends and relatives, took a picture of Mrs. de Graaff sitting in the garden of the old barrack at Unterlengenhardt. The original print of this photograph is in the Isaac Don Levine collection.

On August 27, just three months later, Mrs. de Graaff departed the Netherlands for South Africa, accompanied by her oldest son, Antoon van Weelden, and his wife. They returned on February 2, 1954, when Mrs. de Graaff took up residence in Doorn.

There is no reason to believe that either woman was inaccurate in setting the time when they first met as being prior to 1952. Both obviously chose to keep this information confidential, however, and some of the Anastasians aided in this conspiracy.

Baroness Miltitz told Baron Ulrich Gienanth that Mrs. de Graaff first made contact with Anastasia in 1959. Certainly the photograph taken on June 5 of that year, showing Mrs. de Graaff with a group of people at Unterlengenhardt, places her in Germany during this period. In addition, 1959 is the year that she told her children that she had visited Anastasia.

Several other facts, however, demonstrate that the Baroness simply was not telling the whole truth. In 1959, she sent Gleb Botkin the picture of Mrs. de Graaff taken by Anastasia at Unterlengen-hardt in 1952. The Baroness's accounting of the meeting between Anastasia and Mrs. de Graaff is further suspect because she claims to have been the only person to have met Mrs. de Graaff, when the 1959 photograph itself clearly shows the Dutch woman surrounded by other people. This picture further confirms Anastasia's statement to Milukoff that "here [in Unterlengenhardt] the ladies know." Finally, the intimate nature of the English-language letter of Mrs. de Graaff to Anastasia, dated June 2, 1959, seems to belie the Baroness's assertions.

Thus 1959 seems to have been a year when Anastasia and Mrs. de Graaff brought more people into their confidence, including the Dutch woman's children. Perhaps it is for this reason that they determined to allow everyone else to believe it was the beginning of their relationship.

It was not until August 15, 1965, when Anastasia began working on a book collaboration, that she revealed to Milukoff the story of the fifth daughter and Mrs. de Graaff's claim. Milukoff immediately wrote to Gleb Botkin for his reaction, and within two weeks, Botkin answered, saying that he was not convinced that the story was a hoax.

Later, Milukoff visited Mrs. de Graaff at Anastasia's suggestion and reported to her that Mrs. de Graaff could not speak English or German, despite the fact that she had previously written to Anastasia in English. In July 1967, Prince Frederick, holder of Anastasia's power of attorney, also visited Mrs. de Graaff in Doorn at Anastasia's suggestion. He wrote to her suggesting she meet Mrs. de Graaff, although it is obvious from the evidence of his note that Mrs. de Graaff did not tell the Prince she knew Anastasia.

All of these personages were at times among those closest to Anastasia, a fact that must have been known to her correspondent Mrs. de Graaff. Still, both women chose to keep the true nature of their long friendship hidden. Why?

In July 1968, Anastasia traveled with Milukoff to the United States, took up residence in Virginia, and made it clear to her friends in Europe that she did not plan to return. Just two and a half months later, two articles appeared, the first publicized reports of Mrs. de Graaff's claim.

Quite possibly, Mrs. de Graaff decided to reveal herself at this time because she felt that Anastasia would not be returning to Europe. Whatever criticism or ridicule she might suffer, Anastasia was now somewhat immunized from the derision and skepticism that had plagued her through all the long years of court trials in Europe. Perhaps she thought Anastasia would suffer the least now from the revelation of her claim than at any other time since they had first met. She might also have felt that the recent investigative visits made by Prince Frederick and Milukoff meant that her story was becoming more widely known. If so, she likely would have wanted to avoid the manipulations previously suffered by Anastasia, who had been unable to control her own fate. Moreover, she probably never knew Anastasia had told Milukoff in 1965 that the two women had met each other "sixteen or seventeen years ago, for he had dismissed the remark almost immediately." That would explain why the newspaper reports stated that she had met Anastasia eight or ten years previously.

We can also only postulate why Anastasia waited so long to acknowledge her relationship with Mrs. de Graaff and endorse the Alexandra story. As we have seen, Anastasia lived from 1918 until the very day of her death in fear of imminent assassination, especially by poisoning. She felt deeply that Mrs. de Graaff could face the same danger, at one point on a Milukoff tape telling Jack she "would like that some experts see what she [Alexandra] is, and how she looks, before maybe she is killed . . . she is in danger." Certainly she would never do anything on her own to put the Dutch woman in peril. Once contacted by the press to comment on Mrs. de Graaff's claim, however, it would have been uncharacteristic for Anastasia to deny what she felt to be the truth.

Mrs. de Graaff passed away of a sudden heart attack on November 25, 1968, in Doorn. She is buried, next to her daughter Addy and second husband, in a quiet shaded cemetery on the edge of town. Loved by her family, renowned in her own village, she did not reveal her story to the world until shortly before her unexpected death, robbing historians of the possibility of further, more thorough investigation. We can all speculate, but in the end, Anastasia's words spurring this quest remain most appropriate. Whether Suzanna Catharina de Graaff was merely a deluded psychic or another lost Russian princess "stays a mystery."

Epilogue

Anastasia screamed in vain.

—MICK JAGGER and KEITH RICHARDS
"Sympathy for the Devil"

WHETHER ALEXANDRA DE GRAAFF WAS a genuine Romanov is a question that may never be completely answered. I have presented the evidence I have been able to gather. It is to others, if they so desire, to continue the research and attempt to determine the dispositive truth behind her claim to be the fifth daughter of the Czar.

There can be no doubt, though, about Anastasia. For seven decades writers and historians have allowed the confusion and deception created by some of her relatives to cloud their perceptions or influence their interpretations. Such duplicity continues even today. In 1987 the British government established a Russian Compensation Fund, administered by the accounting firm of Price Waterhouse, to compensate holders of pre-revolutionary czarist bonds. Reports in London newspapers quoted spokesmen for the Fund indicating that the money had come from Czar Nicholas II's "multi-million dollar London bank account," whose existence had been denied for more than sixty years. In addition, the Danish royal family still refuses to make public the papers collected by Ambassador Herluf Zahle. No purpose can be served in Queen Margarethe II's refusal to release these crucial documents.

Faced with these continued efforts to suppress evidence, no one was ever able to present a clear exposition of the *facts* that supported Anastasia's authenticity. Instead, her supporters—Gleb included—used selected details to bolster her case. Her detractors simply lied. Regardless of whether their intentions were admirable or despicable, their image of her became more important than the real person she was. That is the crucial aspect I have tried to illustrate in fulfilling her request that I present her true story.

What has been lost in previous portraits of Anastasia is the fact that she was not simply a personality. Above all, she was not the fairy tale princess popularized and commercialized for nearly sixty years. The Anastasia I knew was charming, delicate. Like a child, she enjoyed toys and taking long rides with Jack in one of his old cars. She loved her cats and dogs but never exerted any discipline over them. They were companions who deserved what she had never been given—freedom and unconditional love. Anastasia appreciated receiving gifts, although their monetary value was of no consequence to her. Much more important was that someone gave her a present she could enjoy—a paperback mystery, a set of crayons or water-color paints, a mechanical gadget, or simply an old magazine clipping of a photograph of her parents.

At the same time, she was an animated conversationalist with a brilliant wit. Anastasia could lucidly explain the most intricate details of her life and the events that had shaped it. The stories she told were fascinating and full of irony. She was equally engaging when she and Jack would begin reciting the genealogies of European royal families. She had clearly come to accept the course of her life, even if she did not understand why it had all gone so wrong.

I also saw Anastasia when she was angry and unreasonably demanding. She could suddenly erupt with shouts and screams after hours of complete silence. These outbursts were never predictable. Nor were they readily understandable. The ones I witnessed were directed at Jack, the man who obviously—in his own way—loved his wife.

As I would learn after a much more thorough reading of the Anastasia literature, the quiescent woman who had shown me nothing but the greatest kindness was only one manifestation of an extremely complex personality. I saw enough of her treatment of Jack to understand what Harriet Rathlef must have endured. Harriet, like Jack, had an unyielding devotion to Anastasia. In both cases the devotion was so strong that even her vitriolic and irrational tirades could not drive them away. That was certainly not the case with Xenia Leeds or Annie Burr Jennings. When she became abusive towards them, they simply abandoned her.

That Anastasia was so self-absorbed and demanding should surprise no one. She had been born the daughter of the wealthiest man in the history of the world. She was a rebellious child, cosseted and raised to believe that she was entitled to such a life. A fusillade of bullets was all it took to shatter this safe and secure existence.

The loss of her parents and the protection they had provided was the most devastating event in her life. After being dragged from the filthy waters of a Berlin canal, her one desire had been to somehow recapture that sense of belonging. The surviving members of her family knowingly denied her solace. What the world tried to refuse her was something much more fundamental. The words of Baron Curt Stackelberg, her last legal advocate, remain the most eloquent: "The right to identity . . . is included in the basic rights of human dignity and the free development of the personality. . . ."

Each of us takes for granted our right to an identity. Anastasia was no different. She was ever secure in her own self, even if the world sought to remake her into something she was not. She accepted the fact that she had come to live as an old woman in a country and a time far removed from her childhood. More importantly, she understood how it had happened. The one question that neither she, nor any of us, could ever answer is why.

Anastasia would often despair that God had forsaken, or forgotten, her. She was not a deeply religious woman, but was of a highly spiritual nature. Although she never fully accepted the tenets of the Anthroposophical movement, its mystical aspects appealed to her. She believed fervently in reincarnation, so much so that even the pruning of a tree was to her mind the mutilation of a living soul. Anastasia must also have felt some connection to those portions of Anthroposophy that emphasized the spiritual nature of Russia. Yet no set of beliefs could ever erase her greatest agony. She could no longer comprehend or find comfort in the God of her childhood.

Her father, Czar Nicholas II, was regarded by his people as God's personal representative. Czarina Alexandra, her mother, had been a fanatic convert to Russian Orthodoxy. As a youth, Anastasia had been imbued with a belief that God was omniscient and omnipotent. Alexandra turned to mysticism, trusting that God had answered her prayers by sending Philippe Vachot and Rasputin. Anastasia believed He had seen her mother's tribulations and had sent these two "friends" to guide her. Her mother had been deserving and had, therefore, received the blessing of God's assistance.

Anastasia had not. To her mind, the real mystery of her life was not her identity, but why God had abandoned her.

It is a question no biographer can answer.

Appendices

IN THE HIGH COURT OF JUSTICE

The Principal Probate Registry

BE IT KNOWN that HER IMPERIAL HIGHNESS THE GRAND
DUCHESS XENIA ALEXANDROVNA (otherwise XENIA ALEX-
ANDROVANA) OF RUSSIA of Wilderness House Hampton Court
Twickenham Middlesex Widow

died there on the 20th day of April 1960

AND BE IT FURTHER KNOWN that at the date hereunder written
the last Will and Testament with a Codicil thereto

(a copy whereof is hereunder annexed) of the said deceased was proved and
registered in the Principal Probate Registry of the High Court of Justice and
that Administration of all the estate which by law devolved to and vests in
the personal representative of the said deceased was granted by the
aforesaid Court to

    Baring Brothers & Co. Limited of 8
    Bishopsgate in the City of London and Count
    Wladimir Kleinmichel of 52 Woodstock
    Road Golders Green London banker the
    executors named in the said will

And it is hereby certified that an Inland Revenue affidavit has been delivered wherein it is shown that the gross value of the said estate in Great
Britain (exclusive of what the said deceased may have been possessed of or
entitled to as a trustee and not beneficially) amounts to £119467-1-10 and
that the net value of the estate amounts to £117272-16-2

And it is further certified that it appears by a receipt signed by an Inland Revenue on the said affidavit that £58870-19-0 on account of estate duty and interest on such duty has been paid.

Dated the 25th day of August 1960

Registrar

Extracted by Lewis & Lewis and Gisborne & Co.
10.11.12 Holy Place
Holborn London E.C.1.

THIS IS THE LAST WILL
—of me—

HER IMPERIAL HIGHNESS THE GRAND DUCHESS XENIA ALEXANDROVNA OF RUSSIA now domiciled in England REVOKING all former Wills,

1. I APPOINT BARING BROTHERS & CO. LIMITED OF 8 Bishopsgate in the City of London and COUNT WLADIMIR KLEINMICHEL of 52 Woodstock Road Golders Green in the County of London to be the EXECUTORS and TRUSTEES of this my Will (hereinafter called "my Trustees" which expression shall include every other the trustees or trustee for the time being hereof).

2. I GIVE the following pecuniary legacies free of duty:
   (a) to Count Wladimir Kleinmichel if he shall prove my Will the sum of Five hundred pounds.
   (b) To each of the following persons namely the children of my sons the Princes Andrew Nikita Dimitri Rostislav and Vassili of Russia the children of my daughter Princess Irina Youssoupoff and my grandson Michael (the son of my son Prince Theodor of Russia) who are living at my death and attain the age of Twenty one years or being female marry under that age the sum of One thousand pounds.

3. I DEVISE AND BEQUEATH all my real and personal property whatsoever and wheresoever of or to which I shall be possessed or

462

entitled at my death or over which I shall then have a general power of appointment or disposition by Will (including the property comprised in a Settlement dated the Thirty first day of December One thousand nine hundred and twenty nine and made between myself of the one part and The Right Honourable Sir Frederick Ponsonby G.C.B., G.C.V.O., His Excellency Peter Bark G.C.V.O., and Edward Robert Peacock of the other part and all entailed property of which I can dispose by Will except property hereby or by any Codicil hereto disposed of) to my Trustees UPON TRUST to sell call in collect and convert into money the said real and personal property at such time or times and in such manner as they shall think fit (but as to reversionary property not until it falls into possession unless it shall appear to my Trustees that an earlier sale would be beneficial) with power to postpone the sale calling in or conversion of the whole or any part or parts thereof (including leaseholds or other property of a terminable hazardous or wasting nature) during such period as they shall think proper and to retain the same or any part thereof in its actual form of investment without being responsible for loss and without being liable especially to account therefor I DIRECT that the income of such of the same premises as for the time being remain unsold (including the income of property subsequently required for the payment of my funeral and testamentary expenses and debts and the legacies and duties in payment whereof the proceeds of such sale calling in and conversion on are hereinafter directed to be applied) shall from my death be applied as if the same were income arising from investment hereinafter directed to be made of the proceeds of sale thereof and that no reversionary or other property shall be treated as producing income for the purposes of this my Will.

4. MY Trustees shall out of the moneys to arise from the sale calling in and conversion of or forming part of my real and personal property pay my funeral and testamentary expenses (including all estate duty leviable at my death in respect of my residuary estate) and debts and legacies given by this my Will or any Codicil hereto and all death duties and other moneys which under or by virtue of any direction or bequest free of duty contained in this my Will or any Codicil hereto are payable out of my general personal estate.

5. MY Trustees shall stand possessed of the residue of the said moneys and the investments for the time being representing the same and of such part of my estate as shall for the time being remain unsold and unconverted (all of which premises are herein called "the Trust Fund") UPON TRUST for my children living at my death if more than one in equal

shares PROVIDED NEVERTHELESS (a) if any such child (other than my son Prince Theodor) shall die in my lifetime leaving a wife husband or issue living at my death my Trustees shall hold the share of the Trust Fund to which such deceased child of mine would have been entitled if living at my death upon trust as to the income of one half of such share for such wife or husband (as the case may be) upon protective trusts during her or his life and subject thereto as to capital and income for all or any the issue living at my death of such deceased child of mine who being male shall attain the age of Twenty one years or being female marry under the age if more than one in equal shares but so that the children of any deceased child of mine shall take equally between them only the share which their parent would have taken if living at my death and (b) if my son Prince Theodor of Russia shall die in my lifetime leaving my said grandson Michael living at my death my Trustees shall hold the share of the Trust Fund to which my son Prince Theodor of Russia would have been entitled if living at my death upon trust as to capital and income for my said grandson Michael.

6. TRUST moneys may be invested in the purchase of or upon the security of such investments of whatsoever nature and wheresoever situate (including the purchase of any interest in land) whether or not authorised for the investment of trust moneys and whether involving liability or not or upon such personal credit with or without security as my Trustees in their absolute discretion think fit to the intent that my Trustees shall have the same full and unrestricted powers of investing and transposing investments in all respects as if they were absolutely entitled thereto beneficially.

7. MY Trustees may at any time or times in their sole and absolute discretion appropriate any part of my estate in its then actual condition or state of investment in or towards satisfaction of any legacy or share in my estate whether or not the same be settled.

8. THE Statutory powers of maintenance and advancement shall be applicable hereto save that my Trustees shall in exercising their power of maintenance not be bound to have regard to what other income is available for that purpose and that the money payable or applicable for the advancement or benefit of any person shall not be limited as provided in proviso (a) Section 32 (1) of the Trustee Act 1925.

9. I DECLARE that any income received after the date of my death in respect of any period previous thereto shall be treated as income and not as capital.

10. ANY Executor or Trustee hereof (i) being a Corporation may in all matters including the exercise of any discretionary or other powers set by its proper officer or officers (ii) whether an individual or a Corporation instead of acting personally or by its own officer or officers (as the case may be) may employ and pay out of the Trust Funds a Solicitor Broker Banker or other Agent to transact all or any business required to be done in the execution or carrying out of the Trusts hereof, (iii) being a Corporation engaged in any business may be employed and may act in the transaction of any such business as aforesaid on terms and conditions as to remuneration and otherwise similar to those on which it is in the habit of transacting similar business on behalf of its ordinary clients or customers and shall be paid out of my Estate or the Trust premises or some part thereof for its services in the transaction of such business in the same manner as if not being an Executor or a Trustee it had been employed in the ordinary course of business for a client or customer for whom it was not a Trustee and in addition to any such remuneration as aforesaid such Corporation shall be paid out of my Estate or the Trust premises or some part thereof as remuneration free from all duties for its general services as a Trustee according to its usual scale of fees in force at the date of its acceptance of the Executorship and/or Trusteeship.

11. MY Trustees shall have full and absolute power and authority to determine out of what fund or funds any such remuneration as aforesaid shall be paid and whether out of income or capital and in what manner the value of my Estate or the trust funds or any part thereof shall be ascertained for the purpose of fixing such remuneration and any such determination shall be binding and conclusive against all parties claiming hereunder.

IN WITNESS whereof I have hereunto set my hand this 22nd day of September One Thousand nine hundred and forty six.

SIGNED by the above named	} (Signed "Xenia")
Testatrix in the presence of }	
both of us and by both of us in }	
her presence:-	}

I, XENIA ALEXANDROVANA HER IMPERIAL HIGH-
NESS THE GRAND DUCHESS OF RUSSIA now domiciled in
England DECLARE this to be a FIRST CODICIL to my Will
which bears date the Twentysecond day of September One thousand nine hundred and fortysix.

1. IN Clause 2 (b) of my said Will ONE THOUSAND POUNDS
   shall be read as TWO HUNDRED AND FIFTY POUNDS. I
   regret having to make this reduction which has been necessitated
   on account of the great increase in Estate Duty since I made my
   original Will.

2. I GIVE a legacy of FIVE HUNDRED POUNDS free of all
   duties to MISS VERA MASLENIKOFF of Wilderness House,
   Hampton Court, Surrey, as a token of my gratitude to her for her
   devoted care given to me over very many years past.

   IN ALL OTHER respects I confirm my said Will.

   IN WITNESS whereof I have hereunto set my hand this
   Fifteenth day of March One thousand nine hundred and fif-
   tythree.

SIGNED by the above named	}	(Signed "Xenia")
Testatrix as and for a	}	
First Codicil to her last	}	
Will in the presence of		}
both of us and by both of	}	
us in her presence: -		}

Note: This document is reprinted exactly as it was issued; mistakes of fact and punctuation remain uncorrected.

From:

FOR IMMEDIATE RELEASE   Robert Speller & Sons, Publishers, Inc.
10 East 23rd Street
New York, New York 10010
Tel. MU 2-4599

To clarify contradictory stories being circulated in official, social and financial circles, Robert Speller & Sons, book publishers of New York City, confirmed today that they have refused to make any further royalty payments to Eugenia Drabek Smetisko (Eugenia Smith), and have demanded the payment of monies expended by them at her request in futile efforts to prove her alleged identity, together with the return of all royalties previously paid to her for her book *The Autobiography of H. I. H. the Grand Duchess Anastasia Nicholaevna of Russia*, published by them in November 1963, and widely promoted that year in the magazines *Life* and *Quick*.

The Spellers have denounced Mrs. Smetisko as an impostor and have accused her of fraudulently mispresenting herself to be the Grand Duchess Anastasia Nicholaevna, fourth daughter of the late Emperor Nicholas II and the late Empress Alexandra Feodorovna of Russia.

The case of Smetisko vs. Speller is docketed for trial before a jury in New York State Supreme Court for early fall. This will mark the first time that an alleged Romanoff claimant will make a personal appearance in any court anywhere. Although Mrs. Anna Anderson has also been claiming to be the Grand Duchess Anastasia Nicholaevna and has had her suit in the German courts for many years she has never made a personal appearance in the courtroom. On June 10th the Hamburg Supreme Court postponed making any decision in her case for a period of at least a year.

Mrs. Smetisko will be asked to prove that she is not Eugenia Drabek Smetisko as her United States naturalization papers, granted in 1928, state, and then prove that she is the Grand Duchess Anastasia Nicholaevna of Russia as she alleges. In her U.S. naturalization papers she stated that she was born in 1899 in Bukovina. The real Grand Duchess Anastasia Nicholaevna was born in 1901 in Peterhof, Russia. Other information stated in her U.S. naturalization papers is inconsistent with her alleged Romanoff identity.

Mrs. Smetisko has charged that the Speller firm "invented" another heir

467

to the throne, the Czarevich Aleksei Nicholaevich, only son of the Emperor and Empress, in the person of Colonel Michael Goleniewski, former Polish army intelligence officer, who fled from Poland in 1960 through the aid of the Central Intelligence Agency and who was brought to the United States in 1961 in company with his German-born fiancee, Irmgard Margareta Kampf. The couple was married on March 7, 1961 in a civil ceremony in Virginia. A religious ceremony uniting the colonel, under the name of Aleksei Nicholaevich Romanoff, and his German-born wife, was held on September 30, 1964 in New York, at which Father Georgi Grabbe, proto-presbyter of the Holy Synod of the Russian Orthodox Church Outside Russia officiated. Among those present at the wedding ceremony were Mrs. Luise Henschel Kampf and Mrs. Margarete Kampf Mische, whom the colonel alleges are respectively the Grand Duchesses Olga and Tatiana Nicholaevni. Some months later Father Georgi Grabbe denied that he had recognized the colonel as the Czarevich. The colonel also alleges that Janina Goleniewska is the Grand Duchess Maria Nicholaevna, and that she is at present held in isolation by private persons.

Contrary to Mrs. Smetisko's statement that the Speller firm "invented" the colonel as the Czarevich, she herself introduced him as her brother the Czarevich and recognized him as such before witnesses on December 31, 1963. Their mutual recognition scene was recorded on tape. Some months later Mrs. Smetisko circulated stories that he was not the Czarevich, and repeated that she and only she survived the Ekaterinburg massacre of the Russian Imperial Family on July 16/17, 1918.

Mrs. Smetisko will be asked to prove in the trial whose "invention" he is. The Colonel categorically denies that he is the "invention" of the Speller firm, and likewise denies the charges "that he is the creation of the American secret service", which was printed on January 14, 1965 in *Red Star*, the official organ of the Soviet Ministry of Defense, Moscow. The Central Intelligence Agency has declined to make any official comment as to the identity of the mysterious colonel.

The Colonel will be subpoenaed as a witness in the trial, and will be asked to prove that there was no massacre and that the entire family of the Emperor escaped to exile as he has printed in various advertisements in the press both in the United States and Germany.

Mrs. Smetisko will have to prove that she not only is the Grand Duchess Anastasia Nicholaevna as she alleges but also that she is the only survivor of the massacre as she claimed in an affidavit dated April 1, 1963, and in her book.

It will be recalled that *Life* Magazine published a lengthy cover story about Mrs. Smetisko in October 1963, in which both positive and negative arguments were stated with a preponderance of the latter. *Life* published a similar article about Mrs. Anderson in February 1955, with a preponderance on the positive side. Mrs. Anderson's career has been widely publicized through the play and two film versions, *"Anastasia"* as well as in several books including her so-called autobiography, *"I Am Anastasia"*, published in 1957. Her story will once again be presented to the public in the musical comedy *"Anya"*, to be produced in the fall on Broadway.

Many promises were made by Mrs. Smetisko to the Speller firm that she would produce documents that would legally prove that she is the Grand Duchess Anastasia Nicholaevna as she claims. More than two years have elapsed since her promises were made and she has failed to produce any such documents. In fact, all evidence uncovered to date concerning Mrs. Smetisko and her activities are negative, including handwriting, anthropological and personal identification. Mrs. Smetisko stated in her April 1, 1963 affidavit that she had no living descendants, yet subsequently told members of the Speller firm as well as many other people, and produced handwritten statements that she has a daughter, a son-in-law, and two granddaughters, all living in Rumania, and produced photographs of her daughter, her son-in-law, and her elder granddaughter to prove it. Her son-in-law is a Judge in Communist Rumania. In addition she has produced photographs of her own alleged husband, who is, interestingly enough, not the man depicted and quoted in *Life* as never having known anybody named Eugenia, anybody from Chicago, or as ever been married before his present marriage.

Mrs. Smetisko also stated in her April 1, 1963 affidavit that her main purpose in publishing the fact of her claimed identity was to counteract the claims of Mrs. Anna Anderson. However, in spite of her promises to do so, she has failed to bring suit against Mrs. Anderson, and in spite of all the publicity Mrs. Anderson has failed to bring suit against Mrs. Smetisko. Neither of the two Anastasia claimants has brought suit against Colonel Goleniewski or any other claimant. All the Romanoff relatives closely related to the Emperor and most the Hesse relatives of the Empress have denounced Mrs. Anderson as an impostor. Although Mrs. Anderson is suing the German House of Hesse for her rights as the alleged sole living heir to the Romanoff fortune held in trust in a German bank, neither Mrs. Smetisko nor Colonel Goleniewski nor any other claimant has done so.

Russians have always followed the position allegedly taken in the Nicholas Sokoloff investigation of the Ekaterinburg assassination that all members of the Russian Imperial Family and their entourage perished, and have urged that the matter be settled once and for all in a legal decision concerning the various claimants to Romanoff identity. No doubt a variety of Romanoff buffs and "experts" will be given an opportunity to present their testimony in the case. Much evidence of Mrs. Smetisko's fraudulent deceptions and misrepresentations have come to light, thereby prompting the Speller firm to denounce her as an impostor and to ask the New York State Supreme Court to establish her legal identity, be it Smetisko or Romanoff.

New York, July 9, 1965

DRAMATIC ADAPTATIONS

1928   film: *Clothes Make the Woman*; Tiffany-Stahl Studios, Hollywood

          cast: Eve Southern as Anastasia; Walter Pidgeon

1953   play: *Anastasia*,* by Marcelle Maurette and Guy Bolton; produced by Laurence Olivier; London, England

          cast: Mary Keeridge as Anastasia; Helen Haye as the Dowager Czarina; Guy Bolton

1954   play: *Anastasia*, by Maurette and Bolton; produced by Elaine Perry; New York

          cast: Viveca Lindfors as Anastasia; Eugenie Leontovich as the Dowager Czarina

1956   film: *Anastasia*, based on Maurette-Bolton; screenplay by Arthur Laurents

          cast: Ingrid Bergman (Academy Award for Best Actress) as Anastasia; Helen Hayes as the Dowager Czarina; Yul Brynner

1956   film: *Anastasia, Die letzte Zarentochter* ("*Is Anna Anderson Anastasia?*") Distributed by Cameo

          cast: Lilli Palmer as Anastasia (German Federal Film Prize for Best Actress); Turhan Bey as Gleb Botkin

1965   musical: *Anya*, based on Maurette-Bolton, with themes based on Rachmaninov music; New York

          cast: Constance Towers as Anastasia; Lillian Gish as the Dowager Czarina

1967   television: *Anastasia*, adapted from Maurette-Bolton; "Hallmark Hall of Fame" special broadcast

          cast: Julie Harris as Anastasia; Lynn Fontanne as the Dowager Czarina

1967   ballet: *Anastasia* by Kenneth MacMillan

          cast: Lynn Seymour as Anastasia

---

* The Maurette-Bolton play has also been performed in Spain, Holland, Finland, France, Austria, Germany, Canada, Australia, Mexico, Brazil, Argentina, Kenya, Turkey, Greece, Italy, Portugal, Denmark, Norway, Sweden, and Belgium.

1972 film: *Nicholas and Alexandra*, screenplay by James Goldman; produced by Sam Spiegel

 cast: Fiona Fullerton as Anastasia

1982 play: *I, Anastasia*, adapted from Maurette-Bolton; Miami, Florida

1982 play: *I Am Who I Am*, by Royce Ryton; New York

1986 television: *Anastasia: The Mystery of Anna*, NBC mini-series

 cast: Amy Irving as Anastasia; Olivia de Havilland as the Dowager Czarina; Rex Harrison as Grand Duke Cyril

1988 play: *Suddenly Among Strangers*, by James Dupont; unpublished, not yet produced

1989 ballet: *Anastasia*, by Sir Kenneth MacMillan, a one-act adaptation of the 1967 production; London Festival Ballet at the Metropolitan Opera House, New York

 cast: Lynn Seymour as Anastasia

1989 video: *The Last Night of Rasputin*, written and produced by Eleanor Antin

 cast: Lisa Welti as Anastasia; Luke Theodore Morrison as Rasputin

1991 play: *The Anastasia File*, by Royce Ryton; London

 cast: Jo Steele as Anastasia

DISCOGRAPHY

1956 *Anastasia*, sung by Pat Boone. Orchestra and Chorus directed by Billy Vaughn. Lyrics by Paul Francis Webster. Music by Alfred Newman. Dot Records: MW-9405.

1956 *Anastasia*, Twentieth Century-Fox movie soundtrack album. Composed by Alfred Newman. Decca Records: DL 8460.

> Side One: *Anastasia-Paris/Russian Easter/Paris-Gaity Bar/Self-destruction/ Who Am I/The Troika/The Beginning/Riberhouse Marsch-Marche de Bataille/ The Tivoli-The Sleeping Princess.*
> Side Two: *The Meeting-Recognition/Valse/Frustration/Wildfeuer Polka/Anastasia Waltz/End Title-Anastasia.*

1965 *Anya*, original Broadway cast soundtrack album. Music and Lyrics by Robert Wright and George Forrest, based on themes by Serge Rachmaninov. United Artist Records: UAS 5133.

> Side One: *Choral Prelude: Anya/A Song From Somewhere/Vodka, Vodka!/So Proud/Homeward/Snowflakes & Sweethearts: The Snowbird Song/Six Palaces/ Hand in Hand.*
> Side Two: *On That Day/This is My Kind of Love/Reprise: On That Day/That Prelude!/A Quiet Land/Here Tonight, Tomorrow Where?/Leben Sie Wohl/If This is Goodbye/Little Hands/All Hail the Empress/Choral Finale: Anya.*

1977 *Anastasia*, written and performed by Elliott Murphy, with the Boys Choir of St. Paul's Cathedral, London. From the album, *Just a Story from America.* Columbia Records: PC 34653.

1986 *Anastasia: The Mystery of Anna*, original television soundtrack album. Composed and conducted by Laurence Rosenthal. Southern Cross Records: SCRS 1015.

> Side One: *Main Title, Pt. 1/The Ballroom/To Siberia/The Sled; Ekaterinburg/ Family Only; The Cellar/Berlin Bridge/Confronting Sophie/After the Interview/ The Railroad Car.*
> Side Two: *Main Title, Pt. 2; Faces From the Past/The Denial/Shopping Spree/ The Romanoffs/At the Astor/Russian Antiques/Darya Says No/The Luncheonette; Back to Europe; Anna and Erich.*

Source Notes

In addition to the published works cited in the Bibliography, I have used unpublished materials gathered from various private collections.

Jaap Bottema supplied me, via Ronald Trüm, with an original copy of a fifty-page memoir of Anastasia's youth dictated in German by her to Baroness Monica Miltitz, 1948. The Baroness entitled the manuscript: "*Die Kindheitserinnerungen der Grossfürstin Anastasia von Russland. Diktat an Monica, Freifrau von Miltitz, im Jahre 1948*" ("The Childhood Remembrances of the Grand Duchess Anastasia of Russia. Dictated to Baroness Monica Miltitz in the Year 1948"). It has never been translated from the original German, and has never been published in full.

Marina Botkin Schweitzer provided me unlimited access to Gleb Botkin's archive. Mrs. Schweitzer imposed no restrictions or stipulations upon my use of her father's papers.

Andrew Hartsook and Greg Rittenhouse supplemented the Schweitzer material with hundreds of letters written by Gleb Botkin, Nina Chavchavadze (Xenia Leeds's sister), Prince Frederick, Baroness Miltitz, Peter Kurth, Gertrude Lamerdin, and others. Mr. Hartsook also provided me access to many photographs and pieces of memorabilia.

Baron Ulrich Gienanth generously supplied materials from the Anastasia Archives at Neuwied Castle, including two unpublished essays about Anastasia written by Baroness Miltitz.

Anastasia disavowed publication of the purported "autobiography," *I Am Anastasia*, because it was compiled without her knowledge or participation. However, during a conversation in 1976, she reviewed for me several passages which she said were factually correct and which accurately represented her feelings on certain matters. At her

suggestion, I have quoted those passages, but only sparingly, in deference to her dislike of the work in general.

The surviving cousins of Jack Manahan kindly allowed use of materials they obtained from Jack's library after his death.

Gretchen Haskin let me read her unpublished non-fiction work,
Rescuing the Czar.

Without doubt, the most important unpublished material used in
Anastasia: The Lost Princess is that collected by Alexis Milukoff, primarily his recorded conversations with Anastasia. The tapes include more
than one hundred hours of dialogue, enough for several volumes of
"Conversations with Anastasia." I have attempted to use the material
contained on the tapes judiciously by quoting statements that aug-
ment the basic chronology of her life and reflect Anastasia's long-held
beliefs. It is my intention to donate the tapes, as well as other materials
from my collection, to a permanent repository at an appropriate time.

There are four major collections of Anastasia materials: the uncatalogued papers of Edward Huntington Fallows (including some of
Harriet Rathlef's papers) at the Houghton Library at Harvard University; the Anastasia Archives at Neuwied Castle in Germany, whose
primary focus is the question of her identity, as contained in the
papers of Prince Frederick; the Ian Lilburn collection in London,
consisting of the official records of the German court cases, as well as
other documents and photographs collected by Anastasia and Prince
Frederick; and my own archive, which I believe is the largest.

BOOK ONE: *The Court of the Double Eagle*

The Russian legend about the double-headed eagle at the future site of
the Kremlin appears in many English-language texts, including Alexandrov's *The Kremlin*. The assassination of Alexander II is recounted in
standard works of Russian history, several sources of which were
used. The description of the Youssoupov palace in St. Petersburg is
found in the October 1990 issue of *Architectural Digest*. The quotations
from Anastasia about her early life are found in the memoir dictated to
Baroness Miltitz in 1948. Robert Massie's *Nicholas and Alexandra*, Greg
King's *Empress Alexandra*, Lili Dehn's *The Real Tsaritsa*, Felix Youssou-
pov's *Lost Splendor*, Anna Viroubova's *Memories of the Russian Court*,
Gleb Botkin's *The Real Romanovs*, Pierre Gilliard's *Thirteen Years at the
Russian Court*, and Post Wheeler and Hallie Erminie Rives's *Dome of
Many-Colored Glass* were used to draw the portrait of life at the
Russian imperial court. Anastasia's comments on her parents' drug

use and the expedition to Mount Ararat were made to the author in December 1976. Her remarks about Rasputin appear on the Milukoff tapes. Anastasia's recollection of Baroness Sophie Buxhoeveden is cited in Peter Kurth's *Anastasia: The Riddle of Anna Anderson*. The "theory of history" remark is also Kurth's. Yurovsky's account of the assassination of the imperial family has been widely published in several languages. Perhaps the best English translation appears in Richard Pipes's *The Russian Revolution*. Anastasia's recollections of the events at the Ipatiev House are taken from Roland Krug von Nidda's *I Am Anastasia* and sources cited in Kurth. The machinations of King George V and the British government concerning the fate of the Romanovs is detailed in Kenneth Rose's brilliant work, *King George V*.

BOOK TWO: *The Lost Princess*

Descriptions of Anastasia's escape from Russia are found in Harriet Rathlef's *Anastasia*, Kurth, and Nidda. Information on weather conditions during the night of February 17, 1920, was obtained from the *Meteorologischer Dienst der Deutschen Demokratischen Republik* (Meteorological Service of the German Democratic Republic) and translated from the original German before analysis by meteorologist Bill Kamal. Anastasia's movements in Berlin the night she fell into the Landwehr Canal are also found in Nidda and Kurth. The information sheet prepared by the Berlin police listing Anastasia as "Unknown Female Person" is in the Anastasia Archives at Neuwied Castle. Life at Dalldorf and with the Kleists is recounted in Kurth and Nidda and in the Rathlef papers. Grünberg's report is quoted in Nidda. Harriet Rathlef's *Anastasia* is the primary source of information about Anastasia's hospitalization at St. Mary's and Mommsen. Grand Duchess Olga's letters to Anastasia disappeared from the new barrack in Unterlengenhardt in 1968. They had been quoted in part by Bella Cohen in the March 28, 1926, edition of *The New York Times*, and thus were a matter of public record. Kurth quotes them in a slightly altered form. Grand Duchess Olga's reputed remarks about her meeting with Anastasia at Mommsen are quoted in Vorres's *The Last Grand Duchess*. Dr. Rudnev is quoted in Rathlef. Some of the Zahle letters are deposited at the Hoover Institution. Tatiana Botkin's recognition of Anastasia at Stillachhaus is found in several texts, including her own books. The photo album she gave to Anastasia is in the author's collection. Anastasia's reaction to the news that Harriet Rathlef had written a book about her is from the Milukoff tapes. Gleb Botkin's activities following his escape from Russia and through the period at Seeon are recounted in his books, *The Real Romanovs* and *The Woman Who Rose Again*. Felix Dassel's remembrances of the hospital at Czarskoe Selo and Seeon are found in his book, which was suppressed by the Grand Duke of Hesse. The archive at Neuwied Castle supplied the author with a photocopy. A copy of Grand Duke Andrew's letter is in the Gleb Botkin papers.

BOOK THREE: *"That I Have Been Through"*

The description of the *Berengaria* is found in John Malcolm Brinnin's *The Sway of the Grand Saloon*. Anastasia's memories of her arrival in New York are from the Milukoff tapes. Gleb Botkin's actions are recounted in his letters and *The Woman Who Rose Again*. Grand Duke Andrew's letter to Grand Duchess Olga was reprinted in the French press in the 1960s and also appears in Kurth. The actions of Xenia Leeds and her husband are from Gleb Botkin's recounting in *The Woman Who Rose Again*. Kurth offers a different account, written some fifty years after the fact, based on the memories of Xenia Leeds's daughter, who was only three years old at the time. As an eyewitness to the events, Botkin's accounts carry more credence. Hallie Erminie Rives's encounter with "a Russian duchess or something" is from her memoir, cited above. Marina Botkin Schweitzer's memories of her father's involvement in Anastasia's case were recounted to the author in several interviews. Gleb Botkin's letter to Grand Duchess Xenia was made public at the time it was written and copies of it are in his papers. Rachmaninov's meeting with Grand Duchess Xenia is described in Botkin's *The Woman Who Rose Again*. The disposition of the Dowager Czarina's jewels is recounted in various books; the best are Leslie Field's *The Queen's Jewels*, Suzy Menkes's *The Royal Jewels*, and Andrew Morton's *Theirs is the Kingdom*. Anastasia's remark about the incident was made to the author in May 1972. The Leeds family's involvement in the restoration of the Greek monarchy is found in G. Nicholas Tantzos's *The Inheritors of Alexander the Great*. A description of the Jennings residence modeled after a Youssoupov palace is found in Monica Randall's *The Mansions of Long Island's Gold Coast*. The document signed by Miss Jennings affording Anastasia charge privileges at B. Altman is in the author's collection. Anastasia's remarks about the marriage of Kaiser Wilhelm to Princess Hermine of Reuss were recorded by Milukoff. Grand Duchess Xenia's will referring to the "Settlement" with Ponsonby, Bark, and Peacock is appended to this text. Anastasia's recollections of her meeting with Hitler were given in an interview with the author in December 1976. Baroness Miltitz's recollections of Anastasia at Seven Oaks are included in two unpublished essays written by the Baroness at Unterlengenhardt; the original German texts are at Neuwied Castle. Anastasia's story of her experiences during the bombing of Hanover are from the Milukoff tapes.

BOOK FOUR: *"Who I Am and Who I Pretend to Be"*

All quotations of Anastasia are from the Milukoff tapes. Gleb Botkin's statements are from his unpublished letters to Anastasia, Anneliese Thomasius, and Milukoff. Baroness Miltitz's recollections are from her unpublished essays. Lord Mountbatten's comment about Prince Sigismund was published in *Royalty Monthly*. Sources vary about the party in the meadow at Unterlengenhardt. Anastasia told Milukoff it took place "not long after the death of poor [Mrs.] Heydebrand," or about August 1959. Baron Gienanth believes it may have been after Tatiana Botkin's visit in the summer of 1960. Equally obscure is the date Anastasia moved into the new barrack. Knowing that Anastasia's memory for dates was almost unerring, this text reflects the chronology she gave to Milukoff. The material on the court cases is derived from various sources. The trial transcripts and briefs are entirely in German, so this text uses English translations, occasionally those quoted in Kurth. The film taken by Milukoff described in the text is in the author's collection.

BOOK FIVE: *"The Czarina of Charlottesville"*

These chapters are based in part on the Milukoff tapes recorded during Anastasia's first three days in Charlottesville in 1968. Mildred Ewell was helpful with information about Jack Manahan's early life and Anastasia's reaction to the assassination of Lord Mountbatten. Evidence of Anastasia and Jack's concern about the disposition of her possessions at Unterlengenhardt is well known and exists in several forms. A letter written by Jack to the Schweitzers and a tape recording of Anastasia and Jack made in 1972 are quoted on this subject. The visits to Charlottesville by Maria Rasputin received international press coverage at the time. In addition to Gleb's letters describing his reactions, the recollections of Rey Barry and Wilbur Crews, who witnessed the meetings, have been used. The record of Anastasia's marriage to Jack is located in the Charlottesville City Hall. Jack's pamphlet, *Anastasia's Money & The Czar's Wealth* (1974), copies of which he deposited in libraries throughout the Commonwealth of Virginia, is the source for Jack and Gleb's feelings about the marriage. The Manahans' travels were well chronicled by the press wherever they went; various newspaper accounts have been consulted. Jack's discussion of Anastasia's genealogy and "Spanish personality," the story of the portrait of the Czar, and Jack's theory of history are from a tape recording made in May 1972 by the author. Discussion of the Manahans' problems with the Farmington Country Club come from interviews with the author. The description of the house at 35 University Circle quoted in the text is from *Argosy* magazine, April 1977. All of the conversations between Anastasia, Jack, and the author are transcribed from notes made immediately afterward. Moritz Furtmayr's conclusions based on the PIK tests have been published in numerous newspapers, magazines, and professional journals. Michael Thornton's interview with Lord Mountbatten about the PIK results appeared in *Royalty Monthly*. The canonization ceremony of the Russian imperial family is described in Greg King's biography, *Empress Alexandra*. Jack's "kidnapping" of Anastasia was international news at the time, and various press accounts were used to establish the facts. Anastasia's stay at the adult-care facility operated by Jane Holt has been unreported until now. Mrs. Holt graciously consented to the only interview she has ever given on the subject. Anastasia's final illness at Martha Jefferson Hospital was described in interviews with Mildred Ewell and Robert Crouch. Dr. James D. Aller's comment on the cause of Anastasia's death is contained in a letter to the author. Anastasia's memorial service was well attended and widely reported. Reverend Ramsey Richardson, Robert Crouch, Richard and Marina Botkin Schweitzer, and Mildred Ewell were present and supplied the author with their various recollections. The account of the interment of Anastasia's ashes at Seeon is based on reports in the German press. Jack's comment about Anastasia's "unnecessary demise" is taken from a letter written to the Schweitzers. The account of Jack's relationship with Althea Hurt is based on his own comments to Wilbur Crews, Robert Crouch, Mildred Ewell, James Hingeley, Stephanie Looney, several citizens of Charlottesville, and the author. Althea Hurt spoke to the author several times about the nature of her friendship with Jack. The account of Jack's funeral is based on the observations of his cousins, Ken Scott, and the author.

BOOK SIX: *"This Is Such a Great Mystery"*

The transcripts of Anastasia's conversations with Alexis Milukoff and Annemarie Mutius are taken from the Milukoff tapes. The conversations between the author and Jack Manahan at Heritage Hall were witnessed by Stephanie Looney. All published sources and archives used are cited in the text. The photographs of Mrs. de Graaff taken by Anastasia are in the Isaac Don Levine collection, Washington, D.C. The postcards written by Prince Frederick, the letters of Gleb Botkin, and the letter to Anastasia written by Mrs. de Graaff quoted in the text are in the author's collection.

Bibliography

NON-FICTION

Alexander, Grand Duke. *Always A Grand Duke* (New York: Garden City Publishing Co., 1933).
———. *Once A Grand Duke* (New York: Garden City Publishing Co., 1932).
———. *Twilight of Royalty* (New York: Ray Long & Richard R. Smith, Inc., 1932).
Alexandrov, Victor. *The Kremlin: Nerve-Centre of Russian History* (London: George Allen & Unwin Ltd., 1963).
———. *The End of the Romanovs* (Boston: Little, Brown and Company, 1966).
Auclères, Dominique. *Anastasia, qui êtes-vous?* (Paris: Hachette, 1962).
Barton, George. "The Fate of Nicholas II—the Greatest Mystery of the War," in *Celebrated Spies and Famous Mysteries of The Great War* (New York: Farrar, Straus and Giraux, no date).
Bergman, Ingrid and Burgess, Alan. *Ingrid Bergman: My Story* (New York: Delacorte Press, 1980).
Birmingham, Stephen. *The Right People: A Portrait of the American Social Establishment* (New York: Dell Publishing Co., 1969).
Botkin, Gleb. *The Real Romanovs* (New York: Fleming Revell, 1931).
———. *The Woman Who Rose Again: The Story of the Grand Duchess Anastasia* (New York: Fleming Revell, 1937).
———. *In Search of Reality* (Charlottesville: no date).
Botkin, Tatiana (Melnick). *Vospominanyo o Tsarskoi Sem'i* (Belgrade: Stefanovitch, 1921).
———. *Au Temps des Tsars* (Paris: Grasset, 1980).
———. *Anastasia retrouvée* (Paris: Grasset, 1985).

Brinnin, John Malcolm. *The Sway of the Grand Saloon: A Social History of the North Atlantic* (London: Macmillian Limited, 1972).

Chavchavadze, David. *The Grand Dukes* (New York: Atlantic International Publications, 1990).

_____. *Crowns and Trenchcoats: A Russian Prince in the CIA* (New York: Altlantic International Publications, 1990).

Cohen, Daniel. "Anastasia," in *The Encyclopedia of the Strange* (New York: Avon Books, 1987).

Curley Jr., Walter J. P. *Monarchs-In-Waiting* (New York: Dodd, Mead & Company, 1973).

Dassel, Felix. *Grossfürstin Anastasia Lebt!* (Berlin: Verlagshaus für Volksliteratur und Kunst, 1928).

Decaux, Alain. *L'Enigme Anastasia* (Paris: La Palatine, 1961).

Dehn, Lili. *The Real Tsaritsa* (Boston: Little, Brown and Company, 1922).

de Jonge, Alex. *The Life and Times of Grigorii Rasputin* (New York: Coward, McCann and Geoghegan, 1982).

Dobson, Christopher. *Prince Felix Yusupov: The Man Who Murdered Rasputin* (London: Harrap, 1989).

Duff, David. *Hessian Tapestry* (London: Frederick Muller, Ltd., 1967).

Eilers, Marlene A. *Queen Victoria's Descendants* (Baltimore: Genealogical Publishing Co., Inc., 1987).

Encausse, Philippe. *Le Maitre Philippe, de Lyon* (Paris: La Diffusiion Scientifique, 1954).

Escaish, Réné. *L'Enigme Anastasia* (Paris: La Palatine, 1961).

Fens, Jack. *Gebouwd in de Wijk: Monumenten en Andere Historische Gebouwen in Hillegersberg - Schiebroek - Terbregge* (Rotterdam: 1983).

Field, Leslie. *The Queen's Jewels* (New York: Harry N. Abrams, Inc., 1987).

Fenyvesi, Charles. *Splendor In Exile* (Washington, D.C.: New Republic Books, 1979).

Fourgeron, Marie. *Anastasie, la fille survivante de Tsar Nicholas II, oui ou non? Je Plaide Oui!* (Cannes: Devaye, 1958).

Frederick-Ernest, Prince of Saxe-Altenburg. "Descubrimiento de un Cementerio Indigena en Santa Maria de Dota - Costa Rica" (San Jose: Instituto Geográfico de Costa Rica, 1959).

Fülöp-Miller, René. *Rasputin: The Holy Devil* (New York: The Viking Press Inc., 1929).

Gilliard, Pierre. *Le Tragique Destin de Nicolas II et de sa Famille* (Paris: Payot, 1921).

———. *Thirteen Years at the Russian Court* (New Hampshire: Ayer Company, Publishers, Inc., 1987).

Gilliard, Pierre, and Savitch, Constantine. *La Fausse Anastasie: Historie d'une pretendue grande-duchesse de Russie* (Paris: Payot, 1929).

Gray, Pauline. *The Grand Duke's Woman* (London: Macdonald & Co., Ltd., 1976).

Halliburton, Richard. *Seven League Boots* (Indianapolis: The Bobbs-Merrill Company, 1935).

Hardwick, Mollie. "Anastasia," in *Great Unsolved Mysteries* (Seacaucus, N.J.: Chartwell Books, 1984).

Kelly, Laurence. *St. Petersburg: A Traveller's Companion* (New York: Atheneum, 1983).

King, Greg. *Empress Alexandra* (New York: Atlantic International Publications, 1990).

Knodt, Manfred. *Die Regneten von Hessen-Darmstadt* (Darmstadt: Verlag H.L. Schlapp, 1976).

Krug von Nidda, Roland. *Ich, Anastasia erzähle* (Frankfurt: Scheffler, 1957); in the U.S. as *I Am Anastasia* (New York: Harcourt Brace and Co., 1958); *I, Anastasia*, in various British editions.

Kurth, Peter. *Anastasia: The Riddle of Anna Anderson* (Boston: Little, Brown and Company, 1983).

Lincoln, W. Bruce. *The Romanovs: Autocrats of All the Russias* (New York: Doubleday, 1981).

Lindfors, Viveca. *Viveka . . . Viveca* (New York: Everest House, 1981).

McGuire, Leslie. *Anastasia: Czarina or Fake?* (San Diego: Greenhaven Press, Inc., 1989).

Manahan, John E. "The Manahan Family 1750-1950 and Allied Families" (Radford, Virginia: privately printed, 1952).

———. "A Kin Study: Manahan of Lissadorn" (Nickelsville, Virginia: privately printed, 1955).

———. "Anastasia's Money & The Czar's Wealth" (Charlottesville, Virginia: privately printed, 1974).

Manahan, John E. and Coppage, Arthur Max. *Coppage Coppedge Chronicle 1542-1975* (Charlottesville, Virginia: privately printed, 1975).

Massie, Robert K. *Nicholas and Alexandra* (London: Victor Gollancz, Ltd., 1972).

Massie, Suzanne. *Land of the Firebird: The Beauty of Old Russia* (New York: Touchstone Books, 1982).

Menkes, Suzy. *The Royal Jewels* (London: Grafton Books, 1985).

Miltitz, Monica. *Novalis: Romantisches Denken zur Deutung unserer Zeit* (Berlin: Oswald Arnold Verlag, 1948).

Morton, Andrew. *Theirs Is the Kingdom* (New York: Summit Books, 1989).

Nakatani, Kazuya. *The Daughter of the Czar* (Tokyo: Kodansha Co., Ltd., 1986).

Nogly, Hans. *Anastasia: Ein Frauenschicksal wie kein Anderes* (Hamburg: Verlag der Sternbucher, 1957); in Great Britian as *Anastasia* (London: Methuen, 1959).

O'Conor, John F. *The Sokolov Investigation* (New York: Robert Speller & Sons, Publishers, Inc., 1971).

Palmer, Lilli. *Change Lobsters - and Dance* (New York: Macmillan Publishing Co., Inc., 1975).

Phillips, Perrott, Ed. "I Survived the Royal Massacre," in *Out of This World: The Illustrated Library of the Bizarre and Extraordinary* (PBC Publishing Ltd., 1978, no place).

Pipes, Richard. *The Russian Revolution* (New York: Alfred A. Knopf, Inc., 1990).

Platnick, Kenneth. "Last of the Romanovs," in *Great Mysteries of History* (New York: Dorset Press, 1987).

Poliakoff, V. *The Tragic Bride: The Story of the Empress Alexandra of Russia* (New York: D. Appleton and Company, 1927).

Randall, Monica. *The Mansions of Long Island's Gold Coast* (New York: Hastings House, 1979).

Rappoport, A.S. *The Curse of the Romanovs* (New York: McClure, Phillips & Co., 1907).

Rasputin, Maria, and Barham, Patte. *Rasputin: The Man Behind the Myth* (Englewood Cliffs, N.J.: Prentice-Hall, Inc., 1977).

Rathlef-Keilman, Harriet. *Anastasia, Ein Frauenschicksal als Spiegel der Weltatas-Harriet von. trophe* (Leipzig and Zurich: Grethlein and Co., 1928); in the U.S. as *Anastasia* (New York: Payson and Clark, 1929).

Richards, Guy. *Imperial Agent: The Goleniewski-Romanov Case* (New York: The Devin-Adair Company, 1966).

———. *The Hunt for the Czar* (New York: Doubleday, 1970).

———. *Rescuing the Romanovs* (New York: Devan Adair, 1975).

Rose, Kenneth. *King George V* (New York: Alfred A. Knopf, 1984).

Savitch, Marie. *Marie Steiner-von Sivers* (London: Rudolf Steiner Press, 1967).

Steiner, Rudolf. *The Course Of My Life* (New York: Anthroposophic Press, 1951).

Summers, Anthony, and Mangold, Tom. *The File on the Tsar* (New York: Harper and Row, 1976).

Tantzos, G. Nicholas. *The Inheritors of Alexander the Great: An Illustrated History* (New York: Atlantic International Publications, 1986).

Thierry, Jean-Jacque. *Anastasia, La Grande-duchesse retrouvée* (Paris: Belfond, 1982).

Tisdall, E. E. P. *Marie Fedorovna, Empress of Russia* (New York: John Day Co., 1957).

Trewin, J. C. *The House of Special Purpose: An Intimate Portrait of the Last Days of the Russian Imperial Family*, compiled from the papers of Charles Gibbes (New York: Stein and Day, 1975).

Vassilyev, A. T. *The Ochrana: The Russian Secret Police* (Philadelphia: J. B. Lippincott Company, 1930).

Viroubova, Anna. *Memories of the Russian Court* (New York: The Macmillan Company, 1923).

———. *Souvenirs de Ma Vie* (Paris: Payot, 1927).

———. *Journal Secret D'Anna Viroubova, 1909-1917* (Paris: Payot, 1928).

Vorres, Ian. *The Last Grand Duchess: Her Imperial Highness Grand Duchess Olga Alexandrovna* (New York: Charles Scribner's Sons, 1964).

Wheeler, Post, and Rives, Halle Erminie. *Dome of Many-Coloured Glass: Memoirs of an American Diplomat and His Wife* (New York: Doubleday, 1955).

Witte, Count Sergius. *The Memoirs of Count Witte*, translated and edited by Abraham Yarmolinsky (New York: Doubleday, Page & Company, 1921).

Youssoupoff, Prince Felix. *Lost Splendor* (New York: G. P. Putnam's Sons, 1953).

Ziegler, Philip. *The Sixth Great Power: A History of the House of Barings* (New York: Alfred A. Knopf, 1988).

FICTION

(Works in which Anastasia appears as a fictional character)

NOVELS:

Appell, Allen. *Time After Time* (New York: Dell Publishing Co., Inc., 1987).

Bowen, True. *And the Stars Shall Fall: A Novel of the Life and Times of the Last Tsaritsa* (New York: A. A. Wyn, Inc., 1951).

Clark, Mary Higgins. *The Anastasia Syndrome and Other Stories* (New York: Simon and Schuster, 1989).

Cosgrove, Vincent. *The Hemingway Papers* (New York: Bantam Books, 1983).

Gavin, Catherine. *The Snow Mountain* (New York: Pantheon Books, 1973).

Green, William M. *The Romanov Connection* (New York: Beaufort Books, Inc., 1984).

Haskin, Gretchen. *An Imperial Affair* (New York: The Dial Press, 1980).

Hoe, Susanna. *God Save the Tsar* (New York: St. Martin's Press, 1978).

Lambton, Antony. *Elizabeth and Alexandra* (New York: E. P. Dutton, 1986).

Lescroart, John T. *Rasputin's Revenge: The Further Startling Adventures of Auguste Lupa—Son of Holmes* (New York: Leisure Books, 1987).

Radziwill, Catherine and Catherwood, Grace Adele. *Child of Pity* (New York: Sears Publishing Company, Inc., 1930).

Steel, Danielle. *Zoya* (New York: Delacourte Press, 1988).

COMIC BOOKS:

Jones, Gerard and Berreto, Eduardo. "Death's Head," No. 1 in Series entitled *The Shadow Strikes!* (New York: DC Comics, Inc., Sept. 1989).

———. "The Lord of Death," No. 2 in Series entitled *The Shadow Strikes!* (New York: DC Comics, Inc., Oct. 1989).

———. " 'Ghosts,' " No. 3 in Series entitled *The Shadow Strikes!* (New York: DC Comics, Inc., Nov. 1989).

———. "Bitter Fruit," No. 4 in Series entitled *The Shadow Strikes!* (New York: DC Comics, Inc., Dec. 1989).

PUBLISHED DRAMATIC ADAPTIONS:

Maurette, Marcelle. *Anastasia* [English adaptation by Guy Bolton] (New York: Random House, 1955).

———. *Anastasia* [English adaptation by Guy Bolton, with an introduction by Edwin Fadiman, Jr.] (New York: Signet Books, 1956).

———. *Anastasia* [with a preface by the playwright] (Paris: Buchet/Chastel corréa, 1957).

Acknowledgments

An undertaking of the scope involved in creating *Anastasia: The Lost Princess* requires the assistance of a great many people. I am deeply indebted to the patience and expertise offered by numerous individuals over the course of a great number of years.

My sincere gratitude to those who have assisted in the conservation of my Anastasia archive and the Milukoff tapes: Herman Badler; Gene Boemer; Sage Hadford; James Hardy; Jim Herrington; Lion and Fox Recordings; Matthew W. McGovern; the staff of Perfect Papers, Washington, D.C.—Joan Bursten and Charlene Kranz; the staff of the Capitol Hill branch of The Riggs National Bank of Washington, D.C.—Elaine B. Trimbell, Dolores J. Dorsey, and Robin Noland; Geoffrey H. Turner.

Romanov scholars Andrew Hartsook, Greg King, and Greg Rittenhouse served as consultants on myriad topics, and provided me with valuable unpublished materials.

Special thanks to Marina Botkin Schweitzer and her husband, Richard, for allowing me unprecedented access to the unpublished portions of the Gleb Botkin archive, and for answering numerous queries.

Janice Manahan Chamberlain, Fred Manahan, and Larry Manahan have added information and insight to the book.

Howard Siegman provided detailed information about the various stage adaptations of the Anastasia story, and encouragement when it was most needed.

Elena Siddall's archive of newspaper clippings about Anastasia's "kidnapping," and her skillful observations of that incident and others provided information and insight that otherwise would have been unavailable. Her many other contributions have been remarkable.

Washington, D.C., meteorologist Bill Kamal took an English-language translation of a highly technical description of the weather in Berlin on February 17-18, 1920, provided by the Meteorological Service of the German Democratic Republic, and made it comprehensible. The state of the weather that night has been a controversial point in Anastasia's story. My thanks to Mr. Kamal for solving this issue.

In Great Britain, Kenneth Pitt provided valuable counsel and research. Thanks also to John Thorneycroft, Architect of the Royal Palaces, Mr. Ottery of The Cabinet Offices for information on the Civil List, and the Archivist of the Royal Bank of Scotland, London, for information on the Anglo-International Bank.

In the Netherlands, Hans Builtjes, Hanca Leppink of Luitingh-Sijthoff, and Ronald A. B. Trüm facilitated research and publication.

My literary representative, Ronald L. Goldfarb of Goldfarb, Kaufman & O'Toole, Washington, D.C., deserves special acknowledgment. So do Anne Clark, Michael Diamond, Nina Graybill, Josh Kaufman, and Jeff O'Toole.

Anne Meadows edited the manuscript in a fashion, and with an attitude, that I believe Anastasia would have appreciated. Thanks also to Daniel Buck.

Gregory D. Hadford kept the business going, and his contributions have my sincerest gratitude.

Rose L. Winters typed and retyped drafts of the manuscript. Her many other contributions are too numerous to mention.

Loretta Divine and Barbara S. Ward read early drafts of the manuscript and made valuable suggestions.

Travel arrangements for my research trips were expertly handled by Lynne Sturtevant and the staff of ACT Travel, Washington, D.C.

The following booksellers have been helpful in locating materials used in my research: The Avid Reader, Chapel Hill, North Carolina; Chapters, Washington, D.C.; Heartwood Books, Charlottesville, Virginia; The Trover Shop, Capitol Hill branch, Washington, D.C.

Suzanne Wyman helped Anastasia and me in ways for which we shall both be eternally grateful.

Matthew W. McGovern has contributed more than even he knows.

Shirley Blair Lovell, James B. Lovell, Jr., Minnie Roark Blair, and Louis M. Bruton contributed to the telling of Anastasia's story, sometimes without knowing that they were doing so. J. C. Blair and John Stephens Lovell inspired us all.

Grateful acknowledgment is made to the staffs of the following institutions and publications: *Albemarle* magazine; the Anastasia Archives of Prince Friedrich Wilhelm zu Wied at Neuwied Castle; the Anthroposophic Press, Hudson, New York; the Archive of the Town Hall of Rotterdam; the Archives of the Municipality of Rotterdam; Bank of England Reference Library; *Bibliotheek der Rijksuniversiteit Utrecht*; the Central Bureau for Genealogy, The Hague; the Charlottesville, Virginia, *Daily Progress*; the Charlottesville, Virginia, *Observer*; the City Clerk's Office, Charlottesville, Virginia; the Fairfield (Connecticut) Historical Society; the Melvin Gelman Library, George Washington University, Washington, D.C.; the Hampton Court Records Office; Holy Trinity Monastery, Jordanville, N.Y.; the Hoover Institution on War, Revolution and Peace at Stanford University; the Houghton Library, Harvard University; the Land Registry Office, Rotterdam; *Meteorologischer Dienst der Deutschen Demokratischen Republik*, Potsdam; the Municipality of Doorn; the Periodicals Division of The Library of Congress; the Netherlands Board of Tourism; *The New York Times*; Keeper of the Royal Archives, Windsor; *Rijksarchief Utrecht*; *The Washington Post*.

Finally, I must give thanks to the following individuals who contributed to my research or to the preparation of the manuscript: Patricia Allen, Dr. James D. Aller, Eleanor Antin, Marie Arana-Ward, James Lee Auchincloss, Kevin Ayers, David Baldwin, Clive Barker, Chip Beaulieu, Marcella Berger, Don Beyer, Stephen Birmingham, Kermit Blaney, Michael Blankenship, Guy Bolton, Jaap Bottema, Don D. Brown, Ellen Butts, Virginia Spencer Carr, Lamar Cecil, David and Eugenie Chavchavadze, John Colozzi, Ellen Coplen Cooper, Robert Crouch, Zula Dietrich, Scott Divine, David J. Dodds, Marlene A. Eilers, Ruth L. Enkiri, Mildred Ewell, Joe Foote, Moritz Furtmayr, Sali Dimond Gelestino, Yvette Gibson, Baron Ulrich Gienanth, Eric Glass, Bernhard Gondorf, John S. Gottdiener, Kay Halle, Jo Hart, Gretchen Haskin, Jeanette Hastrich, James Hingeley, Naomi Hintze, Mildred Hird, Russell Hirshon, Jane Holt, Brien Horan, Steve Jacobs, Mary Keas, C. Brian Kelly, John W. Knott, Jr., Margaret Landon, C. Dean Latsios, Ruth Levine, Ian Lilburn, Viveca Lindfors, Stephanie Looney, Steve Lopez, Pat Loud, Mabel Luman, Tom Mangold, Esther Margolis, Mrs. M. M. Martin, Robin Maugham, Diana McLellan, Richard McLellan, Kate McMains, Connie Monahan, Robin Moore, Sylvia J. Morris, Jeffrey S. Nelson, John F. O'Conor, Jacqueline Onassis, David Osterlund, Mrs. Wallace Pearce, Bernard Portelli, Janice Pottker, Susan Price, Jennifer Reist, William Reit-wiesner, Guy Richards, Reverend Ramsey Richardson, C. Romney-Brown, Mike Roshaven, Carole Schabow, Ken Scott, Susan Shaughnessy, Laura Shay, Stephen Skalsky, Robert Speller, Baron Curt Stackleberg, Dr. and Mrs. Glenn Stoner, David Streitfeld, Bill Sublette, Anthony Summers, Marilyn Pfeifer Swezey, Gore Vidal, J. Lewis Walker, III, Douglas J. Ward, Richard Ward, Annette Weatherman, Guion Wyler.

Index

Compiled by Martha J. Sencindiver, Editorial Experts, Inc., Alexandria, Virginia. This index includes the names of persons, places, and organizations; geographic locations; and subjects related to Anastasia Nicholaievna Manahan and her immediate family.

Members of her immediate family and her relatives and friends among the royal houses of Europe are cited by first name, followed by title and, wherever necessary, the relationship to Anastasia, e.g., Olga, Grand Duchess of Russia (aunt) and Olga, Grand Duchess of Russia (sister).

Cross references are included to lead the user to related persons and subjects and to the preferred name or index term.

T